Envision

WRITING AND RESEARCHING ARGUMENTS

Envision

WRITING AND RESEARCHING ARGUMENTS

SECOND EDITION

Christine L. Alfano and Alyssa J. O'Brien

PEARSON
Longman

New York • San Francisco • Boston
London • Tokyo • Singapore • Madrid
Mexico City • Munich • Paris • Cape Town • Hong Kong • Montreal

Executive Editor: Lynn M. Huddon
Development Editor: Michael Greer
Senior Marketing Manager: Sandra McGuire
Senior Supplements Editor: Donna Campion
Media Supplements Editor: Jenna Egan
Production Manager: Stacey Kulig
Project Coordination, Text Design, and Electronic Page Makeup: Pre-Press Company, Inc.
Cover Design Manager: Wendy Ann Fredericks
Cover Designer: Susan Koski Zucker
Cover Images: *left to right:* Rob Crandall/The Image Works; Benno de Wilde/Punchstock.com;
    and Patrick Broderick/ModernHumorist.com
Photo Researcher: PhotoSearch
Manufacturing Manager: Mary Fischer
Printer and Binder: R. R. Donnelley and Sons
Cover Printer: Coral Graphics

For permission to use copyrighted material, grateful acknowledgment is made to the copyright
holders on pp. 333-334, which are hereby made part of this copyright page.

Library of Congress Cataloging-in-Publication Data
Alfano, Christine L.
    Envision: argument and research in a visual world / Christine L. Alfano and Alyssa J.
O'Brien. — 2nd ed.
        p. cm.
    Includes bibliographical references (p.) and index.
    ISBN 0-321-46251-3
        1. English language—Rhetoric. 2. Persuasion (Rhetoric) 3. Visual communication. 4. Visual
perception. 5. Report writing. I. O'Brien, Alyssa J. II. Title.
    PE1431.A55 2007
    808'.042—dc22
                                                                                    2006028921

Please visit us at www.ablongman.com

ISBN 10: 0-321-46251-3
ISBN 13: 978-0-321-46251-0

1 2 3 4 5 6 7 8 9 10-DOC-10 09 08 07

Contents

Preface xiii

PART I: ANALYSIS AND ARGUMENT

Chapter 1   **Analyzing Texts**   2

Understanding Texts Rhetorically   3

Understanding Rhetoric   5
  Understanding Visual Rhetoric   6

Analyzing Texts Rhetorically   7
  Analyzing a Comic Strip   8

Strategies for Analyzing Persuasive Texts   13
  Analyzing Editorial Cartoons   13
  Practicing Rhetorical Analysis   15
  Reading: Samuel P. Huntington,
    "Under God"   16
  Reading: Doug Marlette, "I Was a Tool
    of Satan"   20

Writing a Rhetorical Analysis   26
  Developing a Thesis Statement   27
  Student Writing: Jason Benhaim, "Tapping
    into the American Psyche"   30

Turning to Texts of Your Choice   34
Prewriting Checklist   35
Writing Projects   36

Chapter 2   **Understanding Strategies
of Persuasion**   37

Analyzing Ads as Arguments   38
  Reading: Seth Stevenson, "You and Your
    Shadow"   40

Understanding the Rhetorical Appeals   43
  Appeals to Reason   44

Logical Fallacies   47
Appeals to Emotion   48
Exaggerated Uses of Pathos   51
Appeals to Character and Authority   54
Misuses of Ethos   58
Exaggerated Ethos Through Parody   59

Considering Context   60

Using Strategies of Persuasion   61
Prewriting Checklist   62
Writing Projects   64

Chapter 3   Composing Arguments   66

Understanding the Canons of Rhetoric   67

Invention in Argument   67

Arrangement in Argument   73

Style in Argument   78
Constructing Persona   78
Choosing a Rhetorical Stance   80
Titles, Introductions, and Conclusions   80

Crafting a Position Paper   85
Student Writing: Angela Rastegar, Position
Papers   86
Writing Multiple Sides of an Argument   90
Student Writing: Aisha Ali, Multiple Sides
Project (excerpt)   91
Synthesizing Multiple Perspectives   93
Reading: Nora Ephron, "The Boston
Photographs"   94

Constructing Your Own Argument   101
Prewriting Checklist   101
Writing Projects   103

PART II: RESEARCH ARGUMENTS   105

Chapter 4   Planning and Proposing Research Arguments   106

Asking Research Questions   107
    Constructing a Research Log   109
    Student Writing: Felicia Cote, Research
      Log (excerpt)   109

Generating Topics   110

Bringing Your Topic into Focus   115
    Graphic Brainstorming   115
    Zooming in on a Topic   117

Planning Your Research Through Writing   120
    Freewriting about Your Research Topic   120
    Student Writing: Bries Deerrose, Research
      Freewrite   121

Drafting a Research Proposal   122
    Student Writing: Susan Zhang, "Little Photoshop
      of Horrors?"   124
    Drafting the Research Hypothesis   129
    Student Writing: Tommy Tsai, Working
      Hypothesis   131
    Student Writing: Tommy Tsai, Final Reflection
      Letter (excerpt)   132

Planning Your Own Research Project   132
Prewriting Checklist   133
Writing Projects   134

Chapter 5   Finding and Evaluating Research Sources   135

Visualizing Research   138
Developing Search Terms   139
Primary and Secondary Sources   141
    Finding Primary Sources   142
    Searching for Secondary Sources   144

Evaluating Your Sources   147
  Evaluating Websites   148
  Evaluating Library and Database Sources   152
  Student Writing: Sean Bruich, Field Research
    Inquiry Letter   159
  Evaluating Fieldwork and Statistics   162

Creating a Dialogue with Your Sources   164
  Student Writing: Amanda Johnson, Dialogue
    of Sources (excerpt)   165

Note Taking and Annotated Bibliographies   167
  Student Writing: Carly Geehr, Visual Annotated
    Bibliography   169

Implementing Your Research Skills   170
Prewriting Checklist   170
Writing Projects   171

Chapter 6   **Organizing and Writing Research Arguments   172**

Organizing Your Draft in Visual Form   173

Learning Outline Strategies   176
  Student Writing: Lee-Ming Zen, Outline:
    "Finding the Woman Who Never Was"   179

Outlines with Subheads and Transitions   184
  Student Writing: Dexian Cai, Research
    Paper Outline   184

Spotlight on Your Argument   188

Working with Sources   190
  Integrating, Not Inserting, Quotations   191
  Documentation During Integration   193

Drafting Your Research Argument   194
  Keeping Your Passion   194
  Collaboration Through Peer Review   195
  Student Writing: Sunthar Premakumar,
    Draft: "Bollywood Sing-Along" (excerpt)   197

Revising Your Draft   201
  Student Writing: Sunthar Premakumar, "Bollywood
    Sing-Along" (excerpt)   204
  Revision As a Continual Process   215

Focusing on Your Project   216
  Prewriting Checklist   216
  Writing Projects   217

PART III: DESIGN, DELIVERY, AND DOCUMENTATION

Chapter 7   Designing Arguments   220

Understanding Document Design
  and Decorum   221

Understanding Academic Writing
  Conventions   223
  Integrating Images in Academic Writing   224
  Design of Academic Papers   225
  Student Writing: Allison Woo, "Slaying the
    Dragon" (excerpt)   226

Tools of Design for Academic Audiences   227
  Composing an Abstract   227
  Student Writing: David Pinner, Research
    Abstract   228
  Shaping Your Bio   229
  Student Writing: David Pinner, Research Bios   230

Combining Visual and Verbal Design Elements   231
  Student Writing: Ashley Mullen, Newsletter   232
  Designing Arguments for Public Audiences   233
  Student Writing: Chris Couvelier and Gene Ma,
    Nonprofit Newsletter and Website (excerpts)   234
  Formatting Writing for Audiences   235
  Reading: London Greenpeace, "What's Wrong
    with the Body Shop?"   236

Designing Visual Arguments   239
   Crafting an Op-Ad   240
   Student Writing: Carrie Tsosie, "Alternative Energy
      for Whom?"   242
   Producing a Photo Essay   242
   Student Writing: Ye Yuan, "Looking Through
      the Lens"   244
   Composing a Website   245
   Student Writing: Sarah Douglas, Website (excerpt)
      248
   Making a Multimedia Montage   249
   Student Writing: Yang Shi, Photo Montage   250

Designing Your Own Arguments   252
Prewriting Checklist   252
Writing Projects   253

Chapter 8   Delivering Presentations   254

Understanding the Branches of Oratory   255

Audience, Purpose, and Persona   257

Transforming Research into a Presentation   259
   Selection   260
   Organization   260
   Student Writing: Tommy Tsai, Presentation
      Outline (excerpt)   262
   Translation   262
   Transformation in Action   263
   Student Writing: Susan Zhang, Presentation
      Script   264

Considering Strategies of Design   268

Using Visuals Rhetorically   270
   Writing for Poster Sessions   270
   Student Writing: Tanja Haj-Hassan, Carlos Ortiz,
      and Jonathan Hwang, Research Posters   270

Writing for PowerPoint or Slide-Based
    Presentations   271
Student Writing: Natalie Farrell, Presentation
    Slides   272
Possibilities for PowerPoint   274
Student Writing: Tracy Hadnott, Sarah Trube,
    Morgan Springer, and Kavi Vyas, Presentation
    Slides   274

Choosing Methods of Delivery   276

Practicing Your Presentation   281
    Anticipating Problems and the Question-and-Answer
        Session   282

Documenting Your Presentation   283

Creating Your Own Presentation   285
Prewriting Checklist   285
Writing Projects   287

Chapter 9   Documentation and Plagiarism   289

Rhetorical Imitation and Intellectual
    Property   290

Understanding Plagiarism   291
    Avoiding Unintentional Plagiarism   292
    Student Writing: Michael Rothenberg, Research Log
        (excerpt)   293
    Reading: Doris Kearns Goodwin, "How I Caused
        That Story"   294

Understanding Documentation Style   296
    Documentation as Cross-Referencing   297
    Using Notes for Documentation   298

MLA-Style Works Cited Lists   300

Student Writing: Sunthar Premakumar, Works Cited and Consulted   301

Student Writing: Dexian Cai, Works Cited   303

Documentation for Print and Online Sources   304

Documentation for Visual, Audio, and Multimedia Sources   308

Copyright and Citing Sources   311

Student Paper in MLA Style   312

Student Writing: Tanner Gardner, "Show Me the Money! The Globalization of the NBA"   312

Documentation for Your Paper   325

Writing Projects   326

Preface

This book emerged from our practical need as writing instructors for an engaging course textbook that would teach students core skills in analysis, argument, research writing, document design, and presentations—but that would do so in a way that captured student interest by using contemporary examples while also building on a solid rhetorical foundation.

Our first edition focused primarily on instructing students how to understand, analyze, and write about visual rhetoric. With this second edition, we've expanded our focus to emphasize a sound base in writing instruction and textual analysis of verbal print documents before broadening to consider other rhetorical texts—such as images, advertisements, films, speeches, and multimedia.

It is our hope that this second edition will accomplish two goals: that it will give teachers the confidence and resources to lead students in an engaging and rhetorically sound pedagogy focused on accessible writing instruction, and that it will capture the interest of students while empowering them to become knowledgeable and skilled writers, researchers, and producers of well-composed rhetorical texts.

To develop students' understanding of rhetorical texts of all kinds—and, along the way, move from written analysis to complex tasks such as argumentation, research writing, and presentation of those ideas—we seek to instruct students in time-honored writing techniques based on classical rhetoric. To that end, we walk students through interactive lessons on crafting thesis statements, structuring argumentative essays, developing research topics, evaluating sources, integrating quotations, revising papers, and, finally, designing and presenting effective presentations and writing projects. At the same time, students will learn key rhetorical concepts for effective communication, such as attending to audience, understanding appeals and fallacies, practicing the canons of rhetoric, differentiating levels of decorum, and using branches of oratory.

What's been most exciting about *Envision* as a project is how our students have continued to collaborate with us: for both the first and second editions, they provided suggestions for examples, extensive feedback on each chapter, unfailing support and enthusiasm, and the ultimate gift of sharing their own writing in this book as well as on the Companion Website: http://www.ablongman.com/envision.

What's New in the Second Edition

Envision: Writing and Researching Arguments—the second edition—has been composed with the student writer and the writing teacher in mind. We have added substantial instruction on composing written texts, on analyzing print materials and articles, and on research topics across a wide range of texts—from written political documents to song lyrics. In this second edition, you'll find a substantial emphasis on written arguments, with most chapters beginning by focusing on words and then expanding to include writing about images and other multimedia.

In addition, we've included more student writing examples and print articles in this revision, largely in response to feedback from our colleagues, reviewers, and students. We've annotated these selections, both to demonstrate the writing lessons presented in each section of the book and to show students how to accomplish the writing tasks and successfully implement rhetorical strategies in their texts.

Moreover, we've added more examples of steps in the writing process: Chapter 1 shows students how to construct a thesis statement; Chapter 3 focuses on introductions and conclusions; Chapter 4 spends time on writing a proposal; and Chapter 6 includes two outlines, a draft, and a revised paper. In this way, *Envision: Writing and Researching Arguments* takes students through all the necessary components for effective writing—from generating an idea, to implementing rhetorical appeals and evidence, to crafting effective transitions, to integrating sources responsibly.

In addition, in an entirely new chapter on documentation, we explain to students why citing sources is important in academic work and offer practical strategies for avoiding plagiarism. We also instruct students in understanding the logic of citation style, concluding with an extensive resource guide to MLA style.

Another new chapter in the book revolves around the conventions for placing words on paper. Since the way an academic paper is formatted represents a type of visual rhetoric, we've taken time to instruct students in academic conventions through our chapter on document design. The end of that chapter moves from papers and abstracts to service-learning projects and visual arguments (op-ads, photo essays, Websites, and more). Thus, we've added and enhanced our instruction for academic writers in college classes, but we've left in guidelines for writing in innovative forms.

We feel that our mission with this book is to teach students how to understand, analyze, conduct research on, and compose arguments about all kinds of texts. We hope to enable students to develop the skills, confidence, and enthusiasm for writing, research, and effective communication about issues that matter to them.

The Structure of the Book

Students of *Envision* will develop the skills to become confident, competent, and effective writers through following the book's three-part structure. At the same time, teachers can use any of the chapters and assignments in any order.

Part I: Analysis and Argument

This section aims to train students in analysis and argument. Students work through exercises to become proficient, careful readers of rhetorical texts and learn practical strategies for writing thesis statements, rhetorical analysis essays, and synthesis essays incorporating various perspectives. Students learn how to analyze the forms of persuasion in verbal and visual texts—from short articles to political cartoons, ads, and photos. Chapters 1 through 3 focus on writing, from thesis statements to formal strategies of argument, and we examine both conventional academic essays and contemporary popular articles.

Part II: Research Arguments

Chapters 4 through 6 focus on strategies of research argument for sustained writing projects. The writing lessons in this section of the book take students through the research proposal, techniques for keeping a research log, learning to locate sources, how to include charts and graphs, methods of outlining, drafting, and revising, and best practices for integrating sources in writing. We spend time instructing students about how to gather and evaluate sources, conduct library and field research, and work collaboratively on a draft. Students can consult sample writing in the form of proposals, outlines, and drafts while they examine textual examples such as articles, propaganda posters, and film trailers.

Part III: Design, Delivery, and Documentation

The final three chapters offer students an opportunity to present their writing. Students learn about document design—both for academic papers and for visual arguments such as op-ads and photo essays. We offer a chapter on translating written work into effective oral and multimedia presentations, with attention to drafting a script, designing a PowerPoint slideshow, and practicing delivery of arguments. Students learn how to design memorable and compelling writing projects for a range of academic and professional purposes, including service-learning courses. We conclude the book with a chapter on plagiarism and MLA documentation.

Sequence of Assignments

Throughout this book, we base our writing assignments on lessons from classical rhetoric. For the second edition, we decided to retain our particular media theme for each chapter—analyzing a range of textual examples, from cartoons, ads, and news photos to propaganda posters, film trailers, and student presentations. Yet our goal is to teach writing skills in analysis, research, and argument. To that end, we've devised our assignments to meet the learning objectives specified by the Council of Writing Program Administrators (WPA), as shown in the accompanying table.

MAJOR ASSIGNMENTS AND LEARNING OBJECTIVES

Chapter Title	Chapter Learning Goals	Major Assignments	Media Focus
1: Analyzing Texts	■ Understanding the rhetorical situation ■ Considering relationships between audience, text, and purpose ■ Textual analysis ■ Developing thesis statements	■ Personal narrative essay ■ Rhetorical analysis essay	Cartoons, comic strips, and editorial cartoons
2: Understanding the Strategies of Persuasion	■ Strategies of argumentation ■ Understanding rhetorical appeals: logos, pathos, ethos ■ Abuses or exaggerated uses of rhetorical appeals ■ Importance of context and *kairos*	■ Contextual analysis essay ■ Analysis of rhetorical appeals and fallacies ■ Comparison/contrast essay	Advertisements

Chapter Title	Chapter Learning Goals	Major Assignments	Media Focus
3: Composing Arguments	■ Introductions and conclusions ■ Arrangement and structure of argument ■ Considering various perspectives on argument ■ Developing persona and rhetorical stance ■ Addressing opposing opinion in an argument ■ Effective titles	■ Position paper ■ Multiple sides of argument assignment ■ Argumentative essay incorporating diverse viewpoints	Photographs, photo essays
4: Planning and Proposing Research Arguments	■ Generating and narrowing research topics ■ Prewriting strategies ■ Developing a research plan ■ Drafting a formal proposal	■ Research log ■ Informal research plan ■ Research proposal	Propaganda posters
5: Finding and Evaluating Research Sources	■ Research strategies ■ Evaluating sources ■ Distinguishing between primary and secondary sources ■ Locating sources ■ Conducting field research ■ Best practices for note taking	■ Critical evaluation of sources ■ Annotated bibliography ■ Field research contact assignment	Magazine and journal covers, websites
6: Organizing and Writing Research Arguments	■ Organizing and outlining arguments ■ Importance of multiple drafts and revision ■ Writing and peer response ■ Quoting from sources	■ Formal outline ■ Peer review and response ■ Using visual evidence ■ Research argument	Film and movie trailers
7: Designing Arguments	■ Understanding the conventions of academic writing ■ Writing abstracts ■ Adopting appropriate voice and tone ■ Considering different genres of argument ■ Relationship between rhetorical situation and types of argument ■ Formatting and genre considerations	■ Writing an abstract ■ Visual argument—opinion advertisement or photo essay ■ Creating electronic arguments using multimedia (audio and visual)	Op-ads, photo essays, Websites, and multiple media

Chapter Title	Chapter Learning Goals	Major Assignments	Media Focus
8: Delivering Presentations	■ Using technology to address a range of audiences ■ Transforming written arguments into visual or spoken texts ■ Strategies of design and delivery ■ Conducting field research	■ Conversion assignment—written to oral discourse ■ Fieldwork assignment ■ Multimedia presentation ■ Collaborative conference presentation	Presentations, poster sessions, PowerPoint
9: Documentation and Plagiarism	■ Best practices in documenting sources ■ MLA style rules ■ Avoiding plagiarism	■ Ethical note-taking exercises ■ Citation practice	

Envision Companion Website

In addition to the exercises and major assignments contained within the pages of *Envision*, we've designed a comprehensive and multi-layered Companion Website to give students access to additional resources for learning to be effective writers, researchers, and rhetoricians through an *active learning* model. From John Dewey to Cynthia Selfe, researchers in rhetoric and composition have shown the advantages of student-centered classrooms and student-focused pedagogy. Moreover, the well-known Learning Pyramid depicting student retention rates demonstrates clearly the efficacy of active student engagement in the learning process (see Figure 1). *Envision* has been designed around the pedagogical philosophy that students learn more when they interact with the course material and when they are challenged to teach each other than when they simply implement the lessons taught to them.

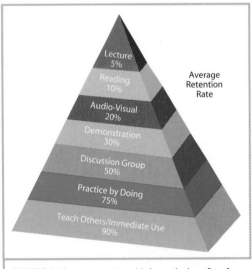

FIGURE 1. The Learning Pyramid shows the benefits of interactive pedagogy.

Accordingly, we have supplemented the rich material found in *Envision* with a Companion Website that contains a wide variety of links and materials designed to facilitate learning as an interactive experience. On the Website, students will find links to writing, research, and rhetoric resources, supplemental readings designed to complement those found in the book itself, additional interactive activities, and over 250 student writing projects to serve as models for their own writing. We aim to maximize student engagement and retention through a variety of interactive, student-centered exercises and assignments. This methodology eschews the "banking model" disparaged by educational theorist Paolo Freire and positions students as experts in their own learning.

Instructors will also find invaluable resources available on the Companion Website, designed to help you with everyday practical instruction in the classroom, with facilitating learning about ways of writing and methods of analysis, with leading your students to becoming adept researchers and confident producers of arguments across a range of media. These include pedagogical resources, like lessons plans and additional classroom activities, sample syllabi, expanded assignment guidelines, assignments for Added Challenge, and supplemental classroom readings.

We hope you will use the *Envision* Website to contribute ideas, suggestions, feedback, and even writing projects of your own. Have students email us with comments on the examples, instruction, and resources we offer in *Envision*. Working on this book has been a collaborative process from the beginning, and we have learned so much from talking with students and teachers across the country about what they need most in a guide to writing argument and research. We hope that you, too, will join the conversation—on the Website, through email, or in person at a conference. Thanks for your interest in *Envision*; we hope you find the book as useful to your teaching as it has been rewarding for us to use in our own classes.

Instructor's Manual

The Instructor's Manual, created by Kristi M. Wilson, Alyssa O'Brien, and Christine Alfano of Stanford University, provides teachers with pedagogical advice for each of the chapters of *Envision*. Each chapter of the Instructor's Manual offers an overview of each *Envision* chapter, teaching tips for working with the main concepts and reading selections in the chapter, suggestions for classroom exercises and writing assignments, and tips for integrating the resources on the *Envision* Companion Website into your classroom. The Instructor's Manual also offers sample syllabi and suggested ways of organizing the reading and exercises according to days of the week.

A Note of Thanks

In the new chapter on documentation, we spend quite a long time discussing the importance of acknowledging your debts as a writer to those who made your ideas and work possible. With this second edition, we'd like to offer our note of thanks to those who made possible the writing of this book.

First, we extend our greatest appreciation to those who envisioned our accomplishment of both editions and rallied us all the way through. To our friends and our families: without your love, support, and understanding, we could never have completed this project.

Chris would especially like to thank those closest to her who kept her grounded and encouraged her during these past few years of writing: her parents, Phyllis and John, as well as Carol and Art, for their input, guidance and support; her sisters, Suzy and Nancy, for listening to the endless tales of *Envision* with such patience and good humor; and her surrogate family, the Dolans, for publishing advice (John J.) as well as therapeutic hot chocolate and pop culture inspiration (Pamela). Most of all, Chris would like to thank Miranda, Max, and the other Chris for tolerating the hours spent away writing and for surrounding her with such love and laughter when she finally turned off the computer.

To Alyssa's parents, Joan and Michael, who publicize the book to friends, colleagues, and teachers while hosting it on coffee tables with delight; to Charmaine, fellow writer, second mother, and supporter; to Jean-Paul, for consistently promoting this book and using it in the "real world" to help with his company Sagefire's marketing communications; to Chris, Lisa, Jen, Will, and Sarah for their enthusiasm and pride in so simple a thing; and most of all to Laird, patient husband who knows this has always been a labor of love, who resists calculating the hourly wage spent in endless rewrites, and who offers instead sweet rewards of life outside work along the California coast—thank you.

Our next note of thanks is for our students. We dedicate this second edition to our students, who make our profession a joy and who served as the impetus and foundation for, as well as the reviewers and recipients of, the writing. We thank our winter and spring 2006 classes for commenting on every chapter through Wiki and chat room feedback sessions. We would like to recognize, with gratitude, the students whose work appears on the *Envision* Website as well as, by name, those who have shared their work in the pages of the book: Aisha Ali, David Baron, Jason Benhaim, Alex Bleyleben, Sean Bruich, Dexian Cai, James Caputo, KiYonna Carr, Michael Chaitkin, Vivian Chang, Felicia Cote, Chris Couvelier, Molly Cunningham, Bries Deerrose, Stewart Dorsey, Sarah Douglas, Lauren Dunagan, Max Echtemendy, Natalie Farrell, Tanner Gardner, Carly Geehr, Tracy Hadnott, Wendy Hagenmaier, Tanja Haj-Hassan, Laura Hendrickson, Tom Hurlbutt, Jonathan Hwang, Aaron Johnson, Amanda Johnson, Derrick Jue, Eric Jung, Liz Kreiner, Alina Lanesberg, Jessica Luo, Gene Ma, Ashley Mullen, Megan Nesland, Carlos Ortiz, Jake Palinsky, Falco Pichler, David Pinner, Sunthar Premakumar, Angela Rastegar, Ben Rosenbrough, Michael Rothenberg, Yang Shi, Allison Smith, Morgan Springer, Albert Thomas, Sarah Trube, Tommy Tsai, Carrie Tsosie, Jessica Vun, Kavi Vyas, Allison Woo, Ye Yuan, Michael Zeligs, Lee-Ming Zen, and Susan Zhang.

Our colleagues at Stanford and in the field of writing and rhetoric deserve our thanks as well. We are deeply grateful for the support from Stanford University and the Program at Writing and Rhetoric: Professor Andrea Lunsford and Marvin Diogenes, who continue to provide inspirational leadership as well as friendship and the opportunity to grow both pedagogically and professionally; Clyde Moneyhun and Claude Reichard, who extend invaluable mentorship and camaraderie under pressure; our teaching colleagues, who generously offered their suggestions for this second edition, particularly Doree Allen, Marjorie Ford, Wendy Goldberg, Serkan Gorkemli, Bump Halbritter, Patti Hanlon-Baker, Jonathan Hunt, Donna Hunter, Sohui Lee, Joyce Moser, Carolyn Ross, Malgorzata Schaefer, John Tinker, Ann Watters, Kristi Wilson, and Susan Wyle. We're appreciative for the administrative expertise and good humor of Cristina Huerta, Vani Kane, Arthur Palmon, and Emily Phillips, as well as the technological expertise of Corinne Arráez and Marilenis Olivera.

We also extend our thanks to the people behind the scenes at Stanford's Wallenberg Hall who have provided both the inspiration and the technological magic to support the writing, computer experimentation, publicity events, and crazy classroom antics that went into the creating of *Envision* over the years: Justin Bryant, Helen Chen, Adelaide Dawes, Eric Grant, Stig Hagstrom, Roy Pea, Melinda Sacks, and especially our friends Dan Gilbert and Bob Smith.

Although we've received feedback from many colleagues along the way, we owe a special debt of gratitude to the writing faculty at Salt

Lake Community College, who welcomed us to their campus and gave us invaluable insight into the way *Envision* was being used in the classroom. The discussions that we had with Ron Christiansen, Sue Briggswere, Lisa Bickmore, Stephanie Dowdle, Allison Fernley, Charlotte Howe, Stephen Ruffus, Jamie McBeth-Smith, and Elisa Stone were instrumental in helping us refine our approach to this second edition.

We'd like to thank as well the colleagues we haven't met—those reviewers who gave Longman the advice that resulted in this edition: David Beach, George Mason University; Matthew Hartman, Ball State University; Carole Clark Papper, Ball State University; Rochelle Rodrigo, Mesa Community College; Erika M. Schreck, Colorado State University, Boulder; Matthew Theado, Gardner-Webb University; Mary Trachsel, University of Iowa.

Finally, we are grateful to those who make publication possible. Lynn Huddon, our editor at Longman, had the vision for this second edition and unfailingly steered us to its completion. Michael Greer, our development editor by title, third co-author in practice, once again made miracles happen by supporting us through the reconceptualization of the book and by gently guiding us with prose and pep talks. Joe Opiela's personal and continuing belief in *Envision* can only be matched by his generosity and stewardship as editor-in-chief. We thank Nicole Solano for her assistance throughout the project. Shaie Dively and Caroline Gloodt rose to the challenge of securing image and text permissions under tight deadlines; Barbara McGowran's electronic copyediting made the final revisions to the manuscript seem almost effortless; and Katy Faria's efficiency, graciousness, and outstanding new design made the book into the final beautiful copy you have before you. Finally, perhaps last in the list but very dear to our hearts, is the entire sales team at Longman, most notably, our buddy Andy Draa, whose charm convinced us to sign with Longman years ago and whose spectacular support of our book retained our own faith in its possibilities; Mike Coons, who hosted a pivotal workshop on *Envision* at Salt Lake Community College; as well as Katherine Bell, Doug Day, Megan Galvin, Rick Perez, and the entire Longman team.

Christine L. Alfano and Alyssa J. O'Brien
November 2006

Part I

ANALYSIS AND ARGUMENT

CHAPTER 1
Analyzing Texts

CHAPTER 2
Understanding Strategies
of Persuasion

CHAPTER 3
Composing Arguments

Rhetoric's classic definition as the art of persuasion suggests a power. So much of what we receive from others—from family and friends to 30-second blurbs on TV—is intended to persuade. Recognizing how this is done gives greater power to choose.

—Victor Villanueva, Jr.

CHAPTER 1

Analyzing Texts

Everywhere around us, words and images try to persuade us to think about the world in certain ways. From "Got Milk?" ads to political campaign posters, words and images combine to move us, convince us to buy something, shape our opinions, or just make us laugh. Living in such a world requires us to pay attention and to think critically and analytically about all the texts we encounter every day. We can see this persuasive power especially in visual texts, such as the political cartoons and comics you might find on your favorite Weblog or in the campus newspaper.

Consider the political cartoon shown in Figure 1.1. How do the words and the images work together to persuade audiences to think or feel or act a certain way?

FIGURE 1.1. Nick Anderson's cartoon from *The Louisville Courier-Journal* uses color and exaggerated form to argue that steroid-using baseball players are popping the dreams of young children.

Nick Anderson's cartoon conveys a powerful message about how steroid use has damaged the relationship between young fans and their baseball-star role models. Notice how when the athlete's steroid needle literally "pops" the child's balloon—and thus, implicitly, the child's admiration for the athlete—the written words "Oh, sorry kid" show a lack of true contrition; the font, selection, and arrangement of words make the player seem anything but sincere. Rather, the brightly colored muscular back takes over the entire space of the cartoon, showing the audience (baseball-loving fans) how steroids not only hurt the players but also hurt the game, the fans, and even perhaps our country's future by demoralizing children.

We can understand how this cartoon works by asking questions about its argument, audience, and author. When we ask questions like these, we are analyzing how texts can be **rhetorical,** how they aim at persuading specific audiences through the careful choices made by the writer in composing the text.

We've chosen to focus on comics and political cartoons in this chapter; by studying these texts, you'll develop skills as both a reader and a writer, learn how to analyze rhetoric, and create powerful arguments about the texts you encounter every day. In the process, you'll come to appreciate how writing as we know it is changing, causing us to approach it with a new set of eyes and rhetorical tools.

Chapter Preview Questions

- How do we read and analyze texts rhetorically?
- How do we write about visual texts?
- How do thesis statements help us make arguments?
- How can we compose titles and draft analysis essays?

Understanding Texts Rhetorically

To approach texts rhetorically means to ask questions about how the text conveys a persuasive message or *argument*, how the text addresses a specific *audience*, and how the writer operates within a *specific context* or *rhetorical situation*.

You encounter many kinds of texts every day, even in just walking across campus. Once you recognize how these texts function *rhetorically*, you'll see that, as rhetoric scholar Victor Villanueva writes, "So much of what we receive from others—from family and friends to 30-second blurbs on TV—is intended to persuade. Recognizing how this is done gives greater power to choose." In other words, once you see how texts try to shape your mind about the world, then you can decide whether or not to agree with the many messages you encounter on a regular basis.

To grasp this concept, let's follow one hypothetical student—we'll call her Alex—as she walks to class and note the rhetorical texts she sees along the way. First stop: the dorm room, your average institutional room, which Alex and her roommate have decorated with Altoids ads they've ripped from magazines.

There's also a large poster for the women's basketball team on one wall and a small Snoopy comic taped above the computer screen. As Alex turns off her computer, we notice what's on the screen: the Website for Slate.com, complete with an animated ad for an online dating service and an annoying pop-up telling Alex she'll win $50 if she clicks now. But Alex doesn't click; she shuts the machine down, piles her glossy-covered textbooks in her backpack, and slams the door shut on her way out.

Alex walks down the hall, past the rooms of other students in the dorm who have photos and graffiti on their doors, pausing in the lounge where several of her friends are watching a rerun of Jon Stewart on a large flat-screen TV. She watches until the show breaks for a commercial for Nike shoes, then she continues, down the stairwell decorated with student event flyers—a charity dance for the victims of Hurricane Katrina, a rally against immigration laws, a dorm meeting to plan the ski trip—and she pushes her way out into the cool autumn air. She only has two minutes to get to class, so she walks briskly past the student union with its event bulletin boards and its large hand-painted sign, "Café, open 6 a.m.–midnight, best crisps on campus." Two students at a small card table have painted their faces blue, and they hand her a small blue card with the cartoon of a surfer on it. "Come to our Hawaiian luau at the fraternity Saturday night!" they call to her as she crosses the quad and heads toward the statue of the university founder on his horse.

Alex then walks over the school crest embedded in the center of the walkway and past a group of students congregated outside the administration building, waving signs that protest the conditions of university janitorial workers. She turns left, weaving along the back of a cluster of gleaming steel and brick buildings that constitute the engineering quad. To her right, she passes a thin metal sculpture called *Knowledge and Life* that guards the entrance to the library. Finally, she reaches her destination: the English department. As Alex jogs up the stone steps, she stops momentarily to pick up the campus newspaper and scan the photos and headlines on the front page before folding the newspaper under her arm. Down the hall and into the classroom she rushes, but she's late. The professor has started the PowerPoint lecture already. Alex picks up the day's handout from the TA and sits down in the back row.

Now that we've seen Alex safely to her seat, how many rhetorical texts did you notice along the way? Ads, posters, cartoons, Websites, textbooks, television shows, flyers, statues, signs, newspapers, PowerPoint slides, even architectural design: each can be seen as an example of rhetoric. Once you begin to look at the world rhetorically, you'll see that just about everywhere you are being persuaded to agree, act, buy, attend, or accept an argument: rhetoric permeates our cultural landscape. Recognizing the power of rhetoric to persuade is an important part of learning to engage in contemporary society. Learning how to read texts rhetorically is the first step in thinking critically about the world.

CREATIVE PRACTICE

The next time you walk to class, pay attention to the rhetoric that you find along the way; take notes as you walk to catalog the various types of persuasion you encounter. Then, write up your reflections on your observations into a *personal narrative essay*. Discuss which types of rhetoric were most evident, which were most subtle, and which you found the most persuasive.

Understanding Rhetoric

In one of the earliest definitions, ancient Greek philosopher Aristotle characterized **rhetoric** as *the ability to discern the available means of persuasion in any given situation.* Essentially, this means knowing what strategies will work to convince your audience to accept your message. As shown in Figure 1.2, this involves assessing and attending to the **rhetorical situation**—that is, to the relationship between writer, text, and audience. Think of the politician who might argue the same political platform but in strikingly different ways depending on what part of his constituency he's addressing; of the various ways mothers, students, or police officers might convey the same antidrug message to a group of middle school students; of how clothing retailers adapt their marketing message to suit the media in which they're advertising—magazines, radio, or television. In each case the *argument* has been determined by the unique relationship between the writer, the audience, and the text.

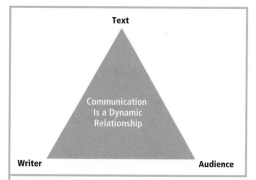

FIGURE 1.2. The rhetorical situation is the relationship between writer, text, and audience.

Student Writing

Read Esmeralda Fuentes's short narrative about the visual rhetoric she observes during the course of one day.
www.ablongman.com/envision/201

In constructing your own arguments every day, you undoubtedly also, consciously or not, evaluate your rhetorical situations. When you want to persuade your coach to let practice out early, you probably make your case face to face, rather than through a formal letter. When you ask for an extension on a paper, you most likely do so in a well-crafted email rather than a hasty after-class appeal. When you apply for a job or internship, you send a formal résumé and cover letter to indicate the seriousness of your interest. Here again we see that the success of your argument depends at least in part on your choice of text (verbal plea, written email, cover letter) in relation to the audience (coach, professor, potential employer) that you're addressing. All these examples are rhetorical acts in the form of oral and written arguments.

Understanding Visual Rhetoric

Yet persuasion happens through visual means as well: how you stand and make eye contact, how you format your professional documents, even how you capitalize or spell words in an email. Moreover, when you insert an image in an essay, create a poster to advertise a club sport, or draw a cartoon spoofing university policy, you are moving into the realm of **visual persuasion**— "writing" with images. From photographs to Websites, political cartoons to advertisements, these visual texts use rhetorical means to persuade an audience. Although some images may be more aesthetic than argumentative, many convey either inherent or explicit persuasive messages. Think about brochures, movie trailers, flyers, commercial Websites, and even comics; these are all created as arguments to convince audiences.

Since such strategies of persuasion occur through images—either alone or combined with words—rather than merely through words, they are called **visual rhetoric**. A documentary is produced and edited specifically to suggest a particular point of view; the illustration in a children's book provides a way to read a story; the sequential cartoons of a comic strip offer powerful commentary on American society. In each example, the writer chooses the best visual representation for the message of the text. The study of visual rhetoric provides you with the means to understand how and why such choices are made, and what the significance of these decisions is in the larger culture in which we live.

Analyzing Texts Rhetorically

Think of your favorite comic strips or political cartoons. Although they may seem purely aesthetic, merely informative about current events, or just plain funny, they do serve as an important mode of communicating ideas. For example, the comic antics of Dilbert or of Pig and Rat from *Pearls Before Swine* may not appear to carry any strong arguments about our society, human nature, or social relations. However, if you look closely at the details—the choice of words, the composition of the image, the particular colors, layout, character placement, and design—then you can gain a deeper understanding of the cartoon's message. This is what we mean by analyzing texts rhetorically.

Consider the following argument, made by cultural critic Scott McCloud as part of his book, *Understanding Comics:*

> When pictures are more abstracted from "reality," they require greater levels of perception, more like words. When words are bolder, more direct, they require lower levels of perception and are received faster, more like pictures.

What's significant about this quote is not only *what* McCloud says about the relationship between words and images but also *how* he says it. In effect, we can look to this brief passage as an example of a persuasive use of rhetoric, in which McCloud makes very deliberate choices to strengthen his point. Notice how he uses comparison-contrast (pictures versus words), qualified language ("reality"), and parallel structure (both sentences move from "When" to a final phrase beginning with "more like") to persuade his audience of the way pictures and words can operate in similar ways. Such attention to detail is the first step in rhetorical analysis—looking at the way the writer chooses the most effective means of persuasion to make a point.

To fully appreciate McCloud's rhetorical decisions, however, we need to consider the passage in its original context. As you can see in Figure 1.3, McCloud amplifies his argument by creating what we call a **hybrid text**—a strategic combination of words and images.

This complex diagram relies on the visual-verbal relationship itself to map out the complicated nature of how we understand both written text and pictures. The repetition and echoes that we found in the quoted passage are graphically represented in Figure 1.3; in fact, translated into comic book form, the division between word and image breaks down. It becomes a visual continuum that strongly suggests McCloud's vision of the interrelationship between these

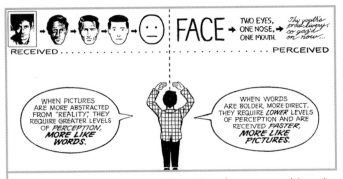

FIGURE 1.3. Scott McCloud writes in the medium of cartoons to explain comics.
Source: Courtesy of Scott McCloud

rhetorical elements. The power of this argument comes from McCloud's strategic assessment of the rhetorical situation: he, the **author,** recognizes that his **audience** (people interested in visual media) would find a **text** that relies on both visual and verbal elements to be highly persuasive.

McCloud's example is also instructive for demonstrating the way word and image can collaborate in modern arguments. Today more than ever, rhetoric operates not just through word choice, but also through choice of multimedia elements—images in a TV commercial, sounds accompanying a radio program, the font and color of a Website or flyer, even the layout strategies of this book. So we need to develop skills of analysis for all rhetorical texts. We need to envision argument as writing across diverse media and in turn develop **multimedia literacy,** or a careful way of reading, analyzing, and understanding media (visual, verbal, and other rhetorical texts).

Analyzing a Comic Strip

Comic strips are a productive starting point for examining how an understanding of the rhetorical situation and compositional strategies work together to produce powerful texts. We can begin with the cartoon in Figure 1.4, looking closely at its detail and composition. Focusing first on the central, circular frame in the middle of the strip, we can see even within this single frame the power of rhetoric at work. When you look at the circular panel, what do you see?

You may see a split screen with two boys and two alien creatures; if you are more familiar with comic strips, you may identify the boy as Calvin from the cartoon *Calvin and Hobbes.* What is the *rhetorical function* of this image? The cartoon provides a dramatic enactment of a moment of crisis in this boy's life. The left side portrays the "real" Calvin, cast in green liquid, an expression of alarm on his face. The white air bubbles surrounding him suggest his panic and amplify the impression of fear. In contrast, the right side of the cartoon

FIGURE 1.4. This *Calvin and Hobbes* cartoon conveys meaning through its colorful combination of sequential images.
Source: CALVIN AND HOBBES © 1992 Watterson. Reprinted with permission of UNIVERSAL PRESS SYNDICATE. All rights reserved.

features a different Calvin, his head opened up to reveal a mechanical brain, his eyes wide and staring like a boy possessed. It seems a standard body-snatcher science fiction scenario, complete with a pair of aliens preparing to refasten Calvin's spiky blonde hair on top of this new brain. As an individual image, this panel taps into a message of fear and childhood imagining, with the aliens readying Robot Calvin to take over the functions of the real Calvin's life.

Let's think about how the meaning of a cartoon changes when it is integrated into a full strip. When we view still frames in succession, we find

Student Writing

Read Jack Chung's interpretation of a *Calvin and Hobbes* cartoon strip.

www.ablongman.com/envision/202

that meaning becomes more complex in a wonderful array of possible interpretations. When read in conjunction with images of a stolen cookie jar, broken lamp, and discarded math book, Calvin's crisis takes on a slightly different meaning. As we arrive at the frame of Calvin gesticulating to his mother, her eyes narrowed with skepticism, we realize that the cartoon itself represents a moment of storytelling; the strip in effect juxtaposes Calvin's version of reality with his mother's. The final frame reveals the end of the tale, with Calvin banished to his room, staring out at the stars. These new elements add levels of meaning to the comic, as we are invited to ponder versions of reality, the power of childhood imagination, and the force of visual detail.

Watterson is hardly alone in the strategy of using his comic strip as a means of producing an argument or cultural critique. For instance, Aaron McGruder's *Boondocks* and Gary Trudeau's *Doonesbury* offer sharper, more critical messages about society through a combination of words and images.

In the *Boondocks* comic strip shown in Figure 1.5, McGruder argues for the power of political cartoons as a form of social commentary by having his protagonist, Huey, draw his own cartoon to comment on electoral politics. The irony in his line "Well, that's the key—not beating the reader over the head with your point" reveals the very way in which *Boondocks* does, in fact, make its point explicit for readers of the strip.

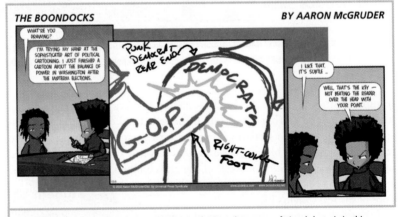

FIGURE 1.5. Cartoonist Aaron McGruder emphasizes the power of visual rhetoric in this comic strip.

Source: THE BOONDOCKS © 2002 Aaron McGruder. Dist. by UNIVERSAL PRESS SYNDICATE. Reprinted with permission. All rights reserved.

Significantly, McGruder subtitled his 2000 collection *The Boondocks: Because I Know You Don't Read the Newspapers.* In choosing these words for the title of his book, he presents his *cartoon* as a means of communicating information and arguments that we might see as equivalent to the news; that is, his comics persuade us to see current events, political controversies, and key issues concerning race in America in a certain light. This is shown in the second frame of Figure 1.5, where the main character, Huey, turns to cartooning itself as a way to craft a persuasive political message. He makes a rhetorical statement with his visual image and accompanying word choice; the drawing here is much more than merely an aesthetic, humorous, or informative text. It is a powerful rhetorical act.

To analyze *Boondocks*, we needed to assess the cartoon's *rhetorical situation* in drawing conclusions; we had to understand the way the writer (Aaron McGruder) took the audience (contemporary Americans) into consideration when creating the text (a comic strip, combining images and words). In fact, we can interpret McGruder's cartoon as offering a particularly striking example of a rhetorical situation: although the Universal Press Syndicate had anticipated that this edgy strip would appear in somewhere between 30 and 50 newspapers, *Boondocks* was published in 160 newspapers for its first run in April 1999 and was so popular with its audience that by the beginning of 2000 it was carried by more than 200 daily papers, and by 2005 it had been converted into an animated television series. McGruder's successful use of visual and verbal rhetoric to engage the topic of American race relations made his strip the most successful debut comic in the Universal Press Syndicate's history.

To apply this understanding of the rhetorical situation yourself, complete the following "Creative Practice." What is your analysis of these texts?

CREATIVE PRACTICE

Look at the *Penny Arcade* comic in Figure 1.6. Jot down your analysis of the elements of the cartoon: color, composition, characters, and action. Pay attention to facial expression, the use of symbols, and the changes between the panels. Then ask yourself: What persuasive statement does the cartoon convey? What is its argument? What is the message for readers?

Having done so, now read the following excerpt from one of the cartoonists' blog posts that accompanied the online publication of

FIGURE 1.6. *The Hipness Threshold* cartoon depicts the adventures of Gabe and Tycho as they accompany their friend Charles into an Apple Computer store, while in a blog entry, the cartoonist Jerry Holkins addresses Apple culture more broadly.

Source: Penny Arcade, Inc. www.penny-arcade.com

this comic. In it, Jerry Holkins makes a very similar argument—but in words. In what ways does this different rhetorical situation (blog versus Web comic) influence the way he makes his argument?

The way Apple projects its brand, however, has nothing to do with the underlying technology. It could not be more divorced from it. So if they want to create largely empty stores staffed exclusively by young hardbodies in ill-fitting t-shirts, it's open season. It's possible that each manifestation of this chain does not resemble the others, that each one is not populated with the scrubbed, tousled young things of the sort one sees in serious teen dramas. You'll forgive me if I don't believe that. I'd say it's far more likely that there is a single Apple Store, connected by a series of geographically distinct portals.

I don't put this out there to imply that the places I have to go to get technology or software are somehow superior, because they aren't. They're horrid. But at least I never feel underdressed.

As these examples demonstrate, we can gather a tremendous amount of information from a seemingly simple comic strip. Indeed, different readers will make different interpretations. This is what we mean by **visual arguments:** each viewer makes a separate interpretation of the image. As we learn to develop our *visual literacy,* we can make more and better-informed interpretations of such intriguing visual texts. And, as we will soon see, these skills of visual analysis will help you approach other kinds of texts rhetorically: political speeches, scholarly articles, letters to the editor about timely issues, even instant messaging and—as we just learned—blog posts.

Strategies for Analyzing Persuasive Texts

We've learned that rhetoric works as a means of persuading an audience to embrace the argument of the author. This is also true for the arguments *you make* about a text. In other words, rhetoric also applies to the texts you craft to persuade someone to accept your interpretation of a specific cultural or political artifact.

Why is it important for you to hone your skills in analyzing texts? Well, as we've seen, a single text visual can yield multiple interpretations. Your task is to argue convincingly—and persuade your audience—to see the text the way you see it. Your challenge as a student of writing and rhetoric is not only to identify the argument contained by a text but also to craft your own interpretation of that text. This involves a careful assessment of the ways in which the elements of the rhetorical situation work together to produce meaning in a text. In many cases your analysis will also address the interplay of words and images. Your analysis can take many forms: a written essay, an oral report, a visual argument, or a combination of these. Practice in analyzing the arguments of others is one of the best ways to develop your own persuasive skills.

Analyzing Editorial Cartoons

We can look at political cartoons—or **editorial cartoons** as they are also called—for another set of visual arguments to help us further develop effective strategies for analysis and interpretation. Editorial cartoons offer a rich resource for this sort of work since, as culture critic Matthew Diamond asserts, they "provide alternative perspectives at a glance because they are visual and vivid and often seem to communicate a clear or obvious message" (270). From the densely symbolic eighteenth-century plates of William Hogarth, to the biting social satire of *Punch*'s illustrators, to the edgy work of political cartoonists such as Ann Telnaes and Mike Luckovich in this century, the editorial cartoon has emerged as a succinct, powerful tool for writers to contribute to public dialogue on contemporary issues.

FIGURE 1.7. This cartoon by Daryl Cagle uses a striking symbol to make its argument.

Source: Daryl Cagle, Cagle Cartoons, Inc.

In the drawing by Daryl Cagle, for instance (see Figure 1.7), the particular face is recognizable to most twenty-first-century readers: the impish smile, the circular, black-frame glasses, and the prep-school tie identify this figure almost immediately as the young actor who plays Harry Potter in the film series. However, through one strategic substitution, Cagle transforms this image from illustration into commentary; he replaces the famous lightning bolt scar on Potter's forehead with a dollar sign. Cagle's Potter has been branded not by his encounter with a nearly omnipotent wizard but by his face-off with American capitalism. In this way, Cagle uses visual elements in his editorial cartoon to comment on the way this children's book hero has become a lucrative pop culture franchise.

For a more politically charged example, let's look at a powerful cartoon created by Pulitzer Prize-winning artist Mike Luckovich, depicting the Statue of Liberty crying in the aftermath of the attacks on the World Trade Center on September 11, 2001. As you examine Figure 1.8, ask yourself: What is the persuasive message of this political cartoon? Write down your interpretation, and be sure to consider the elements of the rhetorical situation as well as specific details that you observe.

Perhaps, in your attempts to write a rhetorical analysis of this cartoon's meaning, you commented on the statue's childlike features, suggestive of innocence or vulnerability. You might have remarked on the nose and hair as seeming particularly Caucasian and asked: What message does this send about who is American? You might also have integrated the history associated with this statue into your interpretation. Is Luckovich offering an argument about how America's role as a haven for the oppressed and as a steward of peace and goodwill was attacked on September 11?

FIGURE 1.8. Mike Luckovich's "Statue of Liberty" circulated widely in newspapers and on the Internet after September 11.

Source: By permission of Mike Luckovich and Creators Syndicate, Inc.

Some students reading this cartoon have argued that it casts an ironic eye on the history of America; they read the Statue of Liberty as crying about the abuses of civil rights in the wake of the attacks. Others claim that the composition of the cartoon—the visual details of the crying eye and childish face—suggests that this country is more vulnerable than previously thought. As you consider the rhetorical situation for the cartoon (the way in which it was written in the wake of the attacks), reflect on how different audiences might respond to its power.

Practicing Rhetorical Analysis

Before choosing your own text for rhetorical analysis, let's look closely at the strategies you can use to analyze a text and arrive at your own interpretation.

In Figure 1.9, for instance, you will find a hybrid argument on the national debate over the Pledge of Allegiance. To get started composing an interpretation of this text, first notice which specific verbal and visual elements stand out as you look at the cartoon.

The drawing itself suggests a generic classroom in America: several elementary school students, diverse in terms of gender and race, face the flag in the standard, patriotic pose, their teacher looking on. The flag, as you might expect, is center stage—but it is significantly limp and uninspiring. This strategic rendering of the flag becomes complicated by the words that accompany the image: "one nation, under nothing in particular." Not only has "God" been removed from the pledge, but with the clever substitution of "under nothing in particular," cartoonist Gary Markstein seems to speaks to the fear of raising a generation of Americans—and a future America—with no faith. His drawing of the disgusted teacher appears to embody the argument of the cartoon. Her mental thought, "God help us," voices an older generation's frustration and worry in the face of these young nihilists. In this way, you might argue, the cartoonist has taken the controversy over the use of "God" in the Pledge of Allegiance to an extreme; he has strategically used both word and image to create a powerful argument about this issue, as powerful as any written article found in a *Wall Street Journal* op-ed piece.

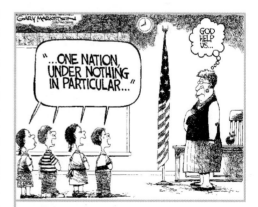

FIGURE 1.9. Gary Markstein conveys the controversy over the constitutionality of including the phrase "under God" in the Pledge of Allegiance.

Source: Gary Markstein and Copley News Service

Like Markstein's editorial cartoon, the following excerpt from an editorial by Samuel P. Huntington comments on the debate over the Pledge of Allegiance. This debate was ignited by Michael Newdow, who filed a lawsuit against his daughter's school district, arguing that the words "under God" in the Pledge amounted to an unconstitutional endorsement of religion. A federal court ruled in favor of Newdow, but the Supreme Court reversed that decision in June 2004. No final decision has been made on the issue of whether or not the words "under God" violate the Constitution's provisions against the endorsement of religion by the government. As you read the excerpt, consider how Huntington's argument compares to Markstein's cartoon. Are they both making the same argument in different ways? Or is there a difference in what each text argues?

"Under God"
Michael Newdow is right. Atheists are outsiders in America.
Samuel P. Huntington

The battle over the Pledge of Allegiance has stimulated vigorous controversy on an issue central to America's identity. Opponents of "under God" (which was added to the pledge in 1954) argue that the United States is a secular country, that the First Amendment prohibits rhetorical or material state support for religion, and that people should be able to pledge allegiance to their country without implicitly also affirming a belief in God. Supporters point out that the phrase is perfectly consonant with the views of the framers of the Constitution, that Lincoln had used these words in the Gettysburg Address, and that the Supreme Court—which on Monday sidestepped a challenge to the Pledge of Allegiance—has long held that no one could be compelled to say the pledge.

The atheist who brought the court challenge, Michael Newdow, asked this question: "Why should I be made to feel like an outsider?" Earlier, the Court of Appeals in San Francisco had agreed that the words "under God" sent "a message to unbelievers that they are outsiders, not full members of the political community."

Although the Supreme Court did not address the question directly, Mr. Newdow got it right: Atheists are "outsiders" in the American community. Americans are one of the most religious people in the world, particularly compared with the peoples of other highly industrialized democracies. But they nonetheless tolerate and respect the rights of atheists and nonbelievers. Unbelievers do not have to recite the pledge, or engage in any religiously tainted practice of which they disapprove. They also, however, do not have the right to impose their atheism on all those Americans whose beliefs now and historically have defined America as a religious nation.

In composing your analysis of this text, you would need to follow a familiar process: First, look carefully at all the elements in the text. You might create a list of your observations or use the prewriting checklist at the end of this chapter to help you read the text more closely. Then, speculate about the meaning of each element. How does it contribute to the whole? Finally, complete the rhetorical triangle (see Figure 1.2) for the text, assessing who the author is, who the intended audience is, and what the argument of the text is, based on your observations of the details.

CREATIVE PRACTICE

Using the political cartoon shown in Figure 1.10, create your own hybrid text. First, jot down your observations about the cartoon; think about its rhetorical situation (its audience, author, and message) and determine a context (when and where you think it appeared). Next, develop an interpretation of the cartoon's meaning. Finally, fill in the blank tablet to clarify that argument for future readers. When you are done, move into a small group and share your work—both your written analysis and your hybrid text. Discuss what you have learned in producing oral, written, and cartoon texts, and how each text conveys your argument.

FIGURE 1.10. In this modified version of John Deering's cartoon, the words on the tablet have been removed, opening up many possibilities for alternative meanings.

Source: By permission of John Deering and Creators Syndicate, Inc.

As you completed your work for the "Creative Practice," you probably found that your additions to the blank tablet altered the cartoon's meaning in fundamental ways. Perhaps you inserted words that referred to religion,

September 11, the war with Iraq, or the 2006 Danish cartoon controversy—in this way, you practiced the art of rhetoric that, through the combination of word and image, contributed a very specific political message or strong social commentary. Or perhaps you drew something in the tablet instead, using *visual persuasion* as your means of practicing rhetoric.

When we gave this exercise to our students, some offered the words "We support the USA" or "Women for equal rights" while others suggested filling in the blank with a visual text—a photo of Hillary Clinton or a drawing of a Muslim woman lifting her burka to expose her heels. In the actual published version from the 2001 *Arkansas Democrat Gazette,* cartoonist John Deering made the tablet present the ironic words "To the Taliban: Give us Osama Bin Laden or we'll send your women to college." Thus, Deering used the ongoing search for Osama Bin Laden as a springboard for lampooning cultural differences in gender roles; his words suggest international and cultural differences among countries. His cartoon practiced visual and verbal means of persuasion, both of which are important to consider when we are analyzing and writing about a text.

Student Writing

See Jeff Enquist's analysis of a cartoonist's commentary on the media representation of Catholic priests as part of a larger social issue dealing with the place of religion in American culture.

www.ablongman.com/envision/203

COLLABORATIVE CHALLENGE

To begin writing about cartoons as powerful rhetorical acts, get into groups of three and turn to the Internet, a vast resource for finding visual rhetoric, to locate political cartoons that address the same issue from diverse national perspectives. Go to the Chapter 1 resource page of the *Envision* Website, and select two or three cartoons from Daryl Cagle's Professional Cartoonist Index. Compare how different countries craft persuasive visual arguments about the same issue with remarkably divergent messages. Working collaboratively, write an analysis of each cartoon, and prepare to share your interpretations with the rest of the class. Be sure to describe elements of the visual text in detail and discuss how each contributes to the rhetorical force of the image.

www.ablongman.com/envision/204

What we can learn from this practice with rhetoric is that the relationship between interpretation and argument is a complex one. Although the author might intend to produce a certain argument, at times the audience may offer a slightly different interpretation. Our task as readers and writers is both to study a text carefully and to learn how to persuade others to see the text as we see it.

One powerful example of how texts can be read in multiple ways occurred in 2002 when Pulitzer Prize-winning cartoonist Doug Marlette created a political cartoon following the 9/11 attacks (see Figure 1.11). The title of the cartoon, "What Would Mohammed Drive?" makes a clear link between the Muslim religion and terrorism, as depicted by the nuclear warhead in the Ryder truck.

FIGURE 1.11. Doug Marlette received death threats after publishing this cartoon.

Source: Courtesy of Douf Marlette

The cartoon caused a firestorm of protest from the Muslim community in America, including death threats on the cartoonist. Marlette responded by asserting that "the objective of political cartooning 'is not to soothe and tend sensitive psyches, but to jab and poke in an attempt to get at deeper truths, popular or otherwise'" (quoted in Moore). Marlette's own words reveal that cartoons are not merely humorous texts but rather, as we have seen, they are rhetorical—they intend to persuade.

Look again at the cartoon and ask yourself *how* it attempts to jab or poke. What elements of composition, framing, shading, and layout suggest to you the target of Marlette's jab? How does the title set up or shape possible readings of the cartoon? How might this cartoon be read differently by an American audience, an Arab audience, and an Arab-American audience? How might it be interpreted in the United States or in the Middle East as conveying a different persuasive message?

Some might argue that the cartoon takes the announced threat of terrorists potentially using trucks to carry out nuclear attacks and reproduces it without irony. Another reader analyzing the cartoon could say that it mocks the government issuing the warning about post-September 11 terrorists. A third reader could point to the caricature of the driver and state that the cartoon makes fun of people of Arab descent. These varied ways of reading and responding to the text depend on both *audience* and *context*, bringing to light the importance of the rhetorical situation. They also reveal the importance of learning effective means of persuading others to see the text through a certain interpretive lens, or way of reading the cartoon.

Let's turn now to Doug Marlette's writing to see how he used the art of rhetoric to persuade his many readers to see the cartoon from his perspective. Marlette's article stands as another persuasive text for us to analyze. As you read this article, originally published in the *Columbia Journalism Review*, use some of the same strategies of analysis that we've used on comics and cartoons throughout the chapter. Ask yourself: Who is his audience? How does he position himself as author? What is his argument? What evidence does he use to support that argument? Which parts are the most persuasive? Which are the least persuasive? What visual images does he convey with words? Are you persuaded by his argument?

Marlette uses a provocative title to capture his readers' attention.

Marlette begins his article by establishing the context behind it. Notice how he implicitly defends the cartoon by describing how it was intended not just to poke fun at Mohammed but at Christian evangelicals as well. The play on words at the end of this paragraph gives the readers their first taste of the humorous, slightly irreverent tone and the close attention to style that characterize this piece.

In the second paragraph, Marlette uses specific examples of the threats he received to construct a rather unfavorable image of the people offended by his cartoon.

I Was a Tool of Satan

Doug Marlette

COLUMBIA JOURNALISM REVIEW, NOVEMBER/DECEMBER 2003, 52

Last year, I drew a cartoon that showed a man in Middle Eastern apparel at the wheel of a Ryder truck hauling a nuclear warhead. The caption read, "What Would Mohammed Drive?" Besides referring to the vehicle that Timothy McVeigh rode into Oklahoma City, the drawing was a takeoff on the "What Would Jesus Drive?" campaign created by Christian evangelicals to challenge the morality of owning gas-guzzling SUVs. The cartoon's main target, of course, was the faith-based politics of a different denomination. Predictably, the Shiite hit the fan.

Can you say "fatwa"? My newspaper, *The Tallahassee Democrat,* and I received more than 20,000 e-mails demanding an apology for misrepresenting the peace-loving religion of the Prophet Mohammed—or else. Some spelled out the "else": death, mutilation, Internet spam. . . . "What you did, Mr. Dog, will cost you your life. Soon you will join the dogs . . . hahaha in hell." "Just wait . . . we will see you in hell with all jews. . . ." The onslaught was orchestrated by an organization called the Council on American-Islamic Relations. CAIR bills itself as an "advocacy group." I was to discover that among the followers of Islam it advocated for were the men convicted of the 1993 bombing of the World Trade Center. At any rate, its campaign against me included flash-floods of e-mail intended to shut down servers at my newspaper and my syndicate, as well as viruses aimed at my home computer. The controversy became a subject of newspaper editorials, columns, Web logs, talk radio, and CNN. I was condemned on the front page of the Saudi publication *Arab News* by the secretary general of the Muslim World League.

My answer to the criticism was published in the *Democrat* (and reprinted around the country) under the headline *With All Due Respect, an Apology Is Not in Order.* I almost felt that I could have written the response in my sleep. In my thirty-year career, I have regularly drawn cartoons that offended religious fundamentalists and true believers of every stripe, a fact that I tend to list in the "Accomplishments" column of my résumé. I have outraged Christians by skewering Jerry Falwell, Catholics by needling the pope, and Jews by criticizing Israel. Those who rise up against the expression of ideas are strikingly similar. No one is less tolerant than those demanding tolerance. Despite differences of culture and creed, they all seem to share the notion that there is only one way of looking at things, their way. What I have learned from years of this is one of the great lessons of all the world's religions: we are all one in our humanness.

In my response, I reminded readers that my "What Would Mohammed Drive?" drawing was an assault not upon Islam but on the distortion of the Muslim religion by murderous fanatics—the followers of Mohammed who flew those planes into our buildings, to be sure, but also the Taliban killers of noncompliant women and destroyers of great art, the true believers who decapitated an American reporter, the young Palestinian suicide bombers taking out patrons of pizza parlors in the name of the Prophet Mohammed.

Then I gave my Journalism 101 lecture on the First Amendment, explaining that in this country we do not apologize for our opinions. Free speech is the linchpin of our republic. All other freedoms flow from it. After all, we don't need a First Amendment to allow us to run boring, inoffensive cartoons. We need constitutional protection for our right to express unpopular views. If we can't discuss the great issues of the day on the pages of our newspapers fearlessly, and without apology, where can we discuss them? In the streets with guns? In cafes with strapped-on bombs?

Although my initial reaction to the "Mohammed" hostilities was that I had been there before, gradually I began to feel that there was something new, something darker afoot. The repressive impulses of

He recounts his response to the protests and comes to one of the most important points of his essay: that he is an equal opportunity offender, having penned cartoons that had enraged many different groups. By moving the question away from an issue of Islam to a larger issue of tolerance, Marlette sets up the issues of censorship and freedom of speech that are the real subjects of this essay.

Notice the way that Marlette also condemns the "murderous fanatics" he describes based on an ongoing pattern of behavior—a rhetorical decision that makes his critique seem less reactionary and more thoughtful.

In this paragraph, he evokes the First Amendment and ends with an implicit comparison between America, with its civil liberties, and more militaristic and war-torn countries. Notice the power of the rhetorical questions that he uses at the end of the paragraph, asking readers to consider the alternatives to American freedom of speech.

that old-time religion were now being fed by the subtler inhibitions of mammon and the marketplace. Ignorance and bigotry were reinventing themselves in the post-Christian age by dressing up as "sensitivity" and masquerading as a public virtue that may be as destructive to our rights as religious zealotry. We seem to be entering a Techno Dark Age, in which the machines that were designed to serve the free flow of information have fallen into the hands of an anti-intellectual mobocracy.

At this point, he returns to describing his career as an equal opportunity offender, shifting the focus off Islam and instead discussing his troubles with evangelical Christians. By mentioning the death threats he received for his cartoons about the PTL Club (a televangelist show hosted by Jim and Tammy Bakker in the 1980s), he draws an implicit comparison here between Christian fundamentalists and what he calls Islamic "fanatics."

Twenty-five years ago, I began inciting the wrath of the faithful by caricaturing the grotesque disparity between Jim and Tammy Faye Bakker's televangelism scam and the Christian piety they used to justify it. I was then working at *The Charlotte Observer,* in the hometown of the Bakkers' PTL Club, which instigated a full-bore attack on me. The issues I was cartooning were substantial enough that I won the Pulitzer Prize for my PTL work. But looking back on that fundamentalist religious campaign, even though my hate mail included some death threats, I am struck by the relative innocence of the times and how ominous the world has since become—how high the stakes, even for purveyors of incendiary doodles.

Although he doesn't reproduce his 1978 cartoon here, he offers a clear description to his readers.

One of the first cartoons I ever drew on PTL was in 1978, when Jim Bakker's financial mismanagement forced him to lay off a significant portion of his staff. The drawing showed the TV preacher sitting at the center of Leonardo Da Vinci's *Last Supper* informing his disciples, "I'm going to have to let some of you go!" Bakker's aides told reporters that he was so upset by the drawing that he fell to his knees in his office, weeping into the gold shag carpet. Once he staggered to his feet, he and Tammy Faye went on the air and, displaying my cartoons, encouraged viewers to phone in complaints to the *Observer* and cancel their subscriptions.

Jim Bakker finally resigned in disgrace from his PTL ministry, and I drew a cartoon of the televangelist who replaced him, Jerry Falwell, as a serpent slithering into PTL paradise: "Jim and Tammy were expelled from paradise and left me in charge."

This exchange brings humor back into the piece and demonstrates Marlette's seemingly flippant response to his critics.

One of the many angry readers who called me at the newspaper said, "You're a tool of Satan."

"Excuse me?"

"You're a tool of Satan for that cartoon you drew."

"That's impossible," I said. "I couldn't be a tool of Satan. *The Charlotte Observer*'s personnel department tests for that sort of thing."

Confused silence on the other end.

"They try to screen for tools of Satan," I explained. "Knight Ridder human resources has a strict policy against hiring tools of Satan."

Click.

Until "What Would Mohammed Drive?" most of the flak I caught was from the other side of the Middle East conflict. Jewish groups complained that my cartoons critical of Israel's invasion of Lebanon were anti-Semitic because I had drawn Prime Minister Menachem Begin with a big nose. My editors took the strategic position that I drew everyone's nose big. At one point, editorial pages were spread out on the floor for editors to measure with a ruler the noses of various Jewish and non-Jewish figures in my cartoons.

After I moved to the Northeast, it was Catholics I offended. At *New York Newsday*, I drew a close-up of the pope wearing a button that read "No Women Priests." There was an arrow pointing to his forehead and the inscription from Matthew 16:18: "Upon This Rock I Will Build My Church." The *Newsday* switchboard lit up like a Vegas wedding chapel. *Newsday* ran an apology for the cartoon, a first in my career, and offered me a chance to respond in a column. The result—though the paper published it in full—got me put on probation for a year by the publisher. That experience inspired the opening scene of my first novel, *The Bridge*.

* * *

But how do you cartoon a cartoon? It's a problem of redundancy in this hyperbolic age to caricature an already extravagantly distorted culture. When writers try to censor other writers, we're in Toontown. We are in deep trouble when victimhood becomes a sacrament, personal injury a point of pride, when irreverence is seen as a hate crime, when the true values of art and religion are distorted and debased by fanatics and zealots, whether in the name of the God of Abraham, Isaac, and Jacob, the Prophet Mohammed, or a literary Cult of Narcissus.

It was the cynically outrageous charge of homophobia against my book that brought me around to the similarities between the true believers I was used to dealing with and the post-modern secular humanist Church Ladies wagging their fingers at me. The threads

Again, Marlette takes time to implicitly defend himself against claims of targeting Islam by describing how he has offended other religious groups as well.

Here Marlette cleverly plays on the idea of cartooning by pausing to assert that the reaction of his critics is "cartoonish" and exaggerated.

Marlette now comes to one of the focal points of his discussion: the way censorship is enforced not by angry critics but by a culture of "niceness" that is afraid to offend.

that connect the CAIR and the literary fat-was, besides technological sabotage, are entreaties to "sensitivity," appeals to institutional guilt, and faith in a corporate culture of controversy avoidance. Niceness is the new face of censorship in this country.

The censors no longer come to us in jackboots with torches and baying dogs in the middle of the night. They arrive now in broad daylight with marketing surveys and focus-group findings. They come as teams, not armies, trained in effectiveness, certified in sensitivity, and wielding degrees from the Columbia journalism school. They're known not for their bravery but for their efficiency. They show gallantry only when they genuflect to apologize. The most disturbing thing about the "Mohammed" experience was that a laptop Luftwaffe was able to blitz editors into not running the cartoon in my own newspaper. "WWMD" ran briefly on the Tallahassee Democrat Web site, but once an outcry was raised, the editors pulled it and banned it from the newspaper altogether.

The cyberprotest by CAIR showed a sophisticated understanding of what motivates newsroom managers these days—bottom-line concerns, a wish for the machinery to run smoothly, and the human-resources mandate not to offend. Many of my e-mail detractors appeared to be well-educated, recent emigres. Even if their English sometimes faltered, they were fluent in the language of victimhood. Presumably, victimization was one of their motives for leaving their native countries, yet the subtext of many of their letters was that this country should be more like the ones they emigrated from. They had the American know-how without the know-why. In the name of tolerance, in the name of their peaceful God, they threatened violence against someone they accused of falsely accusing them of violence.

With the rise of the bottom-line culture and the corporatization of news gathering, tolerance itself has become commodified and denuded of its original purpose. Consequently, the best part of the American character—our generous spirit, our sense of fair play—has been turned against us.

Tolerance has become a tool of coercion, of institutional inhibition, of bureaucratic self-preservation. We all should take pride in how this country for the most part curbed the instinct to lash out at Arab-Americans in the wake of 9/11. One of the great strengths of

The reference to the Columbia journalism school would have extra force considering that this piece was originally published in the *Columbia Journalism Review.* Here, also, he clearly articulates the central point of his extended Mohammed story: that the most "disturbing thing" was that critics were able to influence his editors into refusing to run the cartoon.

Having begun his argument applauding American principles—namely, freedom of speech—he now demonstrates the way that corporate structure and an ideology of tolerance (both hallmarks of American culture) are actually operating in conflict with First Amendment rights.

this nation is our sensitivity to the tyranny of the majority, our sense of justice for all. But the First Amendment, the miracle of our system, is not just a passive shield of protection. In order to maintain our true, nationally defining diversity, it obligates journalists to be bold, writers to be full-throated and uninhibited, and those blunt instruments of the free press, cartoonists like me, not to self-censor. We must use it or lose it.

Political cartoonists daily push the limits of free speech. They were once the embodiment of journalism's independent voice. Today they are as endangered a species as bald eagles. The professional troublemaker has become a luxury that offends the bottom-line sensibilities of corporate journalism. Twenty years ago, there were two hundred of us working on daily newspapers. Now there are only ninety. Herblock is dead. Jeff MacNelly is dead. And most of the rest of us might as well be. Just as resume hounds have replaced newshounds in today's newsrooms, ambition has replaced talent at the drawing boards. Passion has yielded to careerism, Thomas Nast to Eddie Haskell. With the retirement of Paul Conrad at the *Los Angeles Times*, a rolling blackout from California has engulfed the country, dimming the pilot lights on many American editorial pages. Most editorial cartoons now look as bland as B-roll and as impenetrable as a 1040 form.

We know what happens to the bald eagle when it's not allowed to reproduce and its habitat is contaminated. As the species is thinned, the eco-balance is imperiled.

Why should we care about the obsolescence of the editorial cartoonist?

Because cartoons can't say "on the other hand," because they strain reason and logic, because they are hard to defend and thus are the acid test of the First Amendment, and that is why they must be preserved.

What would Marlette drive? Forget SUVs and armored cars. It would be an all-terrain vehicle you don't need a license for. Not a foreign import, but American-made. It would be built with the same grit and gumption my grandmother showed when she faced down government soldiers in the struggle for economic justice, and the courage my father displayed as a twenty-year-old when he waded ashore in the predawn darkness of Salerno and Anzio. It would be

He ends this paragraph by clarifying his interpretation of the First Amendment, specifically with relation to journalism. He then uses a cliché to emphasize his point.

Notice the analogy he makes between political cartoonists and bald eagles. It operates on two levels, on the one hand emphasizing that they are endangered and on the other hand suggesting that cartoonists represent America's freedoms.

His references on this page to important political cartoonists (Herbert Block, Jeff MacNelly, Paul Conrad) underscore his message about the decline of political cartooning as a genre.

In the next paragraph he returns to his metaphor of the bald eagle, developing it into a richer analogy.

As he moves toward his conclusion, Marlette draws his essay together by echoing and slightly revising the title of the cartoon that started the controversy and demonstrating the way that images carry symbolic weight.

fueled by the freedom spirit that both grows out of our Constitution and is protected by it—fiercer than any fatwa, tougher than all the tanks in the army, and more powerful than any bunker-buster.

If I drew you a picture it might look like the broken-down jalopy driven by the Joads from Oklahoma to California. Or like the Cadillac that Jack Kerouac took on the road in his search for nirvana. Or the pickup Woody Guthrie hitched a ride in on that ribbon of highway, bound for glory. Or the International Harvester Day-Glo school bus driven cross-country by Ken Kesey and his Merry Pranksters. Or the Trailways and Greyhound buses the Freedom Riders boarded to face the deadly backroads of Mississippi and Alabama. Or the moon-buggy Neil Armstrong commanded on that first miraculous trip to the final frontier.

What would Marlette drive? The self-evident, unalienable American model of democracy that we as a young nation discovered and road-tested for the entire world: the freedom to be ourselves, to speak the truth as we see it, and to drive it home.

In his written argument, Marlette describes the observations he has made about the public's response to his cartoons. This process parallels the work you have done in walking across campus and observing rhetoric or in listing your observations of the visual detail found in the *Calvin and Hobbes* cartoon. Notice how specific Marlette is in describing the reactions to his cartoons and how concretely he conjures up American identity through the imagery of the bald eagle and the driven vehicle. These are *rhetorical moves,* strategic choices he has made as a writer in deciding how best to persuade his readers (especially those outraged by the cartoons) to see his drawing from a different point of view. Just as Markstein picked the most appropriate words and images for inside his Pledge of Allegiance cartoon, Marlette picked the most appropriate words and metaphors to use in his article.

Writing a Rhetorical Analysis

As you turn now to write a longer, more sustained rhetorical analysis of a text, you'll be putting into practice all the skills you've learned so far in this chapter. You'll need to write down your observations of the text; spend time discussing them in detail, as we have done with the many examples we've worked on so far; and use these observations as evidence to make an argument that will persuade others to see the text the way you see it.

It's crucial to remember that when you write a rhetorical analysis, you perform a rhetorical act of persuasion yourself. Accordingly, you need to include the key elements of analytical writing that we've learned so far: (1) have a point of interpretation to share with your readers, (2) take time to walk readers through concrete details to prove your point, and (3) lead your readers through the essay in an engaging and convincing way. But of all these, the most important is your argument, your "take" or interpretation of the text—your **thesis.**

Developing a Thesis Statement

Perhaps the single most important part of your writing will be your **thesis statement,** the concise statement of your interpretation of your chosen text. To understand thesis statements, let's work through an example. Imagine, for instance, that you want to write an argument about the editorial cartoons in Figures 1.12 and 1.13. Both cartoons comment on recent debates about immigration policy. How might you develop a thesis statement that persuasively conveys your interpretation of how these cartoons contribute to the debate surrounding the status of undocumented immigrants?

Start by jotting down what you see; make close observations about these cartoons. Then use questions to bring your argument into focus

FIGURE 1.12. Cartoon by Daryl Cagle.
Source: Daryl Cagle, Cagle Cartoons, Inc.

FIGURE 1.13. Cartoon by Michael Ramirez.
Source: Michael Ramirez and Copley News Service

and to make a specific claim about the images. The end product will be a *working thesis.* The process of developing your thesis might look like this:

1. Write down your observations.

Close observations: Both pictures focus, literally or symbolically, on the border between the United States and Mexico and on the way that we set up fences (or vault doors) to keep illegal immigrants out. Both also show holes in those barriers: one focuses on people running through a hole in the fence; the other shows a small door in the vault that looks as if it's been propped open from the inside. The words are interesting, too. In the Cagle cartoon, the big sign says "Keep out," while the smaller signs are designed to draw people in. In the Ramirez cartoon, the small sign says "Cheap labor welcome," contradicting the message of the large, high-security door that blocks access to the United States.

2. Work with your observations to construct a preliminary thesis statement.

First statement: Both cartoons focus on the contradiction in American border policy.

3. Refine your argument by asking questions that make your statement less general.

Ask yourself: How? What contradications? To what effect? How do I know this?

4. Revise your preliminary thesis statement to be more specific; perhaps include specific evidence that drives your claim.

Revised statement: The cartoons in Figures 1.12 and 1.13 focus on the contradictions in American border policy by showing that on the one hand, the American government wants to keep illegal immigrants out, but on the other hand, economic forces encourage them to enter the United States illegally.

5. **Further polish your thesis by refining your language and asking questions about the implications of your working thesis statement.**

   Ask yourself: What do you find interesting about this observation? How does it tap into larger social or cultural issues?

6. **Write your working thesis to include a sense of the implications of your claim. Sometimes we call this the "So What?" of your claim.**

   Working thesis: The political cartoons in Figures 1.12 and 1.13 offer a pointed commentary on the recent immigration debate, suggesting ways the official government stance against illegal immigration is undermined by economic forces that tolerate, if not welcome, the entry of undocumented workers into the United States.

This activity should show you that a strong, argumentative thesis does more than state a topic: it makes a claim about that topic that you will develop in the rest of your paper. Let's look at one more example to further consider ways to produce sharp, clear, and persuasive thesis statements. The examples that follow are a series of thesis statements about Mike Thompson's cartoon in Figure 1.14, published in 2006 in reaction to rising gas prices.

Thesis 1: Mike Thompson's cartoon is very powerful.

> *Assessment: This thesis relies too heavily on subjective opinion; the author offers no criteria for evaluating the cartoon or a context for understanding the statement.*

Thesis 2: Mike Thompson's drawing shows his opinion about SUVs.

> *Assessment: This thesis statement rests too much on a broad generalization rather than specific analysis.*

FIGURE 1.14. Cartoon by Mike Thompson.
Source: Mike Thompson and Copley News Service

Thesis 3: In response to rising gas prices, Mike Thompson drew a powerful editorial cartoon about the relationship between driving SUVs and consuming fossil fuels.

> *Assessment: This thesis statement merely states a fact and makes a broad claim rather than offering a focused interpretation of the cartoon. It needs to explain **how** the cartoon was powerful.*

Thesis 4: In his 2006 editorial cartoon "Aptly Named," Mike Thompson persuasively plays with the term *fossil fuel* to suggest that SUVs and the "wanton consumption" of gasoline represent an outdated approach to transportation that needs to recognize its own imminent extinction.

> *Assessment: Of the four examples, this thesis provides the most provocative and specific articulation of the author's interpretation of the significance of Thompson's cartoon.*

A strong argument, driven by a strong thesis statement, is at the heart of any successful essay.

Let's look at how one student, Jason Benhaim, combines effective strategies of analysis with a carefully crafted thesis statement to compose his own rhetorical analysis of a recent editorial cartoon.

AT A GLANCE

Testing Your Thesis

Do you have a specific and interesting angle on your topic?

- Does it offer a statement of significance about your topic?
- Is the thesis sharp enough (not too obvious)?
- Could someone argue against it (or is it just an observation)?
- Is it not too dense (trying to compact the entire paper) or too simplistic (not developing your point thoroughly)?

Notice the way Jason begins his essay with a series of evocative questions that directly engage readers.

Tapping into the American Psyche:

Using Bird Flu to Critique the American Government

What comes to mind when you hear the phrase "Hurricane Katrina"? Does it conjure up pitiful images of human suffering or evoke a sense of anger at the American government's failure to respond? What about the phrases "war in Iraq" or "obesity epidemic"? "Enron scandal"? "Global warming"? "Monica Lewinsky"? Indeed, the media has ground these key phrases so deeply into the American psyche that their mere mention triggers a particular emotional response in even the most socially unaware audience. The fact that all audiences automatically associate these key phrases with certain images, ideas, and feelings makes their invocation a powerful tool for all varieties of social commentators, especially political cartoonists. Certainly, political cartoonists employ several readily apparent methods of condensing as much meaning as possible into a single frame, including the use of symbols, such as having an eagle represent an entire country, or simple artistic decisions, such as portraying Uncle Sam as aging and frail instead of youthful and muscular. However, the cartoonist's ability to take advantage of the associations the public already has concerning certain current events is often overlooked. A recent cartoon by Eric Devericks provides a powerful example of the way in which cartoonists can combine manipulation of classic symbols with allusion to a current event, in this case the imminent bird flu epidemic, in order to construct a visual-verbal argument speaking to issues that extend beyond the current event in question.

Source: Eric Devericks/The Seattle Times

The central image of the Devericks cartoon is a crotchety old Uncle Sam staring intently through a pair of binoculars, his rifle at the ready. Because he faces to the right, the direction in which Americans read, Uncle Sam appears forward-looking and vigilant. However, the details of Uncle Sam's figure hint at his shortcomings. Though armed, Uncle Sam's frail and thin limbs betray his

In his first paragraph, he carefully sets up the context for his argument—that cartoonists tend to work with symbols or issues that automatically provoke a ready-made response in their audience.

By the end of the paragraph, Jason has moved from the context to his thesis statement, which refers to the specific cartoon he will be discussing.

The placement of the cartoon here is quite strategic: by including it in his first paragraph, he presents it as visual evidence to readers, making a much more powerful argument than if he had appended it to the end of his paper.

Jason spends his first main body paragraph describing the cartoon, drawing readers' attention to key details. Notice how, as the paragraph progresses, Jason moves from description to analysis.

weakness. In the context of the cartoon, his white hair only serves to emphasize his old age, and even his characteristic bowtie contributes to his appearing old-fashioned. His antique rifle, so outdated to be equipped with a bayonet, most directly conveys a sense of his being behind the times. The scowl on Uncle Sam's face indicates a certain stubbornness, as though he is obstinately clinging to obsolete means of combating dangerous adversaries.

Uncle Sam's presentation alone constitutes an argument regarding the American government's outdated militaristic obsession and could potentially stand alone as a complete political cartoon. However, when coupled with the image of the sickly bird labeled with the cartoon's only words, "bird flu," the danger for America in focusing solely on military endeavors becomes immediately apparent. The bird's mere presence indicates that the specter of disease is wholly capable of bypassing America's military defense. Indeed, the bird's highly significant position atop the rifle further suggests that America's military might is not only ineffective against disease but actually supports its presence—without the rifle, the disease-carrier would have no place to perch! In light of the bird's position atop his weapon, Uncle Sam's binoculars become useless and even detrimental. His focus on enemy attackers blinds him to the possibility of other dangers. The presence of this sickly bird, representative of an impending costly and potentially life-threatening epidemic, wholly undermines Uncle Sam's vigilant appearance. Despite its simplicity and scarcity of words, the Devericks cartoon makes a clear statement: the American

Jason argues persuasively by using concrete details from his careful analysis of the cartoon.

Jason includes a strong transition here to move readers' attention from the Uncle Sam figure to that of the bird perched on the end of his rifle.

Notice the way Jason revises his own initial description of Uncle Sam to sharpen his argument about how the inclusion of the bird influences the way we read the cartoon as a whole.

government's focus on its military endeavors results in a dangerous ignorance regarding other critical issues.

Though bird flu provides an excellent example of an issue potentially ignored by the American government in favor of war, the bird perched on the end of Uncle Sam's rifle could easily be replaced by a symbol of a different issue facing America. For example, Devericks could just as easily have argued that America's militaristic attitude detracts from its focus on a crumbling educational system or its president's plummeting polls. The bird's tired and sickly appearance indicates that it bypassed Uncle Sam's defenses without much effort, suggesting that America's military defenses are equally susceptible to infiltration by other nonmilitary dangers.

Merely noting America's recent infatuation with war efforts constitutes a mildly effective statement, but using bird flu as a tangible example of why such an attitude is detrimental to the health of the United States brings the message home. Portraying the American eagle as weakened and sickly might make for a startling image, but captioning such an image with a modern phrase forces people to consider bird flu in a different light. Allusion to bird flu adds extra punch to this political cartoon. Even if its audience knows nothing about the details of bird flu, Devericks can at least count on their associating the phrase with a sense of helplessness, panic, or fear. Certainly the mere thought of an epidemic is frightening, but for Devericks bird flu merely shines light on what ought to be the American public's main fear—will their government be able to handle it?

In his penultimate paragraph, Jason strengthens his argument by speculating about alternative ways the cartoon might have been drawn. The summation sentence at the end of this paragraph is a key moment when Jason firmly articulates his interpretation of the cartoon.

Notice the way Jason carefully offers a summary of his argument here without sounding repetitive. He ends his essay with a provocative question that points readers back to his interpretation of this cartoon: that it is ultimately less a commentary on bird flu than a critique of the government.

AT A GLANCE

Visual Rhetoric Analysis Essays

- Do you have a sharp point or thesis to make about the visual text?
- Have you selected key visual details to discuss in support of your main point?
- Do you lead readers through your analysis of the text by discussing important details in sequence? These include:
    Visual composition, layout, and imagery
    Verbal elements in the text
    Color, shading, and arrangement of items
    Caption or title of the image
- Do you have an effective title, main point, introduction, body, and conclusion?
- Have you included the image in the essay?

Turning to Texts of Your Choice

As you turn now to selecting your own texts for rhetorical analysis, consider the ways the lessons you've learned in this chapter can help you approach the task. Keep in mind the need to begin with observations—whether it is of rhetorical texts all around your campus or the most provocative texts in the newspapers or online. As you select a text for analysis, think back to the cartoons or comics you found most striking in this chapter—perhaps the steroids cartoon, the *Boondocks* strip, or the Pledge of Allegiance cartoon. Each of these texts conveys a powerful message through words and images, verbal and visual rhetoric. Spend some time working on your thesis before composing the entire draft. Make sure your angle is sharp and your interpretation is complex. Consider working through a counterargument as well.

When you choose your own text for rhetorical analysis, make sure you pick one that offers a persuasive point. Also, in your own writing, avoid simply describing the elements you see in the work that you're analyzing. Instead, zoom in on specific details and comment on their meaning. Make a persuasive argument by using *specific* evidence to support your analysis of how the text succeeds at convincing an audience to see an issue in a particular way. This is key to crafting a persuasive and effective rhetorical analysis.

PREWRITING CHECKLIST
Comics and Cartoons

❏ **Topic:** What key issue is the comic or cartoon addressing?

❏ **Story:** On the most basic level, what is happening in the cartoon?

❏ **Audience:** In what country and in what historical moment was the cartoon produced? In what type of text did it first appear? A journal? A newspaper? Online? Was this text conservative? liberal? radical? feminist? How does it speak to this audience?

❏ **Author:** What do you know about the artist? What kinds of cartoons does he or she regularly produce? Where does he or she live and publish? What kinds of other writing does this person do?

❏ **Argument:** What is the cartoon's message about the issue? Is there irony involved (does the cartoon advocate one point of view, but the cartoonist wants you to take the opposite view)?

❏ **Composition:** Is this political cartoon a single frame or a series of sequential frames? If the latter, how does the argument evolve over the series?

❏ **Word and image:** Does the cartoon rely exclusively on the visual? Or are word and image both used? What is the relationship between the two? Is one given priority over the other? How does this influence the cartoon's overall persuasiveness?

❏ **Imagery:** What choices of imagery and content does the artist make? Are the drawings realistic? Do they rely on caricatures? Does the artist include allusions or references to past or present events or ideas?

❏ **Tone:** Is the cartoon primarily comic or serious in tone? How does this choice of tone create a powerful rhetorical impact on readers?

❏ **Character and setting:** What components are featured by the cartoon? A person? An object? A scene? Think about how character and setting are portrayed. What are the ethnicity, age, socioeconomic class, and gender of the characters? Do they represent actual people? Are they fictional creations? How are these choices rhetorical strategies designed to tailor the cartoon and its argument to its intended audience?

❏ **Cultural resonance:** Does the cartoon implicitly or explicitly refer to any actual people, events, or pop culture icons? What sort of symbolism is used in the cartoon? Would the symbols speak to a broad or narrow audience? How does the cultural resonance function as a rhetorical strategy in making the argument?

WRITING PROJECTS

1. **Personal Narrative:** Complete the "Creative Practice" on page 5. Recall Alex's observations of rhetoric on her way to class; conduct a similar study of the rhetoric in your world. Write your reflections into a *personal narrative essay.* Discuss which types of visual, verbal, bodily, or architectural rhetoric were most evident, which were most subtle, and which you found the most persuasive.

2. **Rhetorical Analysis:** Choose a political cartoon on a current issue and write a *rhetorical analysis*. You might find an appropriate cartoon in a recent issue of *Newsweek*, in a collection such as Charles Brooks's *Best Editorial Cartoons of the Year*, or online through the *Envision* Website resource page for Chapter 1 (www.ablongman.com/ envision/200). Use the prewriting checklist to help you write a rhetorical analysis of the cartoon. If you choose to analyze more than one cartoon on the same issue, introduce all your texts in the opening paragraph, and spend some time analyzing each one in detail. Make sure that your argument raises a larger point about rhetorical attributes of all the texts you are comparing.

3. **Comparative Rhetorical Analysis of Text and Image:** After you've begun project 2, search through recent newspapers, newsmagazines, or a news database like Lexis-Nexis to find an article that addresses the same issue. Write a *comparative analysis of the text and the political cartoon*. What is each one's argument, and what rhetorical strategies does each one use to effectively make that argument? You may want to use the prewriting checklist in looking at the political cartoon. If you want to take a historical approach to this assignment, choose both a political cartoon and an article that span across the historical spectrum but focus on one issue, such as racial profiling, immigrant workers, or what's "hip" in the entertainment industry. You might consult articles and cartoons from *The Onion*'s "Our Dumb Century" or from online archives available through the *Envision* Website. For whatever texts you choose, write a *comparative historical analysis essay* in which you analyze how the cartoon and article use rhetoric to address a pressing issue of the time. Be sure to include specific details about each text, shape your observations into a thesis using the process on pages 29 and 30, and don't forget a title.

 Visit www.ablongman.com/envision for expanded assignment guidelines and student projects.

CHAPTER 2

Understanding Strategies of Persuasion

Wwhat convinced you to buy that new pair of cross-trainers, to try that new sports drink, to purchase that new cell phone calling plan, or even to decide which college to attend? Chances are some sort of text combining words and image—whether it was a printed advertisement, television or radio commercial, billboard, or brochure—influenced your decision. Consider the street scene in Figure 2.1. What strategies of persuasion does the striking iPod banner ad use? Notice the simple design, the contrast between the bright background color and the dark silhouette, and the strategic use of white that draws your eye from the iPod in the figure's hand to the logo and slogan at the top of the image. How does this ad appeal to you? Does it appeal to your own enthusiasm for music that allows you to identify with the dancer? Or does it draw you in logically, asking you to identify yourself with one type of iPod because of its technical features?

Think now about other advertisements you have seen. How does the look of an ad make you pause and pay attention? Does a magazine ad show someone famous, a good-looking model, or characters you can identify with emotionally? Does a television spot tell a compelling story? Does a brochure offer startling statistics or evidence? Perhaps it was not one but a combination of factors that you found persuasive. Often we are moved to action through persuasive effects that are so subtle we may not recognize them at first; we call these effects **rhetorical strategies**—techniques used to move and convince an audience.

FIGURE 2.1. This eye-catching iPod ad draws the audience immediately into its argument.

Ads offer us a productive means of analyzing rhetorical strategies because they represent arguments in compact forms. An ad has little room to spare; persuasion must be locked into a single frame or into a brief 30-second spot. Advertisements represent one of the most ubiquitous forms of persuasion. The average adult encounters 3000 of these compact, powerful arguments—that is, advertisements—every day (Twitchell, *Adcult* 2). Consider all the places ads appear nowadays: not just in magazines or on the television or radio but also on billboards and computer screens; on the sides of buses, trains, and buildings; in sports stadiums and movie theaters; and even spray-painted on sidewalks.

You probably can think of other places you've seen advertisements lately, places that may have surprised you: in a restroom, on the back of a soda can, on your roommate's T-shirt. As citizens of what cultural critic James Twitchell calls "Adcult USA," we are constantly exposed to texts that appeal to us on many levels. In this chapter, you'll gain a working vocabulary and concrete strategies of rhetorical persuasion that you can use when you turn to craft your own persuasive texts. The work you do here not only will make you a savvy reader of advertisements but also will equip you with skills you can use to become a sharper, more strategic writer of your own arguments.

Chapter Preview Questions

- What specific strategies of argumentation work as persuasion?
- What role do the rhetorical appeals of logos, pathos, and ethos play in persuasion?
- What is the effect of exaggeration in these appeals?
- How does an awareness of context work to create a persuasive argument?
- How can you incorporate strategies of persuasion in your own writing?

Analyzing Ads as Arguments

By analyzing advertisements, we can detect the rhetorical choices writers and artists select to make their points and convince their audiences. In this way we realize that advertisers are rhetoricians, careful to attend to the *rhetorical situation.* We can find in advertisements specific strategies of argumentation that you can use to make your case in your own writing:

- Advertisers might use **narration** to sell their product—using their ad to tell a story.
- They might employ **comparison-contrast** to encourage the consumer to buy their product rather than their competitor's.

- They might rely upon **example** or **illustration** to show how their product can be used or how it can impact a person's life.
- They might use **cause and effect** to demonstrate the benefits of using their product.
- They might utilize **definition** to clarify their product's purpose or function.
- They might create an **analogy** to help make a difficult selling point or product—like fragrance—more accessible to their audience.
- They might structure their ad around **process** to demonstrate the way a product can be used.
- They might focus solely on **description** to show you the specifications of a desktop system or a new SUV.
- They might use **classification and division** to help the reader conceptualize how the product fits into a larger scheme.

These strategies are equally effective in both visual and written texts. Moreover, they can be used effectively to structure both a small unit (part of an ad or, in a more academic text, a paragraph or section of an essay) and a larger one (the entire ad or, in an academic paper, the argument as a whole).

Even a single commercial can be structured around multiple strategies. The famous "This Is Your Brain on Drugs" commercial from the late 1980s used *analogy* (a comparison to something else—in this case comparing using drugs and frying an egg) and *process* (reliance on a sequence of events—here, how taking drugs affects the user's brain) to warn its audience away from drug use. In this 30-second spot, the spokesperson holds up an egg, saying, "This is your brain." In the next shot, the camera focuses on an ordinary frying pan as he states, "This is drugs." We as the audience begin to slowly add up parts A and B, almost anticipating his next move. As the ad moves to the visual crescendo, we hear him say, "This is your brain on drugs": the image of the egg sizzling in the frying pan fills the screen. The final words seem almost anticlimactic after this powerful image: "Any questions?"

These strategies function just as persuasively in print ads as well. For example, look at the advertisement for Rusk hair spray in Figure 2.2, an ad designed to draw the viewer's eye through the visual argument. What the reader notices first are the striking pictures of the golden-haired model, somewhat flat hair on one side and voluminous curls on the other, exemplifying the

RUSK
PROFESSIONAL HAIRCARE

Go from
ordinary...   ...to
    Extraordinary!

PROBLEM: SOLUTION:

FIGURE 2.2. This problem-solution ad for Rusk hairspray uses several strategies of argumentation.

powerful *comparison-contrast* strategy that is echoed in many levels of the ad. The entire ad is bisected to reflect this structure, opposing "problem" to "solution" and literally dividing the main caption— "Go from ordinary . . . to Extraordinary"—in half. What bridges the divide, both literally and figuratively, is the strategically positioned can of hairspray, tilted slighted toward the right to reinforce emphasis on the *example/illustration* of a satisfied Rusk-user. By centralizing the red-capped canister in this way, the ad therefore also establishes a persuasive *cause and effect* argument, implicitly suggesting that using this hairspray allowed this girl to overcome the perceived challenges of limp hair.

Within written texts, the use of such strategies provides a similar foundation for a persuasive argument. As you read the following online article from Slate.com, look carefully to see which strategies author Seth Stevenson utilizes to make his argument about recent iPod commercials.

As part of his online series "Ad Report-card," Stevenson uses a format not usually associated with academic writing—notice here he sets up the commercial under discussion in a separate section before even starting his essay.

You and Your Shadow
The iPod ads are mesmerizing. But does your iPod think it's better than you?
Seth Stevenson

The Spot: Silhouetted shadow-people dance in a strenuous manner. Behind them is a wall of solid color that flashes in neon shades of orange, pink, blue, and green. In each shadow-person's hand is an Apple iPod.

I myself own an iPod, but rarely dance around with it. In part because the earbuds would fall out (Does this happen to you? I think I may have narrow auditory canals) and in part because I'm just not all that prone to solitary rump-shaking. It's a failing on my part. Maybe if I were a silhouette I might dance more.

All that said, these are very catchy ads. I don't get sick of watching them. And yet I also sort of resent them, as I'll later explain.

First, let's talk about what the ads get right. For one, the songs (from groups like Jet and Black Eyed Peas) are extremely well-chosen. Just indie enough so that not everybody knows them; just mainstream enough so that almost everybody likes them. But as good as the music is, the visual concept is even better. It's incredibly simple: never more than three distinct colors on the screen at any one time, and black and white are two of them. What makes it so bold are those vast swaths of neon monochrome.

This simplicity highlights the dance moves, but also—and more importantly—it highlights the iPod. The key to it all is the silhouettes. What a brilliant way to showcase a product. Almost everything that might distract us—not just background scenery, but even the actors' faces and clothes—has been eliminated. All we're left to focus on is that iconic gizmo. What's more, the dark black silhouettes of the dancers perfectly offset the iPod's gleaming white cord, earbuds, and body.

This all sounds great, so far. So what's not to like?

For the longest time, I couldn't put my finger on it. And then I realized where I'd seen this trick before. It's the mid-1990s campaign for DeBeers diamonds—the one where the people are shadows, but the jewelry is real. In them, a shadow-man would slip a diamond ring over a shadow-finger, or clasp a pendant necklace around a ghostly throat. These ads used to be on television all the time. You may recall the stirring string music of their soundtrack, or the still-running tagline: "A Diamond Is Forever."

Like the iPod ads, these DeBeers ads used shadow-people to perfect effect. The product—in this case, diamonds—sparkles and

Stevenson's chatty voice is very appropriate for his online audience.

Notice the way Stevenson defers his thesis, although he gives us a sense of his approach toward the ads (resentment).

In this section, Stevenson relies on **description** to set up the foundation for his discussion of the ads; yet, notice that he is somewhat selective, emphasizing the elements that are most important for his analysis—namely, the way the use of silhouettes emphasizes the product.

The rhetorical question here points to the turn in his piece from description to analysis, the point where the reader will come closer to understanding his resentment.

At this point in the article, Stevenson moves to **description** and **example** to set up the powerful **comparison-contrast** strategy that he develops further in the next paragraphs.

shines on a dusky background. But what bothered me about the spots was the underlying message. They seem to say that we are all just transient shadows, not long for this world—it's our diamonds that are forever. In the end, that necklace is no overpriced bauble. It's a ticket to immortality!

My distaste for these ads stems in part from the fact that, with both the iPod and the diamonds, the marketing gives me a sneaking sense that the product thinks it's better than me. More attractive, far more timeless, and frankly more interesting, too. I feel I'm being told that, without this particular merchandise, I will have no tangible presence in the world. And that hurts. I'm a person, dammit, not a featureless shadow-being! If you prick me, do I not write resentful columns?

Like diamond jewelry, the iPod is designed and marketed to draw attention to itself, and I think (I realize I'm in a minority here) I prefer my consumer goods to know their place. If I did it over, I might opt for an equally functional but slightly more anonymous MP3 player. One that deflects attention instead of attracting it. Because I'm the one with the eternal soul here—it's my stuff that's just transient junk.

Grade: B–. Perfectly executed. Mildly insulting message.

By **comparing** the iPod commercials to the DeBeers campaign, Stevenson can clearly articulate his ambivalent feelings about Apple's ads.
In his semihumorous interjection, Stevenson returns to the **contrast** between himself and the Apple silhouettes with which he started the article.

Notice how he builds on his **comparison** by opening his concluding paragraph with an **analogy**, using a simile ("like diamond jewelry") that reminds the reader of the connection he has established between the two campaigns.

COLLABORATIVE CHALLENGE

Visit an online repository of commercials, such as those linked through the *Envision* Website. With a partner, browse through several commercials, selecting two or three in particular that you find persuasive. Discuss what strategies of argumentation you see at work in these visual rhetoric texts. Try to find an example of each approach listed earlier in the chapter. Write a short paragraph analyzing one of the commercials; compare your interpretation with a partner. Then share your work with the rest of the class.

www.ablongman.com/envision/205

Understanding the Rhetorical Appeals

The rhetorical strategies we've examined so far can be filtered through the lens of classical modes of persuasion dating back to 500 BCE. The formal terms are *logos, pathos,* and *ethos.*

Each type of rhetorical appeal represents a mode of persuasion that can be used by itself or in combination. As you might imagine, a text may employ a combined mode of persuasion, such as "passionate logic"—a rational argument written with highly charged prose, "goodwilled pathos"—an emotional statement that relies on the character of the speaker to be believed, or "logical ethos"—a strong line of reasoning employed by a speaker to build authority. Moreover, a text may use rhetorical appeals in a combination that produces an *overarching effect,* such as irony or humor. You might think of humor as one of the most effective forms of persuasion. Jokes and other forms of humor are basically appeals to pathos because they put the audience in the right emotional state to be receptive to an argument, but they can also involve reasoning or the use of the writer's authority to sway an audience.

Since they appear so frequently in combination, you might find that conceptualizing logos, pathos, and ethos through a visual representation helps you to understand how they relate to one another (see Figure 2.3).

AT A GLANCE

Rhetorical Appeals

- *Logos* entails rational argument: appeals to reason and an attempt to persuade the audience through clear reasoning and philosophy. Statistics, facts, definitions, and formal proofs, as well as interpretations such as syllogisms or deductively reasoned arguments, are all examples of means of persuasion we call "the logical appeal."

- *Pathos,* or "the pathetic appeal," generally refers to an appeal to the emotions: the speaker attempts to put the audience into a particular emotional state so that the audience will be receptive to and ultimately convinced by the speaker's message. Inflammatory language, sad stories, appeals to nationalist sentiments, and jokes are all examples of pathos.

- *Ethos* is an appeal to authority or character; according to Aristotle, *ethos* means the character or goodwill of the speaker. Today we also consider the speaker's reliance on authority, credibility, or benevolence when discussing strategies of ethos. Although we call this third mode of persuasion the "ethical appeal," it does not strictly mean the use of ethics or ethical reasoning. Keep in mind that ethos is the deliberate use of the *speaker's character* as a mode of persuasion.

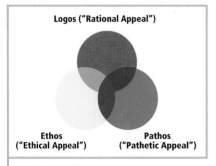

Logos ("Rational Appeal")

Ethos ("Ethical Appeal")   Pathos ("Pathetic Appeal")

FIGURE 2.3. Rhetorical appeals as intersecting strategies of persuasion.

As you read this chapter, consider how each text relies upon various rhetorical appeals to construct its message.

Appeals to Reason

Logos entails strategies of logical argument. As a writer, you use logos when you construct an essay around facts and reason; in general, an argument based on logos will favor the use of logic, statistical evidence, quotations from authorities, and proven facts. In the opening pages of this chapter, for instance, we used logos—quotations and statistics about advertising—to persuade you about the omnipresence of advertising in today's culture. Scholars often rely on logos in this way to make persuasive academic arguments. Consider, for instance, the way Laurence Bowen and Jill Schmid use *logos* as a strategy of persuasion in this passage from "Minority Presence and Portrayal in Mainstream Magazine Advertising: An Update":

> Some might argue that the small number of minorities featured in mainstream magazine advertising may be due to a very deliberate media strategy that successfully targets minorities in specialized and minority media. However, each of the magazines analyzed does have a minority readership and, in some cases, that readership is quite substantial. For example, according to *Simmons 1993 Study of Media and Markets,* the Hispanic readership of *Life* is 9.9%, yet the inclusion of Hispanics in *Life*'s advertisements was only .8%. *Cosmopolitan* has a 11.3% Black readership, yet only 4.3% of the advertisements included Blacks; 13.3% of the magazines' readership is Hispanic and only .5% of the advertisements use Hispanics.

Notice how the authors drive their point home through reference to their research with mainstream magazines as well as to statistical data that they have both uncovered and analyzed. The inclusion of this concrete information and examples makes their argument much more convincing than had they provided a more general rebuttal to the statement that begins their paragraph. In this way, appeals to logic can take on many forms, including interpretations of "hard evidence," such as found in syllogisms (formal, structured arguments), reasoned arguments, closing statements in law, inferences in the form of statistical models, and appeals to "common sense" or cultural assumptions.

In advertising, the mode of persuasion we call logos often operates through the written text; significantly, the Greek word *logos* can be translated as "word," indicating the way in which we, culturally, often look to words as repositories of fact and reason. Let's see how the Chevron ad featured in Figure 2.4 presents a reasoned argument.

The type of logos-based reasoning found in the Chevron ad appears in many ads that you may also be familiar with: think, for instance, of a computer ad that juxtaposes a striking photo of a laptop with a chart detailing its processor type, memory capacity, screen size, and graphics features; a car ad that offsets a glossy showroom photo with safety ratings and positive reviews from *Car & Driver* and *Motor Trend*; or a commercial for a bank that features a smiling agent listing

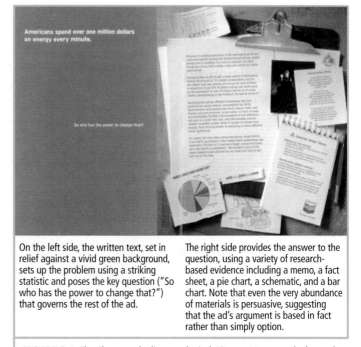

On the left side, the written text, set in relief against a vivid green background, sets up the problem using a striking statistic and poses the key question ("So who has the power to change that?") that governs the rest of the ad.

The right side provides the answer to the question, using a variety of research-based evidence including a memo, a fact sheet, a pie chart, a schematic, and a bar chart. Note that even the very abundance of materials is persuasive, suggesting that the ad's argument is based in fact rather than simply option.

FIGURE 2.4. The Chevron ad relies on a logical argument to persuade the reader.

the reasons to open a checking account at that branch. In each case, the advertisement drives its point through facts, evidence, and reason.

In fact, some might argue that logos as an appeal underlies almost all advertising, specifically because most advertising uses an implicit *causal argument:* if you buy this product, then you or your life will be like the one featured in the ad. Sometimes the associations are explicit: if you use Pantene shampoo, then your hair will be shinier; if you buy Tide detergent, then your clothes will be cleaner; if you buy a Volvo sedan, then your family will be safer driving on the road. Sometimes the *cause-and-effect* argument is more subtle: buying Sure deodorant will make you more confident; drinking Coke will make you happier; wearing Nikes will make you perform better on the court. In each case, logos, or the use of logical reasoning, is the tool of persuasion responsible for the ad's argumentative force.

Student Writing

Fred Chang analyzes Apple Computer's reliance on logos in its advertising battle with Intel.

www.ablongman.com/envision/206

FIGURE 2.5   In this Crest Whitening Strips advertisement, inset images offer visual evidence for the ad's argument.

The ad for Crest Whitening Strips in Figure 2.5 offers us a useful example of how logos can operate in more subtle ways in an ad—through visual as well as verbal argumentation. When we first look at the ad, our eyes are drawn immediately to the model's white smile, positioned near the center of the two-page spread. Our gaze next moves up to her eyes and then down again to the two juxtaposed close-up shots of her teeth.

These two close-ups carry the force of the argument. They are before-and-after stills, demonstrating, in brilliant color, the whitening power of Crest. The contrast between the two images makes a deliberate logos appeal by constructing a cause-and-effect argument. The captions for these two close-ups confirm the message imparted by the images and solidify the visual promise of the ad. The final small box insert is our last visual stop; it shows the product and suggests the solution to the logical equation at work in this ad. The fact that the ad's words, "Your new smile," appear beneath the photo of the product—as the conclusion of the logical argument—reinforces the persuasive message that Crest indeed will give its users such white teeth. To put the logic plainly: if people brush with this product, then they too will achieve this result. In this way, the ad relies on logos to attract and convince its audience.

Logical Fallacies

When crafting your own written analysis of advertisements, be careful not to rely on mistaken or misleading uses of logos, commonly called **logical fallacies.** The causal strategy underlying most advertising can be seen as an example of faulty logic, for surely it is fraudulent to suggest that wearing a certain brand of clothing will make you popular or that drinking a certain beer will make you attractive to the opposite sex. In classical rhetoric, this fallacy of causality is called a ***post hoc ergo propter hoc* fallacy**—namely, the idea that because something happened first (showering with an aloe-enhanced body gel), it is the direct cause of something that happened afterward (getting great grades on your midterms). A similar effect can be produced by the ***cum hoc ergo propter hoc* fallacy**, often called a correlation-causation fallacy. According to this model, because two unrelated events happen at the same time (are correlated), they are interpreted as cause and effect. For instance, the following is an example of a *cum hoc* fallacy: (1) a teenager plays his varsity basketball game wearing his new Air Jordans; (2) the teenager makes many key rebounds and jump shots while playing the game; (3) the Air Jordans caused his success in the game. You can probably think of many commercials that rely on these two particular logical fallacies.

However, in those same commercials, we see more and more cases of advertisers guarding themselves against claims of false causality. For instance, consider the typical weight-loss advertisement. "I lost 31 pounds in 3 months using this nutritional plan!" one happy dieter exclaims on camera. The camera shows an old video clip of the subject at her previous weight, and then it moves to the newly trimmed-down version, usually with a trendy hairstyle and tight-fitting clothes—a clear before-and-after strategy. However, more and more often, you now find these images captioned with one telling phrase: "These results not typical." This disclaimer points to advertisers' recognition that they, like other rhetoricians, need to be careful in their use of logos as an argumentative appeal.

AT A GLANCE

Logical Fallacies

- *The post hoc fallacy:* confusing cause and effect
- *The cum hoc fallacy:* interpreting correlation as causation
- *The hasty generalization:* drawing a conclusion too quickly without providing enough supporting evidence
- *The either-or argument:* reducing an argument to a choice between two diametrically opposed choices, ignoring other possible scenarios
- *Stacking the evidence:* offering evidence for only one side of the issue
- *Begging the question:* using an argument as evidence for itself
- *The red herring:* distracting the audience rather than focusing on the argument itself

Appeals to Emotion

Roughly defined as "suffering" or "feeling" in its original Greek, the term *pathos* actually means to put the audience in a particular mood or frame of mind. Modern derivations of the word *pathos* include *pathology* and *pathetic,* and indeed we speak of pathos as "the pathetic appeal." But pathos is more a technique than a state: writers use it as a tool of persuasion to establish an intimate connection with the audience by soliciting powerful emotions. For instance, consider the way the following paragraphs foster an emotional reaction from the reader:

> Dorsey Hoskins' father Bryan felt a tingling in his arm. The diagnosis—an inoperable brain tumor. Six months later, he died at the age of 33, leaving his wife to raise Dorsey and sister Hattie.
>
> Fortunately, Bryan bought life insurance when he married, and again when his daughters were born. Thanks to Bryan's foresight, Dorsey, Hattie, and their mom are taken care of.
>
> Are you prepared should the very worst happen?

This passage relies on a pathos appeal on many levels. Clearly, the very premise of the piece—moving from tragedy, to a sense of tempered relief, to personal identification—is designed to evoke a sympathetic response. Looking more closely, however, suggests that even the more subtle stylistic choices also contribute to the emotional appeal. Notice, for example, the power of word choice: the author initially introduces Bryan as "Dorsey Hoskins' father," establishing him from the first in terms of his daughter and, ultimately, her loss; the author withholds Bryan's age for three sentences, at which point he can disclose it to accentuate the tragedy of his early death; finally, after the powerful, opening anecdote, the author uses the second person to draw the audience itself into the piece through the pointed rhetorical question.

It shouldn't be a surprise to discover that this passage is in fact taken from an advertisement for life insurance or that the pathos of the text is echoed by the emotional charge of a close-up photograph of 5-year-old Dorsey, which serves as the background for the advertisement. We encounter ads that rely on pathos all the time, and indeed, the visual composition of an ad often taps our emotions in ways we barely recognize.

Let's look closely at another advertisement that relies on creating an emotional connection with the audience to sell its product. In the spring of 2006 Volkswagen launched a new marketing campaign aimed at pitching safety rather than sportiness; the "Safe Happens" commercials revolve around an unexpected moment of collision and its surprisingly reassuring aftermath (Figure 2.6). In this particular commercial, the viewer finds herself transported into the interior of an automobile. At this point, there is no clue as to the car's make or model; the camera shots are all of the car's occupants, a group of friends in their late twenties or early thirties. The camera focuses on each face in turn, identifying them as the points of identification and creating a bond between the characters

Safe happens.

Government star ratings are part of the National Highway Traffic Safety Administration's (NHTSA's) New Car Assessment Program.(www.safercar.gov) All crashes are different and severe injuries can occur. Airbags do not deploy in all accidents. Always use safety belts and seat children in rear using appropriate restraint systems.

FIGURE 2.6. Screen captures from "Safe Happens," a Volkswagen Jetta commercial, demonstrate how the commercial reaches the audience by overlaying a pathos appeal on a narrative structure.

and the viewer. We encounter them in the middle of a friendly, light-hearted conversation, the women gently teasing the men about crying at the end of the movie they have just watched. The exchange is informal and comfortable, the mood light.

In a second, everything changes. Replicating in real-time the experience of a car accident, the commercial cuts the characters off midsentence with a screech of brakes, blinding headlights, and the sound of a collision. The viewer, an invisible passenger in the car, feels the same surprise and horror as the main characters. The camera focus abruptly changes and moves us outside the vehicle; we become bystanders, watching a nondescript SUV plow into the white sedan that we identify as *our* car, the power of the collision captured with harsh accuracy. As the screen goes black, suddenly silence prevails, except for the uneven clatter of a rolling hubcap.

After a couple of seconds, the image reappears, and we see our former companions, unharmed, standing outside the battered vehicle. This first moment of product identification is captioned by an unusual voice-over; the camera zooms in on one of the female passengers, who looks with disbelief at the

Student Writing

Cyrus Chee's rhetorical analysis reads the appeals to pathos in two poster ads for contemporary films about the Holocaust.

www.ablongman.com/envision/207

wreck and whispers, "Holy . . . ." The implied expletive is silenced by a quick cut to a more traditional car-commercial shot: the Jetta, in a spotless white showroom, slowly revolving on a turntable. Even here, beyond the end of the commercial's central narrative, the pathos appeal is reinforced. The rotating car is clearly not a showroom model; the dented driver's side door identifies it once again as *our* car, the one that kept the main characters safe. The written caption reinforces this association, proclaiming "Safe Happens" (playing with the female character's final words) and then announcing that Jetta has received the government's highest safety rating. This moment of logos appeal becomes doubly persuasive because of the viewer's emotional engagement with the commercial: we feel that we ourselves have survived the crash and look to the Jetta as the reason.

Pathos does not only operate through triggering the highs and lows of emotion in its audience; sometimes the appeals, though still speaking to the visceral more than the rational, are subtle. Patriotism, indignation, excitement—all these effects can be linked to the pathos appeal. Consider the Porsche commercial showing a sleek red car speeding along a windy mountain road, the Ford Escape TV spot featuring the rugged SUV plowing through a muddy off-road trail, or the Cooper Mini ad using uniqueness as a selling point for the little car. Each of these ads uses pathos to produce a specific feeling in viewers: I want to drive fast, wind in my hair; I want to get off the beaten path, forge a new frontier; I want to stand out in a crowd, make a statement.

You are probably even more familiar with another type of pathos appeal—the appeal to sexuality. Clearly, "sex sells." Look at Victoria's Secret models posed in near nudity or recent Abercrombie and Fitch catalogs featuring models more likely to show off their toned abs than a pair of jeans, and you can see how in many cases advertisers tend to appeal more to nonrational impulses than to our powers of logical reasoning. Perfume and cologne advertisers in particular often use the rhetoric of sexuality to sell their fragrances, whether it be Calvin Klein's Obsession or Armani's Acqua Di Gio. Such ads work cleverly to sell perfume, not on the merits of the scent or on its chemical composition but through the visual rhetoric of sexuality and our emotional responses to it.

One final—and perhaps most pervasive—pathos appeal deserves mention at the close of this section. Looking at Figure 2.7, we can see yet another typical use of pathos to drive an argument.

It is humor that underlies the visual argument of this ad; by literally bisecting the boyfriend according to his emotional and sexual impulses, this advertisement provides a particularly amusing rendering of how Axe cologne taps into man's split "good-bad" nature. If you think about it, as a culture we tend to be quite persuaded by humor; against our more rational impulses, the ads that make us laugh are usually the ones we remember. To prove this point, you need only think back to last year's Superbowl ads: Which ads do you remember? Which ads did you talk over with your friends during and after the game? Probably most of those memorable commercials relied on humor—or "humos" as one of our students, David Baron, has named it. The arguments made by these ads may not always be the most logically sound, but the way they foster a connection with the audience makes them persuasive nonetheless.

Exaggerated Uses of Pathos

Although these strategies of persuasion successfully move their audience, sometimes advertisers exaggerate the appeal to emotion for more dramatic effect.

Consider the case of exaggerated pathos found in the Listerine campaign from the early twentieth

FIGURE 2.7. This Axe cologne ad relies on humor to market its scent.

AT A GLANCE

Exaggerated Uses of Pathos

- **Over-sentimentalization:** distracting the audience from evidence or relevant issues
- **The scare tactic:** capitalizing on the audience's fears to make a pitch
- **The false need:** amplifying a perceived need or creating a completely new one
- **The slippery slope fallacy:** suggesting that an event or action will send the audience spiraling down a "slippery slope" to a serious consequence

FIGURE 2.8. This Listerine ad uses appeals to pathos to persuade readers to use its product.

century. In the 1920s, Gerard Lambert introduced the term *halitosis* into the popular vocabulary as a marketing strategy; he used it to convince Americans that Listerine was their only alternative to public embarrassment from bad breath (Twitchell, *Adcult* 144). Regardless of the fact that Listerine's primary use at the time was as a hospital disinfectant, Lambert transformed American culture through his successful use of **false needs.**

In Figure 2.8, we see an example from the 1950s of this famous ad campaign. The words of the headline, spoken by the two women in the upper-right corner ("He's Hanging Himself Right Now!"), are a bit cryptic so that the reader has to look to the image in the center of the ad to understand its message. The drawing of the man and woman dancing makes a direct correlation between personal hygiene and romantic relationships, creating a sense of *false need* in the consumer for the product. In this case, the woman's averted head suggests her rejection of the suitor. Moreover, as you can see, the ad also uses the **scare tactic;** the disapproval on the faces of the women at the side table arouses in viewers a fear of rejection. The way the dancing woman's body turns away from the man augments this pathos appeal. Having deciphered the meaning of the ad from the image, the words now seem to confirm the idea in the headline that the man stands little chance of a romantic encounter. Image and text collaborate here to produce a powerful emotional reaction in the audience. Moreover, the threat of impending loss signifies a successful use of the **slippery slope,** an argument asserting that one thing leads to a chain of events that results in an undesirable conclusion: in this case, bad breath leads to solitude and loneliness.

Many contemporary advertising campaigns also operate in a similar fashion, defining a problem and then offering up their product as a solution: think, for instance, of Clearasil's acne cream or Ban Invisible Solid deodorant. Take a moment now to think about times in your life when you may have been motivated to purchase a product through *false need:* have you ever bought a man's or woman's razor? pump-up basketball shoes? an angled toothbrush? curl-enhancing mascara? a transparent band-aid? What other examples of false needs or exaggerated pathos can you recall?

CREATIVE PRACTICE

The written copy that follows is from the Listerine print ad featured in Figure 2.8. As we've seen, the more prominent visual and verbal elements rely primarily on pathos to drive their arguments. Read the copy from the ad over carefully and analyze the rhetorical strategies at work there. Does it also rely on pathos? At which parts? What other strategies or appeals do you see at work in the text? Why do you think the copywriter chose to employ those rhetorical strategies at those points in the argument?

"Mark my words," Edith went on, "by the time they've gone twice around the dance floor, he'll get the complete brush-off from her."

"But why?" Polly queried. "He's so attractive . . . seems so attentive . . ."

"Indeed he is. And he's been wangling this date for weeks. Poor guy . . . he's through before he even starts . . . and he'll never know why*."

This sort of thing can happen, and usually does, when people are careless about halitosis* (unpleasant breath).

How About You?

Are you guilty? The insidious thing about halitosis is that you, yourself, may not realize it is present. So at the very moment you want to be at your best, you may be at your worst . . . offending needlessly.

Sometimes, of course, halitosis comes from some systemic disorder. But usually—and fortunately—it is only a local condition that yields to the regular use of Listerine Antiseptic as a mouth wash and gargle.

Why Run Such a Risk?

Don't risk offending others. And don't trust to makeshifts. Put your faith in Listerine Antiseptic which millions have found to be an *extra-careful* precaution against halitosis. Really fastidious people look up to Listerine Antiseptic as a part of their passport to popularity. It's so easy, so delightful to use, so lasting in effect.

Sweetness for Hours

Listerine Antiseptic is the *extra-careful* precaution because it sweetens and freshens the breath, *not for seconds or minutes . . . but for hours, usually.* Your breath, indeed your entire mouth, feels wonderfully fresh and clean.

Never, never omit Listerine Antiseptic before any date where you want to be at your best. Better still, get in the habit of using it night and morning for that clean, fresh feeling.

Appeals to Character and Authority

The last of the three appeals that we'll look at in this chapter is *ethos*—literally, "character." Perhaps you have used ethos in other disciplines to mean an argument based on ethical principles. But the *rhetorical* meaning of the term is slightly different: according to Aristotle, ethos works as a rhetorical strategy by establishing the goodwill or credibility of the writer or speaker. In fact, as a writer you use ethos every time you pick up a pen or proofread your essay—that is, you construct an argument in which your power to persuade depends on credibility, your word choice, your tone, your choice of examples, the quality of your research, your grammar and punctuation. All these factors contribute to your ethos as an author.

Let's look to one of the articles we've already encountered in this chapter to see the subtle ways in which an author can create his ethos. Below are the opening lines of Seth Stevenson's "Me and My Shadow":

I myself own an iPod, but rarely dance around with it. In part because the earbuds would fall out (Does this happen to you? I think I may have narrow auditory canals) and in part because I'm just not all that prone to solitary rump-shaking. It's a failing on my part. Maybe if I were a silhouette I might dance more.

Notice the way in which Stevenson immediately establishes why he feels authorized to talk about iPods: "I myself own an iPod." He is not an uninformed critic; from the first, he sets himself up as an iPod owner, someone familiar with the product—and by extension the advertising. He also goes to lengths to establish a connection with his audience and gain their trust. By confessing that he rarely dances around with his iPod and then using this as an excuse to draw in his audience ("Does this happen to you?"), he more firmly ingratiates himself with his readers, many of whom have probably had the same experience. In this way, he deliberately constructs his ethos from the opening lines of his essay so that he can then launch into his analysis with the full confidence of his audience.

Clearly, ethos can be a very powerful tool for establishing trust and therefore facilitating the persuasiveness of an argument. Companies have long recognized the persuasive power of ethos. In fact, a brand logo is in essence ethos distilled into a single symbol: it transmits in a single icon the entire reputation of a company, organization, or brand identity. From the Nike swoosh to McDonald's golden arches, the NBC peacock, or the Apple computer apple, symbols serve to mark (or brand) products with ethos.

Yet the power of the brand logo as a seat of ethos relies on the company's overall reputation with the consumer—a reputation that the company carefully cultivates through advertising campaigns. Many companies, for instance, trade on ethos by using celebrity endorsements in their advertising campaigns. Although a rational appeal is at work behind some endorsements—having basketball superstar LeBron James sell basketball shoes, for instance, makes sense—many campaigns rely not only on the celebrity's suitability for selling a product but also on the person's star appeal, character, and goodwill. Consider the power of the famous "Got Milk?" campaign. Here's the argument: if this celebrity likes milk, shouldn't we? Indeed, when we see Kelly Clarkson—or others, such as Serena Williams, Nelly, Ben Roethlisberger, or Jackie Chan—sporting the famous milk moustache, we find the ad persuasive because these celebrities are vouching for the product. We look to their goodwill as public figures, to their character as famous people putting their reputation on the line.

While the impact of a famous spokesperson can be a powerful use of ethos, celebrity endorsement is only one way to create this sort of appeal. Sometimes the *lack* of fame can be a strategic tool of the trade. Consider the Apple "Switch" ad campaign that featured everyday people stepping into the role of spokesperson for the Apple computer system. These ads featured everymen or everywomen of various ages, nationalities, and professions speaking directly into the camera about their reasons for changing from PCs to Apple computers. The combination of an unknown spokesperson, a clear example, a simple white background, and a slightly choppy film style—designed to seem edited and somewhat amateur—brought an ethos to the campaign based not on star power but on no-nonsense use and everyday application. In assessing the rhetorical situation for creating its ads, Apple recognized an important fact: for a large part of its audience, ethos would derive not from the flash of a celebrity smile but from identification with real-life Apple users.

Sometimes an ad features a corporate ethos to establish the credibility of the company. Microsoft's "We See" campaign, for instance, sells not software but a company image. One representative ad from this campaign depicts young children, at work in a classroom. What makes the ad visually interesting is that the image includes white shadowy sketches that transform the children into successful future versions of themselves. Complemented by the header, "We see new skills, tomorrow's inventions," and the closing tagline, "Your potential. Our passion," the ad becomes a window into the future, Microsoft's image of the new generation. The message of the ad relies heavily on ethos: Microsoft cares about America's youth and wants to help them realize their dreams.

In contrast to the Microsoft ad that promotes its corporate ethos rather than a particular product, many ads sell products directly through appeals to character. In Figure 2.9, for example, a Longines watch ad makes its pitch through

FIGURE 2.9. Longines uses corporate ethos to market a particular product; it sells its watches through appeals to character.

words and images: the line, "Elegance is an Attitude" suggests that both the company and the wearer of the company's product can share in elevated ethos. The visual image reinforces this idea through the representation of a well-dressed man standing confidently in a black jacket and pinstriped shirt. He looks directly out at the viewer, potentially catching the eye of possible viewers and literally standing in for corporate ethos.

COLLABORATIVE CHALLENGE

With a partner, look at the car advertisements in Figures 2.10 and 2.11. How does each use specific argumentative strategies and rhetorical appeals to make its argument? Choose one of the ads and brainstorm with your partner a way in which the company might market the same car through an ad that relies primarily on a different strategy or appeal. Sketch out your hypothetical ad—including both image and copy—and share it with the class, discussing how the shift in appeal affected your understanding of the rhetorical situation and the effectiveness of the ad.

FIGURE 2.10. An advertisement for a Saab.

FIGURE 2.11. An advertisement for the Ford Escape hybrid.

Misuses of Ethos

One consequence of relying on ethos-driven arguments is that sometimes we come to trust symbols of ethos rather than looking to the character of the product itself. This tendency points us to the concept of **authority over evidence**—namely, the practice of overemphasizing authority or ethos rather than focusing on the merits of the evidence itself, a strategic exaggeration of ethos that helps entice audiences and sell products.

The most prominent examples of *authority over evidence* can be found in celebrity endorsements; in many commercials, the spokesperson sells the product not based on its merits but based on the argument, "Believe what I say because you know me, and would I steer you wrong?" However, the American public has become increasingly skeptical of such arguments. Living in a world where rumors of Pepsi-spokesperson Britney Spears's preference for Coke circulate on the Internet, Tiger Woods's $100 million deal with Nike makes front page news, and a star like former Sprite spokesperson Macaulay Culkin publicly announces, "I'm not crazy about the stuff [Sprite]. But money is money" (Twitchell, *Twenty* 214), the credibility of celebrity endorsements is often questionable.

Often, companies deliberately attempt to undermine the ethos of their competition as a way of promoting their own products. You probably have seen ads of this sort: Burger King arguing that their flame-broiled hamburgers are better than McDonald's fried hamburgers; Coke claiming its soda tastes better than Pepsi's; Visa asserting its card's versatility by reminding consumers how many companies "don't take American Express." The deliberate *comparison-contrast* builds up one company's ethos at another's expense. At times, however, this technique can be taken to an extreme, producing an ***ad hominem*** argument—that is, an argument that attempts to persuade by attacking an opponent's ethos or character. We see *ad hominem* at work most often in campaign advertisements, where candidates end up focusing less on the issues at hand than on their opponents' moral weaknesses, or in commercials where companies attack each other for the way they run their businesses rather than the quality of their products. In other words, this strategy attempts to persuade by reducing the credibility of opposing arguments.

AT A GLANCE

Misuses of Ethos

Authority over evidence: placing more emphasis on ethos than on the actual validity of the evidence

Ad hominem: criticizing an opponent's character (or ethos) rather than the argument itself

Exaggerated Ethos Through Parody

Another strategy of persuasion is attacking ethos through **parody,** or the deliberate mocking of a text or convention. Parody has long been recognized as an effective rhetorical strategy for making a powerful argument. To see how this happens, let's turn to an ad designed by TheTruth.com, an innovative antitobacco organization (see Figure 2.12). Through the deliberate use of setting, character, font,

FIGURE 2.12. This TheTruth.com antismoking ad attacks ethos through parody.

and layout, this ad deliberately evokes and then parodies traditional cigarette advertising to make its claim for the dangers of smoking.

Even if you are not familiar with the Masters Settlement Act, you probably have seen some of the Marlboro Country ads, often showing the lone cowboy or groups of cowboys riding across a beautiful,

Student Writing

Amanda Johnson, in her analysis of a Barbie parody ad, and Georgia Duan, in her reading of cigarette advertising, explore the construction of body image in the media and the use of parody in ads.
www.ablongman.com/envision/208

sunlit western American landscape. During the early part of its campaign, TheTruth.com recognized the impact of the long tradition of cigarette advertising on the public and decided to turn this tradition to its advantage. In the TheTruth.com parody version, however, the cowboy's companions do not ride proudly beside him. Instead, they are zipped up into body bags—an image that relies on exaggerated ethos and employs pathos to provoke a strong reaction in the audience. By producing an ad that builds on and yet revises the logic of Philip Morris's ad campaign, TheTruth.com could get past false images (the happy cowboy) to get at its idea of the "truth": that by smoking cigarettes "You Too Can Be an Independent, Rugged, Macho-Looking Dead Guy." The visual complexity of the image (and the combination of appeals) resonates powerfully by evoking the audience's familiarity with cigarette advertisements to pack some of its punch.

Considering Context

As you can tell from examining ads in this chapter, a successful argument must take into account not only the *rhetorical situation* but also the context, or the right time and place. That is why promotional trailers for the ABC series *Invasion*—featuring big-budget scenes of a Florida hurricane—could captivate audiences in the early summer of 2005 but horrify and outrage that same audience two months later in the wake of hurricanes Katrina and Rita. In ancient Greece rhetoricians called this aspect of the rhetorical situation ***kairos***—namely, the contingencies of time and place for an argument.

In your own writing, you should consider *kairos* along with the other aspects of the rhetorical situation: audience, text, and writer. As a student of rhetoric, it is important to recognize the *kairos*—the opportune historical, ideological, or cultural moment—of a text when analyzing its rhetorical force. You undoubtedly already consider the context for persuasive communication in your everyday life. For instance, whether you are asking a friend to dinner or a professor for a recommendation, your assessment of the timeliness and the appropriate strategies for that time probably determines the shape your argument takes. You pick the right moment and place to make your case. In other words, the rhetorical situation involves interaction between audience, text, and writer *within* the context or *kairos.*

Consider, for instance, Coca-Cola's ad campaigns. Coke has exerted a powerful presence in the advertising industry for many years, in part because of its strategic advertising. During World War II, Coke ran a series of ads that built its beverage campaign around the contemporary nationalistic sentiment. What you find featured in these ads are servicemen, international landscapes, and inspiring slices of Americana—all designed to respond to that specific cultural moment.

Look at Figure 2.13, an advertisement for Coke from the 1940s. This picture uses pathos to appeal to the audience's sense of patriotism by featuring a row of seemingly carefree servicemen, leaning from the windows of a military bus, the refreshing Cokes in

FIGURE 2.13. This Coca-Cola ad used *kairos* to create a powerful argument for its World War II audience.

their hands producing smiles even far away from home. The picture draws in the audience by reassuring them on two fronts. On the one hand, it builds on the nationalistic pride in the young, handsome servicemen who so happily serve their country. On the other, it is designed to appease fears about the hostile climate abroad: as both the picture and the accompanying text assure us, Coca-Cola (and the servicemen) "goes along" and "gets a hearty welcome."

The power of this message relates directly to its context. An ad such as this one, premised on patriotism and pride in military service, would be most persuasive during wartime when many more people tend to support the spirit of nationalism and therefore would be moved by the image of the young serviceman shipping off to war. It is through understanding the *kairos* of this advertisement that you can appreciate the strength of the ad's rhetorical appeal.

Using Strategies of Persuasion

As you can tell from our work in this chapter, ads convey complex cultural meanings. Recognizing their persuasive presence everywhere, we realize the need to develop our ability to make more-informed interpretations of ads around us. You can pursue your study of ads by conducting your own careful rhetorical analyses of these visual-verbal texts. You'll find over and over again that ads are a microcosm of many of the techniques of persuasion. From billboards to pop-ups on the Internet, ads employ logos, pathos, and ethos to convey strong messages to specific audiences. We've learned how compact and sophisticated these texts are. Now it's time to apply those insights in your own writing.

As you begin to perform your individual analyses of advertisements, consider the way your own writing, like the ads we've discussed, can "sell" your argument to the reader. Consider the rhetorical situation and the specific *kairos* of your argument. What *strategies of argumentation* and *rhetorical appeals* would be most effective in reaching your target audience? Do you want to use narration, a humorous analogy, or a stirring example to forge a connection with your readers based on pathos? Or is your analysis better suited to logos, following a step-by-step process of reading an ad, drawing on empirical evidence, or looking at cause and effect? Perhaps you will decide to enrich your discussion through cultivating your ethos as a writer, establishing your own authority on a subject or citing reputable work done by other scholars. It is probable that in your essay you will use many strategies and a combination of appeals; as we saw in the advertisements presented earlier, from the Crest

Whitening Strips ad to the Coca-Cola campaign, a successful argument uses various rhetorical strategies to persuade its audience.

While focusing on the individual strategies, don't forget to keep an eye on the composition of your argument as a whole. Just as an ad is designed with attention to layout and design, so you should look at the larger organization of your essay as key to the success of your argument. As you approach the organization of elements in your essay to maximize your persuasiveness, even a question like "Where should I insert my images?" has profound implications for your argument. Consider the difference between an essay in which the image is embedded in the text, next to the paragraph that analyzes it, and one with the image attached as an appendix. In your writing, use the persuasive power of visual rhetoric more effectively by allowing the reader to analyze the images alongside the written explanations. Use similar careful attention to organization, placement, and purpose as you begin your own analysis and craft your own rhetorical argument.

PREWRITING CHECKLIST

Analyzing Advertisements

❏ **Content:** What exactly is the ad selling? An object? an idea? both?

❏ **Message:** How is the ad selling the product? What is the persuasive message that the ad is sending to the audience?

❏ **Character and setting:** What is featured by the ad? An object? a scene? a person? How are these elements portrayed? What are the ethnicity, age, socioeconomic class, and gender of any people in the advertisement? How do these choices relate to the ad's intended audience and reflect deliberate rhetorical choices?

❏ **Story:** On the most basic level, what is happening in the advertisement?

❏ **Theme:** What is the underlying message of the ad (beyond "buy our product")?

❏ **Medium:** What medium was the advertisement produced in? Television? print? radio? How did this choice suit the rhetorical purpose of the ad and accommodate the needs of a particular audience?

❏ **Historical context:** In what country and at what historical moment was the advertisement produced? How do the demands of context shape the persuasive appeals at work in the ad? How does the ad reflect, comment on, challenge, or reinforce contemporary political, economic, or gender ideology? How does this commentary situate it in terms of a larger trend or argument?

❏ **Word and image:** What is the relationship between the word (written or spoken) and the imagery in the ad? Which is given priority? How does this relationship affect the persuasiveness of the advertisement?

❏ **Layout:** How are the elements of the ad arranged—on a page (for a print ad) or in sequence (for a television commercial)? What is the purpose behind this arrangement? How does the ad's organization lead the reader through— and facilitate—its argument?

❏ **Design:** What typeface is used? What size? What color? How do these decisions reflect attention to the ad's rhetorical situation? How do they function in relation to the ad's rhetorical appeals?

❏ **Voice:** What voice does the text use to reach its audience? Is the language technical, informal, personal, authoritative? Is the voice comic or serious?

❏ **Imagery:** What choices did the advertiser make in selecting imagery for this ad? If it is a static print ad, does the ad feature a line drawing? a photograph? Is the photograph black and white? a close-up? a panoramic shot? If the advertisement is drawn from television, what are the pace and sequence of the images? Where does the camera zoom in? What does it focus on? Does the ad feature a close-up or a long shot? Is the image centered? completely captured in the frame? Is it cut off? If so, how? Does it feature a head-on shot? a three-quarter shot? Whose point of view, if any, is the viewer supposed to assume?

❏ **Rhetorical appeals:** How does the advertiser use the images to work in conjunction with rhetorical appeals? For instance, does the image reinforce an appeal to reason? Is it designed to produce an emotional effect on the audience? Does the use of a certain style, such as black-and-white authority, contribute to the ethos of the ad?

❏ **Strategy of development:** What strategy of development does the ad rely on? Narration? definition? comparison-contrast? example or illustration? classification and division? How do these strategies contribute to the ad's persuasive appeal?

❏ **Cultural resonance:** Does the ad use ethos—in the form of celebrities, famous events or places, or recognizable symbols—to increase its persuasiveness? If so, how does that establish audience or a particular relationship to a cultural moment?

WRITING PROJECTS

1. **Rhetorical Analysis:** Choose two or three ads for the same product and analyze the strategies of persuasion these ads use to reach specific audiences. To find your ads, you might visit an ad archive such as those linked through the Chapter 2 resources on the *Envision* Website, or look at old magazines in your school library. Alternatively, you can use current print or television advertisements as your sources and select ads that showcase an exaggeration of rhetorical appeals, such as logical fallacies, exaggeration of pathos, misuse of ethos, parody, or self-referential ads. Use the prewriting checklist to help you analyze the appeals at work in the ads and to help you develop your argument about the persuasion in these texts. Be sure to address how strategies of persuasion operate and what the effects are on the audience as well as a description of context: where and when was the ad published and to whom? Refer back to the rhetorical triangle in Chapter 1 to help you.

2. **Contextual Analysis:** Write a contextual analysis on the *kairos* of the Coca-Cola campaign. Examine, for instance, another Coke ad from the 1940s through the Adflip link on the *Envision* Website. Do some preliminary research and read about this era: explore the time, place, and culture in which the ad appeared. Ask yourself: How do the rhetorical choices of the ad you selected reflect an awareness of this context? How does the ad use the particular tools of logos, pathos, and ethos to comment upon or criticize this cultural moment?

3. **Historical Analysis:** Working in groups, look at several ads from different time periods produced by the same company. Some possible topics include ads for cigarettes, cars, hygiene products, and personal computers. Each member of your group should choose a single ad and prepare a rhetorical analysis of its persuasive appeals. Share your analyses and collaborate to explore how this company has modified its rhetorical approach over time. As you synthesize your argument, be sure to consider in each case how the different rhetorical situations inform the strategies used by the ads to reach their target audience. Collaborate to write a paper in which you chart the evolution of the company's persuasive strategies and how that evolution was informed by *kairos*.

4. **Cultural Analysis:** Write a paper in which you compare two ad campaigns and examine the ideology behind specific constructions of our culture. Does one campaign portray gender- or race-specific ideas? How do the tools of persuasion

work to produce each message? What larger message is conveyed by the reliance on such cultural ideals or notions of identity? What representations of sexuality, gender roles, or class are presented by these ads? Write up your findings and then present them to the class, holding up examples of the ads to discuss in support of your analysis.

 Visit www.ablongman.com/envision for expanded assignment guidelines and student projects.

CHAPTER 3

Composing Arguments

I magine that it is September 2005, and the United States is still reeling from the aftermath of Hurricane Katrina. As you visit the newsstand to purchase a paper, you pause to reflect on the various front pages before you. Each showcases a different photograph to comment on the tragedy. One features a striking photo of a military helicopter dropping supplies to the citizens of New Orleans (see Figure 3.1). Another shows an African-American mother clutching two small children to her chest and wading through waist-deep water. Yet another displays the image of a mob of angry people, packed together and arguing as they try to evacuate the city. A final front page uses the picture of a child's dirt-smeared doll, swept into a pile of debris on the road, as its poignant commentary on natural disaster.

Based on these images, which newspaper would you buy? How does each photo make a different argument about exactly what happened? How might the words of the caption or title shape the kind of interpretation you might make about the visual texts? How does the choice of a particular visual-verbal combination present a specific point of view?

Photographs and captions in newspapers work through the tools of persuasion that we examined in earlier chapters. In this chapter, we'll look at photographs to continue our exploration of how visual rhetoric shapes our reality in particular ways. We will also move forward in our understanding of analysis and argument by learning effective ways to

FIGURE 3.1. A photograph of supplies being dropped to New Orleans survivors of Hurricane Katrina.

create arguments. We'll become acquainted with the canons of rhetoric—five classifications of argument from ancient Greece—and we'll work through coming up with ideas, structuring those ideas, and developing a style for your own compositions.

Chapter Preview Questions

- What are the canons of rhetoric, and how do they help us to understand arguments?
- How can you create strong introductions and conclusions?
- What roles do persona and rhetorical stance play in arguments?
- How do photographs function as both visual evidence in arguments and as visual arguments themselves?
- How do writers synthesize multiple perspectives on an issue in an argument?

Understanding the Canons of Rhetoric

In ancient Greece, all communicative acts were classified into five categories, or what scholars call the **canons of rhetoric.** These are the principles by which all writing, speaking, or visual arguments operate: **invention** (coming up with ideas), **arrangement** (organizing ideas in effective ways), **style** (expressing those ideas in an appropriate manner), **memory** (accessing learned materials), and **delivery** (presenting crafted ideas to an audience).

Each of these canons is necessary for persuasive communication, whether that be through spoken word, written discourse, or more recently devised visual/multimedia/hybrid forms of communication. For our discussion of composing arguments in this chapter, we'll focus on the first three canons (you can look to Chapter 8 for discussion of the last two canons).

Invention in Argument

When you craft language with the purpose of persuading your audience, you are **inventing** an argument. That is, you are generating ideas about

AT A GLANCE

Canons of Rhetoric

- *Invention:* creating and constructing ideas

- *Arrangement:* ordering and laying out ideas effectively

- *Style:* developing the appropriate expression for those ideas

- *Memory:* retaining invented ideas, recalling additional supporting ideas, and facilitating memory in the audience

- *Delivery:* presenting or performing ideas with the aim of persuading

a topic. The classical Roman rhetorician Cicero defined invention as the "discovery of valid or seemingly valid arguments to render one's cause probable" (*De Inventione*, I.vii). To develop ideas, you can use a range of rhetorical strategies: invoking pathos, using ethos or good character, or employing logos to reason calmly with your readers or listeners. Your task as a writer is to forge a powerful text that argues a point, to convince others to see a particular perspective, usually your own. In composing arguments you can look not only to writing but also to verbal-visual texts all around you as examples of arguments.

When we look at a photograph, we might think that it provides a window on another person's reality. But in fact photographs, like written texts, are artifacts of rhetorical invention. They are created by a writer or artist. Therefore, the "reality" that photographs display is actually a *version* of reality created by a photographer's rhetorical and artistic decisions: whether to use color or black-and-white film; what sort of lighting to use; how to position the subject of the photograph; whether to opt for a panorama or close-up shot; what backdrop to use; how to crop, or trim, the image once it is printed. In effect, when we see photographs in a newspaper or art gallery, we are looking at the product of deliberate *strategies of invention*. In photography, these strategies include key elements of composition, such as selection, placement, perspective, and framing. In written texts, the same elements—selection, placement, perspective, and framing—are critical to making an argument.

Look at Figure 3.2, an image captured by photojournalist Margaret Bourke-White, showing a line of homeless African Americans, displaced by the 1937 Louisville flood, waiting on line to receive food and clothing from a local Red Cross center. Does the photo merely document a moment in the history of Kentucky? Or have the choice of subject, the cropping, the angle, the background, and the elements within the frame been selected by

FIGURE 3.2. Margaret Bourke-White, "At the Time of the Louisville Flood," 1937.

the photographer to make a specific argument about race and American culture during the first half of the twentieth century?

In your own writing, you could look to this photograph as inspiration for invention. You could use this image to support a historically focused argument, perhaps one that examined the catastrophic 1937 Louisville flood and its impact on the local community. Or, you could refer to this photograph as visual evidence in a paper that examined the link between social status, race, and disaster relief. Either argument could draw on the power of photographs like this one, a power created by the invention strategies of the artist.

CREATIVE PRACTICE

Examine the picture in Figure 3.3, taken by photographer Todd Heisler, of a soldier's coffin returning home on a civilian flight into Reno, Nevada, being draped with the American flag prior to being unloaded from the plane. What argument is Heisler making about Americans' response to the Iraq war and casualties? Now consider this image as the foundation for your own process of invention: What types of arguments might you construct that would use this image as visual evidence? What other sorts of images or evidence would you use to develop your argument?

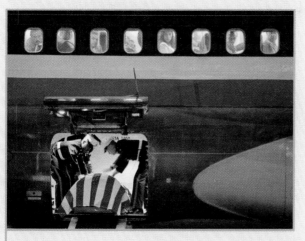

FIGURE 3.3. Photograph of the arrival of a soldier's coffin in Reno, Nevada.

Let's look more closely at how invention factors into the way photographers and writers compose arguments. Consider two famous photographs by Dorothea Lange (see Figures 3.4 and 3.5), which offer very different representations of migrant workers during the Great Depression. In each case, we see a migrant family huddled inside a tent. The subjects seem to be poor, hungry, and struggling to make a living. Their material conditions are bleak.

But notice the effects of the different perspectives. In Figure 3.5, we get an intimate look inside this woman's eyes, where we can see her concern. The lines on her face, visible in this close-up, are evidence of her hard life and worries. The photograph in Figure 3.4 has a wider frame that encompasses the tent and the barren ground. This perspective makes a different kind of argument, one that addresses the condition of the soil, the landscape, the living quarters. We can hardly make out the woman huddled in the darkness of the tent. When we look for visual evidence of the living conditions of migrant workers in the American West during the 1930s, each photograph offers different angles on our argument. Which one would we use to support a thesis about the labor conditions of migrant workers? Which one would we use to argue that the human body is scarred by hardship? Depending on our purpose, we would choose one photograph over the other. Each one makes an

FIGURE 3.4. Dorothea Lange's wide shot gives a stark sense of the experience of migrant farmers.

FIGURE 3.5. The close-up focuses on the struggles of the migrant mother.

argument that we can in turn select as evidence for our claims about the Great Depression. Each photograph uses a particular strategy of invention, creating and constructing ideas in visual form about the "reality" of life for migrant workers. We can, in turn, invent different arguments based on our starting point: which photo do we use as evidence for our thesis?

In written documents, different perspectives on the same topic can yield different arguments. Commentary on Lange's *Migrant Mother* photographs exposes the variety of perspectives not only on the photographs' status as "documentary" evidence from the Great Depression, but also on the way our historical understanding of that period itself is constructed by the invention or arguments of others. For instance, the following excerpt from historian James Curtis's article "Dorothea Lange, Migrant Mother, and the Culture of the Great Depression" demonstrates the way in which Lange's photos are often interpreted as windows into that period:

> In addition to being a timeless work of art, *Migrant Mother* is a vital reflection of the times. Examined in its original context, the series reveals powerful cultural forces of the 1930s: the impact of the increasing centralization and bureaucratization of American life; the anxiety about the status and solidarity of the family in an era of urbanization and modernization; a need to atone for the guilt induced by the destruction of cherished ideals, and a craving for reassurance that democratic traditions would stand the test of modern times.

For Curtis, the images function both as what he calls elsewhere in the article "a timeless and universal symbol of suffering in the face of adversity" (1) as well as the key to understanding Lange's relationship to the evolving genre of documentary photography. For journalist Geoffrey Dunn, however, Lange's series prompts a different response:

> The photographs taken by Lange and her colleagues at the Resettlement Administration (later to become better known as the Farm Security Administration) have been widely heralded as the epitome of documentary photography. The eminent photographer and curator Edward Steichen called them "the most remarkable human documents ever rendered in pictures."
>
> In recent years, however, the FSA photographs have come under a growing criticism. Many view them as manipulative and condescending, to the point of assuming a "colonialistic" attitude toward their subjects. Still others have argued that they are misleading and disingenuous, and in some instances, fabricated.
>
> In a compelling essay entitled "The Historian and the Icon," University of California at Berkeley professor Lawrence Levine has argued that the FSA

photographers focused their lenses on "perfect victims," and in so doing, rendered a caricatured portrait of the era.

"Americans suffered, materially and physically, during the years of the Great Depression to an extent which we still do not fully fathom," Levine asserted. "But they also continued, as people always must, the business of living. They ate and they laughed, they loved and they fought, they worried and they hoped . . . they filled their days, as we fill ours, with the essentials of everyday living."

With the notable exception of FSA photographer Russell Lee, and later, Marion Post Wolcott, whose largely overlooked bodies of work actually capture the dimensions of "everyday living," Lange and her colleagues focused almost exclusively on human suffering. That is most certainly the reason that people like Florence Owens Thompson—and many others who appeared in FSA images—resented their photographic portrayal.

"Mother was a woman who loved to enjoy life, who loved her children," says Thompson's youngest daughter, Norma Rydlewski, who appears as a young child in Lange's classic photograph. "She loved music and she loved to dance. When I look at that photo of mother, it saddens me. That's not how I like to remember her."

Rydlewski noted that while the Depression was hard on her family, it was not all suffering. "Mama and daddy would take us to the movies a lot. We'd go to the carnival whenever it was in town, little things like that. We listened to the radio. If they had any money at all, they'd get us ice cream. In Shafter, we had friends and relatives visiting. We also had our fun."

Troy Owens echoed his sister's sentiments: "They were tough, tough times, but they were the best times we ever had."

Like Curtis, Dunn uses the photographs as the basis for an argument about Lange's practice of documentary photography; however, Dunn's process of invention led him to a different argument, one that prompted him to widen his perspective and consider first-person accounts from other witnesses of that historical moment. The conclusion he reaches through this broader view is that the series exemplifies not reflection but misrepresentation.

All texts—whether written accounts or photographs—are actually shaped by individual perspective and point of view. Texts are "invented" for a specific audience. Your own writing is a text informed by your invention strategies, your purpose, and your point of view. In your writing, you are like a photographer, making important compositional decisions: What will be the subject of your text: an individual, a group, an institution? How will you pose that subject to best convey your own perspective? Should you zoom in, focusing on one particular example as a way of addressing a larger concern? Or should you take a step back, situating your argument in relation to the broader context that surrounds the issue? The choices you make will determine the ultimate impact of your argument: like photographs, effective writing persuades the viewer to look at a topic through the lens of the author's interpretation.

COLLABORATIVE CHALLENGE

In groups of two or three, visit the Collection Highlights of "Suffering Under a Great Injustice: Ansel Adams's Photographs of Japanese-American Internment at Manzanar" through the Chapter 3 resources on the *Envision* Website. Browse through the contents and analyze the framing, cropping, and composition strategies of a selection of the photographs. In some cases clicking on an image will pull up a page comparing the print with the original negative so that you can better understand how Adams cropped his photographs to sharpen the argument conveyed by the images. Working from a comparison of photographs, or of photos and their negatives, make an argument about the perspective offered by each visual text on the experience of Japanese Americans interned during World War II.

www.ablongman.com/envision/209

Arrangement in Argument

After invention, **arrangement** becomes your key consideration because the way in which you present material on the page will shape a reader's response to the ideas. In many cases, attention to arrangement takes the form of the way you order elements in your argument—whether that be the layout of images and text on a newspaper front page or the way you structure a written argument in a more academic paper. It is the arrangement of an argument that gives it structure or that separates a free-form reaction from a carefully developed and proven argument.

Therefore, when we refer to "arrangement" in a written argument, we often are referring to the underlying structure of the essay itself. Although unifying an essay with a smooth flow of ideas is important, it is just as important that the structure of the essay not be completely associational—that is, that it not simply move from one idea to the next through the

process of free association. As we discussed in Chapters 1 and 2, it is important that an essay contain a clear argument or *thesis statement* that gives the
writing direction and that the essay use different rhetorical strategies and
appeals to develop that argument. Fortunately, most essays also adhere to a
foundational structure, one that governs the way the argument is organized.

Among the multitude of possible structures that you might choose for your
essay, here are some common ones you might find useful in composing your
own persuasive arguments:

- **Chronological structure:** Structuring information from the oldest to
  the most recent is perhaps the most intuitive structure to follow for any
  paper that contains examples across time, such as the transformation in
  the Apple computer marketing campaign from Macintosh to iPod.
- **Cause-effect:** An essay confronting the issue of sexist imagery in rap
  music videos might start by exploring how women are represented in
  popular rap videos (*cause*) and then conclude by discussing the impact
  of this representation on the self-esteem and self-perception of young
  girls (*effect*).
- **Problem-solution:** A paper about violence and video games, for
  instance, might devote the first half of the paper to exploring the
  problem of desensitization that occurs through playing violent video
  games and then focus in the second half of the paper on proposing a
  possible *solution*.
- **Block structure:** If you adopt this structure, you would organize your
  paper around a series of examples or case studies—for instance around
  individual films in the James Bond series in a paper about the relationship between the real-world political climate and contemporary spy
  narrative—working your way systematically through each example
  before moving on to the next one.
- **Thematic structure:** Writers who use this structure organize by theme
  rather than example. For instance, a paper on reality television might
  include sections on voyeurism, capitalism, and Darwinism (*the themes*),
  integrating examples from *Survivor*, *American Idol*, and *America's Top
  Model* as evidence in each section.
- **Deferred thesis:** As you become more comfortable with strategies of
  argumentation, you might choose to substitute a thesis question for a
  thesis statement at the beginning of your essay. For instance, rather
  than announcing your argument at the beginning of your paper, you

might ask a question such as "How did images featured in the news define our understanding of the impact of hurricanes Katrina and Rita?" Your thesis—"The news coverage of Katrina and Rita transformed the tragedy into a discussion of class and race in America"—would then appear at the end of your paper as a way of synthesizing the evidence explored in the paper itself.

Let's look again to photography to see in clear visual terms the way a successful argument relies on rhetorically effective strategies of arrangement. Figures 3.6 through Figure 3.9 offer a selection of photographs from the online version of Jane Gottesman's photo essay *Game Face*, a work devoted to redefining the concept of the modern female athlete. A veteran sports writer, Gottesman spent years accumulating a collection of photographs of amateur and professional

FIGURE 3.6. Picture 1 from "Prepare."   **FIGURE 3.7.** Picture 1 from "Compete."

FIGURE 3.8. Picture 1 from "Finish."   **FIGURE 3.9.** Final picture from the photo essay.

women athletes of all ages, races, and socioeconomic backgrounds, a collection that was a museum exhibit and both a print and online photo essay. It is not surprising to find that she gave extra care to strategies of arrangement in composing her visual argument.

Looking at this version of *Game Face*, we can see from the top menu bar that it is divided into four sections: "Prepare," "Compete," "Finish," and "Achieve." Clearly, this is an example of an argument *organized by theme*. This arrangement gives a logical structure to the text: the argument moves along a continuum, from pre-game, to game play, to post-game. Within each of these sections (which roughly approximate the sections of a book or written essay), Gottesman includes several examples (which we might correlate to paragraphs in traditional academic writing). Looking at the individual images, we can see how arrangement plays a strong role in constructing an argument; each page makes its commentary on women's athletics by juxtaposing a powerful photo with a descriptive caption and a relevant quotation from a female athlete. The recurring structure gives the overall photo essay coherence and consistency, despite its variety of examples.

Let's take a closer look at the way the pictures reinforce the underlying structure produced by the section headers; we can do so by carefully examining the lead images for the various sections. The lead image, for instance, (Figure 3.6) centers on an inspirational event: the moment in 1968 when a woman, for the first time, lit the Olympic flame. As the first image in the photo essay, this picture of Norma Basilio symbolizes accomplishment, possibilities, a global perspective, and even more importantly, an auspicious beginning to the argument, the same way in which the lighting of the flame itself marks the beginning of an auspicious event. The next image (Figure 3.7), which heads the "Compete" section, offers a similarly strong statement but shifts perspective from the international to the local, capturing the first moments in a 1994 Pennsylvania triathlon. In this image, as much as we see individual competitors, we also see community—a theme that reappears at many different points in that particular section. The next photograph (Figure 3.8), from the "Finish" section, moves us from the start of competition to its conclusion, focusing on the victory of the female athlete. The series of photographs in this section, from the victorious track star to the weary but triumphant soccer team, celebrate the rewards that come from following through on one's dreams. In the last section, "Achieve," the images escalate in strength, culminating with the inspirational picture of a young girl swinging powerfully toward the stars (Figure 3.9).

COLLABORATIVE CHALLENGE

When we discuss arrangement in reference to photographs like Dorothea Lange's and Jane Gottesman's, we usually refer to the way the photographer stages a shot or orders a series of images. However, in the age of digital photo editing, the canon of arrangement is often used in producing striking arguments in the form of photo illustrations, such as

FIGURE 3.10. Snowball the monster cat fools many viewers with his huge size.

the one shown in Figure 3.10, a hoax photo circulated on dorm chat lists that offers a rather humorous version of photo manipulation. Discuss this image with your group: how were the elements in the photograph altered and arranged to produce the visual joke? Now break into small groups and visit the following sites, linked through the *Envision* Website:

- The Hoax Photo Gallery: a collection of doctored photographs from the online Museum of Hoaxes.
- Frank Van Riper's "Manipulating Truth, Losing Credibility": article from the *Washington Post* about the Brian Walski photo scandal.
- Floyd's Website: before-and-after images that demonstrate the dramatic effects of photo editing.
- "The Case of the Missing Limb": an article from *The Digital Journalist* about how newspaper editors altered a photograph to make it less offensive to readers.

Look through these sites and consider how the canon of arrangement functions in these cases in relation to the ethics of argument. Which altered images are the most convincing? the most disturbing? Why? How do you distinguish between creativity and manipulation? Are there times when photographic manipulation is justified? How can we apply these observations about ethics and arrangement to our consideration of written texts?

Student Writing

See Tiffany Yun's and Chris Mathakul's projects about photo manipulation.
www.ablongman.com/envision/211

Style in Argument

Inventing a thesis or main idea and arranging the elements of your writing are two steps in completing your task of written persuasion. You need also to spend some time considering how you are going to present that idea to your audience. This is where **style**—the third canon of rhetoric—enters the scene. Style concerns choosing the appropriate expression for the ideas of your argument; these choices relate to language, tone, syntax, rhetorical appeals, metaphors, imagery, quotations, level of emphasis, and nuance.

We often translate *style* into *voice* to indicate a writer's unique persona and rhetorical stance as it is manifested in word choice, syntax, pacing, and tone. To construct a successful argument, you need to be able to employ the voice or style that best meets the needs of your rhetorical situation. If you are writing a feature article for *Time* magazine, for instance, you will most likely use accessible language, common expressions, and references to contemporary events. Your paragraphs may be only one or two sentences long, and you may use wit, humor, or pathos to try to move your audience. You might also include a color photograph or even clip art to convey your point to your readers. Such writing choices are all part of your persona as a popular writer. You would make very different composition choices if you were writing for an academic journal that would be read by scholars in the field. In that case you might use disciplinary jargon or diction, longer paragraph structures, and references to other researchers. Those rhetorical choices would distinguish your persona from that conveyed in the popular article. In both cases, your persona and your stylistic choices contribute to building your ethos and persuading your audience.

How do you move from the thesis as a promise of your argument to fostering a strong relationship with your readers so that they will be most inclined to entertain your perspective? The answer lies in careful attention to developing *persona* and *rhetorical stance* in your writing.

Constructing Persona

When you select a certain image, a set of words, or a written phrase to shape your argument and try to persuade your audience, you are constructing a **persona** for yourself as a writer and rhetorician. Your persona is *a deliberately crafted version of yourself as writer.* A public figure will often use *persona* as a purposeful rhetorical tool. President George W. Bush might choose to give a speech about war dressed in army fatigues and flanked by a group of soldiers, but when addressing the state of the economy, he's more likely to hold his press conference from his ranch, wearing a casual shirt and blue jeans. In each case, he constructs a different *persona* designed to be the most appropriate and persuasive for his given rhetorical situation.

The same principle governs the writing process. When you compose a text (written, verbal, or visual), you decide how to use language to present a particular persona to the audience you wish to address. You create a portrait of yourself as the author of your argument through tone (formal or informal, humorous or serious); word choice (academic, colloquial); sentence structures (complex or simple and direct); use of rhetorical appeals (pathos, logos, ethos); and strategies of persuasion (narration, example, cause and effect, analogy, process, classification, or definition). Creating a persona requires care. A well-designed one can facilitate a strong connection with your readers and therefore make your argument more persuasive. However, a poorly constructed persona—one that is, for instance, biased, inconsistent, or underdeveloped—can have the opposite effect, alienating readers and undercutting your text's overall effectiveness.

COLLABORATIVE CHALLENGE

Bring to class a selection of photographs of yourself, including both informal and formal shots (such as your school yearbook photo). In a group, examine each other's photographs and discuss the differences in *persona* evident in each one. Be sure to take into account the details that construct the persona (expression, posture, pose, clothing, background scene, people of various professions in the photo, etc.) as well the composition of the image (color, layout, perspective, angle, lighting). Which picture would you want printed in the newspaper alongside an article describing a prestigious scholarship that you have won? Which photo would you include on the dust jacket of your first published novel? Which photo would you submit to your dorm newsletter? Which would you use on your MySpace or Facebook Webpage? Discuss your decisions and how your assessment of the different rhetorical situations influenced the *argument* you want to make through constructing your persona.

Choosing a Rhetorical Stance

To be persuasive, you must assume a persona that responds appropriately to your specific rhetorical situation. Wayne Booth, one of the most important twentieth-century revivalists of classical rhetoric, defined the writer's position in relation to the rhetorical triangle as the **rhetorical stance** and claimed that it is the most essential aspect of effective communication. He argued that communication failed between people (or a text failed to persuade a reader) if the writer assumed a position that ignored the necessary balance of the rhetorical triangle.

We see examples of inappropriate rhetorical stances constantly: the TV evangelist who moves his congregation with a polished sermon that completely distracts them from flaws in his moral character; the used-car salesman who pads his sales pitch with offers of free gifts, rebate specials, and low percentage rates; the actor who uses her celebrity status to drive a product endorsement, rather than clearly articulating the merits of that product itself. In each case, the *rhetorical triangle*—the relationship between author, audience, and text—is out of balance, and the argument itself, ultimately, is rendered less persuasive. In your own writing, therefore, you need to pay special attention not only to the persona you create but also to the stance you assume in relation to your specific rhetorical situation.

AT A GLANCE

Three Rhetorical Stances That Lead to Communication Failure

- *The pedant or preacherly stance:* the text is paramount and both the audience's needs and the speaker's character are ignored.
- *The advertiser's stance:* the effect on the audience is valued above all, ignoring the quality of the text and the credibility of the speaker.
- *The entertainer's stance:* the character of the speaker is elevated above the text and the audience.

Titles, Introductions, and Conclusions

In writing, you signal your persona and rhetorical stance through your word choice, sentence structure, tone, and strategies of persuasion. Let's zoom in for a moment on three key elements of the written argument to see the way each operates as an important site for these stylistic choices.

Your reader's first encounter with your topic and argument comes through your title; in this way, the title itself operates as a rhetorical act that provides a frame and sets up the argument. Let's return for a moment to Figure 3.1. Many newspapers featured this image on their front pages on September 2,

2005—but with different headlines. Figures 3.11 and 3.12 are two examples. Consider how each paper signals its rhetorical stance through the visual-verbal arguments contained on its front page.

How does the headline "City desperate for help" read in combination with the helicopter image suggest a different argument than "Rising rage: Descent into anarchy" coupled with the same image? The difference in tone, perspective, and rhetorical stance apparent from these contrasting examples underscores the role a headline—and, relatedly, a title—plays in forming a reader's expectations for the argument that follows. In effect, a title is often the first step in writing an interpretation or making an argument.

FIGURE 3.11. Front page of the *Fresno Bee*, September 2, 2005.

Source: © THE FRESNO BEE, 2006

FIGURE 3.12. Front page of the *Deseret Morning News*, September 2, 2005.

In writing your own papers, you should spend some time brainstorming your titles. Some writers find constructing a powerful title to be a useful brainstorming activity to start their composition process and help them with invention; others construct the title only after completing the first draft of their paper, as a way of synthesizing the argument by bringing it into sharper focus. As you work with a title, think about its role in setting up your stance on your topic, indicating to your readers not only the scope of your analysis but also your angle on it. Try to play with language, linking the title to your main point, to a key image you discuss, to an underlying metaphor or motif, or to the larger issue raised by your argument. Test your working title by sharing it with a partner in class.

Like your title, your introduction offers your readers insight into the persona and rhetorical stance that will characterize your essay as a whole. In these opening paragraphs (an introduction may be more than one paragraph), you establish your voice (informal? formal?), your tone (measured? firm? angry? cautious?), your persona, and your topic through careful attention to word choice, sentence structure, and strategies of development. Most introductions also provide the first articulation of your argument as well, moving from a general statement of topic to a more focused statement of your thesis.

However, perhaps even more importantly, the introduction is the moment in which you capture the attention and interest of your reader, often through a device that we call a rhetorical "hook." For instance, looking back at Jane Gottesman's photo essay, we can see how she hooks her online readers in her opening image (Figure 3.6) by framing the 1968 Olympics as a landmark event for women athletes. The reader is drawn in by the ethos of the Olympics and intrigued by the fact that it was only as recently as the late 1960s that women first participated in the torch-lighting ceremony. This hook prompts readers to wonder what other "firsts" they might not be aware of, what other facts about women athletes Gottesman might reveal. This is the hook that gets readers interested—and prompts readers to continue reading.

In written texts, you can use your introduction to hook your readers through one of several methods:

- Defining your terms (especially if you're writing on a subject that not everyone may be familiar with)
- Including a significant quotation or a startling statistic or fact

- Presenting an overview of the issue you're discussing
- Using an anecdote or narration
- Incorporating a vivid example
- Drawing on a relevant analogy or metaphor
- Using the second-person pronoun (*you*) to invite readers to make personal connections

Your choice of hook will depend to a large extent on your broader stylistic decisions about your essay and the way in which you want to develop your argument.

Let's look at how one student, Michael Zeligs, took the canon of style into consideration while composing his introduction to a rhetorical analysis of Robert Frank's photography:

> "Robert Frank, Swiss, unobtrusive, nice, with that little camera that he raises and snaps with one hand he sucked a sad poem right out of America onto film, taking rank among the tragic poets of the world."
>
> In his introduction to Robert Frank's *The Americans,* Jack Kerouac captures the photographer's responsible position as a concerned observer of his time, as the first person to sweep away dominating prejudice and expose what post–World War II America really represented. In his book, Frank pushes the limits of traditional art photography—limits that required clear foregrounds and backgrounds, clear subject and exposure and level tilt—and this enables him to focus more on scenes that dominate his eye and inspire emotional arguments. The America that Frank addresses, however, is not one of fulfilled dreams and two-car garages. It is a struggling foreground for change, founded in the two beautifully conflicting scenes of "Charleston, South Carolina," and "Trolley," where unique photographic elements merge to advance a critique of racial inequality during America's post-war crisis of identity.

What hooks the reader first is the quotation, or epigraph, that heads the introduction: an abstract, lyrical statement that refuses to sacrifice its vision by adhering to conventional punctuation. Commenting on the subject of the paper—the photography of Robert Frank—this quote announces the essay's topic at the same time that it provides a sharp contrast for the writing style of the main body of the introduction that follows. By comparison, Michael's voice seems crisp, focused, and academic, establishing a persona that is both informed on his subject (he clearly not only has analyzed Frank's photographs but has read the introduction to the book as well) and is also able to discuss it articulately. Notice the way that Michael fashions his first sentence to serve as a bridge between his opening hook and the rest of the paragraph. Rather than using the epigraph simply as a snappy device to capture the reader's attention and then abandoning it, Michael creates an ethos appeal by identifying the quotation's author (Jack Kerouac, an iconic critic of American culture) and then restates the meaning of the quote in a way that pulls it in line with his own argument about Robert Frank's photography. The rest of the paragraph moves from general (a description of the project of Frank's larger book, *The Americans,* and a definition of traditional photographic methods) to specific (clarification of the two images Michael is most interested in), ending ultimately with a clear articulation of Michael's rhetorical stance and thesis statement.

If the introduction offers the writer the opportunity to hook the audience's readers' while articulating a personal stance on a subject, the conclusion provides the final opportunity to reinforce an essay's argument while making a lasting impact on readers. For this reason, although a conclusion by its nature should include some elements of summary (synthesizing the key points from the essay), it should also have a rhetorical power of its own. Let's look at how Michael concluded his essay on Frank's photographs:

> Robert Frank, in his images from *The Americans,* takes compelling pictures of a socially conflicted south to expose the growing struggle of race in 1950's America. His images spark from a new ideology of the photographer—a lack of concern for absolute photographic perfection allows him to document situations that really *mean* something. He chooses conflicting lives, black and white together on the page but unequal, his film subtly showing sympathy for the downtrodden worker and the weary traveler. Careful lines and deliberate tones show two opposing worlds where skin color can change the appearance of an entire backdrop, where stark white prison bars show us the walls we have erected within ourselves. These are not simple pictures of ordinary people. They are an artist's whisper about the elusiveness of equality, how in the war against bigotry, we are not done yet.

While offering a summary of his evidence, Michael resists the temptation to center his conclusion on a simple paragraph-by-paragraph reiteration of his argument. Instead he takes care to make his conclusion as stylistically sophisticated as his introduction. Notice his careful use of word choice ("takes compelling pictures," "expose") that works in tandem with the subject of his essay; his return to the task of redefining American photography that he began in his introduction; his implicit reference to his analysis of the images themselves in the main body of his paper ("downtrodden worker and weary traveler," references to "lines" and "tones"); and, finally, the way he broadens his topic to touch on larger, ongoing issues of race relations. His conclusion leaves readers with more than a simple summary of points, prompting them to reflect on the ongoing state of race relations in America.

Consider ways to make your own conclusion a powerful part of your argument. You might use a key quote, example, or reference that either epitomizes or summarizes your points. You might return to an opening example or analogy, offering a slightly different, perhaps more informed perspective on it to connect introduction and conclusion as a frame for your argument. Along similar lines, if you use a chronological structure, you might move from the past to recent times, perhaps ending with a projection into the future. Or, like Michael, you might use your conclusion to suggest broader implications that could increase the reader's sense of personal connection to the topic or its urgency. No matter which strategy you choose, remember to maximize the persuasive potential of your conclusion as a means of reaffirming the strength of your argument with your readers.

Crafting a Position Paper

One way to experiment and put into practice these concepts—invention, arrangement, and style—is to draft a position paper on your topic. By definition, a **position paper** presents one side of an issue, allowing you the opportunity to construct a strong thesis statement and actively argue your main points. A position paper also can be an ideal medium for developing your own particular style, persona, and rhetorical stance. Angela Rastegar, for instance, experimented with persona during a project on photographic coverage of the war in Iraq. She tried out two very different ways of writing. First she composed an argument about the issue from the perspective of an unnamed academic or journalistic commentator. Then she revised the argument by writing a short paper representing an extreme position on the toppling of a Saddam Hussein statue by U.S. troops. Her first "position" offers the academic voice with an ostensibly objective perspective. Notice that there is no obvious "I" speaking, and yet an argument about the power of the media clearly emerges.

Angela Rastegar

Academic Position Paper

Imagine a chaotic world in which you cannot trust the media—newspapers, television reports, and magazines are full of lies about the world and politics. Picture trying to decipher current events or important situations without knowing whom to turn to or what to believe. Sounds far-fetched? Unfortunately, this is not far from the truth. Current newspapers are filled with subtle, clever methods used to deceive the public.

As you look at photographic images in widely respected newspaper articles, consider the techniques used to deceive the public. Concerning one incident—the April 9th destruction of Saddam Hussein's monument in Baghdad—the actual events of this day have been carefully concealed from the public. Although the media portrayed a "heroic" destruction of Saddam's symbol by American forces and mobs of Iraqi supporters, this event was essentially staged by the media.

We must use a cautious eye when viewing news stories and alert ourselves to subtle biases. The media has been called the "fourth branch of the government" because of the undeniable power it yields over the American public. No other source of information is so readily and unquestionably accepted. The government realizes this, and it often takes great measures to work with the media to create effective, captivating stories that not only portray Americans in a positive light but will also sell papers. Examples of the media's

Rastegar 2

influence are not by any means limited to this single event; however, wars provide the perfect opportunity for the media to influence the public. They open wounds in all Americans, leaving viewers vulnerable, easily influenced, and starving for more information. As a result, studying the media's influence on any war opens a vast field of controversy. In this time of crisis, we must read the news with a wary eye.

Finding this voice to offer too much of the "advertiser's stance," Angela then experimented with first person to shape her argument into an analysis of a specific photograph (see Figure 1 in her letter to the editor). She developed this position paper as an examination of the image and named her persona "Elizabeth Grant," a concerned media activist.

Angela Rastegar

Writing a Letter to the Editor as "Elizabeth Grant,"

Left-Wing Media Watchdog

I am writing in response to the astonishing display of deceit attempted by President G. W. Bush and the American government on Thursday, April 10th. President Bush's public address began with the words, "Iraqi citizens support overthrowing Saddam," which was illustrated by the enclosed photograph. It depicts an American marine tying the Iraqi flag around the neck of Saddam Hussein's 15-foot monument. Seconds later, U.S. troops connected the ropes and cables to the statue's neck and brought it crashing to the ground.

The photograph, which contains a brightly colored red and white Iraqi flag in the center, focuses the viewer's attention on this emblem. Did the Iraqi citizens request to use this flag? We don't know, but we can see how the government attempted to appeal to those watching by having a soldier tie Iraq's own flag to the chains.

Figure 1. Laurent Rebours, Associated Press. *The New York Times: On the Web.* "Scenes from Baghdad." Online Posting. 9 April 2003. *The New York Times Company.* 14 April 2003.

The flag falsely suggests that the Iraqi people were behind the destruction of the monument and that America can work in harmony with the people of Iraq to overthrow Saddam. This message drastically distorts the truth; in fact, the soldier originally held an American flag, but his commanding officers ordered him to tie this particular flag to the chains. Thus, the government's use of logos in this photo subtly attempts to convince the public that Iraq wanted to bring down Saddam's statue—when, in reality, the citizens there had nothing to do with it.

In this photograph, the picture also appeals to the viewers' emotions by placing a rope and chains around the neck of Saddam's

Rastegar 3

image. In this sense, it evokes the American hatred for Saddam and creates a clear, understandable aim. The military is able to put a noose around the neck of a symbolic Saddam, displaying the government's ability to destroy him. The government draws on these emotions from the viewers to increase patriotism. Bush applies these same tactics to his public speeches, focusing on American strength to justify our intervention.

In addition, the photo strategically includes a U.S. marine to add to the photo's visual credibility. This symbol of America—a solider in uniform—forces the viewers to place more trust in the photographer and what we see here. My greatest fear is that the average American will hear Bush speak and see this photo without realizing that their goal is to convince the world of Iraqi support for American intervention. They claim that they are fighting to "free Iraq," but in reality, our government simply ties Iraq's fate to Saddam and destroys them both.

In her first position paper, Angela writes about the power of photographs from a generalized, academic perspective, the voice of analytical assessment. But in her subsequent paper, she explores a specific point of view about media coverage of international politics. The persona of Elizabeth Grant—whose style Angela develops through careful attention to word choice, rhetorical appeals, and prose style—relies on the use of "I" and repeated use of strong language. As you can tell, the experimentation with *voice* itself was the most important product of her revisions: it allowed her both to reach into her topic and to examine differences in *style* and *rhetorical stance,* in particularly powerful ways. As she moved into the final stages of her project, she brought the power of this writing to bear on her longer researched argument; although she wrote the final paper from her own perspective, working with the pro and con points of view enabled her to construct a sharper thesis statement and a more persuasive approach to the photographs she was discussing.

Writing Multiple Sides of an Argument

Angela Rastegar's project opens up some interesting possibilities for developing your own persuasive arguments. Sometimes when we write from our own points of view, we get so locked into our individual perspectives that we fail to take into account the diverse or multiple sides of our topics. Such limited vision can weaken our persuasiveness; if we fail to consider or acknowledge alternative positions on our topics, we produce one-sided arguments that lack complexity or credibility with our readers. Recall our earlier discussion of photographs: each photograph suggests a different angle, a unique "version" of an event, and the perspective of a particular persona. When we bring these different sides to light, we find that suddenly an incident or issue that seems polarized—or "black and white"—is actually much more complex. The same holds true for the issues we confront every day as writers and rhetoricians: it is only through exploring the multiple sides of our argument that we can engage it persuasively and effectively.

Begin experimenting with inventing diverse perspectives to achieve a thorough understanding of a complex situation. Although you may be tempted to think of these various perspectives in oppositional terms—as the "pro" or "con" of an issue—such a point of view closes off the richer complexity of the issue. Try to think of arguments not in terms of right or wrong but rather as a spectrum of differing perspectives. As you turn to write your own arguments, consider how you can explore different viewpoints by trying out personas; by inventing diverse responses to your own point of view; and by exploring various writing strategies through experimentation with diction, syntax, style, image selection, arrangement of argument, and voice.

Student Writing

See persuasive position papers by Katie Jones about photography depicting the civil rights era, and by Ryan Kissick on media depictions of baseball star Pete Rose.

www.ablongman.com/envision/212

When writing arguments, you might choose to explore more than one *persona* or *rhetorical stance* to see different sides of an issue. Student Aisha Ali, for instance, developed her project on the conflict in the Middle East by creating three articles, or sides, around a single photograph (see Figure 3.13). Using the image as the foundation for each discussion, she assumed the personas of an African photojournalist, an Israeli soldier, and a Palestinian boy. Aisha's contrasting personas offered a series of riveting snapshots of the Palestinian conflict. To create this effect, she took extra care with word choice, sentence structure, and the development of her arguments. In her first side, she opens the piece by exploring the context of the Middle Eastern situation and then moves with fluid and articulate language to the central narrative: the freeing of the doves in front of an oncoming tank. Her second side adopts a different approach: using direct, informal speech, and biased language suitable to a soldier hardened by armed conflict, this persona launches immediately into the narrative itself. The last side also presents the story of the doves' release; however, as the excerpt from her work shows, the voice is clearly that of a child. Using simple sentence structures and word choices to build a narrative with an underlying pathos appeal, Aisha has brought to life the perspective of the young boy forced to free his doves in the shadow of military occupation.

 Student Writing

Read Aisha Ali's complete project and other student Multiple Sides projects.

www.ablongman.com/envision/213

FIGURE 3.13. The powerful image of doves in front of a tank in the Middle East offers multiple interpretations.

Mohammed al-Durra

Occupation: Elementary School Student

Age: 8

My birds are gone. I had to let them go. I didn't want to, but we had to leave the house and I couldn't carry them. Mommy told me this morning that we would go to my Aunt Fatema's house in

Jenin. I didn't want to go, but she made me. And today, in school, we were going to have Show and Tell, and I told her that, but she said that I could bring in Ali another time. Now I won't get to. Because I had to let him and Nayla and Hassan go free. They were my three doves, and every day I gave them food and talked to them. I knew that sometimes they were scared because of the loud noises that came from town, but I would talk to them in their cage and let them know that it was okay. Mommy said that nothing bad would happen to us because we didn't do anything bad—but Daddy had to leave us, and now I lost my three best friends.

Together, the variety of perspectives in Aisha's writing enabled her to avoid producing a simplistic argument about the violence in the Middle East, and instead to demonstrate its complexity. Although the photograph Aisha used in her series of articles constitutes a powerful visual argument in itself through its striking juxtaposition of fluttering doves (a symbol of peace) and military tanks (a symbol of war), she was able to convey the meaning of the image for diverse viewers through powerful writing. You can try this strategy of writing multiple sides of an argument in your own compositions.

COLLABORATIVE CHALLENGE

Download two to three images from MSNBC.com's "Week in Pictures," accessible through the Chapter 3 resources on the *Envision* Website. As a group, select photos that convey different sides of a situation or event. Come up with three personas—the voice of the person in the photo, the voice of the photographer, and the voice of an observer. Now develop a thesis for each side and write a brief description of your imagined persona. Allow each person in the group to contribute a new perspective. Write up each of these sides; format them into a feature article or cover story for a news-paper or magazine, and, when you are done, present your work as a group to the class.

www.ablongman.com/envision/214

Synthesizing Multiple Perspectives

Although experimenting with writing in different styles from the perspectives of different personas, incorporating diverse strategies of arrangement for each piece, and inventing opposing arguments allow you to develop a deeper understanding of the complexity of an issue, in many academic contexts you will be asked to **synthesize** these perspectives into a single, thesis-driven text. The task then is to incorporate discussion of multiple perspectives (including positions you might find through research) in a way that reveals the complexity of the issue but ultimately advances your own, final rhetorical stance on the topic at hand.

We find an outstanding example of successfully balancing multiple perspectives with a clear, authorial thesis in Nora Ephron's article "The Boston Photographs," published in *Scribble, Scribble: Notes on the Media* (1978). This essay offers a useful model of the canons of rhetoric we've been discussing so far—invention, arrangement, and style.

Ephron offers us insight into the constant struggles that newspaper editors face in selecting photographs for publication—in this case, deciding whether or not to print the "sensationalist" images of a woman and child falling from a fire escape during a 1976 apartment fire (Figure 3.14). Ephron brings into her article at least three perspectives, each embodying a unique rhetorical stance: from her own

FIGURE 3.14. The *Boston Herald American* chose to print the most sensational photograph on its cover.

perspective to those of Stanley Forman, photographer, and Charles Seib, the *Washington Post* ombudsman (the editor who monitors the content of the paper to ensure that it is not offensive to readers). She also represents in miniature other points of view through a series of brief quotations from letters to the editor that appeared shortly after the publication of the controversial photographs. The writers of these letters each get a turn to argue their unique points from the basis of their own rhetorical stance. However, the argument that ultimately is most persuasive is Ephron's own; in this way, she *synthesizes* the arguments to arrive at her own, persuasive conclusion.

The Boston Photographs
Nora Ephron

Ephron begins with the voice of the photographer, Stanley Forman, using a direct quote to present his perspective.
Her next two paragraphs provide background for Forman's recollections.

Notice Ephron's use of the second person to establish a rapport with her reader built on a sense of shared cultural experience.

Although this section is ostensibly description, look closely at her stylistic choices—especially word choice—to see the way she is setting up her stance on the topic.

"I made all kinds of pictures because I thought it would be a good rescue shot over the ladder . . . never dreamed it would be anything else. . . . I kept having to move around because of the light set. The sky was bright and they were in deep shadow. I was making pictures with a motor drive and he, the firefighter, was reaching up and, I don't know, everything started falling. I followed the girl down taking pictures. . . . I made three or four frames. I realized what was going on and I completely turned around, because I didn't want to see her hit."

You probably saw the photographs. In most newspapers, there were three of them. The first showed some people on a fire escape—a fireman, a woman, and a child. The fireman had a nice strong jaw and looked very brave. The woman was holding the child. Smoke was pouring from the building behind them. A rescue ladder was approaching, just a few feet away, and the fireman had one arm around the woman and one arm reaching out toward the ladder. The second picture showed the fire escape slipping off the building. The child had fallen on the escape and seemed about to slide off the edge. The woman was grasping desperately at the legs of the fireman, who had managed to grab the ladder. The third picture showed the woman and child in midair, falling to the ground. Their arms and legs were outstretched, horribly distended. A potted plant was falling too. The caption said that the woman, Diana Bryant, nineteen, died in the fall. The child landed on the woman's body and lived.

The pictures were taken by Stanley Forman, thirty, of the *Boston Herald American*. He used a motor-driven Nikon F set at 1/250, f5.6-S. Because of the motor, the camera can click off three frames a second. More than four hundred newspapers in the United States alone carried the photographs: The tear sheets from overseas are still coming in. The *New York Times* ran them on the first page of its second section; a paper in south Georgia gave them nineteen columns; the *Chicago Tribune,* the *Washington Post* and the *Washington Star* filled almost half their front pages, the *Star* under a somewhat redundant headline that read: Sensational Photos of Rescue Attempt That Failed.

The photographs are indeed sensational. They are pictures of death in action, of that split second when luck runs out, and it is impossible to look at them without feeling their extraordinary impact and remembering, in an almost subconscious way, the morbid fantasy of falling, falling off a building, falling to one's death. Beyond that, the pictures are classics, old-fashioned but perfect examples of photojournalism at its most spectacular. They're throwbacks, really, fire pictures, 1930s tabloid shots; at the same time they're technically superb and thoroughly modern—the sequence could not have been taken at all until the development of the motor-driven camera some sixteen years ago.

Most newspaper editors anticipate some reader reaction to photographs like Forman's; even so, the response around the country was enormous, and almost all of it was negative. I have read hundreds of the letters that were printed in letters-to-the-editor sections, and they repeat the same points. "Invading the privacy of death." "Cheap sensationalism." "I thought I was reading the *National Enquirer*." "Assigning the agony of a human being in terror of imminent death to the status of a side-show act." "A tawdry way to sell newspapers."The *Seattle Times* received sixty letters and calls; its managing editor even got a couple of them at home. A reader wrote the *Philadelphia Inquirer:*"*Jaws* and *Towering Inferno* are playing downtown; don't take business away from people who pay good money to advertise in your own paper."Another reader wrote the *Chicago Sun-Times:*"I shall try to hide my disappointment that Miss Bryant wasn't wearing a skirt when she fell to her death. You could

[Margin notes]
She establishes her ethos in the beginning of this paragraph by demonstrating her knowledge of photography.

While here Ephron finally gives her own assessment of the images (that they "are indeed sensational"), she refrains from a definitive thesis statement at this point.

Word choice once again hints at her argument: Notice how the term "sensational" (with slight negative connotations) has become "spectacular," which suggests awe and appreciation.

She focuses here on audience reaction to the photographs. The accumulation of quotations increases her those as a researcher and also gives weight to their outrage, even though it is a reaction that Ephron does not share.

have had some award-winning photographs of her underpants as her skirt billowed over her head, you voyeurs." Several newspaper editors wrote columns defending the pictures: Thomas Keevil of the *Costa Mesa* (California) *Daily Pilot* printed a ballot for readers to vote on whether they would have printed the pictures; Marshall L. Stone of Maine's *Bangor Daily News,* which refused to print the famous assassination picture of the Vietcong prisoner in Saigon, claimed that the Boston pictures showed the dangers of fire escapes and raised questions about slumlords. (The burning building was a five-story brick apartment house on Marlborough Street in the Back Bay section of Boston.)

For the last five years, the *Washington Post* has employed various journalists as ombudsmen, whose job is to monitor the paper on behalf of the public. The *Post*'s current ombudsman is Charles Seib, former managing editor of the *Washington Star;* the day the Boston photographs appeared, the paper received over seventy calls in protest. As Seib later wrote in a column about the pictures, it was "the largest reaction to a published item that I have experienced in eight months as the *Post*'s ombudsman. . . .

"In the *Post*'s newsroom, on the other hand, I found no doubts, no second thoughts . . . the question was not whether they should be printed but how they should be displayed. When I talked to editors . . . they used words like 'interesting' and 'riveting' and 'gripping' to describe them. The pictures told of something about life in the ghetto, they said (although the neighborhood where the tragedy occurred is not a ghetto, I am told). They dramatized the need to check on the safety of fire escapes. They dramatically conveyed something that had happened, and that is the business we're in. They were news. . . .

"Was publication of that [third] picture a bow to the same taste for the morbidly sensational that makes gold mines of disaster movies? Most papers will not print the picture of a dead body except in the most unusual circumstances. Does the fact that the final picture was taken a millisecond before the young woman died make a difference? Most papers will not print a picture of a bare female breast. Is that a more inappropriate subject for display than the

---

Consider the order in which she arranges the quotes: the last two are the most colorful and memorable.

Her final parenthetical aside slightly undermines the power of this perspective by pointing out an inaccuracy.

At this point in the essay, she features the Washington Post editor who decided to run the photographs in that newspaper. The fact that she follows the reader-response with Seib's reaction is clearly strategic because her own stance most closely resembles his.

picture of a human being's last agonized instant of life?" Seib offered no answers to the questions he raised, but he went on to say that although as an editor he would probably have run the pictures, as a reader he was revolted by them.

In conclusion, Seib wrote: "Any editor who decided to print those pictures without giving at least a moment's thought to what purpose they served and what their effect was likely to be on the reader should ask another question: Have I become so preoccupied with manufacturing a product according to professional traditions and standards that I have forgotten about the consumer, the reader?"

It should be clear that the phone calls and letters and Seib's own reaction were occasioned by one factor alone: the death of the woman. Obviously, had she survived the fall, no one would have protested; the pictures would have had a completely different impact. Equally obviously, had the child died as well—or instead— Seib would undoubtedly have received ten times the phone calls he did. In each case, the pictures would have been exactly the same—only the captions, and thus the responses, would have been different.

But the questions Seib raises are worth discussing—though not exactly for the reasons he mentions. For it may be that the real lesson of the Boston photographs is not the danger that editors will be forgetful of reader reaction, but that they will continue to censor pictures of death precisely because of that reaction. The protests Seib fielded were really a variation on an old theme—and we saw plenty of it during the Nixon-Agnew years—the "Why doesn't the press print the good news?" argument. In this case, of course, the objections were all dressed up and cleverly disguised as righteous indignation about the privacy of death. This is a form of puritanism that is often justifiable; just as often it is merely puritanical.

Seib takes it for granted that the widespread though fairly recent newspaper policy against printing pictures of dead bodies is a sound one; I don't know that it makes any sense at all. I recognize that printing pictures of corpses raises all sorts of problems about taste and titillation and sensationalism; the fact is, however, that people die. Death happens to be one of life's main events. And it is

She gently qualifies Seib's argument, asserting the side or perspective while at the same time suggesting her own interpretation of the issue.

It is only now, after showcasing these many voices on the issue, that Ephron moves to her own argument.

By using the phrases "all dressed up and cleverly disguised," Ephron exposes her own impatience with some of the reactions elicited by the publication of the photos.

Her clever play on words (puritanism/ puritanical) further clarifies her stance.

Look at her use of rhetorical questions to make her point and to throw the issue back at her readers.

irresponsible—and more than that, inaccurate—for newspapers to fail to show it, or to show it only when an astonishing set of photos comes in over the Associated Press wire. Most papers covering fatal automobile accidents will print pictures of mangled cars. But the significance of fatal automobile accidents is not that a great deal of steel is twisted but that people die. Why not show it? That's what accidents are about. Throughout the Vietnam war, editors were reluctant to print atrocity pictures. Why *not* print them? That's what that was about. Murder victims are almost never photographed; they are granted their privacy. But their relatives are relentlessly pictured on their way in and out of hospitals and morgues and funerals.

The use of the first person here marks a moment where Ephron begins to clearly assert her own opinion, rather than reporting on the perspectives of others.

In her conclusion, Ephron ends with a concession to those who were offended and then a strong articulation of her position on the topic that links to larger issues in photojournalism.

　　I'm not advocating that newspapers print these things in order to teach their readers a lesson. The *Post* editors justified their printing of the Boston pictures with several arguments in that direction; every one of them is irrelevant. The pictures don't show anything about slum life; the incident could have happened anywhere, and it did. It is extremely unlikely that anyone who saw them rushed out and had his fire escape strengthened. And the pictures were not news—at least they were not national news. It is not news in Washington, or New York, or Los Angeles that a woman was killed in a Boston fire. The only newsworthy thing about the pictures is that they were taken. They deserve to be printed because they are great pictures, breathtaking pictures of something that happened. That they disturb readers is exactly as it should be: that's why photojournalism is often more powerful than written journalism.

　　How does Ephron present her own argument despite allowing so many voices in her piece? How does she achieve the synthesis of multiple sides while developing her own argument through invention, arrangement, and style?

　　Let's first determine her main idea, the *invention* in her thesis statement. Where is her thesis? What new perspective on the issue of representing death in photographs has she invented in this essay in order to share it with her reading audience? Look at the final paragraph for the answer.

　　Now let's analyze the *arrangement* of her essay. As we read through the essay, we see that Ephron strategically allows the multiple viewpoints on the issue

Strategies of Arrangement

A Classical Speech or Oration

1. Introduction
2. Statement of facts
3. Division
4. Proof
5. Refutation
6. Conclusion

Option A

Use when you want to ground the reader in your argument before bringing up opposing perspectives.

1. Introduction, identification of rhetorical stance
2. Thesis
3. Statement of background, definition, or context
4. Evidence and development of argument
5. Opposing opinion, concession, qualification, refutation
6. Conclusion

Option B

Establish opposing opinion up front so that the entire piece functions as an extended rebuttal or refutation of that line of argument.

1. Introduction and opposing viewpoint
2. Thesis and identification of rhetorical stance
3. Evidence and development of argument
4. Conclusion

Option C

Treat diverse viewpoints as appropriate during the development of your argument and presentation of your evidence.

1. Introduction, identification of rhetorical stance
2. Thesis
3. Statement of background, definition, or context
4. Evidence, opposing opinion, concession, qualification, refutation
5. Conclusion

to play themselves out in the early part of her article, providing the reader with a firm grounding in the debate, before concluding with her own very strong point of view. By arranging her essay in this way, Ephron focuses the audience reaction to the images and to the editor's decisions to run them through the lens of her own argument. However, Ephron's strategy is just one of many patterns of arrangement that take into account incorporating counterarguments while producing a persuasive text. You have multiple options available to you when dealing with opposing viewpoints. You can follow the classical method of arrangement (see table) or select a modified version, depending on your purpose.

AT A GLANCE

The Arrangement of Ephron's Argument

1. Quotation from photographer (1 paragraph)
2. Background (2 paragraphs)
3. Ephron's general assessment of images (1 paragraph)
4. Reader reaction to photos (1 paragraph)
5. Editor's point of view (4 paragraphs)
6. Qualification of Seib's point of view (1 paragraph)
7. Her own argument (final 3 paragraphs)

The models of arrangement in the table are not designed to be rigid parameters. Instead, they should suggest possibilities and potentially productive strategies of arrangement; in your own writing, you will have to select the most productive way to lay out your topic and the diverse opinions that surround it.

You'll need to consider first the strength of the other perspectives on the issue. Do they corroborate your argument? Then you could include them as supporting evidence. Do they offer points of view that you can disprove? Then you might present the opinion and provide a **rebuttal,** or refutation of the points, demonstrating why they are not valid. Do they offer points of view that you can't disprove? Then you might *concede* the validity of their argument but go on to *qualify* their points by showing why your own argument is nonetheless persuasive. The key is to treat these other voices with respect; always represent their points of view fairly and without bias, even if you disagree with them. In a sense, when you are dealing with multiple perspectives, some of which may run counter to your own argument, you face a question of ethics quite similar to that the editors faced with the Boston photographs: How do you present possibly volatile material in a way that is both fair and yet advances your persuasive purpose?

We can see how Ephron herself answered that question by assessing her use of the canon of *style,* specifically in the persona and rhetorical stance she developed in her essay. As a careful analysis of her essay demonstrates, Ephron presents the background on the issue as if through an objective lens; however, her word choice, her selections of quotations, and even the sentence structures themselves collaborate to produce a rhetorical stance that seems all the more persuasive for its earlier objectivity when she moves to the strong statement at the end of her essay. For this reason, when her voice becomes more clearly argumentative in her conclusion, the reader does not automatically resist her argument. Instead, because of Ephron's stylistic choices, readers are more likely to be persuaded by her thesis, "That they [the photographs] disturb readers is exactly as it should be," and to welcome Ephron's fundamental redefinition of the purpose and characteristics of good photojournalism.

AT A GLANCE

Dealing with Multiple Perspectives in Your Arguments

When incorporating other viewpoints into your writing, you can use them in one of three ways:

- *Evidence:* you can use the diverse viewpoints to support your own thesis statement.

- *Concession/Qualification:* you can admit that the person has a strong point but then explain why it doesn't diminish the persuasiveness or validity of your argument.

- *Rebuttal:* you can present an opposing opinion, fairly and respectfully, and then demonstrate why it is not a valid argument in this case.

CREATIVE PRACTICE

Rewrite the Nora Ephron piece from the perspective of one of the personas that she mentions in her text: the editor, the photographer, or a disgruntled reader. As you do, incorporate the other perspectives into your argument, experimenting with arrangement and style to produce a piece that synthesizes diverse viewpoints while still making its own strong argument.

Constructing Your Own Argument

In this chapter, you've learned to harness the canons of rhetoric—invention, arrangement, and style—to compose effective arguments of your own. You've developed strategies for crafting titles, introductions, and conclusions; you've explored the importance of persona and rhetorical stance in argument. You've experimented with developing a position paper, crafting multiple sides of an argument, and then integrating diverse perspectives through a synthesis paper. Now it's time to implement these skills. Practice inventing a position on an issue, arranging claims and evidence for your argument (including working with images as evidence for your points), developing a rhetorical stance, and working on persona through style by crafting your prose with care. You might want to brainstorm first with the help of the prewriting checklist and then try out the longer writing projects described below.

PREWRITING CHECKLIST
Analyzing Photographs

❑ **Content:** What, literally, does the photograph depict? Who or what is the subject of the photo? What is the setting?

❑ **Cultural context:** What is the historical context of the photograph? If it "documents" a particular event, person, or historical moment, how prominently does this photograph factor into our understanding of this event, person, or place? (For instance, is it the only known photograph of an event, or is it one of a series of pictures taken of the same subject?)

(continued)

❏ **Material context:** Where was this photograph reproduced or displayed (an art gallery, the cover of a magazine, the front page of a newspaper)? If it was published elsewhere originally, does this source credit the original?

❏ **Argument:** What, thematically, does the photograph depict? What is its message to the audience? For instance, while the photo might *show* a group of people standing together, its argument might be about love, family unity across generations, or a promise for the future.

❏ **Photographer:** Who took this photograph? What was the person's purpose?

❏ **Genre:** Is this a news photo? a self-portrait? a piece of art? How does it fulfill or confound the expectations of this genre? (For example, the expectation for a news photo is that it clearly captures a person, moment, event; the expectation for a self-portrait is that it evokes an artist's sense of his or her own persona.)

❏ **Audience:** Was the photograph intended to persuade a larger audience or to function as a more personalized expression of a point of view?

❏ **Purpose:** What is the photograph's purpose? Is it intended to be overtly argumentative and to move its audience to action? Or is the argument more subtle, even to the point of "seeming" objective or representational?

❏ **Rhetorical stance:** How does the composition of the photo convey a sense of the rhetorical stance or point of view of the photographer? Pay attention to issues of focus (what is "in focus"?This may differ from the ostensible "focus" of the picture); cropping (what is "in" the picture, and what has been left "out"?); color (is the picture in black and white? color? sepia?); setting (what backdrop has the photographer chosen?); and perspective (are we looking down? up?).

❏ **Representation versus reality:** Does this photograph aspire to represent reality, or is it an overtly abstract piece? Is there any indication of photo manipulation, editing, or other alteration? If so, what rhetorical purpose does this serve—what argument does this alteration make?

❏ **Word and image:** Does the photo have a caption? Does it accompany an article, essay, or other lengthy text? How does the image function in dialogue with this verbal text? Does it offer visual evidence? Does it argue an independent point? Does it provide a counterargument to the print text?

WRITING PROJECTS

1. **Written Argument:** Write an argument about an issue that moves you; base your argument on your analysis of a powerful image, and include your interpretation of the image as part of your writing. Invent a strong thesis, pick your persona, decide on your strategy of arrangement, and write with particular attention to style. You might choose to write a popular article, such as a letter to the editor of the campus newspaper, a Weblog entry, or a newspaper column such as *Newsweek*'s "My Turn."

2. **Three Position Papers:** Write three position papers or articles, with each one commenting on the previous one in turn so that the project forms a coherent whole. Give each persona a name, an occupation, a geographic location, and a strong perspective to argue in words. Each position can offer a new point of view on one image or can develop complexity about an issue by bringing in a new image as visual evidence. You might choose to format your project as a feature article for a specific magazine or reading audience. To do so, first conduct a rhetorical analysis on the features of a chosen publication (*The New Yorker, The Economist,* a national newspaper, or a campus journal) and then format your three arguments as part of that publication. Include a cover page with an introduction by the editor and a closing assessment page, perhaps by a staff writer. You could also format your project as a Website or multimedia text (a bound book, a flash montage, or photo essay).

3. **Multiple Sides Collaboration:** Collaborate on composing multiple position papers by assigning the writing of each argument to a different member of your group. You might, for instance, write about the conflict between your college campus and the surrounding town: have someone interview locals, the sheriff, the administrators, and the students. Provide a series of arguments from each perspective and images to function as argumentative texts for each side. Be sure to include concession and refutation. Collaborate in the writing of the introduction and the conclusion as well as in the design, arrangement, and style of the project as a whole. The last writer in the group should compose a synthesis paper, incorporating the positions of everyone and providing a closing argument.

4. **Argument Presentation:** As a class, present your arguments in a conference format; set up the day as a showcase of arguments. Each speaker can project his or her argument and images on a screen and deliver the words of the argument in a powerful

voice. You might pursue this option either individually, by having each person present the project in turn, or collaboratively, by having each member of a team present an argument and the images that inform and direct that point of view. Decide if you want to provide written feedback for each person, and award a prize to the most effective use of visual rhetoric, the most persuasive argument, and the best style.

 Visit www.ablongman.com/envision for expanded assignment guidelines and student projects.

Part II

RESEARCH ARGUMENTS

CHAPTER 4
Planning and Proposing
Research Arguments

CHAPTER 5
Finding and Evaluating
Research Sources

CHAPTER 6
Organizing and Writing
Research Arguments

Research is never completed. . . . Around the corner lurks another possibility of interview, another book to read, a courthouse to explore, a document to verify.

—Catherine Drinker Bowen

Planning and Proposing Research Arguments

W hat's going on in the poster shown in Figure 4.1? Why the juxtaposition of a menacing Soviet officer with a contemporary college student listening to downloaded music? Why the deep red background color and the placement of characters with the officer looking over the student's shoulder? Why is *Communism* so large and visually echoed by the hammer and sickle? At some point, you begin to realize that this poster is intended as a parody and that it pokes fun at recent publicity campaigns by the Recording Industry Association of America (RIAA) to combat file sharing and unauthorized music downloading. These observations will help you begin to make an argument about the poster, but in order to back up or substantiate your claims about its meaning, you would need to do some research. That is, you would need to place the rhetorical elements of the poster in their historical and critical contexts.

FIGURE 4.1. How does this parody propaganda poster use visual elements to undermine the RIAA's stance on file sharing?

One important point of reference for this poster is the 1950s cold-war era, in which anti-Communist propaganda posters originated. You would need to study the history and culture of that period to support your claims about this contemporary visual parody. A second is the current debate about music downloading and copyright law. As you try to grasp the significance of representing the RIAA's position through a parody of anti-Soviet propaganda, you would need to investigate the political and legal controversies surrounding file sharing.

Research is one way to gain access to a specific period of time or set of issues. You can also conduct research to find out how other writers have approached and analyzed texts such as these. Your research might entail interviews with experts about your topic area or a survey of your peers.

Doing research lends depth and complexity to your interpretation of a given text and positions your argument within a larger discussion on an issue. Such research involves more than going to the library and gathering sources. It's an inquiry that you pursue by exploring a variety of sources: online, in libraries, and through fieldwork. In this chapter, you will learn the first steps of becoming an active participant in a research community and begin to develop the skills for turning a research topic into an effective research plan and a solid research proposal.

Chapter Preview Questions

- How do I generate a productive topic for a research paper?
- What prewriting techniques can I use to develop ideas and focus my topic?
- How do I keep a research log?
- What are the steps for conducting a research inquiry and writing a strong research plan ?
- How do I transform my plan into a formal research proposal?

FIGURE 4.2. This World War I propaganda poster offers a wealth of detail for historical analysis.

Asking Research Questions

The discussion in this chapter focuses on a specific subset of persuasive images—propaganda posters—because such texts make very powerful public statements and because, for many of us, to understand the motivations behind a propaganda poster, we have to perform a certain amount of research. Often this research involves pursuing answers to questions we have formulated about the poster. In fact, most research papers begin with the act of asking questions.

One way you can get started on your research is to pick a text that moves you and start brainstorming questions about it. Let's say that you came across the 1917 American enlistment poster shown in Figure 4.2 in an exhibit on campus or as part of a class discussion about World War I posters. Approaching it for the first time, you and your peers probably will start to analyze the visual rhetoric, much as we did in the earlier chapters of *Envision.*

What are your eyes drawn to first, the words or the image? Maybe you look first at the simian figure in the middle, roaring menacingly at you, and then at the swooning, seminaked woman in his arms. In contrast, maybe the person next to you explains that her eyes first are attracted to the bold yellow text at the top and then move to the bottom, where the words "U.S. Army" in black are superimposed on the imperative "Enlist." In synthesizing various responses to the text, you most likely would find yourself with more questions than answers. This is actually good, for those questions can be the beginning of your research inquiry.

You might ask, Is that gorilla King Kong? Following up on that question through research, you could confidently answer, No, since you would discover that the poster was made decades before the movie was released. During that same research, you might find several books that discuss the wartime practice of casting enemies as subhuman creatures, offering a possible explanation for why the enemy nation is portrayed as a menacing gorilla in this poster. Adding to that your observation that "*culture*" is spelled "Kultur" (on the club the gorilla is holding), you probably would realize that the enemy symbolized here is in fact Germany.

Then you might ask: What is the significance of that bloody club? Why is the woman unconscious and partly naked? More research might provide insight on how bestiality emerged as a wartime theme in World War I enlistment posters. The idea was that if a nation's women were threatened with potential attack by such "monsters," then the men would surely step up to save and protect their wives, daughters, sisters, and mothers.

These very specific observations and questions about the posters should lead you to look up sources that will provide compelling answers and, eventually, to acquire new knowledge. In other words, by asking questions about your text, you can move beyond an initial response and into the realm of intellectual discovery.

In fact, your first questions about a text will lead you to ask more pointed questions about the context, political environment, key players, and social trends informing your text. For the propaganda poster in Figure 4.2, such questions might include: What conflicts was America involved in during 1917? What was the meaning of the word on the gorilla's hat, "Militarism," at that time? How would an appeal to enlist factor into that historical situation? Who is the audience for this poster, and how is this poster part of a series of wartime propaganda images? If you were to work through these questions, you might begin to develop ideas for a feasible research topic—one that could yield an interesting paper on war propaganda and the relationship between America and Germany in 1917.

As you investigate your research topic, your questions will likely become more specific: Do other posters of the same historical period use similar imagery and rhetorical strategies? How do the techniques used in early twentieth-century posters differ from those used during World War II? How are the rhetorical strategies used in this poster similar to or different from enlistment posters you might encounter today? In what ways have enlistment posters changed over time?

To answer these questions, you might perform an online search to yield useful information. Perhaps you might visit the library, talk with a history professor, or visit a museum. In all cases, what these questions lead to is a focused *research topic* and, ultimately, a written project that draws on and contributes to the arguments that others have made about such texts. Generating a range of interesting and productive questions is the first step in any research project; the process of inquiry itself helps you to define a project and make it your own.

Constructing a Research Log

As you move from asking questions about a text to producing a feasible research topic for your paper, keep track of your ideas in a **research log.** This log will help you organize your ideas, chart your progress, and assemble the different pieces of your research.

It can contain primarily written text, or it can include images as well, as does the example in Figure 4.3. The log itself can take many

FIGURE 4.3. Felicia Cote uses a preliminary brainstorm generated from a news photograph of a homeless man to develop a topic in her research log.

forms, from a handwritten journal, to a series of word processing documents, to an online Weblog. The key lies not in what form you choose, but in the way you use your chosen form to help you develop your topic into an interesting and provocative research project.

Generating Topics

One of the most crucial aspects of starting a research project is selecting a viable and engaging **topic.** The word *topic,* in fact, comes from the ancient Greek word *topos,* translated literally as "place." The earliest students of rhetoric used the physical space of the papyrus page—given to them by their teachers—to locate their topics for writing. Similarly, your teacher may suggest certain guidelines or parameters for you to follow when it comes to your topic; for instance, you may be given a specific topic (such as representations of race in Dr. Seuss cartoons) or you may be limited to a theme (the rhetoric of political advertisements on television, radio, and the Internet).

In some cases, you may not have any restrictions at all. But regardless of the degree to which your topic has been mapped out for you, you still can—and should—make it your own. You do this partly by generating your own range of questions and path of inquiry and partly by responding to the rhetorical situation provided by your assignment. Even if your whole class is writing on the same topic, each person will present a different argument or approach to the issue. Some will use a different stance or persona, some will rely on different sources, some will use different rhetorical appeals, and all will argue different positions about the topic.

To see how this works, let's look at one student's project on propaganda posters to see how he moved from a series of images to a more fully developed research topic. When asked to choose a topic for a research paper, student Tommy Tsai found he was interested in propaganda posters from

FIGURE 4.4. This Uncle Sam poster from 1917 was reissued for World War II.

FIGURE 4.5. Anti-Nazi propaganda relied on religiously charged rhetoric.

FIGURE 4.6. American war efforts employed extreme visual messages to galvanize support.

World War II. Looking at selection of images (see Figures 4.4 through 4.6), Tommy started by asking some questions, such as the ones that follow:

- Who is depicted in these posters? Are these depictions positive or negative?
- What is the purpose of each poster?
- What strategies are these posters using to persuade their audiences?
- How do these posters reveal cultural prejudices?

Through the process of asking such questions, he was able to identify his preliminary topic as "the rhetoric of World War II propaganda" and began to frame it more formally in his research log notes. He wrote in one research log entry that he wanted to analyze these posters in their historical contexts: "In particular, I plan to focus on the propaganda posters that appeared in the three most active countries in that time period: the United States, Germany, and Japan. My research paper will report my findings from the comparison of the different rhetorical strategies employed by the three nations." By generating a set of preliminary research questions, he was able to focus more clearly on the dialogue between those posters and his interest in them. In this way he was able to turn an overly broad initial topic into one that was more specific and workable.

COLLABORATIVE CHALLENGE

Get into groups of three or four and look at the series of posters in Figures 4.7 through 4.10, which fall under the broad topic of World War I enlistment posters. As a group, come up with a list of three research questions that you might explore based on two to four of the posters. Now exchange your list with another small group and discuss the differences in your questions. By the end of the session, come up with three or four concrete research topics you might pursue.

FIGURE 4.7. An American woman wears a Navy suit in Christy's propaganda poster.

FIGURE 4.8. A group of British women watch male soldiers leave for battle in Kealey's 1915 poster.

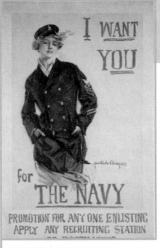

FIGURE 4.9. This 1917 U.S. poster presents a direct message from a woman dressed for war.

FIGURE 4.10. Great Britain's John Bull points straight at the viewer in this 1915 poster.

As you completed the "Collaborative Challenge," your responses to the posters undoubtedly varied. Perhaps you generated some of these topics:

- Women in World War I recruitment posters
- Cross-dressing and enlistment posters
- The use of sexuality in Navy propaganda
- The differences in portrayals of men and women

No matter what topics you and your collaboration partners wrote down, you all probably have one thing in common: you were drawn to themes that interested you. This is key: successful research topics need to interest you, inspire you, or even anger you. Even with assigned topics, you should be able to find some aspect of the assignment that speaks to you. In general, there needs to be a *connection* between you and your topic to motivate you to follow through and transform it into a successful argument.

In addition, while selecting your topic, you might consider the type of research you'll need to do to pursue it; in fact, you might select your topic based mostly on the sorts of research it allows you to do. For instance, a student writing on propaganda of the Prohibition era will work extensively with paper sources, which might involve archival work with original letters, posters, or government documents from that time period. A student writing on visual advertising for ethnic-theme

AT A GLANCE

Looking for the "Perfect" Topic

1. *Look inward.* Ask questions about yourself: What issues, events, or ideas interest you? Are there any hot-button topics you find yourself drawn to again and again? What topic is compelling enough that you would watch a news program, television special, film, or relevant lecture on it?

2. *Look outward.* Ask questions about the people, structures, and issues you encounter every day. Walk through campus or your neighborhood and look around: What are the central issues of student life on campus? Do you walk by a technology-enhanced classroom and see the students busy writing on laptops or using plasma screens? Topic: technology and education. Do you see a fraternity's poster about a "dry" party? Topic: alcohol on campus. Do you see workers outside the food service building on strike? Topic: labor relations at the college.

3. *Use creative visualization.* Imagine that you are at a party; you are chatting casually with a friend when you overhear someone nearby talking about something. Suddenly, you feel so interested—or so angry—that you excuse yourself from your companion to go over and participate in the conversation. What would move you so strongly?

4. *Use the materials of the moment.* Perhaps the *topos* might be closer to the classical Greek model; although not a roll of papyrus, your class reading list or a single issue of a newspaper can house many topics. Scan the front page and opinion section of your school or community newspaper to see what events or issues people are talking about. Be sure to look at the pictures as well for hot issues or events. You might shift your perspective from local to global and pick up a national or international newspaper or a newsmagazine; what is gripping the community at large?

dorms on campus will be more likely to complement paper sources with interviews with the university housing staff, student surveys, and first-person observations. A student writing on sexualized rhetoric in student campaign materials might take a poll, gather concrete examples, and research the newspaper's written coverage of past and present elections. Think broadly and creatively about what kinds of research you might use and what types of research (archival work versus fieldwork involving interviews and survey taking) appeals most to you. A final important consideration is whether you can actually get your hands on the source material you need to construct a persuasive argument.

CREATIVE PRACTICE

Examine a copy of a school, local, or national newspaper for compelling stories or images that might offer interesting topics for research. Which have you seen in the news for several days? Which focus on issues you've discussed before? Which seem to be workable topics that you can explore through a sustained research inquiry? What type of research would each one entail? Select two or three of these issues, and for each one ask yourself the screening questions listed in the "At a Glance" box. Finally, look over your answers and consider: Which topic would you be most likely to pursue and develop into a full research paper? Why? Write these ideas down in your research log.

AT A GLANCE

Screening Questions for Topics

1. *Am I interested in the topic?* We write best about ideas, events, and issues that touch us somehow—through curiosity, passion, or intellectual interest.

2. *Can I argue a position on this topic?* At this stage, you may not have developed a stand on the issue, but you should see promise for advancing a new perspective on the topic.

3. *Will I be able to find enough research material on this topic?* Brainstorm some possible sources you might use to write this paper.

4. *Does this sort of research appeal to me?* Since you will be working with this topic for an extended period of time, it is best to have a genuine interest in it and in the type of research that it will require (archival work or fieldwork).

Bringing Your Topic into Focus

Once you have settled on a topic, the next step in the research project involves exploring your knowledge—and the limitations of your knowledge—about it. A productive way to do this is through **prewriting.** Defined literally, prewriting is writing that precedes the official drafting of the paper, but, practically speaking, it can take many forms. Lists, scribbled notes, informal outlines, drawings—all different types of prewriting serve the same goal: to help you and your peers explore and focus a topic.

Graphic Brainstorming

The practice of **graphic brainstorming** provides writers with a great way to develop topics. This technique transforms traditional **brainstorming**—jotting down a series of related words and phrases on a topic—into a more visible process. Also called *webbing, clustering,* or *mapping,* the goal of *graphic brainstorming* is to help you develop your topic by exploring relationships among ideas. You can brainstorm by hand or on a computer; in either mode, begin by writing a topic in a circle (or square or rectangle, if you prefer). Figure 4.11 shows the first step you might take in brainstorming for a paper generated from the World War I posters discussed earlier (Figures 4.7 through 4.10).

Next, brainstorm ideas and questions about that topic, and then arrange them in groups around your main circle to indicate the relationships among them. As you answer each question and pose more developed ones in response, you begin to bring your topic into focus. You'll notice that Figure 4.12 shows how we might start to do this by writing questions that differentiate between various posters and by grouping them by gender issues. In addition, in our brainstorm, we use various types of notations—including words, phrases, and questions—and insert lines and arrows to indicate the relationship between the concepts. We even use color to further emphasize

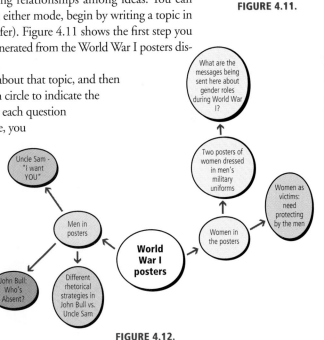

World War I posters

FIGURE 4.11.

FIGURE 4.12.

these associations. These techniques help us develop the argument and eventually can lead to a more narrowed topic and perhaps even a preliminary thesis.

As we continue to brainstorm—whether for an hour or over several sessions—it becomes clear why some people call this technique **webbing.** As Figure 4.13 shows,

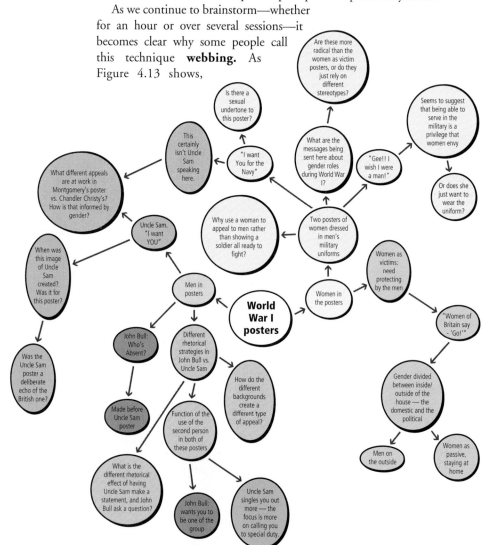

FIGURE 4.13.

our graphic turns into a web of ideas. By using this technique, in fact, we have done more than simply develop our topic: we have made it visually apparent that our topic is too broad for a standard research paper assignment. Our web now offers enough ideas for an entire book on the subject. But our diagram also provides us with clues about the direction in which to take our project. We can pick a *subsection* of ideas to focus on in our writing.

Zooming in on a Topic

Let's zoom in on one part of our diagram—the part, color-coded yellow, that asks key questions about representations of women in military posters. Working with this part of the web, we could write a focused paper that examines the implications of the way women are depicted in these texts. We could write about how cross-dressing is used as a deliberate appeal to the audience, or about how military posters evoke the image of wife and mother to mobilize troops. However, to effectively narrow our topic, we should continue to sharpen our questions about these images.

Focusing Questions for a Research Topic

1. **Write down your topic.**

   Topic formulation: gender roles in World War I.

2. **Work with that topic by asking a pointed question based on close analysis of the text at hand.**

   First question: Is there a sexual undertone to the posters?

3. **Refine the topic by answering that question.**

   Topic narrowing: Yes, in one of the posters, the woman is standing in a provocative pose, looking at the audience in a sexual manner, but in another, the women seem more identified with family (mother, daughter) than with sexuality.

4. **Revise the narrowed topic to be more specific.**

   Revised topic formulation: the different constructions of femininity in World War I propaganda posters.

5. Identify significant aspects of that topic to explore.

Second question: How so? In what way? What is the significance?

6. Use the answers to these questions to focus the topic.

Final topic focus: the use of the Madonna-whore stereotype as a persuasive strategy in World War I recruitment posters.

In working with the webbing process and then asking key questions in this way, we have just completed one of the most important steps in developing a viable research topic: **narrowing** a large subject to a more manageable one. By asking such questions—and we could come up with many others along different lines of inquiry (such as race, sexuality, international representations, and nationalism)—we begin to develop a *focused* topic that will offer us the opportunity for close analysis, rigorous research, and a sharp argumentative stance. That is, we can move from "World War I posters" to "changing gender norms reflected in World War I posters." With this focused and narrowed topic, we'll be able to contribute a new opinion about war posters and add to the ongoing dialogue that we find in our secondary sources.

CREATIVE PRACTICE

Try out this practice of *narrowing a topic* with a pair of early twenty-first-century posters that protest the U.S. war with Iraq. Examine the posters shown in Figures 4.14 through 4.17, and then complete a *graphic brainstorm* to develop a feasible topic for your essay. Be sure that you narrow your topic from "anti-war propaganda posters" to a more focused one that you might pursue in a research paper. You might decide during your graphic brainstorm to focus your topic by identifying which images you'd like to write about or by generating key questions to ask about particular texts: What is the significance of the style that is used in the posters? How do the words and images work together in these posters? How do they work against each other? What is the significance of showing people who have been wounded? How does symbolism operate in these posters? The more specific the questions you ask, the more focused your topic will be.

FIGURE 4.14. This recent anti-war poster uses strong language to catch the reader's attention.

FIGURE 4.15. This striking poster implies a connection between the war with Iraq and the oil trade.

FIGURE 4.16. This poster solidifies the visual agument through a caption.

FIGURE 4.17. Originally composed to protest the Vietnam war, this poster recently re-emerged in reference to the Iraq war.

AT A GLANCE

The Research Freewrite

• Write your ideas in full sentences.

• Use a three-paragraph model to focus your answers:

  • Paragraph 1: Announce the topic and state your thesis.

  • Paragraph 2: Identify key sources.

  • Paragraph 3: Anticipate problems.

Planning Your Research Through Writing

In completing the "Creative Practice" you most likely constructed a set of web diagrams that, like those in Figures 4.12 and 4.13, alternated between asking and answering questions. This process will narrow your focus and provide you with a direction for your research inquiry. But did you find yourself concerned that you don't have the knowledge necessary to write this essay? Are you worried that the gaps in your own knowledge will prevent you from answering those questions in a satisfactory way? If so, then you are in good company. All researchers and scholars fear the limitations of their knowledge. The key is to use that lack of knowledge as a motivation to put ideas on paper—the first step in the writing process for your research argument. We'll discuss three ways of putting ideas on paper: freewriting about your topic, drafting a formal research proposal, and developing a research hypothesis.

Freewriting about Your Research Topic

One way to start planning your research process is to freewrite about your ideas in your research log. Testing out your research plan in this way will move you from the work you did in narrowing your topic to the work you need to do in gathering sources and developing a research outline. This method also will provide an informal structure for your research, giving it shape and sharper focus as you move deeper into the research process.

In completing your freewrite, you may find it helpful to follow a **three-paragraph model:** in the *first paragraph,* announce your topic and state a preliminary thesis so that you can begin the project with a critical and focused perspective; in the *second paragraph,* identify the sources you plan to use to investigate this topic; in the *third paragraph,* speculate on obstacles or problems you might encounter in your research and how you might avoid or solve these problems. Let's look at a freewrite from student Bries Deerrose, who shaped his research inquiry around questions concerning a piece of contemporary propaganda: a leaflet dropped in Afghanistan by the U.S. military in the 2002–2003 campaign there.

Student Writing

See Joseph Yoon's research freewrite on the Vietnam War Memorials in the United States and in Vietnam.

www.ablongman.com/envision/215

Research Freewrite

America's image has come increasingly under the scrutiny of our allies and enemies alike. In response, President George W. Bush established the Office of Global Communications, the stated purpose of which is "to advise . . . on utilization of the most effective means for the United States Government to ensure consistency in messages that will promote the interests of the United States abroad, prevent misunderstanding, build support for and among coalition partners of the United States, and inform international audiences." In this paper, I will examine how this office has gone about this, especially through visual rhetoric. I will examine how the world has responded to such propaganda, especially the Middle East, and I will examine what image the office portrays, whether this is an accurate image of America or an example of political rhetoric. Finally, I will discuss whether such marketing is beneficial or detrimental, from both a foreign and American perspective. **_Tentative thesis:_** America is actively projecting an image of itself using various forms of visual rhetoric; this image is both accurate and necessary for the dissemination of various liberal perspectives, in the hopes of providing more choice for the public and private lives of individuals worldwide, as well as ensuring meaningful, peaceful dialogue between America and the world.

To research this topic, I hope to examine firsthand government-generated materials: flyers, commercials, radio broadcasts, publications, etc. I will also attempt to find any commentaries on this effort as well as on domestic conceptions of what America is and what its image should be. I will compare this

This first paragraph introduces the research topic and describes what Bries thinks the main focus of his paper might be. At the end of the paragraph, he includes a tentative thesis to help him focus his interest and argument as he begins researching this topic.

In the second paragraph, Bries discusses the sources he intends to use. Notice the broad range of possibilities he considers: flyers, television commercials, radio broadcasts, and both American and international sources.

with foreign opinions regarding America's image and reactions to the American marketing techniques. To do this, I will need to find foreign commentaries, including visual rhetoric responding to our own visual rhetoric. I will need secondhand sources concerning foreign opinions.

The most difficult part of this assignment will be determining foreign opinion, since I am not fluent in other languages. I will also need to form my own opinion about the effectiveness, morality, and accuracy of these rhetorical tactics (are we really projecting the objective truth, what is the objective truth, and should we really market ourselves at all?). Such philosophical issues are always sticky, and will require much thought and a wide array of perspectives.

This freewriting process allowed Bries the opportunity to work through his topic, his sources, and his methodology as a way of moving to a concrete research plan.

Office of Global Communications leaflet air-dropped in Afghanistan.
http://www.psywarrior.com/afghanleaf08.html.

In the third paragraph, Bries anticipates the difficulties he might face and how he can solve them.

Bries concludes with a concrete example of the visual rhetoric he will use in his research paper, a leaflet dropped in Afghanistan by the United States in the 2002-2003 campaign.

Drafting a Research Proposal

In many academic contexts, you will be asked to move beyond freewriting and formalize your research plan through composing a full-length **research proposal.** This type of text is common in many disciplines and professions and is used by writers to develop agendas for research communities, secure funding for a study, publicize plans for inquiry and field research, and test the interest of potential audiences for a given project. In the writing class-room, the research proposal provides a similar formal structure for develop-ing a project, but it also serves another purpose: it is a more structured means of organizing your thoughts to help you solidify your topic and move into the next stages of the research process. For these reasons, the *genre, organization,* and *con-tent* of the research proposal differ in important ways from other kinds of popular and academic writing that you might do. In drafting out your proposal, include the following elements:

- *Background:* What do I already know about my topic? What do I need to find out more about?
- *Methods:* How am I going to research this topic? What research questions are driving my inquiry?
- *Timeline:* What are my goals for the dif-ferent stages of research and how can I schedule my work to most effectively meet these milestones?
- *Ultimate goal and significance:* What do I hope to accomplish in my research? What are the broader issues or implications of my research?

AT A GLANCE

Key Functions of the Research Proposal

- It introduces the narrowed *topic.*
- It presents the *rhetorical stance* or *thesis* that the writer will develop.
- It explains the *significance* of the research project.
- It lists possible *sources* for investigation.
- It outlines your research *methods* or planned approach to the research.
- It delineates a detailed *timeline* for investigating the topic.
- It often anticipates any *difficulties* that might arise in pursuing this topic.
- It often includes a brief *biography* of the researcher (usually a one-paragraph description of the writer's credentials, interests, and motivations).
- It includes, if appropriate, a carefully chosen and analyzed visual rhetoric text as a case study or concrete example of the topic.

As this list suggests, in your proposal it is important to explain your interest in your chosen subject and establish a set of questions to guide your inquiry. You should also use the proposal to delineate the timeline for your research and writing process. Although this part may seem obvious, it is crucial for time management. Some proposals may require you to have done some preliminary work with sources, while others may be designed to facilitate the very earliest stages of the research process.

As the last item on the "At a Glance" list indicates, you should incorporate an appropriate visual text—a sample propaganda poster to be analyzed or an editorial cartoon that introduces the issue—into your proposal to show readers an example of the materials about which you'll be conducting your research.

If your research project focuses on visual texts, you might incorporate an appropriate image to introduce an issue, present the context, captivate your audience, provide a rhetorical stance, or offer insight into the complexity of your topic.

As you craft your research proposal, realize that while it serves to clarify your research intentions, it should also *persuade* an audience of the feasibility and significance of your project. In fact, perhaps the most important step in launching your research inquiry is to address the issue of your project's significance or, as some writing instructors call it, the "So What?" part of the project. It is the "So What?"—an awareness of the significance of the topic you're addressing and the questions you're asking—that moves the proposal from being a routine academic exercise to a powerful piece of persuasive writing. When addressing the "So What?" question, consider why anyone else would care enough to read a paper on your topic. Ask yourself:

- What is at stake in your topic?
- Why does it matter?
- What contribution will your project make to a wider community?

These are difficult questions to answer, and they may be ones that you defer until later in your research when you have gathered evidence and developed your argument to support your thesis. However, the sooner you clarify the significance of your work, the faster you will move toward producing a rigorous and interesting piece of writing. Keep notes in your research log on how the answers to these questions change as you proceed with your research and your thinking about the topic.

Let's look at an example: a research proposal Susan Zhang developed on digital manipulation.

Susan Zhang

Little Photoshop of Horrors?: Digital Manipulation

of Media Images

Susan begins with a specific example to hook the audience and to set up the context for her proposal.

When O. J. Simpson was arrested in the summer of 1994, Newsweek and Time magazines featured his mugshot on their covers. But while Newsweek's photo was unaltered, Time had darkened the color of his skin and reduced the size of his prisoner ID number. To anyone who saw the two magazines on the news rack, the difference was obvious. To some it was even unethical: minority groups protested that the digital manipulation made O. J. look darker and more menacing, thereby presuming his guilt. The Time illustrator who altered the image later claimed that he only "wanted to make it more artful, more compelling." The impartiality of the photography was widely contested.

You can't always believe what you read in the news, but a photograph doesn't lie, right? Because the photographer and the camera are perceived to be mere vehicles for converting reality into image, people are more apt to trust a photo, believing it to be the product of a machine rather than a human, and consequently free of bias. But with the advent of digital imaging, that credibility has been compromised. Image-editing programs such as Photoshop make it possible to perform cosmetic touch-ups, graft parts of pictures onto others, even construct a picture entirely from scratch. In many ways, digital imaging has redefined the field of photography. With words like "composograph" and "photoillustration" being coined to describe altered images indistinguishable from the real thing, people have grown wary of deeming the photograph a purveyor of truth.

For my research project, I want to explore how the capacity of image manipulation has affected the way we perceive photos in the news and media. Has it led to a permanent loss of faith? Or, on the flip side, to the establishment of stricter standards for allowable alterations? By examining past incidences of digital manipulation and current guidelines for photographs in the media, and the

In the proposal she turned in for class, Susan also embedded images from the *Newsweek* and *Time* covers in her introduction as visual evidence for her claims. She uses questions to identify common assumptions that her audience might hold about her topic.

She then clearly states her research goals. She suggests some key research questions and then ends with a declarative sentence that underscores her intentions as a researcher. Notice how she mentions the significance—or importance—of the project early on in the proposal.

contexts in which they apply, I hope to gain a better understanding of the credibility of news and media imagery in the digital age.

Methods

First, I want to approach my topic through its historical context. I will start with the pre-digital era and look at whether photo manipulation existed then. Surely there were tricked, staged, and doctored photos also? To what extent were photos altered using darkroom techniques? What kind of ethical considerations governed the editing of media images then? By comparing past precedents with the types of digital manipulations commonly used today, I can determine whether digital imaging really has made photo manipulation a bigger and more prevalent problem.

Next, I will look at digital manipulation from the public's point of view. In the past when a digital image was altered, how did the public respond? For example, if a photograph is altered in an obvious or humorous manner, it could be perceived as satire or social commentary, but if it is altered subtly and the change not announced, it could be perceived as deception. How easily can people recognize an altered photo? And when a magazine or newspaper is exposed for digitally manipulating a photo, does this automatically discredit it in the public eye?

I will also consider the photographer's point of view. Do photographers consider photo manipulation a recent development stemming from digital imaging? What are the moral and ethical justifications for manipulated photographs? What kinds of standards exist in the field of photojournalism and media photography? How do these standards regulate the integrity of digital photojournalism?

Susan writes her "Methods" section by using her research questions: the historical perspective, the audience's perspective, and the photographer's perspective. She carefully thinks through each line of inquiry.

Sources

To begin my research, I will look at books on the ethics of photojournalism. So far I have checked out Paul Lester's *Photojournalism: An Ethical Approach* and Julianne Newton's *The Burden of Visual Truth: The Role of Photojournalism in Mediating Reality.* These books will help me understand the history of ethical photojournalism, the ways in which a photograph conveys a message, and the public's response to photographs.

Then, moving toward the digital side of media images, I will turn to books such as Thomas Wheeler's *Phototruth or Photofiction?: Ethics and Media Imagery in the Digital Age* and Larry Gross's *Image Ethics in the Digital Age.* The first book examines specific examples of photo manipulation and later provides an ethical framework for considering image manipulation in photojournalism. The second book is a collection of articles on aspects of digital image ethics.

I will also search online databases such as EBSCO and LexisNexis for articles on digital manipulation and recent controversies over digital manipulation. Search terms I might use include "photo manipulation," "digital photojournalism," and "digital image ethics." Through these databases I hope to find authoritative opinions from photojournalists as well as public reactions to altered images in magazines and the news.

As a primary source, I will look at photojournalism Websites. I will visit large news and magazine sites and smaller photojournalism communities, browsing their photographs to see if they use digital manipulation, and if so, how it is addressed. Also, there are many web resources that explain the guidelines that have

Although this was written before she began serious research, Susan increased her proposal's persuasiveness (and her own ethos as a researcher) by including the titles of specific texts she located through a computer search of her library's holdings. She carefully groups her intended sources and also explains briefly why these types of sources would be useful for her research.

By including search terms and specific database names, Susan shows that she is ready to move to actual research.

Susan finishes her discussion of sources with attention to primary sources—the actual photographs themselves—that she intends to find to use in her paper.

been development by photojournalists. For example, the National Press Photographers Association's Website features a digital code of ethics. These sites will clarify the guidelines of digital photojournalism and how closely they are being followed.

Timeline

In her timeline, Susan lists not only deadlines imposed by her instructor but also key steps in the research process: finding books, evaluating sources, taking notes, constructing a thesis, peer review, a second round of research, drafting, and revising.

1/20 Research proposal due

1/20–1/22 Search for articles on photojournalism and digital manipulation using online databases

1/22–1/27 In-depth research using books

Primary research using photojournalism sites

1/27–1/31 Review notes and write a thesis

Talk with classmates and instructor for advice on my thesis

Evaluate which sources to use

2/1–2/5 Outline paper: decide on the major arguments, draft topic sentences, and choose support for each argument

2/5–2/12 Write first draft of paper

With this detailed timeline, Susan shows her careful time management and builds her ethos by demonstrating her understanding of the research process; she even uses colored font for due dates to highlight their importance.

2/12 Research paper draft due

2/15–2/28 Obtain and reflect on feedback

Additional research and revision as necessary

3/3–3/6 Review second draft for polish, errors

3/6 Revision of research paper due

Significance

In her conclusion, Susan reasserts the importance of her project, broadening to address the "So What?" that she needs to answer as she enters into her research.

With advancements in technology, photography has moved from the darkroom to the computer lab, making it possible to alter photographs beyond what is considered ethical. The abuse of this technology has resulted in manipulated photos being passed off as real in the media, and a resulting public skepticism over the

> reliability of all media images. A closer look at the occurrences of digital manipulation today, as regulated by the evolving guidelines of photojournalism, could reveal to what extent such skepticism is warranted.

Drafting the Research Hypothesis

In reading Bries's freewrite and Susan's proposal, you might have noticed that as they developed their topics, they were simultaneously trying their hands at formulating their arguments. For instance, in Bries's first paragraph, he moves from the open-ended language of a proposal ("I will examine," "I will dis-cuss") to a restatement of his subject in terms of a tentative thesis statement at the end of the paragraph. Many times as you draft your research plan, you will find that you enter into your project relying on broad questions ("What do the leaflets that Americans dropped on Afghanistan in 2003 say about our country and our international policy?") or on statements of intention (i.e., "In this paper, I will explore how . . . image manipulation has affected the way we perceive photos in the news"). However, as we see in the examples from Bries and Susan, it is also useful to use your research plan as an opportunity to try to define your rhetorical stance in relation to that topic.

So how do you make a claim about a topic that you have not yet researched completely? This is a key question, and it is often a frustrating one for many writers. Realize, however, that you've already taken the first step just by asking pointed questions about your topic. From these questions, you can develop a working thesis that makes an argumentative claim that you'll attempt to prove. At this point, you might call it a **hypothesis,** rather than a *thesis,* to suggest its tentativeness. It is crucial for you to try to formulate a working hypothesis for your research plan as a way of looking at your project with an analytical eye. Of course, you may revise your hypothesis—and maybe your entire approach to the subject—several times over the course of your research. Indeed, most writers do modify

Student Writing
See many examples of research proposals.
www.ablongman.com/envision/216

Student Writing
Examine Anastasia Nevin's research proposal on the historical mystery of the Romanov assassination, a study of archival photographs and artifacts.
www.ablongman.com/envision/217

their thesis statements, and this revision process is a natural part of what happens when you actually begin to read your sources and take notes about them in the research log. Nevertheless, trying to state your thesis or hypothesis is an important first step in focusing your argument and making the most out of the timeline available to you for research.

One way to develop your detailed hypothesis is to rewrite one of your more narrowed questions from the research proposal as a polished declarative statement that you intend to prove. For example, if you asked yourself, "How were representations of race used in World War II propaganda?" then you might turn that question into a potential thesis: "Representations of race deployed in World War II propaganda functioned as a way to justify the internment of innocent civilians." As you continue your research, you may come to disagree with that statement, but at least beginning with a tentative thesis gives you somewhere to start your research.

Let's consider how this process might play out for a research argument on propaganda posters. We're going to follow Tommy Tsai's research process as he developed his paper on propaganda posters entitled, "This is the Enemy': Depravation and Deceitfulness of America's World War II Political Art."

To develop his research hypothesis, Tommy worked his way through a series of questions:

1. **First, he clarified his own familiarity with the topic, even before doing any research.**

   Question: What do I already know about my topic?

   Tommy: The different styles of propaganda posters of three countries during World War II. The United States exploited the nationalist feelings of Americans with their posters by using images like the American flag to represent the glory associated with "fighting for your own country." Germany also exploited nationalist feelings among its citizens; the German government did so by using the *ethos* appeal associated with its political leader Adolf Hitler. Japan used a more logical approach; many of their posters show images of Japanese soldiers as victors of a battle.

2. **His next question moved him toward a specific argument.**

   Question: What do I want to know more about?

   Tommy: The people who designed the posters and the work that went into the design process. Also, I would like to know more about the historical context (I've never taken history before, so basic information about the war would be really helpful).

3. **With the last question, he began to create his hypothesis for the project.**

Question: What are the specific aspects of this topic I hope to explore?

Tommy: The specific rhetorical strategies employed by each country. I also want to look at how these rhetorical strategies affected people, and how effective each country's propaganda was.

Notice that at this point Tommy's hypothesis relies more on his intentions than any firm conclusions; however, by refining his writing in this way, he could approach his research with clearer goals in mind. Accordingly, he was soon able to craft a more polished working hypothesis.

Working Hypothesis

I have conjectured that German propaganda made use of the *ethos* appeal of its fascist leader Adolf Hitler; that Japanese propaganda utilized the *logos* appeal by continually portraying images of a victorious Japanese army; and that American propaganda for the most part employed the *pathos* appeal by evoking nationalistic feelings and associating war

Figure 1. Uncle Sam poster.

with glory and patriotism (see Figure 1). These conjectures coalesce into my argument that the government of each nation is able to bring its political messages across effectively by employing the appropriate rhetorical appeal in its propaganda posters.

Student Writing

See Tommy Tsai's complete research plan and proposal.
www.ablongman.com/envision/218

Working with this hypothesis, Tommy launched his research project, and he eventually wrote a compelling paper that examined U.S. propaganda posters against both the German and Japanese nations. Some of this material was rather disturbing (see Figures 4.4 through 4.6), but Tommy felt compelled to work with these images. In his final reflection on the research paper, Tommy looked back at the development of his argument and even proposed ideas for future study. His reflection letter should show you that a research paper is only the beginning of your engagement with the issues that matter to you.

Final Reflection Letter, March 2003

The final paper turned out to be very different from what I envisioned it to be at the beginning. First of all, my topic changed from World War II propaganda posters in general to a criticism of America's portrayals of their World War II enemies. Also, for my final draft, I had to cut out an entire section from my paper (the one about how America portrayed the political leaders of other nations) since it did not work well with my thesis. Instead, I concentrated on the two remaining sections in order to give my paper more focus. . . . I have also developed an interest in the topic. Perhaps the world wars will make another appearance in one of the many other research papers I will have to write in my four years at the university.

Planning Your Own Research Project

Now that you've learned about the process of generating a topic, focusing the research questions for your topic, developing a hypothesis, and then writing up your plans for research in a structured freewrite or a formal proposal, what can you argue about the first propaganda poster of this chapter (Figure 4.1)?

In answering this prompt, you might start to work through the projects related to the research process. You might develop a research focus that begins with questions and ends with a "So What?" statement of significance. You might try to incorporate visual images into a proposal that will conclude with a clear statement of your future authority on this topic as a researcher. Try the strategies for keeping track of your ideas and work in progress in a research log, a key tool that you'll be using in the next chapter as we turn to gathering and evaluating sources for your topic. It's time to get started on the research process for writing a persuasive argument about an issue that matters to you.

PREWRITING CHECKLIST

Analyzing Propaganda Posters

❑ What is the underlying message of this poster? What idea is it trying to convey to its audience?

❑ What are the specifics of the rhetorical situation informing this piece of propaganda? Who produced the poster? Who was its intended audience?

❑ What is the historical context for this poster? What country was it produced in, and what was the social and political situation of the time? How does an understanding of its context affect our understanding of its message?

❑ What type of rhetorical appeal does the poster feature? Does it rely primarily on logos, pathos, or ethos to make its point? How does attention to this appeal manifest itself visually in the poster?

❑ What is the relationship between word and image in the poster? How does this relationship contribute to its rhetorical appeal?

❑ How do design elements such as color, font, layout, and image selection (photograph or illustration) work as persuasive elements in this text?

❑ What strategies of argumentation does the poster use? Does it feature narration? comparison–contrast? example?

❑ Recalling the discussion of exaggerated use of appeals from Chapter 2, does the poster rely on any logical fallacies? any exaggerated use of pathos? If so, how do these work to persuade the audience?

❑ Does the poster use stereotypes to convey its message? How do stereotypes figure as rhetorical devices in this situation? How does the stereotype place the poster in the context of a larger cultural discussion?

(continued)

❏ What research questions can you develop about this poster?

❏ What kinds of sources might you look at to understand better what's going on with this propaganda poster?

WRITING PROJECTS

1. **Research Freewrite:** Freewrite about your *research ideas* by first writing out answers to the questions provided in the "Prewriting Checklist" and then developing them into a three-paragraph freewrite. In the first paragraph, introduce your research paper topic and describe what you think the main focus of the paper might be. Include a tentative thesis in this paragraph. In the second paragraph, discuss the sources that you intend to use. In the third paragraph, speculate on what obstacles you foresee in this project and/or what you anticipate to be the most difficult part of the assignment. If appropriate, use an image to complement your written text. Show your answers to your instructor or your peers for feedback.

2. **Research Proposal:** Write a detailed research *proposal* that discusses your topic, planned method, and purpose in depth. Be sure to cover your topic, your hypothesis, your potential sources and problems, your method, timeline, and, most importantly, the significance of the proposed project. For more specific instruction consult the Writing Guidelines on the *Envision* Website. When you are done with the writing, present your proposal at a roundtable of research with other members of your class. Answer questions from your classmates to help you fine-tune your topic and troubleshoot your future research.

3. **Peer Review:** Collaboratively peer review your research proposals. Assume that you are on the review board granting approval and funding to the best *two* proposals of each group. Complete research proposal review letters for each member of your group. When you are done, discuss your letters and what changes you can recommend. Then revise your proposals to make them stronger, better written, and more persuasive. For more specific instructions and for **peer review forms** for the research proposal, consult the *Envision* Website.

 Visit www.ablongman.com/envision for expanded assignment guidelines and student projects.

CHAPTER 5

Finding and Evaluating Research Sources

As you move from planning to conducting research, you'll need to investigate resources of all kinds and evaluate them for use in your project. You can use your analytical skills to make important distinctions when locating, evaluating, and using sources for your research project. Look, for instance, at the magazine covers in Figures 5.1 and 5.2. Although they focus on the same topic—global warming—the visual rhetoric of the covers suggests that the content of each journal will be quite different. The audience for *Time* magazine differs from that of *Science*, and, consequently, the writing styles within the articles will be different as well. The cover of each magazine previews the distinct content inside.

FIGURE 5.1. Cover of *Time*, April 3, 2006.

FIGURE 5.2. Cover of *Science*, March 24, 2006.

Chapter Preview Questions

- What is the best way to locate research sources?
- What is the difference between a primary and a secondary source?
- How do I critically evaluate both print and electronic sources?
- How do I pursue field research for my project?
- What is an annotated bibliography, and how can it help me?
- How should I take notes while researching?

Specifically, the cover of *Time* in Figure 5.1 conveys how the editors chose to represent global warming to their audience. Ask yourself: What is the argument conveyed by the visual rhetoric of the cover? What is the significance of the choice to use a polar bear as the main character in their image? How is color used strategically? How does the "spotlighting" of the polar bear and the positioning of the image in relation to the words contribute to the rhetorical effect? What kind of stance toward the dangers of global warming does the cover suggest?

In contrast, the *Science* cover (Figure 5.2) features a photograph of an ice-covered lake. The photo appears to have been taken with a "fish-eye" lens, bringing several ice fragments into prominence in the foreground. How do such different rhetorical strategies appeal to the journal's very scientifically informed audience?

Clearly, the editors deliberately located, evaluated, and used materials for the covers that would reflect their magazine's contents. As a researcher, you can use your skills in rhetorical analysis to help you evaluate sources for your own research project, looking to the different elements of a text—from the cover design, to the table of contents, to the index—to better understand the text's perspective on your topic and its usefulness for your project.

COLLABORATIVE CHALLENGE

Working in small groups, compare Figures 5.1 and 5.2 to another image depicting the topic of global warming, the one on the cover of the August 26, 2002 issue of *Time* (see Figure 5.3). What similarities and differences are clear from the use of visual and verbal rhetoric? What stance does the cover suggest that *Time* will take on the topic? How is that stance represented in the cover design?

Now look at other *Time* covers that have addressed the issue of global warming and climate change over several years (the April 9, 2001 cover; the February 17, 1992 cover; the October 19, 1987 cover), through the *Envision* Website. How do these covers take different approaches to this issue? How does context seem to inform this approach? Look in the table of contents for each issue; do the article titles seem to support the position suggested by the covers? Finally, as a group, develop your own stance on this issue. Together, sketch a design for a new cover for an upcoming issue of *Science, The Economist,* or *Time.* Use the cover to suggest an argument for a specific perspective on global warming and to provide a visual preview for the contents inside. Share your design and argument with the class.

FIGURE 5.3. Cover of *Time,* August 26, 2002.

www.ablongman.com/envision/219

Your task as a researcher will be quite similar to that of the editors of *Science* and *The Economist.* As you begin gathering and evaluating sources for your own research-based argument, keep in mind that you will need to shape the argument into a paper addressed to a particular audience: your writing class, a group of scientists, a lobbying organization, an advertising firm, or browsers on the Web. To take part in any of these conversations, a researcher needs to learn what is being talked about (the *topic*), how it is being discussed (the *discourse*), and what the different positions are (*research context*). But your conversation about your research project also will extend beyond your audience; you will, in fact, be engaged in a discussion with the sources themselves.

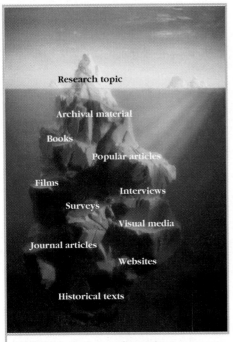

FIGURE 5.4. The iceberg of research.

Visualizing Research

When you think of the act of research, what comes to mind? Surfing the Web? Looking through a library? Interviewing experts in the field? All these images represent different research scenarios. The material you gather in each situation will compose the foundation for your research; this body of knowledge will inform your essay, but not all of it will find its way into your final paper. Nevertheless, you need to research widely and thoroughly to be fully informed about your topic and write a compelling research-based argument. One helpful way of visualizing the relationship between the *process* and the *product* of research is through the metaphor of the **iceberg of research** (see Figure 5.4). In essence, your topic represents only a starting point for your research project; beneath it lie the many different sources you should explore to lend depth and body to your argument. Published books, journal articles, Websites, and field research all constitute the materials of your potential research. As you move beyond a surface knowledge of your topic, you will gather, assess, keep, throw out, and ultimately use a variety of sources. Moving into the depths of your project can therefore be quite exciting as you encounter a rich array of voices, knowledge, and opinions on your topic.

Sometimes, however, this process can be a bit overwhelming. We all share anxieties about writing a research argument. Many times we think of brilliant words penned by minds of genius and fear that we will have nothing new to add to the conversation. Or we worry that we won't find anything interesting to say despite the richness of our sources. Both of these views are extremes. It is more helpful to think of research sources as texts written by people who were once, like yourself, struggling to add substance to their research ideas and seeking to fulfill the plan of their research proposals. In this way, you might consider the process of gathering and assessing sources as a very social one, a process in which you respect and acknowledge the ideas of others and then seek to add your own voice to an ongoing conversation. One way to begin that conversation is to discover what others before you have said, thought, written, and published and to keep track of that process in your research log.

This chapter addresses the fears and anxieties that can be obstacles on the research path. We'll use the metaphor of the *conversation* to accentuate the point that the research process is an act of *composing a response to an ongoing dialogue about a topic.* By gathering, synthesizing, and sorting the perspectives of others, you begin to shape your own stance on a research topic. By adding your voice as a writer, you are responding to others. Research is a *relationship* that you develop with the source material and the writers you encounter along the way.

AT A GLANCE

Using Your Research Log

As you begin gathering sources, follow the crucial steps below.

1. Note where and when you find new ideas.
2. Keep a detailed and careful record.
3. List all the search terms you try and note how helpful each is.
4. Write a short paragraph on your discovery of source leads.
5. Keep notes on your developing ideas about this argument.
6. Jot down quotes from sources, including page numbers and direct quotes.
7. List your sources in full, including author, title, place of publication, and date.
8. Copy down complete URLs for Web articles and image sources online.
9. Feel free to brainstorm new ideas and ways you could develop your argument or change your research direction.

Developing Search Terms

The first step in the research process lies in locating relevant and interesting sources to draw into your conversation. This involves finding the best **search terms** to use in looking for sources on your topic. Your search terms will change depending on whether you are searching the Web, a library catalog, or an academic database. You will need to identify the most productive keywords for searching in each of these situations.

AT A GLANCE

Tips for Using Search Terms

- **Web:** Use popular or colloquial terminology in your Internet searches because search engines pick up actual terms from pages as they crawl across the Web.

- **Library:** The Library of Congress has created a set of terms used by librarians to catalog information. These Library of Congress Subject Headings (LCSHs), as they are called, may not be obvious to you. (For example, the Library of Congress calls the Vietnam War the "Vietnamese Conflict, 1961–1975," so you won't find anything if you put "Vietnam War" into a subject heading search in a library catalog.) You can find the LCSH terms in two ways: by looking at a library record online or by consulting the print index. By plugging the terms into your library catalog, you can access information for your project more efficiently.

- **Databases:** Since databases can house a wide range of materials, from academic publications to popular articles, you will have to customize your language based on the database you have selected. Match your search terms in diction and formality to suit the type of resource you are exploring.

Let's take as our example a project about Internet advertising. In a preliminary Web search, you would find that specific terms such as "pop-up ads," "banner ads," and "ethics & advertising online" would yield more results than generic terms like "Internet advertising" and "Internet advertisements." Moving to your library catalog, you would likely find that a successful search requires *different terms* than you used in your broader Web search. That is, you might instead use academic terminology, such as "electronic commerce" or "Internet marketing," because those phrases appear in scholarly book titles. However, if you search a database such as Lexis-Nexis (a resource for news articles as well as legal, medical, and business articles), your keywords might change again to be closer to your preliminary Internet search. In this case, searching a database using the term "Internet advertising" would provide you with more than 90 citations in popular magazines and journals, while "pop-up ads" would yield only 16 hits, an inverse amount from your Internet search. As you can see, experimenting with a range of terms can help you narrow your sources by finding materials relevant to your topic. For instance, you might use the more specific term "Internet advertising & law" to narrow your search and focus on the legal aspect of the issue if that interests you. Through such experimentation you will find the search term that yields the most productive results.

CREATIVE PRACTICE

Perform a search on your topic, first on the Web, then in your library catalog, and then in a database. Experiment with your search terms and record your results in your research log. Now locate the Library of Congress Subject Headings for your topic (often located in library citations under the "subject" header), and use those terms in another catalog search. Do you achieve different results? Are your results more tailored to your needs or more general? In your research log, assess which search terms function best.

Primary and Secondary Sources

Your initial searches will yield a range of sources—from magazine articles to books, video recordings, and perhaps even manuscripts or a photograph collection. Each of these sources can play a vital role in your research. Scholars divide research into primary and secondary research, and sources, likewise, into **primary sources** (original texts you analyze in your research paper) and **secondary sources** (sources that provide commentary on your primary material or on your topic in general).

Consider, for instance, Tommy Tsai's project, examined in detail in Chapter 4. Propaganda posters were Tommy's *primary sources,* and the articles, books, and transcribed interviews providing analysis of those posters were his *secondary sources.* His paper is now *another* secondary source, one that contributes to an ongoing intellectual discussion about the meaning and power of the posters.

But as you search for your research materials, keep in mind that no sources are *inherently* primary or secondary; those terms refer to *how you use them* in your paper. For instance, if you were working with the topic of Internet advertising, you might use actual banner ads and Flash animations as your primary sources, as well as press releases and advertising Websites. For secondary sources you might turn to articles that discuss innovations in online marketing, a Website on the history of digital advertising, and perhaps even a book by a famous economist about the impact of technology on corporate marketing strategies. However, imagine that you shift your topic slightly, making your new focus the economist's theories about the corruption of traditional advertising by multimedia technology. Now, that same book you looked at before as a *secondary* source becomes a *primary* source for this new topic.

As you can see, your inquiry will determine which sources will be primary and which will be secondary for your argument. In most cases, you will need to use a combination of primary and secondary materials to make a persuasive argument. The primary sources allow you to perform your own analysis, whereas the secondary sources offer you critical viewpoints that you need to take into account in your analysis and integrate into your argument to build up your ethos. How you respond to and combine your primary and secondary sources is a matter of choice, careful design, and rhetorical strategy.

Finding Primary Sources

Searching for **primary sources** can sometimes be challenging; they come in many forms but can also be some of the most exciting sources to work with in your research process. Consider, for instance, the sources that student James Caputo used in his project on the media representations of the early years of the NASA space program. James had many fascinating primary resources to work with: John F. Kennedy's inspirational speeches about the formation of the space program; front pages of both American and Russian newspapers detailing the successful completion of the first Apollo mission; publicity shots of the astronauts; the first images—both still and moving—from the moon's surface; and advertisements published after the first moon landing that showed the space program's attempts to win public support through publicity. He chose to focus on multiple magazine covers and images from magazine articles for his primary source materials (see Figures 5.5 and 5.6).

FIGURE 5.5. James used this illustration, "The Rocket Blitz from the Moon," which originally accompanied a 1948 *Collier's* magazine article, as a powerful primary source for his research paper.

The image in Figure 5.5 originally appeared in an article published in *Collier's* magazine on October 23, 1948, concerning the military applications of space travel. James analyzed it and found that it was intended to warn American readers of the consequences of falling behind in the "space race" with the Russians. Similarly, Figure 5.6, a cover shot from *Time*'s July 25, 1969 issue, relied on pathos to persuade the American readers to view the U.S. space program in a certain light. James found that the image, with its strong nationalistic overtones, cast the successful Apollo 11 mission once again in terms of the Cold War and the American-Soviet space race. He placed these primary sources at the center of his research argument, and then he turned to secondary sources to substantiate his own claims about them.

FIGURE 5.6. James also analyzed other primary sources, including magazine covers like this one from a 1969 issue of *Time*.

Primary materials like the one James found are more accessible than you might think. They can be found in your library—whether in the general stacks, archives, or multimedia collections—or at community centers such as library exhibits, museums, and city hall. Many public libraries have special collections and archives with particularly rich primary source materials, including the following:

- Original documents (perhaps a handwritten letter by Mahatma Gandhi, correspondence between Charles Dickens and Charlotte Brontë, or Charles Lindbergh's journals)
- Rare books and manuscripts (such as an illustrated first edition of William Blake's *Songs of Innocence and Experience* or Roger Manvell's manuscripts on the history of the Third Reich)
- Portfolios of photographs (photos of Japanese American internment camps or of Black Panther demonstrations from the 1960s)

- Other one-of-a-kind texts (for example, AIDS prevention posters from South Africa, a noted artist's sketchbook, or a series of leaflets produced by the U.S. Psychological Warfare Department, distributed to the Vietnamese during the Vietnam War)
- Government documents (including U.S. censuses and surveys, reports from the Department of Agriculture, or even congressional papers).

In many cases, you can work directly with these materials so you can perform your own first-hand analysis of that piece of cultural history.

While the best way to determine the holdings of your college library or community museum may be to search a catalog or contact a reference librarian, an increasing number of academic institutions and organizations digitize their collections to make them widely available to an international community of researchers. Your school's electronic access to primary sources might be as simple as a list on the library Website of holdings you can explore at the library itself. Alternatively, it might be as extensive as a complete set of digital reproductions or links to Internet archives of primary materials that you can analyze.

Searching for Secondary Sources

Just as important as your primary materials are your **secondary sources**—texts that provide commentary on your topic and often analyze the texts you have chosen as primary sources. The writers of these texts offer the voices with which you will engage in scholarly conversation as you develop the substance of your argument.

Your first stop in your search for secondary sources should be your library's reference area, the home of dictionaries, guides, encyclopedias, bibliographies, and other resource materials. These storehouses of important information can be invaluable in providing you with the *foundational information* for your project, including basic definitions, historical background, and brief bibliographies. Yet, while such "background" materials are necessary to help you construct a framework for your research argument, they represent only one part of your *iceberg of research.* For more rigorous analysis, you should turn to books and articles that provide critical analysis and arguments about your specific research subject. To locate these more specific secondary sources, you might search your library catalog for relevant books and films and other published materials. However, you also have another valuable type of resource available to you: databases and indexes.

You'll find databases and indexes indispensable to your research because they provide you with bibliographic citations for academic articles on your topic of interest. Keep in mind that databases can come in many forms: they can be housed on CD-ROMs, online, or as collections of electronic journals. Additionally, although some databases provide only a bibliographic citation that you can use to locate the source in your library catalog, many include a detailed abstract summarizing a source's argument, and others link you to full-text electronic copies of the articles you are searching for.

As you continue to search for sources, remember that the best strategy for keeping careful track of your research process entails recording the dates, details, and relevance of your searches in your *research log;* you might also want to keep a running list of your sources by call number and title, or include printouts of relevant articles or database entries, as Vivian Chang did for her research log on a project discussing the fantasy world of *The Lord of the Rings.* (See Figure 5.7)

Although databases, catalogs, and search engines provide indispensable tools for conducting your research, don't overlook the resource you have in

AT A GLANCE

Using One Source to Locate Additional Sources

Here's the process for finding sources:

1. Locate one relevant source through the library catalog.
2. Retrieve it from the library stacks.
3. Spend some time looking over books in the same area to discover additional books on the same topic.
4. Assess briefly the applicability of each text to your project, and check out the ones most valuable to you.
5. Look at the bibliographies in the backs of your most useful books to locate sources that were helpful to the authors and may be of use to you.
6. Repeat the process often to build your iceberg of research.

Finding Secondary Sources

You can use the following library resources to locate secondary material:

- *Dictionaries, guides, encyclopedias:* Such foundational texts provide helpful background information for your topic.
- *Library catalog:* This engine allows you to search the library holdings for relevant books or documentaries.
- *CD-ROM indexes and bibliographies:* These CDs contain vast amounts of bibliographic information, but often they can be used only in the reference section of the library.
- *Electronic databases and indexes:* These databases are available on the Internet through subscription only; many provide access to full-text versions of articles from a range of sources.
- *Electronic journals:* Many libraries offer access to the full digital versions of academic journals for a range of disciplines.

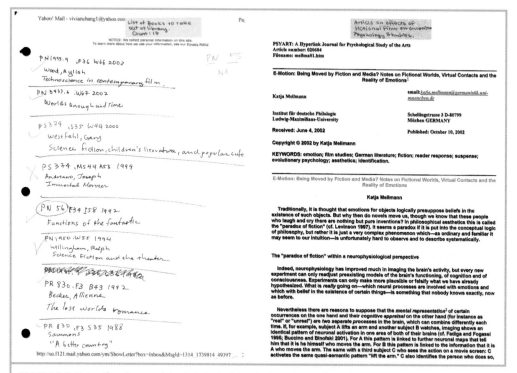

FIGURE 5.7. Vivian Chang's research log includes both handwritten notes and annotated article printouts.

AT A GLANCE

Recording Searches in Your Research Log

- Date each entry in your log to keep track of your progress and show the evolution of your ideas.

- Write down complete identifying information for any source you consult, including images on the Web, articles online, journals or magazines in the library, articles from library databases, and chapters in books.

- Double-check transcribed quotations for accuracy while you still have the source before you, and include page numbers (or paragraph numbers for Website articles).

- Annotate the entry by including an evaluation of the source and an indication of how you might use it as part of your final paper.

- If you are using Web sources, be aware that Websites tend to be updated or to simply disappear. To avoid losing important source material, print out significant Webpages and insert them into your log or download them to your hard drive and include them on a CD-ROM with your research log.

your peers. As colleagues in the research journey, your peers will have discovered helpful print sources, databases, and indexes. Ask others who are working on similar topics to share their research logs, and help each other along the route of your research. This is particularly true for the stage in your research when you produce a perliminary bibliography—a working list of the sources for your iceberg of research.

COLLABORATIVE CHALLENGE

Form groups of three or four and share your preliminary bibliographies. To prepare, each person should practice locating and evaluating sources. First, each person should come up with three to six keywords as well as Library of Congress Suject Heading about your topic. and then perform a search for both primary and secondary sources. Make sure each person explores print sources through the library catalog as well as online texts through databases and e-journals. Then, each person should produce a preliminary bibliography for your research project—a list of eight to ten potential sources. Next, get into your groups and share your preliminary bibliographies. Each person in the group should spend five minutes presenting a narrative of his or her research process: What sources have you found so far? Which databases were unexpectedly fruitful to your search? What journals hold the most helpful secondary sources? How are you formatting your research log? Then, have each person in the group lend another person a particularly useful source. Broaden the base of your research argument by incorporating more sources.

Evaluating Your Sources

Implementing these research strategies to locate primary and secondary materials will provide you with access to many interesting sources, but how do you discriminate among them to find those that will be the best for your argument? The key rests in understanding the argumentative perspective, or *rhetorical stance,* of each source. At times, the source's stance may be self-evident: you may automatically gravitate toward experts in the field, well known for their opinions and affiliations. It is just as likely, however, that you may not be familiar with the names or ideas of your sources. In either case, it is essential to develop a method for evaluating the sources you encounter.

Evaluating Websites

For many of us, when we hear the words "research paper," our first impulse is to log onto the Internet and plug our topic into a search engine such as Google (http://www.google.com). However, because you are likely to encounter a vast number of hits, you will need a method for assessing the credibility and usefulness of your findings.

To understand effective methods of evaluating different types of sources, let's take the example of a research paper on the stem cell debate. What would be the best way to evaluate sources for this project? For instance, if you search the term "stem cells," you are likely to generate close to a million results. On the one hand, such a plentiful search gives you ample means to "eavesdrop" on the ongoing conversation about your topic; on the other hand, the sheer magnitude of hits can be overwhelming. Faced with such a massive amount of material, how do you begin to sort through them to identify those most helpful to your research?

Your best resource in this situation is your skill as a rhetorician. While opening various Webpages, consider how their visual and verbal elements suggest the sites' rhetorical stances and points of view on topic. The CNN.com "In-Depth Special" on the stem cell debate provides a good example of how rhetorical analysis factors into the research process (see Figure 5.8). As you study this page, three prominent aspects of the site probably stand out: the large CNN.com logo in the upper-right corner, which establishes the ethos of the site; the topic header, "The Stem Cell Debate," which identifies the focus and approach of the page; and the picture of the scientist at work. From here you can perform a more careful analysis of the way this homepage suggests CNN's approach to the stem cell issue, including the written words categorizing this debate into "issues," "science," "politics," and "analysis."

The writing is very scientific and logos based in tone, providing a credible source for your project. You can even analyze the words of the opening blurb:

> A year after President Bush's decision on stem cell research, scientists say they are being hindered by federal rules governing the use of embryonic stem cells because access to stem cell lines approved for research is limited. But the director of the National Institutes of Health said the agency is "diligently working" to make more cell lines available.

Notice how the paragraph begins with an appeal to an authority, President Bush, and then uses strong language to convey its stance on the issue—that

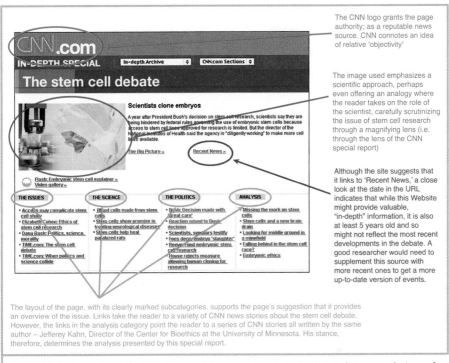

The CNN logo grants the page authority; as a reputable news source. CNN connotes an idea of relative 'objectivity'

The image used emphasizes a scientific approach, perhaps even offering an analogy where the reader takes on the role of the scientist, carefully scrutinizing the issue of stem cell research through a magnifying lens (i.e. through the lens of the CNN special report)

Although the site suggests that it links to 'Recent News,' a close look at the date in the URL indicates that while this Website might provide valuable, "in-depth" information, it is also at least 5 years old and so might not reflect the most recent developments in the debate. A good researcher would need to supplement this source with more recent ones to get a more up-to-date version of events.

The layout of the page, with its clearly marked subcategories, supports the page's suggestion that it provides an overview of the issue. Links take the reader to a variety of CNN news stories about the stem cell debate. However, the links in the analysis category point the reader to a series of CNN stories all written by the same author – Jefferey Kahn, Director of the Center for Bioethics at the University of Minnesota. His stance, therefore, determines the analysis presented by this special report.

FIGURE 5.8. A careful analysis of this CNN.com Webpage demonstrates its rhetorical stance on the issue of stem cell research; notice the words of the title bars.

scientists are "hindered by federal rules." These words give you a clue to the stance of the article: it is pro-science, anti-government. The words work together with the image of the scientist to provide one side on the issue of stem cell research.

Consider how this works for another example from your Google search. A quick glance at the stem cell page for the American Association for the Advancement of Science, shown in Figure 5.9, might indicate that it is also a prime candidate for your work. It is directly related to your topic, it showcases a comprehensive report on the topic, and it even offers links to other sources on stem cell research. However, more careful scrutiny of the site is necessary to fully gauge the organization's stance on the issue. Through rhetorical analysis, you can evaluate this source for your project.

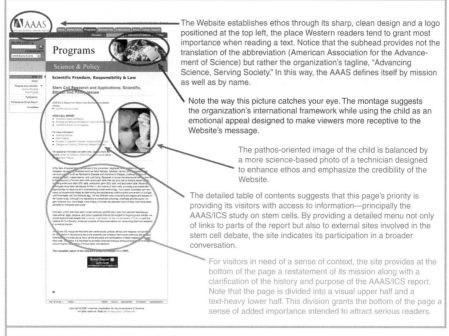

The Website establishes ethos through its sharp, clean design and a logo positioned at the top left, the place Western readers tend to grant most importance when reading a text. Notice that the subhead provides not the translation of the abbreviation (American Association for the Advancement of Science) but rather the organization's tagline, "Advancing Science, Serving Society." In this way, the AAAS defines itself by mission as well as by name.

Note the way this picture catches your eye. The montage suggests the organization's international framework while using the child as an emotional appeal designed to make viewers more receptive to the Website's message.

The pathos-oriented image of the child is balanced by a more science-based photo of a technician designed to enhance ethos and emphasize the credibility of the Website.

The detailed table of contents suggests that this page's priority is providing its visitors with access to information—principally the AAAS/ICS study on stem cells. By providing a detailed menu not only of links to parts of the report but also to external sites involved in the stem cell debate, the site indicates its participation in a broader conversation.

For visitors in need of a sense of context, the site provides at the bottom of the page a restatement of its mission along with a clarification of the history and purpose of the AAAS/ICS report. Note that the page is divided into a visual upper half and a text-heavy lower half. This division grants the bottom of the page a sense of added importance intended to attract serious readers.

FIGURE 5.9. The American Association for the Advancement of Science stem cell page combines words and images to encourage readers to access—and trust—its report on the issue.

Source: Screenshot of AAAS science & Policy web page: http://www.aaas.org/spp/sfri/projects/stem/index.shtml. Reprinted with permission from AAAS.

Specifically, assess the written language. The header—*Scientific Freedom, Responsibility and Law*—encapsulates the tensions inherent in the stem cell debate between the desire to maintain the researcher's freedom to conduct research as he sees fit with questions of moral responsibility and legality; in this way, the page suggests that it provides a balanced approach to the issue. Yet phrases in the central paragraph, such as *extraordinary advances* and *unprecedented opportunities,* indicate a stronger position on the topic. The question is not whether stem cell research should continue (a question that might concern other organizations), but how to carry on stem cell research "in an ethical manner." Having identified the stance, your task as a researcher is not only to take this position into account while reading, but also to broaden your research to include many different perspectives on the issue.

As you can see, you need to take special care in evaluating Webpages since the reliability varies widely across the Internet. Attention to the visual and verbal rhetoric of a site's homepage—its "cover"—is essential to understanding its argument and therefore its suitability as a research source. After assessing the "cover" pages of each Website, the next step is to move deeper into the site to analyze its content and argument.

CREATIVE PRACTICE

Compare the Websites shown in Figures 5.8 and 5.9 with two others generated from searching "stem cell" on Google: the Stem Cell Research Foundation site and the DoNoHarm site (see Figures 5.10 and 5.11).

What rhetorical decisions are apparent from each site's homepage design? How do the images suggest different approaches to the stem cell issue? How does the organization of information, the menu, and the written text contribute to this impression? Follow the site links to explore how the rhetorical stance suggested by the "cover" is reflected in the site's contents. Evaluate these two pages as sources for a paper on stem cell research. Develop a list of criteria for evaluating Webpages, and share it with the class.

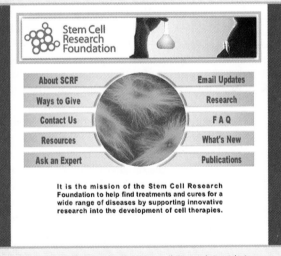

FIGURE 5.10. Homepage for the Stem Cell Research Foundation.

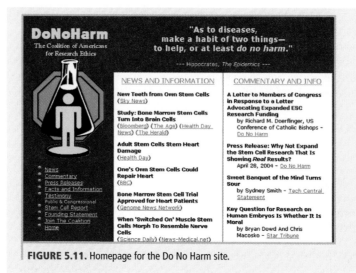

FIGURE 5.11. Homepage for the Do No Harm site.

The list of criteria generated by the "Creative Practice" may have varied from person to person, but most likely everyone focused on issues of authority, accessibility, and suitability in assessing the Webpages. After your preliminary rhetorical analysis, you might have looked at the URL to establish the author or host of a Website, or you might have examined the selection of images or the word choice for indications of bias or sensationalism. Perhaps you looked for the "last updated" note to check the currency of the site or for the "contact" link to evaluate the author's sense of accountability for his or her work. You may have followed the links to see if the site was self-contained, linking only to its own materials, or whether it contained external links, connecting it to the broader conversation on the topic. In addition, you most likely evaluated the *type* of material the site contained: primary documents or secondary commentary. Each of these steps inevitably took you beyond the cover, deeper into the contents of the site and closer to assessing its appropriateness as a source for your own research.

Evaluating Library and Database Sources

Clearly, popular Websites provided a multitude of sources for your project on stem cells. However, it's important to remember that no matter how

AT A GLANCE

Evaluating Websites

- Who is the author of the Website? Is it a personal Website or is it institutionally affiliated? What sort of authority does it draw on?
- Does the author take responsibility for the page by offering a place for comments or an email link for feedback?
- Who is the audience?
- What is the purpose?
- What is the rhetorical stance of this Website? Does it deal with both sides of the issue or only one side?
- Does it offer links to other sites on the Web?
- How timely is the page? Does it have a date? Does someone maintain the Website? Are there broken links?
- Is it an archive of primary material? If so, does it cite the original sources in a correct and complete manner?
- Is it easy to navigate? Does it have a search engine?

productive a Google search may be, for almost all college research papers, you will need to seek out sources through library shelves and databases since they host scholarly materials that will be more useful for your project.

Let's see how you might evaluate library and database sources for your stem cell research paper. Your first stop would be the library's reference area, where you look up foundational information in the *Encyclopedia of Bioethics*. Then you would search the library catalog for book-length sources, generating a long list of citations. You then decide to track down some journal articles that, you reason, will provide balance to your research because they often represent the most current discussions on a topic. To find relevant articles, you begin searching the electronic databases that most closely suit the specific focus of your project: SciSearch, MEDLINE, LegalPeriodical, BIOSIS. You produce an impressive list of citations and even retrieve a few full-text articles. You also search some sources that are more news related, including LexisNexis and ProQuest, to find a selection of references to popular newspaper and magazine articles that will balance the scholarly sources. Finally, armed with your list of citations, you head into the library stacks, returning shortly after with a rather heavy collection of books and bound periodicals.

Your first search complete, you can now retreat to a quiet space and assess the significance and value of your findings. You can be relatively confident in the quality of the texts you've accumulated because library holdings and scholarly databases tend to contain materials that have been more rigorously screened than those found through an Internet search engine. However, keep in mind that you'll still need to apply the same evaluation criteria to these texts as you would to Web sources.

You can start by assessing the visual rhetoric of some of the journal covers spread across your desk, beginning the process of assessing topic, stance, and reliability. You might, for instance, have come across the two covers found in Figures 5.12 and 5.13. A rhetorical analysis reveals differences in purpose, audience, and focus. *Stem Cells,* by using an actual image of embryonic cells, signals its focus on cellular biology and scientific applications; in addition, by listing its table of contents—complete with authors and article titles—on the front cover, it privileges ethos as an appeal. *Yale Scientific* chooses a different approach, using a powerful visual

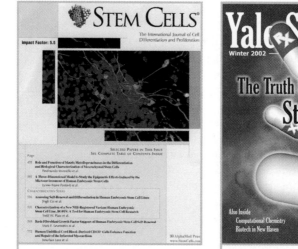

FIGURE 5.12. The cover of *Stem Cells* emphasizes its scientific approach in choices in cover image and text.

FIGURE 5.13. The cover of *Yale Scientific* zooms in on the debate rather than on the science of stem cells.

metaphor coupled with the term "Truth" to suggest its engagement with the debate surrounding stem cell research.

However, in many cases you may not be able to use a cover image as a guide to evaluation; many scholarly journals and books have been re-covered in plain library bindings. In that case, what steps should you take to select those that would be most productive for your research?

First, assess the **author.** Perhaps your teacher recommended the author to you or you notice that the author has written many books and articles on the topic. You can look this person up in a bibliography index or on the Web to assess the ethos of the writer. If the author turns out to be disreputable or affiliated with an extreme organization, would the source still be an important one to consider? Would the exaggerated stance help you argue for the existence of extremist positions on your topic?

Check out the **place of publication.** Is it a university press (suggesting peer-reviewed scholarship) or a trade press (suggesting a commercial venture)? Is it published by a foundation or organization (suggesting a political agenda) or self-published (suggesting the author's struggle to have his or her views accepted for publication)?

Look also at the **date.** Is it a recent contribution or an older study? An older source can provide historical context, but sometimes it can be too outdated to be useful. Usually, you should pick the more recent sources to engage the most timely perspectives on your topic.

Next, go beneath the cover of the book or journal. Open it and turn to the **table of contents** and the **index** to see exactly what the book contains. Is it a collection of articles by different authors, or does it reflect the viewpoint of a single author? Now flip through the pages, looking for interesting arguments and judging the quality or complexity of the writing. You may note its **voice** or **tone:** Is it written for

AT A GLANCE

Evaluating Academic Sources

- *Author:* Is the author an expert in his or her field? What professional or personal affiliations or experiences has this author had that might have influenced his or her argument or ethos?

- *Date:* When was the text published? If not recently, might it be outdated? Is it a text that sets a certain framework for discussion that other writers have since built on? Or does it offer a new perspective to an ongoing discussion?

- *Publisher:* Is the publisher an academic or popular press? Which would be most appropriate for your topic? Does the publisher have any connection to the topic under discussion?

- *Rhetorical stance:* What is the author's point of view on the topic? Is it moderate or extreme? How does that affect his or her treatment of the issue?

- *Audience:* For whom was this work intended: an academic or a popular audience? What level of specialized knowledge does the author assume that the audience has?

- *Relevance to your project:* How does this text relate to your argument? Does it provide background material? an opposing opinion? a supporting argument?

specialists in the field or for a popular audience? Does it focus on issues relevant to your research?

This rhetorical attention to the writing—the language, tone, date, context, and stance of the author—even at this early stage, is crucial to successful assessment of each of your sources. For the articles you collected for your stem cell research project, you might come across Gretchen Vogel's "Can Old Cells Learn New Tricks?" from the February 25, 2000 issue of *Science* (see Figure 5.14). Opening to the first page, you can perform a quick rhetorical analysis of its visual and verbal elements to evaluate its usefulness.

The first things that probably catch your eye are the colorful images of stem cells, as close up as if they were being viewed through the lens of a microscope. This imagery suggests that the article will have a scientific focus, and yet the arrows leading to each of the images suggest that it will teach a popular audience something new about stem cells. The first paragraph confirms the more popular focus of the piece; rather than starting with detail about the characteristics or applications of stem cells, the introduction zooms in on an individual biologist and her own reluctant participation in the ethical debate. By skimming, you see that the writing is clear and engaging, even when it is describing technical issues. Furthermore, you find that the rest of the article both explores some of the more recent scientific discoveries and, true to its introductory frame, continues to position that science in relation to the ethical debate. Since you are concerned as much with the debate as with the mechanics of stem cells, you can quickly ascertain that this article will be very helpful in your formulating your own analysis of the issue.

As our analysis of Vogel's article reveals, the most important assessment question is how *useful* a source will be for your project and your potential argument. Then you are on your way to knowing *how* you will use that text from your iceberg of research to craft your own research-based argument on the issue. Depending on your project, you might decide that you want to use not only print and electronic sources but also **field research** in the form of interviews or surveys. Collecting these sources often involves fieldwork, gathering and collecting your own evidence and data. For instance, one student, Megan Nesland, used fieldwork prominently in her research project about elevated asbestos levels at a local reservoir. In her preliminary research, she found many articles by community activists, geologists, and

STEM CELL RESEARCH AND ETHICS

NEWS

Can Old Cells Learn New Tricks?

Stem cells found in adults show surprising versatility. But it's not yet clear whether they can match the power of cells from embryos

Stem cell biologist Margaret Goodell has never seen her work on muscle and blood development as particularly political, so she was surprised when last month the Coalition of Americans for Research Ethics (CARE), a group that opposes the use of embryos in research, invited her to speak at a congressional briefing in Washington, D.C. She was even more astonished to find herself quoted by conservative columnist George Will a few weeks later.

Goodell gained this sudden notoriety because her work, and that of other teams around the world, just might provide a way around the moral and political quagmire that has engulfed stem cell research to date. Since their discovery in 1998, human embryonic stem cells have been

says bioethicist and CARE member Kevin Fitzgerald of Loyola University Medical Center in Chicago.

But can adult stem cells really fulfill the same potential as embryonic stem cells can? At this stage, the answer is by no means clear. Indeed, scientists caution that it is too early to know if even ES cells will produce the cornucopia of new tissues and organs that some envision. "It is still early days in the human embryonic stem cell world," says stem cell biologist Daniel Marshak of Osiris Therapeutics in Baltimore, which works with adult-derived stem cells.

From a scientific standpoint, adult and embryonic stem cells both have distinct benefits and drawbacks. And harnessing either one will be tough. Although scientists have

Studies with rodents also indicated that cells derived from ES cells could restore certain missing nerve functions, suggesting the possibility of treating neurological disorders. Last summer, Oliver Brüstle of the University of Bonn Medical Center and Ronald McKay of the U.S. National Institute of Neurological Disorders and Stroke and their colleagues reported that they could coax mouse ES cells to become glial cells, a type of neuronal support cell that produces the neuron-protecting myelin sheath. When the team then injected these cells into the brains of mice that lacked myelin, the transplants produced normal-looking myelin (*Science*, 30 July 1999, p. 754). And in December, a team led by Dennis Choi and John McDonald at Washington University School of Medicine in St. Louis showed that immature nerve cells that were generated from mouse ES cells and transplanted into the damaged spinal cords of rats partially restored the animals' spinal cord function (*Science*, 3 December 1999, p. 1826). Although no one has yet published evidence that human ES cells can achieve similar feats, Gearhart says he is working with several groups at Johns Hopkins to test the abilities of his cells in animal models of spinal cord injury and neurodegenerative diseases, including amyotrophic lateral sclerosis and Parkinson's disease.

While Gearhart and his colleagues were grappling with ES cells, Goodell and others were concentrating on adult stem cells. Conventional wisdom had assumed that once a cell had been programmed to produce a particular tissue, its fate was sealed, and it could not reprogram itself to make another tissue. But in the last year, a number of studies have surprised scientists by showing that stem cells from one tissue, such as brain, could change into another, such as blood (*Science*, 22 January 1999, p. 534). Evidence is mounting that the findings are not aberrations but may signal the unexpected power of adult stem cells. For example, Goodell and her colleagues, prompted by the discovery of blood-forming brain cells, found that cells from mouse muscle could repopulate the bloodstream and rescue mice that had received an otherwise lethal dose of radiation.

Bone marrow stem cells may be even more versatile. At the American Society of Hematology meeting in December, hematologist Catherine Verfaillie of the University of Minnesota, Minneapolis, reported that she has isolated cells from the bone marrow of children and adults that seem to have an amazing range of abilities. For instance, Verfaillie and graduate student Morayma

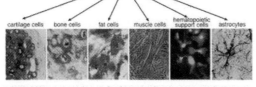

MSC

cartilage cells   bone cells   fat cells   muscle cells   hematopoietic support cells   astrocytes

Multitalented. Mesenchymal stem cells (MSC) from adult bone marrow can become bone, cartilage, and even brain cells in lab culture.

one of the hottest scientific properties around. Because these cells can theoretically be coaxed to differentiate into any type of cell in the body, they open up tantalizing possibilities, such as lab-grown tissues or even replacement organs to treat a variety of human ills, from diabetes to Alzheimer's. Politically, however, human stem cells have been a much tougher sell, as they are derived from embryos or fetuses. Indeed, most research is on hold as policy-makers grapple with the ethics of human embryo research.

Enter Goodell, whose work suggests that stem cells derived from *adults*, in this case, from mouse muscle biopsies, can perform many of the same tricks as embryonic stem (ES) cells can—but without the ethical baggage. Both CARE and George Will seized upon her work as an indication that research on ES cells could remain on hold with no appreciable loss to medicine. "There's a lot less moral ambiguity about the adult stem cells,"

been working with mouse ES cells for 2 decades, most work has focused on creating transgenic mice rather than creating lab-grown tissues. Only a handful of groups around the world have discovered how to nudge the cells toward certain desired fates. But that work gained new prominence in late 1998, when two independent teams, led by James Thomson at the University of Wisconsin, Madison, and John Gearhart of The Johns Hopkins University, announced they could grow human stem cells in culture. Suddenly the work in mouse cells could be applied to human cells—in the hope of curing disease.

The beauty of embryonic stem cells lies in their malleability. One of their defining characteristics is their ability to differentiate into any cell type. Indeed, researchers have shown that they can get mouse ES cells to differentiate in lab culture into various tissues, including brain cells and pancreatic cells.

FIGURE 5.14. The first page of Vogel's article on her innovations in stem cell research.

environmental experts on the extent and dangers of the contamination. However, she soon realized that her argument would be much more powerful if it drew on her own firsthand impressions. Consequently, she took an afternoon to visit the reservoir, where she interviewed hikers about their awareness of the asbestos issue, took a tour with a local geologist who pointed out key rock formations to her, and even took photographs that highlighted the incipient asbestos problem to use as visual evidence in her paper (see Figure 5.15).

This field research added depth to her argument by allowing her to uncover her own evidence to support her argument. Not all fieldwork involves trips to local sites. Sometimes you gather your own primary data about a topic from carefully determined sample groups or individuals. If you were interested in studying grade inflation at your campus, for instance, you might do a survey of a sample of students and professors. If you were studying the layout and impact of a new proposed park in your community, you might interview a city planner or the landscape architect involved in the project. One student, Sean Bruich, writing on recent marketing strategies used by the Oakland Athletics baseball team, wrote a letter to the team's marketing coordinator. Consult his letter to learn how to begin your field research.

FIGURE 5.15. Megan's photo and caption: "A large serpentinite outcrop alongside the Crystal Springs Reservoir, already showing signs of its hidden asbestos."

April 7, 2003

Lynne Tibbet

Sales & Marketing Coordinator

Oakland Athletics

Dear Ms. Tibbet,

My name is Sean Bruich and I am a freshman at Stanford University. As part of Stanford's required courses in writing, I am enrolled in Dr. Alyssa O'Brien's course on Visual Rhetoric. Writing a sizable research paper that focuses on visual rhetoric is a required portion of this class. As a long-time fan of the Oakland Athletics, I was hoping to write my paper on the marketing strategies employed by the Athletics over the course of the last few years (specifically, I'm hoping to focus on the "Baseball Country" and "Baseball: A's Style" ads since they are so memorable).

At this point I'd like to request some materials from the Athletics. Specifically, if the A's could send me, by either email or by mail, the print materials from these campaigns, I would be really appreciative. In addition, if possible, I would love to also get copies of some of the commercial spots that are shown on TV. I will reimburse your office for any and all expenses incurred, including materials and mailing costs.

At some point, I'd like also to discuss with you or one of your colleagues how the A's create and direct their marketing campaigns, if you have the time available.

I only need ads that are now or have been in the market-place—I'm not in any way requesting unpublished work. I will

Sean writes a formal letter to the contact he has found for his field research.

He introduces himself and his project fully, relying on ethos and stating the purpose of his letter early.

He makes his request specific and feasible, taking into account any potential obstacles.

He offers to sign a confidentiality agreement, a rhetorical strategy to convince his audience to send him field research materials.

talk to my professor to ensure that none of these materials extend beyond this project, and are not republished or retransmitted in any way without prior permissions from the Athletics. In addition, if the A's need me to sign any confidentiality agreements, I would be happy to do so.

Basically, I'm going to start working on this term paper in the course of the next week or so, although I do have several smaller writing assignments that could be aided greatly by these materials if I can get hold of them sooner.

Please do not hesitate to contact me if you have questions or want to discuss this situation further.

Thank you very much for your time!

Regards,

Sean

Sean Bruich

P.O. Box 12345

Stanford, CA 54321

He ends politely, with an invitation for the person to contact him. He lists his full contact information, including email address.

(650) 555-1878 (dorm)

(650) 555-7694 (cell)

seanstudent@university.edu

You also can take advantage of resources closer to home by interviewing faculty members from your university who have written or lectured on subjects related to your topic. This is a great way to make contacts and develop your iceberg of research because, in addition to interviewing the faculty member as another secondary source, you can usually ask him or her to recommend two or three key books in the field that you might consult as you continue on your research journey.

AT A GLANCE

Conducting Interviews and Surveys

1. *Target your population:* Identify the best sources for your field research: a professor at your college who is expert in this area? a professional from the community? peers in your class, dorm, athletic team, or town?

2. *Develop questions:* Compose a list of questions to ask in your interview or survey. Review them with a peer or show them to your instructor. For interviews, avoid general questions; design your questions to elicit quotations you can use in your paper. For surveys, you want to balance short, multiple choice questions (that yield primarily statistical data) with some short answer question that will produced more nuanced responses. Keep your survey short; the longer your form, the fewer completed surveys will probably be returned to you.

3. *Prepare:* For interviews, look up the biography of the interviewee online or in the paper. Read any publications by the person so you can show you already know a little about the person's stance on the issue. Also, be ready to talk about your background knowledge in this area. For surveys, prepare by getting to know the population's stance on the issue and by researching the best mode of distribution for that population (for instance, an electronic form might not be the best choice when surveying populations with limited Internet access).

4. *Make contact:* For interviews, make initial contact by email, mail, or phone. Explain clearly your purpose, your identity, and your goal for the field research. Offer two or three concrete times that might work for the interviewee (check a professor's office hours or a professional's working hours); also offer to interview over the phone or by email. If your interviewee does not reply at first, send a polite follow-up email, asking for just 15 minutes of time, or requesting the name of someone who would be available instead. Don't hesitate to persist, but do so respectfully. For surveys, find a reliable means of distribution—in person or electronic—and, just as importantly, make clear on the survey a deadline and where/how the forms should be returned if you're not going to collect them immediately yourself.

5. *Record and document:* Ask permission from interviewees and survey subjects for you to use their words in your paper. If you record an interview with a tape recorder or cell phone device, be sure to ask permission first and to create a transcript as soon as possible after the interview. Document all uses of the interview with quotation marks in your paper.

6. *Follow-up:* If you do complete your field research successfully, send a thank you note to any interviewees and even offer a copy of your completed paper. Although it is more difficult to follow up with survey subjects, consider sharing your findings with them through a local newsletter or college newspaper article.

Evaluating Fieldwork and Statistics

When you conduct interviews and surveys, you are looking for materials to use in your paper as supporting arguments, evidence, or statistical data. But as you pursue your interviews and surveys, keep in mind the need to evaluate your field research sources as carefully as you assess your print and electronic sources. If you interview a professor, a marketing executive, a witness, or a roommate, consider the rhetorical stance of that person. What kind of bias does the person have concerning the topic of your project? Similarly, if you conduct a survey of your peers or in your dorm, remember to assess the value and credibility of your results as rigorously as you would evaluate the data of a published study. It's easy to fall into the trap of misusing statistics when making claims if you haven't taken into account the need for **statistical significance,** or to paraphrase the social psychologist Philip Zimbardo, the measure by which a number obtains meaning in scientific fields. To reach this number, you need to design the survey carefully, conduct what's called a *random sample,* interview a *large enough* number of people, and ask a *range of different* people. These are complex parameters to follow, but you will need to learn about them to conduct survey research that has reliable and credible results. It's easy to draw improper conclusions without a clear understanding of statistics. Your teacher—or a psychology professor who is familiar with these concepts—can help you to design effective surveys and incorporate statistical evidence accurately into your research paper.

Let's turn again to Professor Zimbardo's explanation of statistics to understand how careful you need to be when using scientific data—whether your own surveys or a secondary source that relies on scientific studies and statistics—as evidence in your paper: "Statistics are the backbone of research. They are used to understand observations and to determine whether findings are, in fact, correct and significant. . . . But, statistics can also be used poorly or deceptively, misleading those who do not understand them" (595). The point is that statistics—though we often think of them as Truth—actually function rhetorically. Like words and images, numbers are a mode of persuasion that can mislead readers. Thus, you need to be especially vigilant when using a survey or statistics as a supposedly "objective" part of your iceberg of research, particularly if you plan to depend on such materials in your argument.

For example, the information graphic "Estimated number of new cancer cases, 1997-2006" provides an example of the argument that charts can be misleading in the way that it mixes and matches the years it samples. Clearly, you need to take as much care with how you convey information visually as you do with how you convey it in writing. We see this in David Pinner's writing project about grade inflation at the university level. David accumulated enough quantitative information through fieldwork and primary research to compose his own charts. He discovered a wealth of information in archived faculty senate minutes, which he sorted through during his research. From that work, he came across

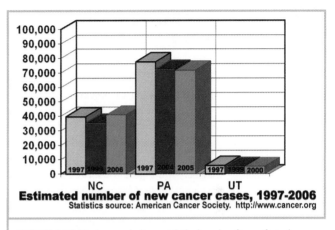

Estimated number of new cancer cases, 1997-2006
Statistics source: American Cancer Society. http://www.cancer.org

FIGURE 5.16. The bar graphs here might be based on figures from the American Cancer Society, but the random sampling of years produces a misleading argument about the rise of cancer rates in these states.

important statistical data that reflected the change in grade distribution at Stanford over the course of 25 years. In addition to including the numbers in his written text, he created two powerful pie charts (see Figure 5.17), using a visual comparison of statistics to underscore his point. His argument was more powerful not just because of his impressive primary research but also because of how he represented it in his paper through responsible use of statistics.

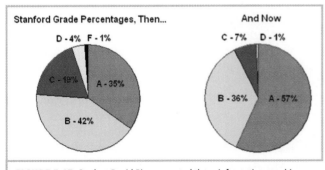

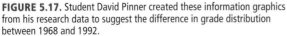

FIGURE 5.17. Student David Pinner created these information graphics from his research data to suggest the difference in grade distribution between 1968 and 1992.

Creating a Dialogue with Your Sources

Throughout this chapter we have emphasized the point that research is social, a relationship with the people whose ideas and writing came before yours. You are contributing to this conversation, building on the work of others, and adding a new perspective. Indeed, this notion of writing as communal is the reason why you need to use the author's name when citing a quotation or an idea; remember that all your sources are authored sources. From the DoNoHarm Website shown in Figure 5.11, to Gretchen Vogel's article depicted in Figure 5.14, each source mentioned in this chapter was composed by a person or a group of people. If you think of these texts as written *by people like you,* you will have an easier time remembering to acknowledge their ideas and integrate their quotations into your essay. You can begin this process through an exercise we call a **dialogue of sources**—a fictional conversation among the primary and secondary sources of your research paper designed to help you identify each one's central argument and main idea.

You can find a visual equivalent for the dialogue of sources in comedian Jon Stewart's video sketch from *The Daily Show,* "Bush v. Bush," in which he moderated a "debate" between President George W. Bush and his younger self, Texas governor George W. Bush, on matters of foreign policy (see Figure 5.18). In reality, the debate was composed of carefully edited excerpts from speeches from different points in Bush's career; the result was a provocative look into his changing opinion on U.S. foreign intervention. Although the video dialogue was comic, the premise was a sound one: many news commentary shows feature "round-table" discussions among a diverse group of people, with the idea of promoting a conversation about a relevant social or political topic.

FIGURE 5.18. Screen shot from "Bush v. Bush," a debate staged by Jon Stewart on *The Daily Show.* Still courtesy of Comedy Central.

You may find it helpful to create your own *dialogue of sources* in which you write out the diverse opinions you've encountered in your research:

Student Writing
See the dialogues of sources by Andrew Timmons on PetCo Park and by Amanda Johnson on tobacco advertisements.
www.ablongman.com/envision/220

- First, identify the key players from your research log. Which ones have the most influential or important arguments?
- Then, create a cast of characters list in which you create a short "bio" for each speaker, including yourself, describing each person's credentials and rhetorical stance—their ethos and their argument. You may even want to create identifying icons or pictures to give "faces" to the participants.
- Now, draft the script. Begin by writing key questions to ask your sources about your topic. As they articulate their positions, use quotes from your sources where possible, and include page numbers.
- Next, consider what your sources would say in response to each other. Write their fictional conversation by using quotes from your sources.
- Don't just play the "objective" moderator. Respond to the sources and, in the process, start to develop your own argument.

To prepare for her research paper on tobacco advertisements, Amanda Johnson (AJ) wrote this dialogue between several sources she had found: RJ Reynolds Tobacco Co. (RJRT); Larry C. White, author of *Merchants of Death* (LW); and Hugh High, a professor of Economics, Finance, and Law who published a collection of tobacco studies titled *Does Advertising Increase Smoking?* (HH), among others.

Dialogue of Sources

AJ: I would like to thank the panel for joining us this afternoon. We have quite a diverse group of writers, researchers, spokespeople, and a professor here to discuss the focus and objectives of current tobacco advertising. Since I know your comments on this subject vary widely, I suppose I will start off by asking you to talk

---

Amanda's complete dialogue begins with a list of speakers and their bios. Then she introduces the topic of her research project. She reproduces the argument of each source, both print and interview, through paraphrase.

about what you believe to be the focus of tobacco advertising as it exists today.

By allowing debate to evolve, Amanda begins to see how she might use quotations from these sources in her paper.

RJRT: RJ Reynolds tobacco products are among the best advertised in the industry, and we take pride in our commitment to maintaining honest advertising to the public. We do not intend for our advertising to manipulate nonsmokers into trying our products, nor do we choose to target these audiences. Advertising is simply a method by which we are able to maintain our share of the market and compete with other tobacco manufacturers.

Most importantly, she begins to develop her own argument for her research paper in the context of these other perspectives.

LW: How can you possibly claim to avoid targeting specific audiences and replenishing your older dwindling population with new younger smokers!?! The whole point of advertising is to get more people to buy your product, and, since market shares don't change all that much for large companies like yours, the best way to get more people to buy your product is to increase the number of overall smokers. Youth are your best option because if you can get them hooked now, you will have a steady flow of income for several decades to come.

HH: Mr. White, you make a good point about general economic objectives. However, studies show that advertising does very little to change the number of new smokers. Countries that have banned advertising for tobacco-related products have seen very little decline in the number of consumers that buy their product. As RJRT stated previously, advertising is only successful at making adjustments within the market concerning the relative amounts each company is able to sell.

AJ: I recently reviewed a chart concerning the prevalence of smoking among U.S. adults and found that over the past 40 years since the surgeon general first warned about cigarettes' cancerous effects, the steady decline in smokers has slowed to rest around 25 percent of the population over the age of 18. With the number of people dying each day, it is surprising that this number does not continue to go down. How would you account for the slowed change?

She does this by questioning the responses, adding facts from her research, and moving the argument forward as she will need to do in her paper.

As you can tell, the dialogue of sources is a process of literally responding to the main arguments in your texts. It can produce a helpful interchange about the research topic and move you toward refining your own argument.

Note Taking and Annotated Bibliographies

You can use the dialogue of sources as a note-taking strategy while you work through your research sources. Indeed, many students find this approach to note taking to be the best way to create thorough research logs for their projects, one that keeps their own thesis evident. However, there are many methods of note taking, and at this point in your research process, you probably have developed some techniques of your own: taking notes right in your research log or on note cards, on loose-leaf paper, in a spiral notebook, or on your laptop.

AT A GLANCE

Note-Taking Strategies

As you read through your sources, take notes on materials that you could use in your paper:

• Particularly memorable quotations

• Background information you can summarize

• A well-written passage providing context or a perspective useful to your argument

Be sure to double-check your notes for accuracy and to include complete source information and page numbers.

AT A GLANCE

Composing an Annotated Bibliography

1. Put your sources into alphabetical order; you can also categorize them by of primary and secondary sources.

2. Provide complete identifying information for each source, including author's name, title, publication, date, page numbers, URLs for Websites, and database information for online sources.

3. Compose a three- to five-sentence annotation for each source:

   • First, summarize the main argument or point of the source; use concrete language. Include quotations if you wish.

   • Next, indicate the writer's stance. How credible or biased is this source?

   • Finally, and most importantly, describe the relevance of this source to your research argument. Will the source be used as background for the opening part of your paper? Does it offer a key counterargument? Will it provide the main authority to back up your claims?

AT A GLANCE

Constructing a Visual Annotated Bibliography

1. List your sources in alphabetical order; you can separate your list into primary and secondary sources or provide one complete list.

   • Include images for your primary sources and the covers or Website images of secondary sources to show each source's stance through visual rhetoric.

   • For each source, include all identifying information.

   • Briefly state the argument of each source, the possible audience, and the bias or slant of the writer and include any specific passages of particular interest.

   • Most importantly, explain the relevance of this source to your own research project and even where and how you might use it in your paper.

As you move further into your research, you might want to synthesize your notes in what researchers call an **annotated bibliography**—a list of research sources that provides informational notes about each source and how you might use it as you turn to drafting your paper.

Realize that composing entries in the annotated bibliography involves much more than merely recording information: it is a way for you to synthesize arguments and add your response to what the source has to say about your research topic. Be sure to name the sources in your notes so you start to create the same type of interactive dialogue with your sources as you might have with faculty members or interviewees. Moreover, if you quote from textual passages either in your notes or in your annotated bibliography, include name prompts, use quotation marks, and show clearly the distinction between direct quotes from your source and your own summaries or commentaries. In this way, you can avoid potentially misquoting or plagiarizing sources later.

As you compose your annotated bibliography, consider including images that you might use as primary or secondary sources as well. In this way, you are crafting a **visual annotated bibliography**—a working list of potential sources in which you include images. This is very helpful if you plan to analyze images in your paper or if your rhetorical analysis covers visual and multimedia texts, such as James Caputo's project on the government's space program.

Consider, for instance, Carly Geehr's visual annotated bibliography for her research project on the representations of swimming as a gendered sport in the American media throughout history (see Figure 5.19).

Student Writing
See samples of visual annotated bibliographies on a wide range of topics.
www.ablongman.com/envision/221

Both the image of a swimmer from the early 1920s in the secondary source by Douglas Booth and Colin Tatz, as well as the more recent advertising from *U.S.A. Swimming* were key images that Carly analyzed in her paper to make an argument about the feminization of swimming in American sports culture.

Carly Geehr
Visually Annotated Bibliography

Dr. Alyssa O'Brien
May 13, 2003

The American Media and Swimming: Investigating the "Uphill Battle"

Booth, Douglas and Colin Tatz. *One-Eyed: a View of Australian Sport.* Australia: Allen and Unwin, 2000.

In order to make my argument that swimming could be a more popular sport in the United States, I will need to present strong evidence: this book provides it to me. Booth and Tatz chronicle the history of Australian sports in both society and in the media. From their descriptions of media coverage and the role of gender in sports, I can find out why, culturally and historically, swimming has been able to achieve such a high level of popularity in Australia. Of particular interest to me so far has been their focus on the traditional, accepted role of women in sports—it is drastically different in US history. By comparison to my sources about American sports culture, I will find out the key differences between the two countries and hopefully draw some concrete conclusions as to why swimming is not as popular in the United States as it is in Australia. This photo is the image of a female Australian swimmer whose look and demeanor demand respect, unlike her beautified American counterparts (212). I will be able to compare the Australian images of swimmers with the American images of swimmers, hopefully noting some key differences in visual rhetoric techniques employed—preliminarily, I suspect that the American images will focus much more on aesthetics while Australian images will focus on intensity and ruggedness (more pertinent to the sport itself).

"Duel in the Pool Advertisement." 3 Apr 2003. <http://www.usaswimming.org/Duel>.

[A little background: USA Swimming recently staged its first "made-for-TV" dual meet versus the Australian national team. The goal was to attract network attention and draw the people who would normally be watching sports on weekend afternoons into watching swimming for a change. According to Mary Wagner, the ratings were good but not exceptional.] This image is one of the advertisements put out by USA Swimming before the event to attract its target audience of teenagers and others (particularly males) who would be watching television on Saturday and Sunday afternoons. It appeals mostly to ethos, citing Michael Phelps as a world record holder, but also appeals more subtly to pathos in using the national colors and the national flag to create a sense of nationalism and passion for the event. However, this image helps me support my claim that USA Swimming's promotions have fallen short of successful in that it is not an exciting image—if the intent was to attract teenagers and adults who typically watch traditional, exciting American sports, then this image fails to create sufficient energy to generate interest or a desire to deviate from watching normal weekend sports on TV.

FIGURE 5.19. Well-chosen images and detailed annotations show Carly Geehr's progress on her research project.

Implementing Your Research Skills

As you begin to articulate your contribution to the dialogue about your topic, use the strategies that you've learned in this chapter. These include visualizing research as a conversation that you are joining and understanding the process of researching your argument as a movement from surface to depth. As you learn to search and locate both primary and secondary sources, you can engage in critical evaluation of these texts in your research log. You can also engage in innovative fieldwork of your own to generate original resource material to use in your argument. In writing your own annotated bibliography, remember that effective annotations and note-taking practices can help you develop the strategies of an academic writer and that these practices will move you toward finalizing your own argument about the topic. By moving from covers to contents, you will watch your iceberg take shape, and you will begin to let your own voice be heard.

PREWRITING CHECKLIST

Focus on Evaluating Websites, Magazines, and Journals

❏ What images are featured on the cover? Do the images lend themselves to an appeal to logic? to an appeal to emotion? to an appeal to authority?

❏ Do the words included as headings and subheads on the cover contribute to any of these appeals?

❏ What do the cover images suggest about the contents of the larger text? Do they suggest a specific rhetorical stance or point of view? What is the effect of each visual choice?

❏ How do the words on the cover or homepage work in conjunction with the image to suggest the entire text's rhetorical stance? Do the words complement the image? Do they offer a contrast to the image?

WRITING PROJECTS

1. **Research Log Entries:** Continue to write in your *research log*; keep a running commentary/assessment of potential research sources for your project. Realize that careful research notes are a crucial part of the process and will help you avoid unintentional plagiarism of material (see Chapter 9 for more tips on avoiding plagiarism. Include in your log a combination of typed notes, highlighted photocopies, emails to yourself, a CD-ROM of sources from databases, note cards, scanned images, and other means of processing all the information you encounter.

2. **Working with your preliminary Bibliograbhy:** Create a *dialogue of sources* or an *annotated bibliography* to showcase the primary and secondary sources you'll employ in the major paper. Be sure that your writing provides a range of primary and secondary sources. Include both print and electronic sources and, if appropriate, include images to demonstrate the kinds of materials you'll be analyzing in the project.

3. **Collaborative Peer Review:** In groups of three or four, present your annotated bibliographies to one another. Pull the "greatest hits" from your research log, create a multimedia annotated bibliography, and tell the class about how your research is going. In other words, *present a discussion of your work in progress*. You should identify your thesis, key points, obstacles, and successes so far. You'll get feedback from the class about your developing research project.

 Visit www.ablongman.com/envision for expanded assignment guidelines and student projects.

CHAPTER 6

Organizing and Writing Research Arguments

A s you've seen, constructing a research argument is a complex and ongoing process. From selecting a topic to locating and evaluating sources and taking notes, it involves a series of interrelated steps. This is true of the *drafting* stage as well. In fact, organizing, drafting, and revising information is a prominent part of the process of creating any text, whether it be an academic essay, a television commercial, a radio essay, or even a film. Figure 6.1, for instance, offers us a rare glimpse at the drafting process behind a major motion picture—in this case, *Serenity* (2005). You might have watched this exciting scene in the theaters or on DVD; in it, one of the main characters, River, single-handedly fights an entire roomful of Reavers—the cannibalistic bad guys of the film—to protect her brother and friends. What you see in Figure 6.1 are the storyboards for this scene—an artist's draft that lays out the action in chronological increments, mapping out not only the movement of the characters but also the camera angles and thus the audience's experience of the events depicted. Notice the way it captures a sense of motion by rapidly changing perspectives and how it creates a narrative tension in the last panel with the close-up of the Reavers grabbing River to drag her back during her attempted escape. Storyboards like this one clearly operate as a visual outline, a type of organizational strategy that underlies almost all films. The polished final version seen in the theater is actually made possible by drafting steps like this one.

In many ways, the process of writing is like film production: both have many small steps that support a grounding vision or main idea, both have a carefully planned structure, and both involve rigorous editing. Because producing a film and producing a research argument

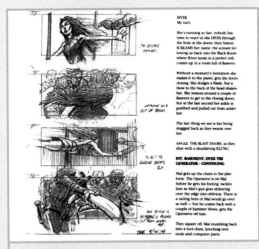

FIGURE 6.1. This storyboard for Joss Whedon's film *Serenity* shows an initial draft for one of the film's climactic action scenes.

share such rich similarities, we'll use the medium of film throughout this chapter to explore various aspects of the process of writing a research paper: from constructing a visual map and formal outline to integrating sources, key quotations, and evidence. We'll talk about incorporating sources responsibly in a way that sustains the conversation you began in the previous chapter, and we'll walk through the drafting and revision process. Just as filmmakers leave many scenes on the cutting room floor, you too will write, edit, cut, and rearrange much of the first draft of your research paper before it reaches its final form. You'll find that the process of completing your research argument is as collaborative as film production. Additionally, both film and writing involve parameters of length, cost, and time that you need to contend with to produce the best possible text. No matter what your topic, you can think of the way in which film works to help you visualize the final product and move from notes to writing the completed paper.

Of course, you have been writing all along: conducting analysis and forming arguments, drafting the proposal, completing the research log, and building an annotated bibliography. These are all ways to develop your argument through writing. Recognizing the connection between these shorter writing activities and the supposedly all-consuming task of "writing the research paper" can help the process seem more enjoyable and productive; it can help you avoid "writer's block" as you see that you've been making progress all along.

Chapter Preview Questions

- What strategies of organization work best for my paper?
- What are the best ways to get started writing a full draft?
- How do I know when to quote, paraphrase, or summarize?
- How can collaboration and peer review help me revise?

Organizing Your Draft in Visual Form

It can be quite challenging to turn on the computer and try to crank out a complete draft without first arranging materials into some kind of order. Using storyboards like those shown in Figure 6.1, or the bubble webs or graphic flowcharts described in this section, can be productive ways to prewrite through visual means. In fact, filmmakers and screenwriters often begin the production process by visually mapping out movie ideas, key scenes, and plot progressions. Similarly, you can use various forms of visual mapping to organize your research notes and argumentative points in order to sort, arrange, and make connections between ideas.

The most basic way to get organized is to physically stack your research books and materials and then write labels for each pile. This organizational strategy functions as a concrete way of categorizing the resources you have and figuring out, visually, how they relate to one another. Next, you can produce a visual map of these sources by using colored pens and paper or by cutting out shapes and constructing a three-dimensional model for your paper's organization.

If you have access to a computer, you can turn your hand-written visual map into a **bubble web,** in which you arrange your ideas into categories using shapes and colors. Figure 6.2 shows Lee-Ming Zen's visual map for his project on the video game Lara Croft: Tomb Raider titled "Finding the Woman Who Never Was: Gender Exploration Through Lara Croft." As Lee's legend for the visual map explains, each color represents his categorizing process for the many points he wishes to cover in his paper. By grouping his research and his ideas into categories contained within colored circles and then drawing relationships

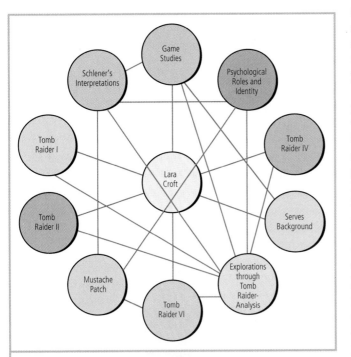

FIGURE 6.2. The bubble web by Lee-Ming Zen helped him organize the ideas of his argument into categories and, ultimately, sections he wanted to cover in his written paper. His categories include content- (or detail-) related materials for rhetorical analysis, idea or broad concept-related materials from his research, and material that requires Lee's own synthesis of ideas of analysis.

between these categories using colored lines, Lee can sort through the sources he has read, the ideas he has encountered, and the many points and sections he wishes to cover in his written research paper. Ultimately, Lee turned this visual map into a formal written outline (see page 176). But it was crucial for him to make sense first of the research he had gathered. Through this map, he began to see how he could articulate his argument about gender roles played out in the video game.

In addition to such free-form visual maps, you could try more hierarchical or linear graphic flowcharts as a means of organizing your materials. In **graphic flowcharts,** you list one idea and then draw an arrow to suggest cause and effect and to show relationships among items. Figure 6.3, for example, presents Ye Yuan's graphic flowchart of his ideas about war photography, arranged in a tree structure. This visual hierarchy helped him assess his project by asking questions:

- Is each point developed thoroughly?
- Do I have a balance among the sections?
- Is there a coherent whole?

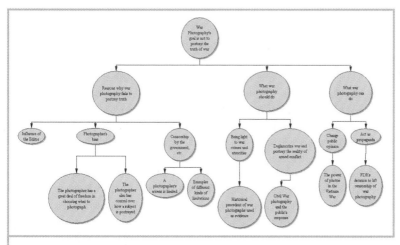

FIGURE 6.3. This graphic flowchart by Ye Yuan, created with the software program Inspiration, allowed him to visualize the sections of his written paper.

COLLABORATIVE CHALLENGE

Using the visual-mapping technique of your choice, begin to arrange your ideas for the research paper. Create a bubble web of ideas or make a graphic flowchart of concepts. If you'd rather work with physical materials, gather colored pens, pencils, papers, scissors, and tape and then "create" relationships among ideas by arranging them visually on paper: cut out shapes, draw lines and links, tape pieces of paper together. When you are done constructing your visual map, explain your organizational plan to your peer review partners. Ask for feedback on what areas seem under-developed, isolated, or extraneous. Use this feedback to think about the balance of materials and arrangement of sections in your written essay.

Learning Outline Strategies

Visual maps can help you sort out your materials and prepare you for the next step: the detailed, written outline. For a longer, more complex paper, such as a research-based argument, an outline is an extremely useful method of arranging ideas and expediting the drafting process. Outlines offer a plan for your paper and should show the relationships among the various sections in your argument. If your outline simply consists of a list of topics, you won't be able to see the argument of the whole paper, nor will you be able to check for connections and progression between your individual points. In other words, the secret to producing a successful outline—and by extension a successful paper—is to pay special attention to the flow or development of ideas.

It's often hard to know for certain what the best way of organizing your paper will be without some trial and error. We can learn a lot from films about the ways in which various texts are organized. Consider how a film's **trailer,** or short prerelease video, provides a brief outline of the key scenes, the main conflict, the crucial characters, and the message of the movie. Figure 6.4 shows still shots from the theatrical trailer of *Kill Bill: Volume 1.*

FIGURE 6.4. Still shots from the trailer for *Kill Bill: Volume 1*.

Structured loosely as a narrative, this segment of the trailer suggests an outline of the film, moving from an identification of conflict, to defining the main character's central nemesis, to a scene of confrontation and physical combat. In doing so, the trailer reproduces one of the central themes of the *Kill Bill* series: the identification of evil and the quest for revenge through violence. But there are many ways to arrange these elements, each of which suggests a different argument for the film. The power of the trailer as an organizational tool is that it allows the filmmakers to experiment with order and meaning.

COLLABORATIVE CHALLENGE

In groups of three or four, visit the movie trailers site on Apple.com through the *Envision* Website and view two or three trailers, either for the same film or different ones. Write down the main features of each trailer. How does each one function as an outline of the film's key scenes, characters, conflict, and message? What tone or style is conveyed through the selection of imagery, the choice of music, and the emphasis on a particular plot or character? What can you apply to your own outline strategies of arrangement?

www.ablongman.com/envision/222

Keeping the idea of the trailer in mind, take your ideas from the visual map you have created and craft them into a **formal outline,** a detailed list that uses numbers and letters to indicate subsections of your argument. Rather than list three sections only—such as Introduction, Body, and Conclusion—create several points within the body to show the development of your argument. Lee-Ming Zen, for example, developed a formal outline from his visual map on video game character Lara Croft. He broke the body of his paper into several points he wished to cover, taking readers through the history of Lara Croft, various interpretations of gender roles in the game, and then a close analysis of the games in chronological order, from earliest to most recent.

Lee-Ming Zen

Research Paper Outline

April 23, 2003

Dr. Alyssa O'Brien

Finding the Woman Who Never Was: Gender Role Exploration Through Lara Croft

I. Introduction

A. "Hook" line

B. Background

C. Thesis: By examining the various expressions of Lara Croft and the evolution of her aesthetic character, we are offered a chance to explore the various cultural and sociological aspects of our understanding of gender, especially in relation to videogames. In particular, her evolution parallels the different stages of gender exploration that adolescents experience and struggle through. Yet, at the same time, Lara Croft is a paradox acting as an objectification of women that both stereotypes and empowers women by allowing anyone to explore gender through her body.

D. Organizational hints

II. The Woman Who Never Was

A. Origins of Lara Croft

1. concept

2. reasons

Lee drafted a working title on his outline to help him focus the argument.

Lee includes a complete, detailed statement of his working thesis to guide and shape his outline.

B. *Tomb Raider* Series

   1. general information

   2. statistics to show the import and impact

C. Schleiner's role interpretations of Lara Croft

   1. female Frankenstein

   2. drag queen

   3. dominatrix/femme fatale

   4. female role model

   5. lesbian idol

D. University of Michigan's proposed stages of gender-role development

E. Ideas and concepts of masculinity/femininity

   1. Girls

   2. Boys

III. Evolution of Lara Croft

A. Version 1.0

   1. *Tomb Raider* box cover

   2. Lara Croft's features

   3. Schleiner's analysis's applications to this image

   4. Relation to Stage I in Parsons and Bryan

B. Version 2.0

   1. Mustache patch image

   2. Mustache patch background and information

   3. Schleiner's analysis's applications to this image

   4. Relation to Stage II and especially Stage III in Parsons and Bryan

Lee lists his argument points briefly in the body sections of his outline. If you prepare a more detailed outline, you may want to identify sources you will use to support your claims. Include quotations and page numbers.

C. Explorative Analysis
1. Flanagan's take
2. Gender role exploration in Stages I-III through Lara Croft versions 1 and 2
3. Game concept relation in gender exploration
   a) Game immersion
   b) Character identity

D. Version 4.0
1. Version 3.0 is the same as the 2.0 engine but tweaked
   a) brief explanation of game engines
   b) lack of major change in her image
2. A sexier Lara Croft – image analysis
3. Analysis of changes in her image since versions 1 and 2
4. Schleiner's analysis's applications to this image
5. Relation to Stage III and IV in Parsons and Bryan

E. Version 6.0
1. Concept art and the new 'realistic' look
   a) The new 'Gen-X' Lara Croft
2. Changes since versions 1, 2, and 4
3. Comparative analysis in regards to Schleiner and Flanagan (hopefully in order to begin tying everything back together)
4. Relation to Stage IV and V in Parsons and Bryan

F. Explorative Analysis
1. Gender role exploration in Stages III-V through Lara Croft versions 4 and 6

2. Change in the trend of Lara as a parallel to the adolescent development

   a) Significance of this trend

   b) Applications of this trend to other research on gender identity, roles

3. Game concept relation in gender exploration

   a) Game spaces

   b) Gender difference in technology use

IV. Conclusion

  A. Quick look back

  B. Overall import of these findings

  C. Further reaching impacts of this study

Indicate where your argument will lead to in your conclusion. Rather than just restate your thesis and summarize your argument, discuss the significance of your points.

As you can tell from Lee's example, formal outlines can help you work step by step through the process of arguing your position. Additionally, they can save you a lot of time as you approach the writing process itself. Consider using full sentences to most clearly articulate your thoughts or inserting sources right into the outline; these techniques can help you troubleshoot areas where you might need to do supplemental research or expand your argument.

One benefit of outlining as a prewriting practice is that it allows you to experiment with different organizational structures to discover which one works best for your paper. Depending on your topic, you can try several approaches, just as filmmakers rearrange a film to create a variety of trailers. Do you want to start your paper with a question, move through evidence, and then arrive at a declarative thesis statement? Or do you feel that your argument is best served by a firm thesis statement up front, followed by an accumulation of supporting evidence that ultimately touches upon larger related issues? The key in organizing your paper is to consider the relationship

AT A GLANCE

Useful Organization Strategies

- *Chronological:* relevant for historical discussions
- *Thematic:* helps with diverse case studies
- *Cause and effect:* focuses on consequences
- *Problem-solution:* useful for social issues papers
- *Illustrative:* emphasizes examples of a pattern
- *Macro to micro:* moves from the general to the specific
- *Micro to macro:* moves from the specific to the general
- *Narrative:* employs the personal experience

between *form* and *content,* or the way your structure can facilitate your argument.

Lee centered his argument principally on a **chronological** model, but as the "At a Glance" box demonstrates, that is only one of many strategies available to you. Let's look again to film for an organizational example you may wish to follow. If you visit the PBS Frontline Website to view the documentary *The Merchants of Cool,* for instance, you would find the film chunked into thematic "chapters." The first chapter, "hunting for cool," establishes a definition and sets up the research problem: how do advertisers successfully market products to teens? The next segment, "under-the-radar marketing," shifts the thematic focus from advertising to company image; and "the mtv machine" chapter narrows to examine MTV as a marketing tool. In its sixth and final chapter, "teen rebellion: just another product," the documentary reinforces its thesis, using the band Limp Bizkit to demonstrate how extreme materials can be successfully marketed to a mass audience. In this way, the organization functions as part of the film's argument. Structure (*form*) fits argument (*content*).

CREATIVE PRACTICE

Watch Frontline's *The Merchant of Cool* (available through the *Envision* Website), paying close attention to how the argument as a whole is organized. Notice that when you roll your mouse over the image, a one-sentence summary of each segment appears. Explore the way the film addresses its target audience, incorporates sources and evidence, and arranges its argument into subthemes. Write a detailed outline that reveals the organizational structure of this documentary. What can you learn and apply to the research paper you will be writing?

 www.ablongman.com/envision/223

Outlines with Subheads and Transitions

Outlines can also help you develop the complexity of your research argument if you incorporate subheads and transitions into your writing. **Subheads,** or labeled headings for each subsection of your outline, are a terrific way to structure your ideas into discrete units to show the progression of your argument and help your readers make sense of a complex argument. Subheads work particularly well for longer, research-based essays. You can transform the key parts of your outline into a short list of argumentative subheads.

If you were writing a detailed outline, you might insert into the body of your paper subheads that indicate specific parts of your argument. For a paper on film marketing, a subhead could be "A Look at Website Marketing of Films." You can feel free to get creative by connecting your subheads thematically or by using a single metaphor to add a rich layer of vivid words to your essay. For our film-marketing paper, the body might include the following subheads: "Movies Online Are a Big Splash," "Surfing for Movies," and "The Next Wave in Viral Marketing." After you write a list of working subheads, exchange them with a partner. Suggest modifications and new ideas to each other; keep focused on using subheads to advance the argument of the essay. Let's take a look at how Dexian Cai met this challenge by incorporating argumentative subheads into his outline.

Dexian Cai

PWR1 H-1

Dr. Alyssa O'Brien

Research Paper—Outline

November 12, 2003

I. Introduction

> Notice how Dex includes the opening line for his paper, the hook, right in the outline, setting the tone for the paper.

    1. Hook: A brief description of a current McDonald's advertisement for 2003. While ostensibly American and Western, the interesting aspect is that this ad is in fact for an Asian market.

---

   2. Thesis: McDonald's advertising in East Asia has evolved over
      time, adapting to trends and changes in Asian societal values.
      The paper will argue that McDonald's both shapes and is
      shaped by these evolving trends, creating a dynamic
      relationship between the restaurant and consumers.
   3. Implications: What are the effects of McDonald's influence on
      Asian values and societal evolution? Is this is a healthy trend
      or merely a restaurant moving with the times? Are accusations
      of cultural imperialism or degradation of morals justified?
II. Background
    • A brief history of McDonald's entry into the various East Asian
      markets. In particular, research will center on Japan, Hong
      Kong, Korea, Taiwan, China, and Singapore.
    • A summary of McDonald's image and ethos in the United States.
III. McDonald's: From Homely to Hip
     Then
    • Rhetorical analysis of ads from the 1970s and 1980s, when
      McDonald's first broke into the Asian markets.
    • Argument that McDonald's was attempting to portray itself
      as a family restaurant that made children feel special.
      Highlight the fact that the campaigns differed across the
      various countries because McDonald's tailored each campaign
      to the specific market's characteristics and perceived needs.
    • Compare and contrast with contemporary American campaigns.
      Family vs. fast food.
    • Sources: McDonald's Corporation. (Pending the approval of a
      request sent via e-mail.)
    • Secondary Source: Watson, James L. Golden Arches East:
      McDonald's in East Asia. Palo Alto, CA: Stanford University
      Press, 1997.

His thesis comprises
two sentences since
this argument is
complex.

He ends the intro with
questions to engage
the reader.

After a brief back-
ground section, Dex
moves on to the heart
of his argument.
The subhead "From
Homely to Hip"
reflects in words the
point Dex will make
in this section, namely,
that McDonald's has
changed its brand
image from conserva-
tive to trendy. The
play on words in the
subhead helps keep
Dex on track and to
interest the reader.

Note that he includes
his sources right in his
outline so he'll be sure
to weave them into
his paper.

Since his paper focuses on the visual rhetoric of McDonald's advertising in Asia, it is appropriate for Dex to include images in his outline. These images will serve as evidence for his argument. [Images were removed for copyright purposes but appeared in Dex's original outline.]

He includes a key research question as a transition into this section. His next subhead again uses language to convey this point in the progression of his argument; with such argumentative subheads, he can be certain that his argument is building in significance.

He is still working on points of the argument, even in the outline, as shown in his question whether to bring in Joe Kincheloe's argument as a secondary source here.

Now

- Rhetorical analysis of ads for 2003.

- Argument that McDonald's marketing strategy has evolved to embrace East Asia as an "assimilated market," as the campaign and slogan are standardized the world over. There is no longer a uniquely Asian campaign; instead it is replaced by the homogeneous American set of ads.

- Image of fun and relaxation is interspersed with images of McDonald's products. Using youth to drive the campaign is a clear signal of the target audience and the aim of creating a "cool" and "hip" image for the franchise. This contrasts the familial tone of ads from the "early days."

- Sources: McDonald's Country Websites

IV. Getting Behind the Arches

- Key Question: What has brought about this evolution in advertising strategies in East Asia? Why the shift in image?

- Argument: The dynamics of influence are mutual and interactive. Although McDonald's largely responds to perceived societal trends, it also seeks to influence attitudes and sell its version of "hip" or "cool," especially to Asian youth.

- Analyze how the Asian case is reflective of McDonald's marketing strategy internationally. Discuss the moral/ethical implications of such strategies.

- Consider the McDonald's "Culture of Power" argument in Kincheloe's book. Are the claims leveled against the franchise valid?

- Source: Kincheloe, Joe L. The Sign of the Burger: McDonald's and the Culture of Power. Philadelphia: Temple University Press, 2002.

IV. Amer-Asia? A Peek at the Future of Asia
- Summarize/recap the arguments of the paper.

Larger Questions
- Given the trend of increasing global integration, is homogenization under American leadership an inevitable end of modern civilization?
- Discuss ways in which this is not so ("dissenting opinion"). Asia's cultures continue to greatly influence McDonald's, causing wide variations between McDonald's image in Asia and in America.
- What are the implications of changing societal trends for Asian youth? How does McDonald's advertising affect and influence these trends? Do the ads exacerbate/speed up the "Americanization" of Asian youth? or merely reflect what is already present?

The final section is not titled "Conclusion" but instead uses an argumentative subhead to transition into the closing argument of the paper, namely that the presence of McDonald's is potentially changing distinctions between nations, blurring cultures into a combined identity Dex calls "Amer-Asia."

As you can see from Dex's example, using an appropriate metaphor in a subhead provides consistency in language that in turn can help the flow of your essay. Similarly, you can enhance the flow of your writing with careful attention to **transitions**—phrases that provide the connections between the paragraphs or sections in your paper. When creating transitions, even during your outlining phase, think about how you can signal the next idea, build on the previous idea, or reiterate the key terms of your thesis as you advance your argument. Many students like to think of the game of dominoes when composing transitions: each domino can only touch another domino with a matching number; two connects with two, three with three. Using this notion of progressive, connecting terms, you can incorporate transitions within sections of your outline to give it overall structure and flow. Then, when you turn to writing the paper, you will avoid big jumps in logic. Instead, by incorporating the transitions from your outline, you will produce a polished piece of written work.

COLLABORATIVE CHALLENGE

Using scissors, cut your outline into pieces so that each main subject heading (with its related subcategories) is on a separate piece of paper. For example, for a five-paragraph essay, you would end up with five pieces: an introduction, a piece for your first section, a piece for your second section, a piece for your third section, and a conclusion; for a research outline, you should have at least eight pieces. Be sure to cut *off* the heading numbers from each piece of paper to eliminate any sense of the way the headings were originally arranged on your outline. Now shuffle your pieces so they are out of order, and give them to your collaborative partners. Have your partners reassemble the pieces in the order they feel is most appropriate for your argument and then explain their reasons. Now discuss your original organization, and the rationale behind it.

Spotlight on Your Argument

As you turn now from writing an outline to fleshing out the full draft, consider the decision before you concerning what kind of voice or rhetorical stance to take in the language of your prose. Again, we can learn a lot from filmmakers as they face similar decisions.

In *Fahrenheit 9/11,* Michael Moore is careful to introduce and acknowledge his sources, but even while he includes many other voices in his film, he ultimately emphasizes his own argument. Of course, the film relies on research as background material, offering the narrator's comments as interview segments, in which a primary or secondary authority speaks directly to the audience, and as quoted material spoken directly by the narrator or through voice-over. But, as the promotional movie poster in Figure 6.5 suggests, Moore's opinion provides the foundation for everything disclosed in the film, making his rhetorical stance a prominent part of the text.

As you approach writing your paper, consider diverse ways to present your argument. Think of the power of a casting director on a film set. In a film such as Franco Zeffirelli's version of *Hamlet* (1990), for instance, the entire sexual politics of the narrative was influenced by the decision to cast Glenn Close (age 43 at the time) as Queen Gertrude, mother to Mel Gibson's Hamlet (Gibson was 34). Their close proximity in age set in relief an incest plot at which Shakespeare himself had only hinted. In essence, what audiences watched in the movie theater was less Shakespeare's *Hamlet* and more Zeffirelli's interpretation of it. In your own writing, you have a comparable power; the way you "cast" your sources can influence your reader's understanding of your argument.

In fact, your treatment of your sources will define your approach to your topic. Consider the "objectivity" of a celebrity biography shown on TV: although the text purports to offer no explicit argument, the selection of quotations used, the identities of people interviewed, and the emphasis given to certain stages of the artist's career collaborate to produce not some objective *truth* but a single *version* of that artist's life. Or think about Oliver Stone's *JFK* (1991) and the controversy it stirred. The film was in fact an argument: Stone used primary and secondary evidence to create his own interpretation of the events surrounding President John Kennedy's assassination. Even years after its release, *JFK* sparks heated debate; many of the film's most vocal critics continue to argue about the validity of Stone's version of events.

As seen in the examples presented here, sometimes you want to put your sources center stage and direct from behind the scenes, and sometimes you will want to step out of the shadows and articulate your argument more explicitly to the audience. Whichever way you go, you should decide what role you, the writer, will play in your paper. The key is to choose the role that

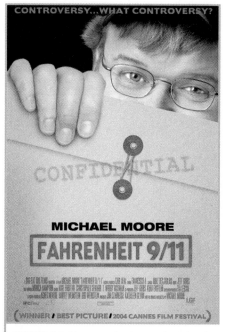

FIGURE 6.5. The promotional poster for *Fahrenheit 9/11* reveals the way Michael Moore emphasizes his own argument in the film.

will produce the most effective argument on your topic, one that fits the needs of your rhetorical situation. Your voice is your spotlight on your argument; it should have rhetorical purpose and complement the content of your project.

CREATIVE PRACTICE

Watch "Protesting the Protesters" through the link on the *Envision* Website. How does the filmmaker convey his opinion about the war protest? How does he direct the interplay between image and spoken word to reproduce his argument? How does his voice-over commentary function as a spotlight developing his research argument?

www.ablongman.com/envision/224

Working with Sources

After you decide on your approach to working with sources—as a strong explicit narrator or as the synthesizer of information—you need to start turning your outline into a rough draft. But how will you introduce and weave these other voices—your sources—into your written prose?

As you work on the balance between your sources and your own argument, you will need to include your sources not only appropriately (to avoid plagiarism) and strategically (to decide on how much of a presence you will have in the paper) but also purposefully (to provide a range of quotations and supporting evidence for your paper). We call this process **integrating sources,** and it's a complex process that occurs in three basic ways:

- **Summary:** synthesizing a great deal of information from a source
- **Paraphrase:** putting a source quotation into your own words
- **Direct quotation:** excerpting a specific passage from a source, enclosing it in quotation marks

AT A GLANCE

Reasons to Use Direct Quotation

- *Evidence:* The quotation provides tangible evidence for part of your argument.
- *Ethos:* The original author is a primary source or an expert on the subject, and including a direct quotation would increase the ethos of your argument.
- *Language:* The original author used memorable phrasing or has a particular voice that would be lost in paraphrase.

You'll want to alternate between methods while incorporating your sources with stylistic variety. This means knowing your options as a writer and selecting the best method for each rhetorical situation within your research essay. There is no single "correct" way to integrate sources. Instead, to accomplish the goal of purposeful citation with variation, you'll need to make some important choices. When should you paraphrase? insert a direct quote? summarize material? Your decisions will be dictated by the specific needs of each part of your argument, but there are some guidelines that you should follow.

If a quotation does not fit into any of the categories listed in the "At a Glance" box, consider paraphrasing or summarizing it. What you want to avoid is a paper dominated by unnecessary quotations; in such a case, your voice—what readers expect most in your paper—gets buried. It's similar to what happens in film when the filmmaker splices together too many different scenes; the audience becomes lost in the montage and can no longer follow the narrative. If you're worried that you have integrated too many sources (and lost your own voice), spend some time reviewing the draft and ask yourself:

- Am I still the moderator of this conversation?
- Is my voice clear, compelling, and original?
- Do I allow my own argument to emerge as foremost in this piece?

Source material should *support* your argument, not supplant it.

Integrating, Not Inserting, Quotations

But how, practically, do you go about integrating sources appropriately and effectively rather than simply inserting them? To work successfully with quotations, try using the three R's: *read, record, relate.*

Although a direct splice may be a successful film technique, in argumentative writing, we need clearer signposts of transition and context. Consider the stylistic options available to you to integrate sources by reading through the quotation examples from a paper on Al Gore's 2006 film about global warming, *An Inconvenient Truth.*

- **Using an introductory clause/phrase:** With this technique, the writer formally introduces the quote with a clause or phrase—one that often,

AT A GLANCE

How to Integrate Sources Appropriately and Effectively

- **Read.** Read a text carefully and actively, underlining passages that move you or suggest moments of deep meaning, or passages that might contribute to your argument/interpretation. If you are working with online texts, cut and paste the citation into a computer document, noting the paragraph number (for Websites) or page number (for regular texts) in parentheses. Always keep track of the page number and source information if you transcribe citations as you read.

You'll need this part in order to provide the citation in your writing.

- **Record.** Keep a notebook or an annotated computer file of quotes in which you *record* your reactions to a particular passage you've read. Does this passage move you? How so? Does it reveal the theme of the

text, the climax of the scene, the point of the argument, the purpose of the passage? Always engage critically with a citation, developing your reason for including it later.

You'll need this part in order to provide your interpretation of the citation.

- **Relate.** Place the citation and your interpretation in an appropriate place in your essay. Where in the paragraph should the quotation and the comment appear? What is around it? above it? after it? Make sure that you *relate* the inserted text to the material that precedes and follows your citation and interpretation. Never just "stick in a quote" without explanation and strategic placement.

You'll need this part in order to achieve the most successful quotation integration.

but not always, refers to the author and/or the original text title. For example:

> Reacting strongly to the environmentalist message, online columnist Joseph Blast argues, "'An Inconvenient Truth' contains very little truth, and a big helping of propaganda."

- **Using an incorporated structure:** Using this strategy, the writer seamlessly melds the quotation into a sentence of the essay so that it flows smoothly with the rest of the prose. For example:

> Joseph Blast articulated one of the most common critiques of Al Gore's global warming film in a June 2006 online editorial when he claimed that "'An Inconvenient Truth' contains very little truth, and a big helping of propaganda."

- **Using an interrupted structure:** In this variation on the previous two models, the writer breaks the quote into two halves, embedding information regarding the author and/or the original text in the middle of the quotation itself. For example:

> "In the style of a previous generation of propaganda films," Joseph Blast argues in his June 2006 editorial, "Gore substitutes vivid images of the alleged effects of global warming for an accurate account of the scientific debate."

- **Using an end comment:** In this technique, the writer inserts the quotation and then provides an interpretation, or closing comment, that importantly advances the argument. For example:

> Joseph Blast's claim that "'An Inconvenient Truth' contains very little truth, and a big helping of propaganda" exemplifies the critical tendency to undermine the legitimacy of an opposing point of view by categorizing it as "propaganda."

Experiment with these strategies in your own writing to determine which best serves your rhetorical purpose. For instance, if you want to draw attention to the *author* of a quotation to add ethos to your argument, you might opt to integrate using an introductory clause; however, if you want to emphasize *information* rather than authorship, an incorporated structure might be more effective. One key to remember is to avoid overusing any one type of integration strategy; otherwise, your writing style might become monotonous, like a film that relies too heavily on the same types of shots.

Documentation During Integration

As you incorporate sources into your draft, be sure to include citations for each quotation or paraphrase. This would also be a good time to begin drafting your works-cited list or bibliography, to save time later. The purpose of this is not only to provide a "list of credits" for your references but also to supply interested readers with the resources to continue learning about your topic. Just as you undoubtedly found certain articles inspiring while investigating your topic and used them as springboards for more focused research, so too might your paper serve as a means of leading your readers to intriguing ideas and articles. You can go back over the correct format for citations in your final edit, following the guidelines in Chapter 9 for documentation to do so.

AT A GLANCE

Final Check for Integrating Sources

- Did you *introduce the quote* in various ways?
- Did you *link the reference* to your argument to show the relevance?
- Did you *comment* on it afterward to advance your argument?
- Did you *cite* it properly using the appropriate documentation style for your subject area?

COLLABORATIVE CHALLENGE

To check if you need to cite information you've paraphrased, or if you are worried about citing information that is "common knowledge," you can ask your roommate or your peer review partner to assess your outline or draft. Any passage that stands out as unfamiliar should be marked with a highlighter. Then return the favor by examining your reader's work in progress with highlighter in hand. You can help point out to your peers what knowledge is most probably not readily available to you (or other readers) without the help of sources. Your peer reviewers can also point out material that is "common knowledge" and doesn't need to be cited.

AT A GLANCE

Strategies for Drafting

- **Following the linear path:** Start at the beginning, write the introduction, and then move sequentially through each point of argument.

- **Fleshing out the outline:** Gradually transform the outline into a full draft, moving from a keyword outline to a prose outline by systematically expanding each of the sections; as you add more detail, the keywords fall away, leaving behind drafted paragraphs.

- **Writing from the middle:** Start writing from a point of greatest strength or start with a section you can complete easily; then write around it and fill out sections as you go.

- **Freewrite and then reverse outline:** First, produce pages of freewriting; then compose a detailed **reverse outline** in which you record the point of every paragraph to assess the argument's flow and structure; and finally, reorder and rewrite the paper multiple times until it begins to take the proper form for the argument.

Drafting Your Research Argument

As you continue to forge ahead with your research argument, turning from an outline to a full draft or composing sections of your argument in separate time blocks, realize that there are many strategies for getting it done. For each of these ways of working, the key is to start and then just keep writing. Try out one of the many methods described in the "At a Glance" box.

Also realize that to write is to struggle with the process, as noted by Stanford psychologist David Rasch: "Almost all writers are familiar with the experience of feeling stuck, blocked, overwhelmed, or behind schedule in their writing." What can help? Staying motivated and relying on others.

Keeping Your Passion

As you move deeper into the writing process, integrating quotations and working out the flow of your argument, don't lose sight of your enthusiasm for your subject. Reread your earliest freewrites and your entries in your research log. What goals, what motivations prompted you to begin the project? What aspects of your topic excited you, angered you, or inspired you? What contribution did you imagine yourself making to this discussion? As you begin synthesizing your information and creating a unified argument, you are in effect realizing that initial vision. Remember, your audience will be reading your paper to learn *your* particular point of view on the subject. Your drafts are your shooting scripts, if you will—the versions of your paper that ultimately you will transform, through careful review, editing, and revision, into your "release" of the text into final form.

You should also allow yourself well-needed energy breaks. Brief periods away from the writing process can often recharge and reinvigorate your approach to the paper and help you think through difficult points in the argument. Ironically, a pause in drafting can also help you avoid writer's block by allowing you to remember what interested you about this project in the first place. Finally, if you are having trouble getting through the draft process, allow yourself to write what Anne Lamott, author of *Bird by Bird,* famously calls the "shitty first draft." In the words of Anne Lamott, "All good writers write them. This is how they end up with good second drafts and terrific third drafts." In other words, you should realize that the first version by no means has to be perfect or even close to what the final paper will look like. It is instead simply your first attempt at getting your ideas on paper. Freeing yourself to write something—anything—can help you escape from the weight of perfectionism or the fear of failure that often paralyzes writers. You will have plenty of opportunities to rework the material, show your draft to others, and move forward with the writing process.

Collaboration Through Peer Review

In addition, take advantage of the community of writers in your class to talk through your ideas and share work in progress. You might find your organizational plan confirmed by your peers, or you might be pleasantly surprised by their suggestions for alternative structures, ways of integrating sources, or images to include in the paper. Such discussions can help you get back your fire for your project as well as give you extremely useful advice to implement in the writing of the draft. Moreover, your peers' responses to your work in progress can help you determine if your writing is persuasive or not.

Consider how collaboration works in the film industry. Even though a film is generally recognized as a unified expression of a single idea, in reality it is the product of the collaborative effort of dozens of individuals, from the screenwriter and actors to the key grips and camera operators. But there is another, often less recognized collaborator: the audience. Think about how novels are adapted to the large screen: whether by adding a romantic subplot or substituting a "Hollywood ending" for a less palatable one, many scriptwriters deliberately revise original texts to accommodate the perceived desires of a mass audience. Sometimes an entire narrative is recast to make it more marketable; the 1995 hit, *Clueless*, and the 2001 teen film *O,* are good examples of films in which literary classics (Jane Austen's *Emma* and William Shakespeare's *Othello*) were updated to appeal to a mainstream modern audience.

Sometimes the audience's intervention is more direct. It is common practice for many filmmakers to hold "advance screenings" of major releases, designed to gauge audience reaction. In 1986, a preview audience's reaction to the ending of the film *Fatal Attraction* was so negative that director Adrian Lyne reshot the final scenes. When the film was released in the following year, it featured a markedly different conclusion. Similarly, the version of *BladeRunner* released in 1982 was significantly edited in an attempt to increase its box office appeal; however, director Ridley Scott changed the ending yet again years later, premiering his *BladeRunner—The Director's Cut* 11 years after the movie first appeared. In each case, collaboration shaped the final version and made evident the rhetorical triangle between audience, writer, and text. Similarly, writing needs to take into consideration the audience's expectations; we write to show an audience our work, so we need to respond to audience needs when we write and revise our texts.

As a writer you can benefit from "advance screenings" of your argument; the collaborative work you do on the structure and content of your outlines and drafts should guide you to a revised product that satisfies both you and your audience. But to do so, you need feedback from your audience in the form of peer review; then you will need to revise your draft to accommodate the suggestions you receive.

Consider the draft written by Sunthar Premakumar about the words within songs of Bollywood cinema, an Indian film genre that involves many long dancing numbers similar to Broadway musicals. Sunthar was curious about the messages in the song lyrics and the reasons the films are so popular (nearly twice as many are produced annually as Hollywood films) despite taxing demands of time and corniness on their audiences. He conducted a range of academic and field research, wrote a detailed outline, and then composed his first draft, keeping his passion in view. He would go on to revise the draft substantially by incorporating feedback from his teacher and his peers. But his first draft shows how you, too, can overcome your concerns and get your research argument down on paper.

Premakumar 1

Sunthar Premakumar

PWR2: Cross Cultural Rhetoric

Dr. Alyssa O'Brien

Research Paper—Draft

February 21, 2006

Bollywood Sing-Along

Introduction

I am sitting at the movie theatre in Sri Lanka with my family excited to watch the newly released Bollywood movie Yuva. The theatre is packed with people who have pledged the next three hours of their life to this movie, the latest hit film of the year. While everyone is busy eating their pop corn, the lights get dimmer in preparation for the screening of the movie. As the title is displayed the crowd starts cheering enthusiastically with young boys whistling as loud as they could. A five minute song follows the title by which time the crowd is already on its feet dancing to the upbeat tune. The crazy frenzy finally dies down as the crazy fans finally settle into their seats; a few minutes after the song had concluded. There is a long silence in the audience for a while as they are indulged in the intricate love story which involves six different characters. The whole love plot requires three hours to be developed

---

Sunthar's draft title identifies his topic, but it does not yet indicate his argument. His revised paper addresses the "What about it?" question through a subtitle that reveals his sharper focus.

Sunthar chose an organizational strategy in which he opens with a personal narrative. He thereby enables his readers to understand the power of Bollywood movies on an audience.

The details in Sunthar's opening paragraph set up the key elements he'll explore in the research paper: the complicated plot lines, the long songs, and the magical allure of Bollywood films as a genre.

effectively and intense concentration on the viewers' part for complete comprehension. However the random song and dance sequences that occur at frequent intervals absorb some of the tension accumulated through this intense plot. Twenty minutes into the movie the crowds go wild again. The hit number of the movie had just begun and in the spur of the moment the audience suddenly transforms into a giant chorus to start singing along with the song. Silence follows the song once again.

This procedure repeats many times over and finally the credits of the movie are displayed. As we walk out, my sister asked me what I thought of the movie and I respond with my usual 'the songs were amazing but the movie wasn't good'. This would have been the two hundredth time that I had responded in this manner, but I would still go to watch more movies. Why? Well, the great songs would transform an ordinary movie into an extraordinary movie and thus making the time worth the while. However, I always wonder why these Bollywood film songs attract such fans like me and my friends time and time again.

Bollywood: An overview

Before we further explore the reasons behind the attractive force of these film songs, it is important to understand the nature of such songs. India is home to many 'ollywoods' such as Mollywood, Tollywood and Bollywood. The word Tollywood refers to the not-so- well know Telugu film industry in India. The word Mollywood is not used too much, however it refers to the Tamil film industry in South India.

Named after the Indian city renowned for movies, Bombay (now called Mumbai), Bollywood is the most prominent one of the three and is usually used to represent the entire Indian film industry. In his article

In this draft, Sunthar ends his introduction by posing one of his key research questions: why do people watch Bollywood films if the movies really aren't very good? He then states his hypothesis: that the music transforms an ordinary movie into an extraordinary one. During his final revision, he will develop this line into a substantial thesis paragraph, allowing readers to contemplate his argument in full and making them curious to read on and learn more about his claims.

Sunthar uses an argumentative subhead to set up his next section: providing background on Bollywood films.

Premakumar 3

titled "Bollywood", author Alex Ninian gives and overview of the
Bollywood industry in a nutshell.

> On average, 800 films are produced and distributed every year, that
> is more than two per day, and shown to 11,000,000 people every day
> in 13,000 cinemas across India. To these statistics can be added the
> export of film to over a hundred countries where they are watched by
> millions of expatriate Indians, or NRIs (non resident Indians), mostly
> in Britain, the United States, and Europe. (235)

All these movies have many similarities such as abundant singing
and dancing, cheesy love stories and unbelievable action sequences
while catering towards the regional tastes. These elements differentiate
the Indian movies from the ones made by its western counterparts,
Hollywood. One might wonder why these songs have such an attractive
impact on its audience and whether this attraction is used constructively
to achieve something that transcends into ones daily life.

Indian film music has influential power on its Indian audience
due its immense appeal to the public through the upbeat rhythms and
classical tunes that are present in most of these songs. However, these
film songs fail to make a revolutionary impact on the community since
the public is more attracted to the entertaining dance numbers and
don't pay much attention to the important message conveyed through
the lyrics of the songs.

Religion and Music

It is interesting that music has such a power over the public in
South Asia. The reason for this seems to be the importance given to
religion and religious practices in this part of the world. Since the time

---

Sunthar integrates his research effectively, not relying on sources too much. He introduces his source and gives a brief summary of the point before providing a direct quotation of statistical information that proves his point about the popularity of Bollywood cinema

Sunthar has buried his thesis, though he has buried it at the end of the second section of his paper. However writing his thesis out is still a helpful first step in clarifying his argument; during revision, he can circle it and then, when he writes his next draft, he can move it up earlier into his introduction. When he does so, he'll also need to strengthen his transition to his next section.

Premakumar 4

I was born, music and religion have been integral parts of my life. My religion, Hinduism, has been instrumental in shaping my interest in music since from a young age I have been made to sing many spiritual songs during Hindu festivals. This is not just unique to me but rather something that I have in common with most of my friends in Sri Lanka, the country where I am from. The close relationship between music and religion is explained well by the famous Indian Sitar player, Pundit Ravi Shanker, in his book *"My Music, My Life"* as the following:

> Many people have asked me if one must read, absorb, learn, and know about India's religions, philosophies, and spiritual atmosphere, or even come to India to visit and travel in order to understand our music, let alone play it. To this I would say yes, all this is necessary since our music is so closely connected to the complete unfolding of India's history and development. (Shanker 9)

In most Indian religions such as Hinduism, which is the most prominent religion in India, music one of the main tools that are used to promote spirituality and religious values. Most of the religious songs advocate love toward God and mankind while addressing importance social issues. It helps to guide the devotee towards nirvana by destroying his ungodly qualities, such as hatred, selfishness. Therefore there are numerous songs in Hinduism that focus on helping the follower to get rid of these bad qualities.

* * *

Integrating another key source, Sunthar opts for the block quote. He doesn't have the MLA format for block quotes down correctly yet, but it's crucial for him to integrate this source so he can continue to write in what we have been calling "a conversation" with his sources.

Sunthar forgets to comment on the quote after integrating it. That is, he needs to explain the evidence he has offered and then relate it to his argument before moving forward in his paper. He does a wonderful job revising this portion for his final paper, as you can see in the full version of his revision on the Envision Website.

As you notice from the draft excerpt here, Sunthar decided to use the pronoun "I" throughout his paper. His instructor suggested that he deploy the pronoun consistently, not to present unfounded opinion but to make a point based on his research or unique personal experience. The "I" has

AT A GLANCE

Questions for Assessing Your Draft

- **Argument consistency:** Are your introduction and conclusion arguing the same points, or have you changed your argument by the end? Either revise the end to be consistent with your original thinking, or embrace your new vision and rework the beginning.

- **Organization and progression:** Does your paper flow logically, developing one idea seamlessly into the next? Do you provide important theoretical foundations, definitions, or background at the beginning of the paper to guide the audience through the rest of your argument?

- **Your voice versus sources:** Do you foreground your own argument in your paper or

do you focus primarily on your sources' arguments, locating your point of view primarily in the conclusion? If the latter is true, bring your voice out more in commentaries on the quotations.

- **Information:** Are there any holes in your research? Do you need to supplement your evidence with additional research, interviews, surveys, or other source materials?

- **Opposition and concession:** Do you adequately address opposing arguments? Do you integrate your opposition into your argument (i.e., deal with them as they arise), or have you constructed a single paragraph that addresses opposing opinions?

authority in these cases, but if you are not sure if you should use it in your paper, talk with your instructor about your options.

Revising Your Draft

As many professional writers can attest—and Sunthar would agree with this based on his drafting experience—a text goes through numerous drafts on its way to becoming a polished final product. Even filmmakers produce multiple drafts of their movies before they release their film, experimenting with different sequencing, camera shots, and pacing to create what they consider to be the fulfillment of their artistic vision. We've all seen the results of this process: deleted scenes or *outtakes* from popular film or television programs. What these segments represent are moments of work (writing, producing, and shooting) that, after review and editing, were removed to streamline the film.

As you might imagine, often it's difficult or even painful to reshape your work during revision; it's hard to leave some of your writing behind on the cutting room floor. However, as your project develops, its focus may change: sources or ideas that seemed important to you during the early stages of research may become less relevant, even tangential; a promising strategy of argumentation may turn out to be less suitable to your project; a key transition may be no longer necessary once you reorganize the argument. As you turn to your draft with a critical eye, what you should find is that in order to transform your paper into the best possible written product, you'll need to move beyond proofreading or editing and into the realm of macro changes, or **revision**.

That's not to suggest that proofreading is not a necessary part of the revision process; it is. Careless grammatical and punctuation errors and spelling mistakes can damage your ethos as an author, and they need to be corrected. It is very probable that you've been doing such microrevision throughout the drafting process—editing for style, grammar, punctuation, and spelling. However, sometimes it's difficult to do *broader revisions* until you have a substantial part of your paper written. It is only once your argument starts coming together that you can recognize the most productive ways to modify it in order to optimize its effectiveness. This is the key to successful revision: you have to be open to *both* microediting and large-scale, multiple revisions. Think of this process as **re-vision,** or seeing it again with new eyes, seeing it in a new light.

Let's look at decisions some students made during the revision process:

- **Draft:** Reading over her draft about the propagandistic elements in World War II films, Jennifer realized that she had gotten so caught up in presenting background information that her paper read more like a historical report than an argument.

  Revision: Jennifer sharpened her focus, cut down on some of the background information, and brought her own argument to the forefront.

- **Draft:** Miranda had the opposite problem; in her draft she made a compelling argument about the literary status of graphic novels but did not really quote from or mention any of her sources, so she wasn't showcasing her work as a researcher.

  Revision: She more prominently integrated her source material into her argument, both by referring to specific authors and articles she had read and by using additional direct quotations. In doing so, she greatly increased her ethos and the persuasiveness of her argument.

- **Draft:** After drafting her paper on hip-hop and gender identity, Sharita realized that her thesis was too broad and that in trying to cover both male and female imagery, she wasn't able to be specific enough to craft a really persuasive argument.

  Revision: Realizing that her interest really lay in exploring the conflicted stereotype of powerful, sexualized women in hip-hop videos, Sharita cut large sections of her paper revolving around the male imagery and focused on the female. The result was a provocative argument based on concrete, persuasive examples.

- **Draft:** Max, a dedicated Mac user, wrote his draft on the aesthetics of design in the Apple product line. The first version of his paper was visually stunning, detailed, and eloquently written. But it was so one sided that it read more like a marketing brochure than an academic argument.

  Revision: His task in revision was to provide a more balanced perspective on the Apple computer phenomenon. After further research, he incorporated a greater diversity of perspectives in his paper and softened some of his language to be less biased in favor of Apple products.

As these examples indicate, you need to enter into the research process looking not just for mistakes to "fix" but also for larger issues that might relate to your structure, your thesis, your scope, or the development of your ideas.

In addition to your own assessment of your writing, you should take into account **peer evaluations** of your drafts; consider your peer review sessions "advance screenings" with your audience. Sometimes you'll find that your peer reviewers vocalize ideas that echo your own concerns about your draft; other times you may be surprised by their reactions. Do keep in mind that their comments are informed *suggestions,* not mandates; your task, as the writer, is to assess the feedback you receive and implement those changes that seem to best address the needs of both your argument and your audience. Like the filmmaker looking to transform a creative vision into a box office hit, you want to reach your audience without sacrificing your own voice or argument in the process.

One way to facilitate a productive peer session is to use directed peer review questions for one-on-one discussions of your draft, rather than to rely exclusively on oral comments. When exchanging drafts with a peer group, you also may find it helpful to attach a cover memo that points your readers to specific questions you have about your draft so that they can customize their responses to address the particular issues that concern you as a writer.

COLLABORATIVE CHALLENGE

Form a peer review group to exchange the drafts of your research papers. Read your peer reviewers' papers carefully, annotating them with **constructive feedback**—positively framed suggestions about what might be changed and why. You might also complete the questions from the "Checklist for Peer Editing the First Draft" on the *Envision* Website. Then meet with your group and talk about both the strengths in the papers and suggestions for improvement. Next, go back to your computer and revise your paper. Bring a new version to class and exchange your second draft with a group composed of one new reader and one reader who was part of your group for the first draft. Again, read the drafts and write comments on them. This time, complete the questions on the *Envision* Website for the "Checklist for Peer Editing the Second Draft." Meet with your group and consider carefully the responses from both your new reader and your repeat reviewer. What do the suggestions have in common? How has your revision strengthened your argument? What further revisions do your peers suggest? Finally, discuss the extent to which audience feedback factors into your revision process.

www.ablongman.com/envision/225

Let's return now to Sunthar's draft paper and see how he used the peer review suggestions he received to revise the sections we examined earlier.

Premakumar 1

Sunthar Premakumar

PWR2: Cross Cultural Rhetoric

Dr. Alyssa O'Brien

Research Paper—Final

March 8, 2006

Bollywood Sing-Along:

The significance of Music in the Indian Film Industry

Introduction

First, Sunthar added a subtitle to indicate the focus of his research argument.

He made microedits to punctuate and still uses descriptive language that makes his writing vivid and memorable.

I am sitting at the movie theatre in Sri Lanka with my family, excited to watch the newly released Bollywood movie Yuva. The theater is packed with people who have pledged the next three hours of their lives to this movie, the latest hit film of the year. While everyone is busy eating their popcorn, the lights get dimmer in preparation for the screening of the movie. As the title is displayed, the crowd starts cheering enthusiastically, with young boys whistling

Premakumar 2

as loud as they can. A five-minute song follows the title, by which time the crowd is already on its feet dancing to the upbeat tune. The crazy frenzy finally dies down as the fans finally settle into their seats, a few minutes after the song has concluded. There is a long silence in the audience for a while as they are indulged in the intricate love story that involves six different characters. The whole love plot requires three hours to be developed effectively and intense concentration on the viewers' part for complete comprehension. However, the random song and dance sequences that occur at frequent intervals absorb some of the tension accumulated through this intense plot. Twenty minutes into the movie the crowds go wild again. The hit number of the movie had just begun and in the spur of the moment the audience suddenly transforms into a giant chorus to start singing along with the song. Silence follows the song once again.

This procedure repeats many times over, until finally there is an intermission an hour and a half into the movie. As we walk out to buy a drink, my sister asks me what I think of the movie, and I respond with my usual "the songs were amazing but the movie doesn't seem too good". This may be the two hundredth time that I have responded in this manner, but I will still go to watch more movies.

At this point, I began wondering about this strange mindset that I have about Indian film songs. I began wondering why these songs have such an impact on their audience. If they do have such a strong influence on their large audience, is it used constructively to make an important impact on the Indian community? Are the producers and music directors using this music as a medium of

In this revision Sunthar incorporated advice from his peers and added several additional research questions. He also elevated his language, making it more academic in tone and word choice. In this way, he sets readers up for his argument by introducing his key argumentative terms right from the beginning.

Highlighted in yellow, the key terms of his argument revolve around his curiosity about the power of songs—words and music—to impact a community. He questions how song works as a form of persuasion. He wonders

Premakumar 3

if the words can bring about change in listening audiences.

persuasion to bring about a change in the society? Do these songs serve a purpose greater than entertainment? These interesting questions motivated me to pursue the answer to these questions.

In this final revision, Sunthar expanded his one-line hypothesis into a thesis paragraph, a full articulation of argument. Notice how specific his thesis is: he lists how songs appeal through rhythm but then claims fail to make what he calls a "revolutionary" impact. Notice how he resists telling readers what the effect is—he keeps that surprise for his conclusion.

Even though Indian film music has influential power on its Indian audience due to its immense appeal to the public through the upbeat rhythms and classical tunes that are present in most of these songs, these film songs fail to make a revolutionary impact on the community because the public is more attracted to the entertaining dance numbers and do not pay much attention to the important message conveyed through the lyrics of the songs. However, these songs do fulfill their purpose as a source of entertainment that cheers up its audience by having a positive effect on their mindset.

Religion and Music

It is interesting that music has such a power over the public in South Asia. This is due to the importance given to religion and religious practices and the close connection between music and religion in this part of the world. Since the time I was born, music and religion have been integral parts of my life. My religion, Hinduism, has been instrumental in shaping my interest in music from a young age because I have been made to sing many spiritual songs during Hindu festivals throughout my life. This is not unique to me but rather something that I have in common with most of my friends in Sri Lanka. The close relationship between music and religion is explained well by the famous Indian Sitar player Pundit Ravi Shankar in his book My Music, My Life:

For his revision, he decided to move the background section about Bollywood to later in the paper to emphasize here instead his argument's focus on religion and music in history. In this way, his paper flows better from the previous paragraph, where his last point was about music and audiences.

Many people have asked me if one must read, absorb, learn, and know about India's religions, philosophies, and spiritual atmosphere, or even come to India to visit and travel in order to

Premakumar 4

understand our music, let alone play it. To this I would say yes, all this is necessary since our music is so closely connected to the complete unfolding of India's history and development. (9)

Thus, Shanker explains how religion is an important component of understanding Indian music, while at the same time music is an important part of religion. In most Indian religions, such as Hinduism, music has been one of the main tools used to promote spirituality and religious values. Most of these religious songs advocate love toward God and mankind while addressing importance social issues. These songs are composed to help guide a follower toward nirvana by getting rid of his undesirable qualities, such as hatred and selfishness. Therefore, these songs had the potential to motivate a community to change for the better, a common quality found in most Indian classical music songs.

Classical Music

Most classical songs, like their spiritual counterparts, have strong messages embedded within them. The two eminent forms of classical music found in India are Hindustani and Carnatic music forms. Both Hindustani music, which is practiced in North India, and Carnatic music, which is practiced in South India, include many inspirational songs in their repertoires. All Indian dance forms are accompanied by one of the above-mentioned types of classical music during performances. The combination of music and dance in movies was inspired by these classical forms of dance and music. The early movies included only the pure form of Indian classical dance and music.

However, over the years the Western film industry has influenced Bollywood, which was more than willing to adopt Western elements to

Once again, Sunthar integrates his research, this time using proper MLA style: he includes only the page number since he has already mentioned the author's name above, and he eliminates the unnecessary quotation marks that he included around the block quotes in his draft.

Most importantly, Sunthar paraphrases the point of this quoted source so that readers understand the importance to the argument. He then broadens his claim to give more general information about the importance of music in his community.

Sunthar sets up his next section with a transition word, (highlighted) foreshadowing his focus on "classical music."

In this section, he provides background research knowledge to instruct his readers about the history of Indian music and then transitions into the background information on Bollywood as a film genre that had been located much closer to his introduction in his final draft. This new organization helps him reinforce his emphasis on the

Premakumar 5

impact of the words of
Bollywood movie songs
on the audience—
rather than on the
history of film itself.

attract a larger audience. With the development of new technologies, the music industry in India started shifting more toward a fusion path, incorporating Western and Eastern styles. Before talking about Bollywood in detail, it is important to have an overview of this industry and its imperial impact on the Indian community.

India is home to many "ollywoods," such as Mollywood, Tollywood, and Bollywood. The word Tollywood refers to the not-so-well-know Telugu film industry in India. The word Mollywood is not used too much; however, it refers to the Tamil film industry in South India. Named after the Indian city renowned for movies, Bombay (now called Mumbai), Bollywood is the most prominent term of the three and is usually used to represent the entire Indian film industry. In his article titled "Bollywood," author Alex Ninian gives an overview of the Bollywood industry in a nutshell:

He relies on an impor-
tant source he found
during his research.
This one presents
a concise overview
of the popularity of
Bollywood films, so
Sunthar includes a
direct quote here.

On average, 800 films are produced and distributed every year, that is more than two per day, and shown to 11,000,000 people every day in 13,000 cinemas across India. To these statistics can be added the export of film to over a hundred countries where they are watched by millions of expatriate Indians, or NRIs (non resident Indians), mostly in Britain, the United States, and Europe. (235)

Contemporary Film Music

The transformation of Indian film music into its present influential form started in 1993 with the introduction of the music director A. R. Rahman, who single-handedly changed the face of the Indian music industry with his amazing ability to fuse the two kinds of music with the aid of technology in a manner that attracted a huge audience in India. This was a major turning point in the Indian music industry.

Premakumar 6

Since 1993, this reformed version of film music has had a great impact on the general public in India. "Many people go for movies just to watch the wonderful upbeat songs included in them," said Arunan Skanthan, a film music lover in Sri Lanka, explaining the strong appeal these movies have on the public. In India music is played everywhere. From formalized concerts and shows to the songs played over the radio on the street corner, this music seems to flow into every Indian's ears most of the time. As George E. Ruckert states in his book Music in North India:

> In India, one never gets too far from either tea or the sound of Lata's (Lata Mangeshkar is a famous India play-back singer) voice, although today it is mixed with other voices from the films, and popular selections from famous ghazal and bhajan singers, or the energetic qawwalalis of the late Nusrat Fateh Ali Khan. (2)

Music in India seems to be everywhere and one cannot escape its influence.

With the emergence of film music, the focus on classical music has somewhat diminished over the years, although it still attracts quite a few music enthusiasts. However the reason why more and more people in India prefer film music over the traditional forms is that an appreciation of classical music requires formal training or prior knowledge, while film music does not. The increasing popularity of film music encourages most musicians to abandon their classical practice and pursue a career in play-back singing for movies. Renowned classical singers such as Hariharan and Unni Krishnan, who hail from Hinustani and Carnatic music traditions, respectfully, are in the forefront of film music and rarely perform classical music.

Although the argument is flowing nicely here, Sunthar shows that he is having what we call "a dialogue with his sources" by weaving one into the next as evidence for his paper. Included in his research iceberg were books, online articles, journal articles, and four interviews.

Most youngsters who start learning Indian classical music do not intend to become professional classical singers but rather want to become play-back singers for film songs. As a result of this mindset, film music is gaining more influence on the Indian public than its classical predecessor. However, film music does not use this influencing power to advocate social values, something that classical music did effectively during its time as an influential medium.

A Music Director's View on Film Songs

At this point, Sunthar introduces one of his key sources: an interview with the famous music director A. R. Rahman, who happened to be visiting the area and giving a talk during the time of Sunthar's research process. Sunthar was able to conduct field research with this authority and use those quotes in his final paper.

During my research I had the great honor of meeting the Indian music director A. R. Rahman, who is considered to be the best music director in India. During my interview with him I got the chance to obtain his thoughts about the role played by these film songs. During the conversation with him I asked him whether he makes a conscious effort to include messages in his songs. He responded, "I try sometimes if the scope of the movie lets me to do it, but most of the times the producers want commercial dance numbers and that is what I have to deliver." He also mentioned that songs of such nature require a lot of time and attention to make, and in an industry for which he is expected to make many songs a month, it is nearly impossible to invest considerable time into one song.

Just as in his draft, Sunthar continues to use "I," allowing his readers to identify with his research discoveries and begin to be persuaded by his developing argument.

This was a surprising reply to me since I was hoping that he would accept my view that some of the songs in the movies actually carry an important message regarding a social or ethnic issue. Although this is not completely false, it is interesting to see that movie producers and music directors don't try to include songs of this nature but rather prefer the dance numbers.

Premakumar 8

However, A. R. Rahman's first solo album, Vandae Mataram, which was not part of any movie but rather was like any other album, was a huge success in India. This album focused mainly on uniting the different provinces in India to bring about a love for the nation. Vandae Mataram, which means tribute to motherland, was made for the fiftieth anniversary of Indian independence and has sold many copies worldwide. When asked about this album and its effect on people, A. R. Rahman commented that it was made for such a purpose and thus a lot of time was put into making sure that it was "inspiring and powerful." Therefore, one can observe that it is not impossible to achieve this purpose but rather it is the thought and motivation that is required to make the film songs a powerful tool for social reform. Having listened to numerous film songs it was amazing to see the ratio between dance numbers and motivational songs that are prevalent in these movies. The motivational songs are highly outnumbered by the dance numbers.

Sunthar draws logical conclusions from analyzing his evidence. He advances his argument by bringing in his own direct experience and analysis of films and songs, and then he leads readers to his preliminary conclusion, highlighted in yellow.

The Appeal of Songs to the Bollywood Audience

Are the producers and the music directors the only ones to be blamed for the misuse of such a powerful medium of persuasion? It seems that the audience should share blame as well. During an interview with Stuti Goswamy, a junior at Stanford University majoring in economics, I was able to get a good insight as to why so many Indians are crazy over Bollywood songs. Stuti stated that she loves listening to Bollywood songs, dancing to the beats, and singing along with the tunes. When asked whether she feels that these songs carry a strong message, she replied that she usually doesn't pay much attention to the lyrics because most of the songs

Using a question to signal a turn in his argument, he transitions to the next two sections of his paper, in which he will present the evidence of his extensive field research.

Premakumar 9

Specifically, Sunthar incorporates field research that he conducted on campus with some of his fellow students, as evidence for his argument about the impact of words and songs on an audience.

she listens to are dance numbers. When asked whether she pays attention to motivational songs like "bharat hum ko" (a famous motivational song from the movie Roja) she said that she is not fluent enough in Hindi to actually understand the intricate details mentioned in the song.

This is a common phenomenon in these Bollywood films, with both dance numbers made up of simple lyrics and motivational songs using rare words in Hindi that are rich in meaning but are not commonly used in public. Therefore, these motivational songs are not easily accessible to the common folk in India and to the second-generation Indians living abroad. Ironically, these motivational songs are usually targeted toward the common folk in India. For example, the song "malarodu malar," from the famous movie Bombay, addresses the conflicts between religious groups and advocates harmony between religions. However, the poet who wrote the lyrics for this song uses complicated metaphors and deep words to make the song sound pretty and thus makes it hard for the commoner to comprehend it fully. Another example is the song "jana gana mana," from the movie Aayitha Ezhuthu, which is a song that inspires students to get involved with government and social issues. Many who listen to this song for its upbeat rhythm and amazing tune do not understand the entire message embedded in the lyrics because the rhythm and tune overshadow the lyrics.

These shortcomings and the huge demand for dance numbers force most of the producers and music directors in India to abandon the idea of including motivational songs, focusing instead on producing what the audience demands.

Premakumar 10

Parallel Movie Industries in India

Second-year masters student Amritha Appaswami had some interesting insight regarding the other film industries in India that were not as popular as Bollywood: . . .

* * *

Roopa Mahadevan, a first-year masters student at Stanford University, mentioned that most of the "parallel cinemas" (movie industries that do not come under the classification of Bollywood) are based on some important social issue. However, since these movies, which are usually in English, only attract upper-class Indians, they remain underground most of the time and the general public rarely gets to know about them. Roopa commented that the reason for this occurrence was the mindset of most moviegoers in India. She said that most of the people who go to the theaters in India to watch movies are those who live under the poverty line, and the reason they watch these movies is to escape into an alternate reality where everyone is happy and miracles always occur. For them this is the relief after long days of struggles and worries. Therefore, Roopa argued, it is important that these movies are entertaining and have a lot of upbeat songs for the viewing pleasure of the audience. Echoing the nature of the audiences that view most of these movies, Roopa also stated that directors wouldn't concentrate too much on making a movie with a profound message when the majority of their audiences are uneducated.

Conclusion

As the crowd gets ready for the next part of the movie, I walk in slowly with a drink in one hand and popcorn in the other. My

In this section Sunthar discusses parallel texts—other film industries—and presents more of his field research. Note that the asterisks here indicate that we have included only a portion of this section; the full paper is available online through the *Envision* Website.

Building off the field research, Sunthar advances his final argumentative point: that films serve as entertainment and even distraction, but the message of words in the music slips in nonetheless.

As he turns to the conclusion, Sunthar returns to the opening frame of his paper—the personal narrative. He embeds his final argument within this narrative, making it quite clear to readers that though the songs' revolutionary messages may not be discerned by the viewing audience, the films nevertheless give audiences a hopeful escape from the troubles they experience in their lives.

mind is still wondering about the purpose of these film songs as I look around to see whether I see any familiar faces in the audience. Even though I'm disappointed in not finding any, I notice many happy faces that are having a great time at the movie cinema after a long day at work. Then it suddenly strikes me that this could be the purpose of these songs: happiness.

Even though these movies do not send out a message to the community, they do have some significance. While entertaining large masses of people who come to the cinemas to forget their sorrows, these movies also give audiences some hope in life, something to look forward to in the coming week. These movies often show miraculous events, such as someone poor becoming rich through hard work. For the common masses in India who are uneducated, these are small things that give them hope even through the numerous struggles they encounter in their daily lives. By picturing themselves in the context of the movie, they find joy in hoping that it would happen to them someday. With this new revelation, I go into the movie theater once again just to enjoy the songs, hoping that one day I will dance in the Alps with a beautiful lady dressed in a flashy costume, accompanied by numerous dancers who have a choreographed dance prepared just for this occasion.

In the final resion, Sunthar developed his conclusion substantially, incorporating peer review suggestions to explain what the magical allure is for audiences. His tone becomes rhapsodic, and we can tell his argument is coming to a close.

The strong, developed ending of Sunthar's paper shows how careful revision can help you develop a compelling argument that offers a power fully from beginning to end. Be sure to save some energy for your conclusion: you want your parting words to ring memorably in your reader's ears.

Revision as a Continual Process

Sometimes, when writing, we may continue to revise our papers even after we have "finished." Think back to the earlier *BladeRunner* example and how Ridley Scott revised the film for re-release years after its first showing. Similarly, while you may be satisfied with your final research product when you turn it in, it is possible that you have set the groundwork for a longer research project that you may return to later in your college career. Or you may decide to seek publication for your essay in a school newspaper, magazine, or a national journal. In such cases, you may need to modify or expand on your argument for this new rhetorical situation; you may produce your own "director's cut"—a paper identical in topic to the original but developed in a significantly different fashion. Keep in mind that revision is indeed "re-vision" and that *all writing is re-writing*.

AT A GLANCE

Revising Your Draft

1. *Read your essay out loud or have someone read it to you.* You can hear mistakes and inconsistencies that you unknowingly skipped over when reading silently.

2. *Gain critical distance.* Put your essay away for a few hours, or even a few days, and then come back to it fresh.

3. *Answer peer review questions for your essay.*

4. *Don't be chained to your monitor.* Print out your draft, making revisions by hand. We conceptualize information differently on paper versus on a screen.

5. *Use your computer to help you look at your writing in different ways.* Take a paragraph and divide it into distinct sentences, which you line up one under another. Look for patterns (for instance, is the repetition deliberate or accidental?), style issues (is sentence structure varied?), and fluidity of transitions between sentences.

6. *Take into account feedback even if it initially doesn't seem significant.* You might not decide to act on the advice, but at least consider it before dismissing it.

7. *Revise out of order.* Choose paragraphs at random and look at them individually, or begin at the end. Sometimes our conclusions are the weakest simply because we always get to them last, when we're tired; start revision by looking at your conclusion first.

8. *Look at revision as a whole.* As you correct mistakes or prose problems, consider the impact that the revision makes on the rest of the essay. Sometimes it is possible just to add a missing comma or substitute a more precise verb, but often you need to revise more than just the isolated problem so that the sentence, paragraph, or essay as a whole continues to "fit" and flow together.

Focusing on Your Project

In this chapter, you have learned strategies for visual mapping, organizing, outlining, drafting, and revising your research paper. You have explored ways of casting your argument and acquired concrete methods for integrating both written sources and visual texts as evidence for your argument. Chances are you have written the first full draft of your paper. Feel free to approach these writer's tasks creatively, such as creating a hypertext outline or packaging your research paper electronically on a CD-ROM with links to visual material such as film clips, advertisement videos, or audio files. Your work as a writer has only just started, and the "premiere" of your project awaits.

PREWRITING CHECKLIST
Focus on Analyzing Film and Documentary

❏ Assess the genre of the film (comedy? horror? drama? film noire? documentary?) and how this affects the audience's response to its content. Does the film combine elements of different genres? What is the rhetorical effect of this combination?

❏ What is the plot of the film? What is the organizational structure?

❏ Is this plot arranged chronologically? in parallel sequences? thematically? What is the rhetorical significance of arrangement?

❏ What is the message conveyed to readers? Is it persuasive or informative? Is this message conveyed through reliance on pathos, logos, or ethos?

❏ How is the ethos of the filmmaker conveyed to the audience?

❏ What notable types of shots does the filmmaker use? Jot down one or two instances where cinematic techniques (zoom-in, cuts between scenes, fade in/fade out, montage) are used for rhetorical effect.

❏ Is there a narrator in the film? voice-over? What is the effect on the audience?

❏ Is there any framing—a way of setting the beginning and end in context?

❏ How is time handled? Does the film move in chronological order? reverse chronological order? What is the significance of such rhetorical choices on the meaning and power of the film? Are flashbacks used in the film? What effect is achieved through the use of flashbacks?

(continued)

❏ How are pathos, ethos, and logos produced by the different cinematic techniques? For instance, is pathos created through close-ups of characters? Is ethos created through allusions to famous films or filmmaking techniques? Is logos constructed through the insertion of a narrator's viewpoint?

❏ What is the audience's point of identification in the film? Is the audience supposed to identify with a single narrator? Does the film negotiate the audience's reaction in any specific ways? How?

❏ How is setting used to construct a specific mood that affects the impact of the message of the film?

❏ Is the film an adaptation of another work—a play or a novel? To the best of your knowledge, what modifications where made to customize the narrative for a cinematic audience? Does the text as film differ in content or message from the text in its original form? Can you see traces of revision and rewriting?

WRITING PROJECTS

1. **Visual Map or Outline:** Create a visual representation of your argument. This can be in the form of a bubble map, a flowchart, a hierarchal set of bubbles, or a handmade construction paper model. Give your ideas some kind of shape before turning to the outline. Try to write an annotation for each part of your drawing, model, or storyboard to help you move from mass of material to coherent research-based essay.

2. **Detailed Written Outline:** Working with your research materials and notes, create a written outline of your ideas, using numbers and letters to indicate subsections of your argument. Rather than simply calling the second section "II. Body," create several points within the body to show the development of your argument. You may want to start with a topic outline, but ideally you should aim for argumentative headings. Include your working thesis statement at an appropriate place in your outline, and include visuals that you will analyze in the essay itself. After you draft the outline once, go back and insert your primary source images in the outline to show how your research paper will analyze an issue through a rhetorical lens. Finally, add material from your sources at appropriate places: insert actual quotations (with page numbers) from your research sources where possible, and don't forget to cite your sources for both paraphrase and summary. Make sure you include the full names and page numbers for your sources wherever you can. This outline might easily turn into the paper itself. Use it to check the balance of sources, the progression of ideas, and the complexity of your argument.

3. **Research-Based Argument:** Write a 12- to 15-page argumentative research paper on a topic of your choice. If you wish to analyze and research visual rhetoric, consider the images that shape a debate, tell a certain history, or persuade an audience in a certain way. In other words, address an issue through a visual rhetoric lens. You should integrate research materials that can include articles, books, interviews, field research, surveys (either published or that you conduct yourself), TV programs, Internet texts, and other primary and secondary sources, including visuals. Keep in mind that, because this is a research paper, you need to balance primary and secondary materials. In addition, you should use both electronic and paper sources. Ultimately, your goal should be proving a thesis statement with apt evidence, using appropriate rhetorical and argumentative strategies.

4. **Reflection Essay:** After you have completed your essay, attach to the back of the essay a one-page reflection letter that serves as a self-evaluation. Reflect back on your research process and the development of your argument through research and revision. Include comments on the strengths of the essay, the types of revisions you made throughout your writing process, and how the collaborative process of peer review improved your essay. You might want to close by looking ahead to how you can continue to write about this issue in future projects and in future academic or professional situations.

 Visit www.ablongman.com/envision for expanded assignment guidelines and student projects.

Part III

DESIGN, DELIVERY, AND DOCUMENTATION

CHAPTER 7
Designing Arguments

CHAPTER 8
Delivering Presentations

CHAPTER 9
Documentation and Plagiarism

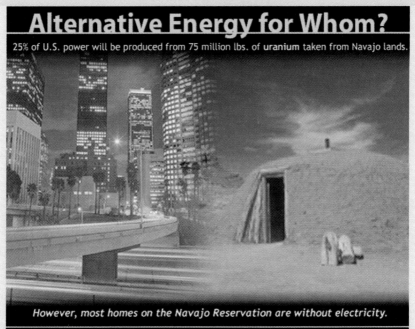

Alternative Energy for Whom?

25% of U.S. power will be produced from 75 million lbs. of **uranium** taken from Navajo lands.

However, most homes on the Navajo Reservation are without electricity.

Diné Citizens Against Ruining our Environment

What a shift in the means of delivery does is bring invention and arrangement into a new relationship with each other.

—Kathleen Yancey

CHAPTER 7

Designing Arguments

This chapter will give you the expertise to design your work for diverse purposes and audiences. We'll provide specific guidelines for academic essays, including line-spacing, margin size, and other formatting considerations. You'll learn how to write an academic abstract, a short biography (bio), and a cover letter. Then we'll examine hybrid document design in the form of newsletters and brochures before turning to visual arguments, such as op-ads, photo essays, and multimedia projects.

Michael Chaitkin, for example, turned the cover of his research paper into a **visual argument**—a graphic representation of a written argument—that served as a compact visual depiction of his thesis (see Figure 7.1). For example, In his paper, Michael explored the significance of Michelle Bachelet becoming Chile's first elected female president; he contended that although she was the daughter of a convicted traitor who was tortured to death by Chilean dictator Augusto Pinochet, she offered the promise of "healing history's wounds" by bridging the political and cultural gap between fighting communities in Chile. Michael encapsulated this argument visually in many ways: by placing the photograph of Bachelet in the center of his collage; by using a picture of Pinochet as a somewhat oppressive top border for the page; by placing images of the Chilean communities on both sides of Bachelet; and by locating his central research question, in blue, between them. In this way, he carefully and deliberately employed the

FIGURE 7.1. The cover of Michael Chaitkin's research essay offers a carefully designed visual argument.

strategies of invention, arrangement, and style to produce a collage that served both as a cover for his written research paper and as an argument in its own right.

Chapter Preview Questions

- What are the best ways to design arguments for specific audiences?
- What purposes do abstracts, "bios," and cover letters serve?
- What is decorum and how does this rhetorical principle govern document design?
- What techniques can you learn for designing your writing in digital and multimedia formats?
- How do visual arguments work, such as opinion advertisements (or op-ads), photo essays, and Websites?

Understanding Document Design and Decorum

Let's return to Alex, our hypothetical student from Chapter 1. Her interest in a Health and Society major led her to write an analysis of antismoking advertisements and a research paper on the urban subculture of teenage runaways. She now needs to format her paper for her teacher, and she also is considering submitting it for publication in her college's undergraduate research journal. Moreover, her teacher wants her to convert her paper into a visual argument to appear in a class exhibit. Alex needs to learn appropriate document design for academic audiences, but she also needs to learn how to write an abstract and bio, and she wants to explore her choices of media for the visual argument. In each case, she has four key decisions to make: Alex must identify her *argument* (her main point), her *audience* (whom she intends to reach), her *medium* (printed article, abstract, advertisement, photo essay, or multimedia montage), and the specific *form* (the layout and design aspects) for her composition. What governs her choices in each case is a matter of document design strategy, or the choices writers make in formatting their work.

To use terms from classical rhetoric, the decisions you face for document design have to do with **decorum**—a word defined as "appropriateness." In everyday language, someone who exhibits decorum in speaking knows the right kinds of words and content to use given the circumstances and audience. For example, you might swear or whoop in joy at a baseball game, but not on a job interview when talking about how your team won the game. But decorum as a rhetorical principle extends beyond choosing the right words and phrases for the occasion.

In the Roman rhetorical tradition, Cicero separated decorum into three levels of style that he assigned to different argumentative purposes. Cicero defined the *grand style* as the most formal mode of discourse, employing sophisticated language, imagery, and rhetorical devices; its goal is to move the audience. He considered *middle style* less formal than grand style but not completely colloquial; although it uses some verbal ornamentation, it develops its argument more slowly in an attempt to persuade the audience by pleasing them. The final level, *plain style,* mimics conversation in its speech and rhythms, aiming to instruct the audience in a clear and straightforward way. By adding decorum to our rhetorical toolkit, we can make decisions about how to design documents. As demonstrated in the "Levels of Decorum" table below, we can attend to argument, audience, medium, and form by understanding the *level of style* for a particular occasion. Like our classical counterparts, we must understand our rhetorical situation and use a style that best suits the circumstance.

LEVELS OF DECORUM

Level	Characteristics	Example: Antismoking Campaign for a Written Argument	Example: Antismoking Campaign for Visual Argument
Grand or high style	Ornate language; formal structures; many rhetorical devices	Academic paper to be published in a scholarly journal	An antismoking advertisement in the *Journal of the American Medical Association*
Middle style	Some ornamentation; less formal language; argument is developed at a leisurely pace	Feature article or editorial column to be published in the campus newspaper	A photo essay or collage for a school exhibit about effects of smoking or lung cancer
Plain or low style	The least formal style; closest to spoken language; emphasis on clarity, simplicity, and directness	Weblog post on family experiences with cigarette's harmful effects	A Website devoted to the physiology and psychology of nicotine addiction

For the rest of this chapter, we'll look at various models for document design, examining the way in which we need to adjust our choice of style according to the formal and rhetorical demands of each situation.

Understanding Academic Writing Conventions

From the perspective of decorum, the conventional academic essay falls under either grand or middle style, depending on the preferences of your audience. If your instructor asks you to compose a formal written paper, you will definitely be writing in grand style.

In addition to mastering the content and using grand style for your word choices, you also need to follow the accepted format for designing your essay, as shown in the "At a Glance" box.

An entire scholarly community has reached consensus on format conventions for academic papers, so that everyone knows what information will be provided where. It's similar to the convention of every car in the United States having the steering wheel on the left; the convention fosters a set of shared expectations designed to promote consistency, order, and ease of use.

But there's a deeper *purpose* for these academic-writing conventions. Most have to do with a rhetorical relationship, the fact that people (your instructor and your peers) will be reading your paper, and these reviewers need ample space to provide written comments. By double-spacing your document and providing 1-inch margins on all sides, you leave room for reviewers to comment on lines or paragraphs. You put page numbers and your name in the upper-right corner to enable reviewers to keep track of whose paper it is and to easily refer to your writing by page number in closing comments. The rationale for stapling or clipping is to keep your pages from getting lost.

AT A GLANCE

Characteristics of Academic Writing in Grand Style

- Language should be be more sophisticated than ordinary speech
- Use formal structures to organize your paper, including:

   A complete introduction containing your thesis

   A transition paragraph predicting your argument

   Clear subsections for each part of your argument

   A substantial conclusion

AT A GLANCE

Key Elements of Academic Document Design

- Double-space all pages.
- Provide 1-inch margins on all sides.
- Number pages at the top right; include your last name.
- Use subheads to separate sections.
- Staple or clip the paper together.
- Use in-text citations to acknowledge research sources.
- Use endnotes or footnotes for additional information.
- Include a list of references at the end.
- For specific examples of documentation, see Chapter 9.

COLLABORATIVE CHALLENGE

Cut and paste a short paragraph from your research paper into a new document in your word processing program. Now copy it, and position the copied paragraph below the original on your screen. Change the font in the newly copied paragraph to one distinctly different from the original. Repeat this procedure twice more, so that you end up with four paragraphs, each with a markedly different font. Print out your paragraphs and exchange them with a partner. As you look at your partner's printout, consider the following questions: How does the font change the way that you understand what is being said in the paragraph? How do you form different expectations about the paper based on the font? How do you form a different perception of the author? Which font would you recommend the author use for the final research paper? Why? Discuss your answers with your partner.

AT A GLANCE

Including Visuals in a Paper

- Does your paper focus on a visual topic, such as the analysis of ads or films? If so, you probably want to include images or screen shots as evidence and as primary materials to analyze in your writing.
- Does your paper rely on images, such as political campaigns from billboards or Websites, as supporting evidence for your thesis? If so, include image of these materials into your paper.
- If you simply insert an image without comment, a readers will skip over it. Make sure you describe its relevance in the text near the image.
- Include a caption with the figure number and a brief description.
- Provide the complete image source in your bibliography.

Integrating Images in Academic Writing

There are many reasons you might want to include visuals in your research paper. If, for instance, your topic concerns hybrid cars, you might want to insert a technical diagram to explain the car's mechanics to readers. If you are analyzing advertisement campaigns for hybrid cars, your argument would benefit from showing readers an example through a strategically integrated image. But realize that randomly inserting a picture into your paper does not serve the *purpose* of using images rhetorically in an academic argument. Instead, you need to integrate visual texts into your document design in a rhetorically effective manner.

Carefully consider your strategy of arrangement and the *placement* of your images: Will you put them in an appendix? on your title page? on a separate page? on the same page as your written argument? Each decision is both a stylistic and rhetorical choice. An image placed in an appendix tends to be viewed as *supplementary,* not as integral to an argument; an image on a title page might act as an epigraph to set a mood for a paper, but it is less effective as a specific visual example. If you want to use your images as *argumentative evidence,* you need to show them to your readers as you analyze them; therefore, placing them beside the words of your argument will be most successful.

Once you have determined the placement that best serves your rhetorical purpose, you need to insert the image effectively. Like a quotation, an image cannot be dropped into a text without comment; it needs to be **signposted,** or connected to your argument through deliberate textual markers. You can accomplish this by making explicit **textual references** to the image—for example, "shown in the image at the right" or "(see Figure 3)"—and by taking the time to explain the rhetoric of the image for readers. Just like words quoted from a book or an interview that you might use as evidence, visual material needs *your interpretation* for readers to view it the way you do. Your analysis of its meaning will advance your argument by persuading readers to see the image as you do, and in the process, readers will pause to contemplate the evidence rather than skip over it.

Moreover, it is crucial to draft a **caption** for the image that reiterates the relationship between the point you are making in the paper and the visual evidence you include. In a paper Albert Thomas wrote about the popular sport of capoeira, a form of Brazilian martial arts that resembles dancing, he included a still image from the film *Ocean's 12* and wrote an effective caption.

Remember, however, that what is most important is the analysis of the image you include in the body of your paper; don't hide the meaning of the image in the caption. Captions should be concise but not do the work of the written argument.

Figure 1. Vincent Cassel's character in *Ocean's 12* uses capoeira to evade this laser grid.

Albert includes a still shot as visual evidence in case his readers haven't seen the film.

His caption includes a figure number, the name of the person and the text (the film), as well as a link to his argument: "Cassel's character . . . uses capoeira to evade this laser grid."

A less effective caption would have simply named the film.

Design of Academic Papers

A page from student Allison Woo's paper on Asian-American female stereotypes in contemporary cinema provides an example of *both* effective academic writing conventions and effective placement and captioning of visuals (see Figure 7.2).

Allison's last name and the page number are in the upper-right corner.

She indents the first line and double-spaces the text.

By embedding the images in the paper, Allison makes readers pause to analyze them as evidence—the way readers would study a poem or a quoted line from a book.

She arranges the visuals so they are in dialogue, reproducing the comparison that is the purpose of her paragraph. In this way, the two figures function effectively as visual evidence for her argument: the striking similarity in pose, costume, and demeanor between actresses Lucy Liu and Michelle Yeoh substantiate Allison's points about the prominence of the "Dragon Lady" stereotype in popular American films.

Woo 9

Meanwhile, the Dragon Lady images of sexuality are equally prevalent in film today. In *Tomorrow Never Dies* (1997), Asian actress Michelle Yeoh plays a seductive Chinese spy, who simultaneously flirts, manipulates, fights, and plays with her costar, James Bond (played by Pierce Brosnan). Screenwriter and novelist Jessica Hagedorn lists Yeoh's character as an archetypical Dragon Lady. Dressed in tight jumpsuit in her favorite color of corruptible black, Yeoh's character double-crosses, connives, and seduces her way through the movie, and it is always unclear whether she is good or evil.

Bond eventually conquers all, winning sexual access to the Asian woman. In *Payback*, Lucy Liu's character Pearl also double-crosses both sides.

Figs. 8 and 9. Michelle Yeoh in *Tomorrow Never Dies*, 1997 (left); Lucy Liu in *Payback*, 2002. (right). Their common characterization, dress, hairstyle, weaponry, and "dangerous" sexuality illustrate the way Hollywood repackages the same stereotyped characters in different movies.

Although she only appears in a few scenes, most of them show her seductively whispering a few lines of sexual prompting. Achieving almost orgasmic pleasure from sexually manipulating and dominating men, she thrives in her sexuality and moral corruption. Even Caucasian movie critic Sam Adams recognizes Pearl as a stereotypical "Dragon Lady," as she makes sexual advances on the hero (Mel Gibson) and the villains in the movie. Her Asian heritage is distinguishable from the Caucasian prostitute in the

---

FIGURE 7.2. Allison Woo, "Slaying the Dragon: The Struggle to Reconcile Modern Asian Identity with Depictions of Asian Women in Past and Present American Film," page 9, showcases visual and verbal arguments working together.

Since Allison's project analyzed female stereotypes in two films, *Tomorrow Never Dies* (1997) and *Payback* (1999), she decided to include two images as evidence. Rather than relegating these pictures to an appendix, Allison positioned them in the paper with text flowing around it, making the visuals an integral part of her arguments.

Allison's caption lists necessary information—figure numbers, descriptive titles, names of the actresses and films, and the years of release—as well as the sources for the images. Moreover, by paraphrasing the written argument, the caption paraphrases the central point of Allison's paragraph. Through this successful union of words and images, Allison constructs an academic argument effectively and persuasively.

Tools of Design for Academic Audiences

In addition to the research paper, you might choose to compose supplemental pages, such as a cover page containing an academic *abstract* and research *bio*— a brief biography of the author. We'll discuss these aspects now so you can add them to your toolkit of writing strategies.

Composing an Abstract

The **research abstract** is a professional academic genre designed not only to present the research topic but also to lay out the argument. There are many versions of abstracts depending on the disciplinary audience and the purpose of the writing. When applying to academic conferences in the humanities, for example, academics often must write a 500-word abstract that predicts the paper's argument, research contribution, and significance. Other times, especially for writers in the sciences or social sciences, abstracts are written *after* the paper has been completed to serve as a short summary of the article. You will undoubtedly encounter these abstracts when you begin searching for research articles; they often precede a published paper or accompany bibliographic citations in online databases.

Abstracts can range from a few sentences to a page in length, but they are usually no longer than two paragraphs. The key in writing an abstract is to explain your argument in one brief, coherent unit. As you compose your abstract, you will need to make several rhetorical decisions.

To understand how your answers to the questions listed in the "At a Glance" box will shape your writing, let's consider three student abstracts each correspond to a different level of decorum, use varying levels of specificity, and implement diverse means of constructing a research persona.

AT A GLANCE

Writing an Abstract

Plan to write 1 or 2 paragraphs about your paper, working through these questions:

- What level of decorum or style do you wish to use?
- How will the style predict the tone of your paper and establish your persona as a researcher?
- Do you want to you use "I"?
- How much specificity should you include from the paper?
  - Do you want to list the concrete examples you analyze in your writing?
  - Do you want to give an overview of your argument?
  - Should you name sources you use in making your argument?
- How can you be both brief and engaging?

- Molly Cunningham, for her abstract on her paper "Illuminating the Dark Continent: Hollywood Portrayals of Africa," writes in the *grand style* of decorum: she uses complex academic terms and a sophisticated vocabulary, including terminology from her discipline of postcolonial anthropology. In three complex sentences, she conveys her theoretical approach to analyzing film, names the films, and provides her thesis before ending with a statement of broader significance.
- Laura Hendrickson's abstract for her paper titled "Plastic Surgery Among Women in South Korea" uses the *middle style* of decorum by combining the use of "I" with specific terms from her research, such as "Neo-Confucian ideals." She identifies her topic—observations about plastic surgery in Korean female role models—and makes a claim about it—that surgery represents a projected Western standard of beauty.
- David Pinner relies more heavily on *plain style* for his abstract on copyright and the Creative Commons movement:

> Since the rise of Napster and mp3s, the battle for intellectual property control of artistic works has exploded. Restrictive measures by the RIAA and MPAA threaten to take control of creative works away from both users and creators, to the point where people can't even control the data on their computer. However, a new alternative has emerged: Creative Commons, a copyright license designed for flexibility, readability and ease of use. In my project, I examine the way that Creative Commons is changing the nature of artistic collaboration in a world where art is increasingly created and distributed through electronic means.

Several elements of this abstract mark it as plain style: the use of the contraction *can't;* the use of the first person; and the concluding statement of purpose that resists providing a fully developed argument. The abstract avoids excessive display or ornamentation and instead is direct, clear, and accessible—all hallmarks of plain style.

Shaping Your Bio

While the abstract offers a concise statement of the argument, the **bio** is a concise paragraph that explains the persona of the writer to the intended audience. The bio functions to persuade readers of the writer's depth of knowledge or connection to the topic. Usually, the bio describes the writer's credentials, interests, and motivations for engaging in research work. Molly Cunningham's bio for her paper on Hollywood depictions of Africa follows this model, resembling the polished "About the Author" paragraph that you might find at the back of a book on the topic or in the headnote of an academic article:

Student Writing

See abstracts and students bios by Molly, Laura, and Sunthar.
www.ablongmam.com/envision/226

Molly Cunningham is a sophomore planning to double major in Cultural and Social Anthropology and English. After spending time in East Africa, she has become interested in exploring cultural definitions of the orphan within the community and family in light of postcolonialism as well as the AIDS pandemic. She is currently planning a summer research project in Botswana to do ethnographic research on this topic. Cunningham is also interested in the politics of humanitarian aid and the interplay between community and international donors. Involved in fundraising for a Kenyan orphanage, she hopes to deconstruct the meanings and attitudes that shape the nature and determine the amount of foreign aid going into Africa. She has utilized this research project to expand her thinking on this topic while learning to convey her findings to wider audiences.

Notice how Molly names specific qualifications and experiences she has had that make her an authority in this area. Moreover, she ends the bio with her future plans in this area of research that suggest her pursuit of a "research line" or academic path of scholarly inquiry.

It is possible, however, that if you are writing a bio to accompany a research proposal you may feel that, at this point in your project, you have no authority on the topic. It is important to keep in mind that as you explore your sources, you will become more knowledgeable about your topic and be able to contribute to dialogue about your area of research. Thus even at an early stage of your research, you can use language, tone, and style to construct a sense of ethos. Look, for example, at David Pinner's bio and the way he establishes his authority even though he had just begun his research:

> David Pinner is a sophomore at Stanford University majoring in physics. His father came from a traditional copyrighted background, while his mother's family had long been in the public domain. Being raised in a multilicensed household was difficult, but thanks to the work of Creative Commons and other copyleft organizations, his situation is finally being recognized by the general public. He enjoys electronic media, sailing, playing music, and Stickin' it to The Man. He is a dues-paying member of the Electronic Frontier Foundation (www.eff.org) and releases his blog under an Attribution-NonCommerical-ShareAlike v2.0 Creative Commons license.

David creates a sense of his credibility as a researcher on this issue in several ways: by demonstrating his familiarity with the sides of the debate (*copyright* versus *public domain*); by using terminology relevant to the topic (*multilicensed, copyleft*); and by referring to some of the prominent organizations involved in the copyright debate (*Creative Commons, Electronic Frontier Foundation*). In addition, his humorous tone in the bio anticipates the original approach he will use in his research paper.

When formatting your own bio, you might decide to include a photograph of yourself. Remember to select your picture carefully, with attention to its rhetorical impact. Many students who choose to write a traditional bio like Molly's opt for a formal photograph such as a school portrait; other students, like David, might choose a more candid or humorous picture to complement the tone of their bios. One student, when writing about online gaming communities, even created a Photoshopped portrait of herself standing next to her onscreen avatar identity to represent the two perspectives she was bringing to her research. As you can tell, the picture works in conjunction with the bio not only to construct a persona for the writer, but also to suggest that writer's rhetorical stance.

CREATIVE PRACTICE

Write a short bio of yourself using plain style, such as you might include on a Facebook profile or MySpace page; choose a picture to accompany your bio. Now translate the plain style bio into grand style and choose a new photo to accompany a hypothetical published version of your research paper. Reflect on this process. How does the level of decorum relate to audience, context, and purpose? How satisfied are you with the success of each version of your bio?

Combining Visual and Verbal Design Elements

So far, we've been talking about design in written arguments. But we also know that the visual rhetoric of a page matters to an audience: from the paragraph indents to the margins and double-spaced lines, to the rhetorical placement of images—all these design decisions are ways of conveying your level of decorum and your purpose to your specific audience. When we say "first impressions," we often mean how well a writer meets the conventions anticipated by the audience.

When your audience allows you to combine visual and verbal elements, you can produce *a hybrid composition* such as a feature article for a magazine, a newsletter aimed at a community audience, or an online article for diverse readers. Research has shown that in such texts, readers tend to focus on the visual part of a text first, before the words. Whether it's a news article, a traditional academic paper with a visual, or a multimedia collage, the visual grabs the attention first. Perhaps the images in this book engage your interest more immediately than the prose. Indeed, according to Adbusters, an organization devoted to cultural criticism and analysis, the visual part of any page is noticed significantly more than any text on the same page. Adbusters uses this finding to provide advice for creating ads, but we can apply the insight to written compositions combining visual and verbal elements.

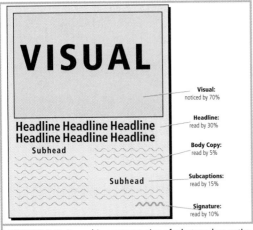

FIGURE 7.3. A graphic representation of what readers notice most on a page: visuals grab attention most.

FIGURE 7.4. Design of Ashley Mullen's hybrid composition.

Figure 7.3 provides a useful diagram for understanding the way readers process information, showing that 70 percent of readers notice visuals and 30 percent pay attention to headlines; much farther down on the attention-grabbing scale are the body, subheads, and the signature. Knowing this, consider the importance of visual as you approach designing your own hybrid compositions. As for your headline—second in importance to viewers—follow a suggestion from Adbusters: "The most important thing to remember here is that your headline must be short, snappy and must touch the people that read it. Your headline must affect the readers emotionally, either by making them laugh, making them angry, making them curious or making them think." Clearly, headlines work through rhetorical appeals: you need to think carefully about which appeal—pathos, ethos, or logos—would provide the most effective way to engage your audience.

Let's look at the design decisions Ashley Mullen made in formatting her writing project on the topic of police brutality. She created a newsletter that featured a cover story in which she arranged words around a powerful image. In designing this text, Ashley took into account not only the argument she sought to make but also, as Figure 7.4 makes clear, the choices of layout, placement of images, font size, color, and overall design. Her painstaking care with the design of this text is evident in the power of her finished product. Inside the newsletter, Ashley selected several photographs—each functioning as an individual argument—as a graphic way of representing the additional points she wanted to make on the issue: each photo anchored her writing and complemented the diverse perspectives she crafted. We can see here how visual rhetoric functions as a powerful tool of argument for her hybrid composition; it complements her careful attention to style through her word choices, imagery, expressions, and argument for each position. You might do the same in your writing through formatting your work in newspaper columns or as a magazine feature article, Website, or personal letter.

Designing Arguments for Public Audiences

Although Ashley Mullen designed her hybrid composition for an academic audience (her class), she could have easily decided to share this writing project with a community group, a public service organization, or a student group dedicated to social change. Often we call such projects **service-learning** or **community service** projects because they combine learning (or writing) with service to the community. The writing you do for this type of class project is likely to be produced for a nonacademic audience, including a nonprofit agency, a city council, or members of an outreach group.

For these writing projects, you might be asked to produce a grant letter, a newsletter article, a fact sheet, a brochure, or even a Website. Such projects benefit both the nonprofit organization and the members it serves; in addition, it provides you with experience producing the kinds of texts you'll be asked to write throughout your professional career.

Let's take a look at the design strategies employed in community service writing projects, which are often multilayered, just like many of the professional projects you might encounter outside the university setting. That is, you might be asked to develop not just one flyer, pamphlet, or poster but rather a series of interconnected texts; thus, design becomes a more complicated process of connecting diverse documents according to purpose and audience.

For example, as part of their service-learning project for the nonprofit organization Alternative Spring Break (ASB)—a program that offers college students an opportunity to use their spring break to help a community by working with the homeless, cleaning out land to grow plants, and building affordable housing—students Gene Ma and Chris Couvelier created an interview questionnaire, a formatted feature article for online publication, and as Figure 7.5 shows, designed a new logo as well as new content for the group's Website.

The logo features a sleek, minimalist approach to engaging prospective students: the red and white letters replicate the university's colors (in place of the blue and yellow used in the old logo); and the faint image of students in

> Community-based writing—whether it is practical or academic—is *writing for real.* It engages tangible issues, uniting thought and action, and it calls for new approaches to writing.
>
> —Carolyn Ross and Ardel Thomas, *Writing for Real,* 17

FIGURE 7.5. Gene Ma's redesigned logo for the ASB Website.

FIGURE 7.6. Chris Couvelier's newsletter design.

San Francisco's Chinatown conveys the location of one of ASB's most successful community programs that focuses on helping the Asian-American population.

The key to the design of this hybrid composition project, as with many nonacademic writing tasks, was collaboration. Here's how it worked: Gene and Chris divided the tasks. First, Chris contacted past participants of ASB through a written survey and follow-up telephone calls, and then he created a newsletter suitable for publication on the Webpage (see Figure 7.6).

After Chris completed his work, Gene analyzed the rhetoric of the organization's Website and found it dull and cluttered. He created a new logo, new content, different pictures, and 40 pages of updated materials (see Figure 7.7). Finally, he created a humorous PowerPoint presentation to convey to his colleagues in class the process of researching, designing, and producing this hybrid composition. The multiple layers of this service-learning project made it much more akin to the kind of work that you will find in the workforce, whether you work for a nonprofit or professional organization; in either case, the total needs of a specific community audience dictated the various steps along the way to completion of the project.

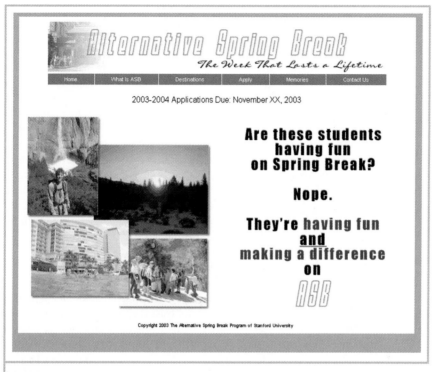

FIGURE 7.7. Screen shot from Gene Ma's newly designed Website for ASB.

Formatting Writing for Audiences

Let's look now at a purely verbal or written example of formatting writing for online audiences before we move to the visual arguments in the next section. In the following reading, the author employs many of the elements from the "At a Glance" box on document design that appeared earlier in the chapter. The selection includes a title, subheads, references, and a reference list at the end. But notice how the written argument has been changed or translated into a *hybrid composition* to meet the expectations of the online reading audience.

Student Writing
View Gene Ma's award-winning Website project for ASB.
www.ablongman.com/envision/227

The title is in plain style and all capital letters, with the subtitle in lowercase. This font decision makes it appealing to online readers.

The article uses argumentative sub-heads, as might an academic paper. They convey points of argument being made in the article. Moreover, they keep readers interested.

The numbers correspond to notes and sources at the end. These notes are *hyperlinked*, so readers can jump there easily while reading on the web.

WHAT'S WRONG WITH THE BODY SHOP?
—a criticism of 'green' consumerism—

REFERENCED VERSION—all the facts and opinions in the London Greenpeace A5 'Body Shop' leaflet validated. Note: most references are given just by way of example.

The Body Shop have successfully manufactured an image of being a caring company that is helping to protect the environment [1] and indigenous peoples [2], and preventing the suffering of animals [3]—whilst selling 'natural' products [4]. But behind the green and cuddly image lies the reality—the Body Shop's operations, like those of all multinationals, have a detrimental effect on the environment [5] and the world's poor [6]. They do not help the plight of animals [7] or indigenous peoples [8] (and may be having a harmful effect), and their products are far from what they're cracked up to be [9]. They have put themselves on a pedestal in order to exploit people's idealism [10]—so this leaflet has been written as a necessary response.

Companies like the Body Shop continually hype their products through advertising and marketing, often creating a demand for something where a real need for it does not exist [11]. The message pushed is that the route to happiness is through buying more and more of their products. The increasing domination of multinationals and their standardised products is leading to global cultural conformity [12]. The world's problems will only be tackled by curbing such consumerism - one of the fundamental causes of world poverty, environmental destruction and social alienation [13].

FUELLING CONSUMPTION AT THE EARTH'S EXPENSE

The Body Shop have over 1,500 stores in 47 countries [14], and aggressive expansion plans [15]. Their main purpose (like all multinationals) is making lots of money for their rich shareholders [16]. In other words, they are driven by power and greed. But the Body Shop try to conceal this reality by continually pushing the message that by shopping at their stores, rather than elsewhere, people will help solve some of the world's problems [17]. The truth is that nobody can make the world a better place by shopping.

20% of the world's population consume 80% of its resources [18]. A high standard of living for some people means gross social inequalities and poverty around the world [19]. Also, the mass production, packaging and transportation of huge quantities of goods is using up the world's resources faster than they can be renewed and filling the land, sea and air with dangerous pollution and waste [20]. Those who advocate an ever-increasing level of consumption, and equate such consumption with personal well-being, economic progress and social fulfillment, are creating a recipe for ecological disaster [21].

Rejecting consumerism does not mean also rejecting our basic needs, our stylishness, our real choices or our quality of life. It is about creating a just, stable and sustainable world, where resources are under the control of local communities and are distributed equally and sparingly—it's about improving everyone's quality of life. Consuming ever more things is an unsatisfying and harmful way to try to be happy and fulfilled. Human happiness is not related to what people buy, but to who we are and how we relate to each other. LET'S CONSUME LESS AND LIVE MORE!

Notice how the article uses all CAPS to draw the online reader's attention and even begins a new section with a two word question?

MISLEADING THE PUBLIC

Natural products? The Body Shop give the impression that their products are made from mostly natural ingredients [22]. In fact like all big cosmetic companies they make wide use of non-renewable petrochemicals, synthetic colours, fragrances and preservatives [23], and in many of their products they use only tiny amounts of botanical-based ingredients [24]. Some experts have warned about the potential adverse effects on the skin of some of the synthetic ingredients [25]. The Body Shop also regularly irradiate certain products to try to kill microbes - radiation is generated from dangerous non-renewable uranium which cannot be disposed of safely [26].

Some sections are very short, a common feature in online writing, where information is "chunked" into accessible packages.

. . .

CENSORSHIP

As the Body Shop rely so heavily on their 'green', 'caring' image, they have threatened or brought legal action against some of those who have criticised them, trying to stifle legitimate public discussion [46]. It's vital to stand up to intimidation and to defend free speech.

The article uses direct address, the pronoun *you,* to engage readers. This design strategy again indicates the use of the plain style.

WHAT YOU CAN DO

Together we can fight back against the institutions and the people in power who dominate our lives and our planet. Workers can and do organise together to fight for their rights and dignity. People are increasingly aware of the need to think seriously about the products we use, and to consume less. People in poor countries are organising themselves to stand up to multinationals and banks which dominate the world's economy. Environmental and animal rights protests and campaigns are growing everywhere. Why not join in the struggle for a better world? London Greenpeace calls on people to create an anarchist society - a society without oppression, exploitation and hierarchy, based on strong and free communities, the sharing of precious resources and respect for all life. Talk to friends and family, neighbours and workmates about these issues. Please copy and circulate this leaflet as widely as you can.

For more information, contact:
London Greenpeace
5 Caledonian Road
London N1 9DX, UK.
Tel/Fax 0171 713 1269
Tel 0171 837 7557
E-mail: lgp@
envirolink.org

REFERENCES

1. See "Fuelling Consumption" paragraphs in the leaflet and associated references.

2. See "Exploiting Indigenous Peoples" paragraphs in the leaflet and associated references.

3. See "Helping Animals?" paragraph in the leaflet and associated references.

4. See "Natural products?" paragraph in the leaflet and associated references.

10. [Numerous publications, statements, advertisements, etc. by the *Body Shop*.] For example, the company's Mission Statement (1998) says that they are dedicating their business "to the pursuit of social and environmental change" and are trying to ensure that their business "is ecologically sustainable, meeting the needs of the present without compromising the future." "For us, animal protection, human rights, fair trade and environmentalism, are not just fads or marketing

The "More Information" column above is an online design version of the bio; the contact information gives readers more knowledge of the persona while building ethos and authority.

Since these notes are positioned far down on the page, they can go into more detail because they assume that only very interested readers will be accessing this part of the composition.

gimmicks but fundamental components in our holistic approach to life of which work and business are a part" [Gordon Roddick (Chairman) quoted in 1996 *Body Shop* publication "Our Agenda".] "I'd rather promote human rights, environmental concerns, indigenous rights, whatever, than promote a bubble bath" said Anita Roddick (the *Body Shop* founder and Chief Executive) [speech at 'Academy of Management', Vancouver (Aug 95).]

Back to 'Beyond McDonald's—Retail' Section

London Greenpeace Press Release

WWW Body Shop FAQ

London Greenpeace reply to Body Shop statement

A5 version of 'What's Wrong With The Body Shop'

From a design perspective, the final series of links for future reading signifies one of the great benefits of writing a hybrid composition in a digital environment.

As you can tell from this article, the same strategies of design that shape academic research papers also apply to other modes: what is most important in each is a consideration of *purpose, audience,* and *argument.* Think about how readers will interact with your writing—whether as a print copy handed in for comments (in which case you double-space and follow academic guidelines); as a newsletter (in which case you might open with a powerful image, lay out the writing in columns or boxes, and use an interesting page size); or as a hybrid piece to be read on the Web (in which case you include hyperlinks, single-space, create shorter chunks, and use font strategically).

Designing Visual Arguments

In essence, *visual arguments* are compact multimedia texts that exist as independent creations, such as op-ads, photo essays, Websites, and montages. We can understand these texts through the levels of decorum (outlined earlier in the chapter): someone surfing the Web might find the student Website dedicated to family members who died from smoking cigarettes (our plain-style example); a person browsing through departmental publications might encounter a student's photo essay about the effects of smoking (our middle-style example); or a visitor looking at an exhibit case in a library might see op-ads created by a Writing and Social Issues class and find in this work powerful pieces of visual rhetoric (our grand-style example).

When you construct a visual argument—whether generated for your research project, as a new argument about a issue, or as an assignment for your class—you have the opportunity to experiment with many forms of media to make a powerful argument. You can apply strategies for inventing, arranging, and producing the design of an innovative visual argument that will persuade viewers to agree with your message.

Keep in mind, however, that each medium structures information in a distinct way. A PowerPoint slide is set up differently than a Webpage, just as a Webpage is set up differently than a magazine advertisement. Therefore, part of creating a powerful visual argument lies in identifying your chosen medium's conventions of structure and style and adjusting the form of your argument—its layout, design, style, and organization of information—to be the most appropriate choice for your project.

FIGURE 7.8. This Body Shop opinion advertisement relies on a powerful visual argument to shock readers into questioning concepts of beauty.

Crafting an Op-Ad

The **op-ad,** or **opinion advertisement,** is one of the most concise forms of visual argument. Most op-ads promote an opinion rather than a consumer product. Many nonprofit organizations, special interest groups, and political parties find the op-ad a particularly effective way to reach their target audiences. Like all ads, the op-ad is a compact persuasive text, one that uses rhetorical appeals to convey its message. In addition, like other types of ads, an op-ad may rely partially on written text, but it tends to work through the visual components of its argument.

In Figure 7.8, for instance, the op-ad makes its point through a strategic combination of visual and verbal elements. The Body Shop has crafted an innovative image that communicates a powerful message: the realistically proportioned doll, set in a confident, casual pose against a natural background of ivy, produces a strong counterstatement against standards of body image in the mass media that promote exceptional thinness for feminine beauty. The words, "There are 3 billion women who don't look like supermodels and only 8 who do," are arranged to reinforce the visual argument of the non-super-model-like body. The image creates an argument based on pathos, while the statistical words rely on logos. The design of the op-ad thus works through visual and verbal strategies to make people think twice about body image. The tiny words under the Body Shop name and logo accentuate and confirm the argument of the image: "Know your mind love your body." In this way, the op-ad uses the way readers attend to information on a page: image first, headline second, caption third.

In many ways, the figure of the heavyset Body Shop doll evokes Barbie; op-ads often rely on this rhetorical strategy—**parody,** or the use of one text's formal properties to subvert the meaning of the original and make an independent argument.

In Figure 7.9, a spoof ad from Adbusters, the iconic figure of Joe Camel has been transformed into Joe Chemo to dramatize the link between cigarettes and lung cancer. Even the mascot's trademark symbol of his "coolness"—his sunglasses—are transformed into a symbol of loss, as Joe gazes on them sorrowfully. Held away from his face, exposing his ravaged eyes, they are now a mere reminder of the ostensibly "cool" life he once had with his cigarette-smoking ways.

To understand how to compose your own op-ad, let's look at the process by which one student, Carrie Tsosie, constructed her visual argument. After writing an effective research paper that presented the dangers of allowing uranium mining on or near Navajo reservations, Carrie decided to reformulate her argument as an op-ad to reach a larger audience. Her initial considerations were her visual format and her headline—two elements of her ad that underwent some revision. She explained:

FIGURE 7.9. This Joe Chemo op-ad derives its power from its parody of the well-known Joe Camel character that appeared on cigarette boxes for years.

AT A GLANCE

Designing an Op-Ad
- Decide on your purpose (to inform, to persuade, to move to action).
- Identify your audience.
- Know your argument.
- Determine which appeals to use (pathos, logos, ethos).
- Select key images for your ad.
- Write your print text; decide how it will function in relation to your image(s).
- Draft a gripping headline to complement your image.
- Experiment with layout—arrangement, image size, organization of text—to arrive at the most effective design.

My first idea was to have an image of a deformed lamb because then the audience would see what radiation poisoning can do. I wanted to use the phrase "Stop mining before it starts," but it seemed like that phrase was overdone, and I don't think that my audience could really relate to the deformed lamb because they do not know how important it is to some Navajo people and their lives. (Tsosie, reflection letter)

As shown in her completed op-ad (Figure 7.10), Carrie decided against the pathos-based image of a sick animal.

She opted instead to feature different human environments through her strategic choices of images. In addition, rather than base her ad on a strong imperative such as "Stop Mining," she chose to soften her voice and reach her audience by asking them to question their assumptions about alternative energy. In her final op-ad, she composed a heading with the provocative question "Alternative Energy for Whom?" and then followed the words with a striking visual argument. It is here, in the image, that we find the main work of argumentation. Carrie combined an image from the urban landscape with a stereotypical image from the reservation to produce a striking effect, using what we call *visual juxtaposition,* or the combination of multiple images, as a rhetorical device to call attention to the discrepancy between these ways of life and inform readers about her critique.

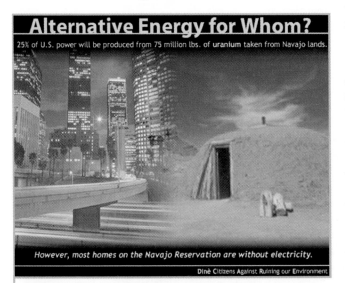

FIGURE 7.10. Carrie Tsosie's op-ad uses visual juxtaposition and a strong headline to make its argument against U.S. mining practices.

Producing a Photo Essay

Although op-ads offer a concise, forceful argument, you may wish to develop your points more thoroughly than one page allows or use visual space to show the range of material with which you've been working. If so, consider the **photo essay**—a text in which photographs, rather than print text, convey the central argument. In a word-based essay, verbal text takes priority, and images are typically used as supplements. In a photo essay, by contrast, the visual either collaborates with the verbal or becomes the *primary mode* of representation and persuasion.

As a genre, the photo essay first emerged in 1936 with the launching of *Life* magazine, whose mission statement was "to see life; to see the world." Over the 63 years it remained in print, *Life* hosted many of America's most famous photo essays, covering a range of topics from the space race to the Vietnam War, the civil rights movement, and rock and roll. But the photo essay can assume many different forms and use diverse media: it could be a series of documentary photographs and articles about southern sharecroppers published together in book form, such as Walker Evans's and James Agee's *Let Us Now Praise Famous Men* (1941); it could be a book-length photo essay that juxtaposes images with first-person narratives, such as Lauren Greenfield's *Girl Culture* (2002); it could be a striking 27-page color spread in a magazine, such as William Albert Allard's "Solace at Surprise Creek" in the June 2006 issue of *National Geographic;* or it could even be an online arrangement of cap-tioned photos, such as *A Rescue Worker's Chronicle,* created by paramedic Matthew Levy. In each case, the photographs and written text work together, or the images themselves carry the primary weight of the argument.

Today electronic photo essays are essential conveyers of important events, a result of Internet news sources like CNN.com, Time.com, and MSNBC.com, which routinely publish photo essays as "picture stories" on their Websites. Such texts are composed of a series of images and words that work together to suggest an argument about a person, event, or story. Each electronic photo essay typically contains (1) a photo, (2) an accompanying caption, (3) an audio option, and (4) a table of contents toolbar that allows readers to navi-gate through the images. The result is an electronic text that maintains many structural similarities to print text: it offers readers a clear sense of progression from beginning to end while investing its argument with the rhetorical force of multiple media (word, image, sound).

COLLABORATIVE CHALLENGE

Perform an Internet search on the term "photo essay." In small groups, select one of the essays that results from the search and ana-lyze how it creates an argument. What is the relationship between text and image? Which is given priority? What is the intended audi-ence, and how does the design of the photo essay reflect attention to audience? How interactive is the experience? After assessing the properties of the photo essay as a group, together map out alternative strategies of design. Present the original and your plan for an alternative version to the class, clarifying the rationale behind the changes you would make and suggesting which project—yours or the original—you feel is the most rhetorically effective photo essay and why. Then, based on what you have learned, compose a photo essay about your university. First, decide on your thesis—that is, the main argument you wish to make about your school: is it an institution that prides itself on academic excellence? on student life? on tradition? on diversity? Then, using a digital camera, take appropriate photos, and design your photo essay, using captions or print text as appropriate, and present it to the class.

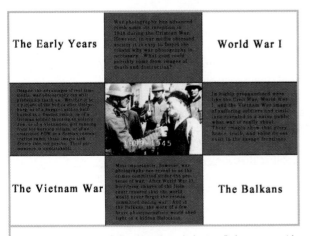

FIGURE 7.11. Ye Yuan's "Looking Through the Lens" photo essay with the rollover graphic activated.

Let's now consider how one student, Ye Yuan, created an online photo essay that uses a dynamic format to give readers control over the way they view the information and the way the argument is assembled.

Figure 7.11 demonstrates this reader-oriented dynamic. The arrangement of information, though it follows a roughly left-to-right, top-to-bottom organization, also opens up the possibility of browsing this photo essay in a less rigidly determined fashion. As you might expect, clicking on a bolded title takes you to a series of sequential images from that time period, offering structure to this broad discussion of war photography. At first glance, this arrangement might seem to rely on a traditional hierarchy of image and word, with the pictures serving as a secondary layer to the word-based introduction. Yet as soon as the reader begins to interact with this photo essay, moving the mouse across the page, this illusion is dispelled. Each bolded title contains a rollover graphic, so that when the reader moves the mouse over the words, a representative image appears. This dynamic relationship between word and image suggests a conjunction of meaning between the two; cooperation between the visual and the verbal is designed to "hook" and move the reader to the next level of the photo essay.

At the subsection level (shown in Figure 7.12), the reader finds a carefully chosen image that represents war photography from that historical period. Here, the photographs function as the arguments, because the heading remains constant for each subsequent image; the pictures change, but the print remains the same.

The photo essay works best if you have a topic that can be effectively argued through an accumulation of visual evidence presented as a sequence of images. Keep in mind that designing a photo essay is like drafting a research paper: you may take pages of notes, but the task of crafting the argument involves sifting through information, deciding between relevant and irrelevant materials, and arranging the most powerful evidence in your finished product. Remember to shape your photo essay around your argument through carefully made rhetorical choices about purpose, audience, and medium.

Composing a Website

If you decide to move your project online and produce a Website, your readers will then encounter your visual argument as **hypertext,** or a series of interlinked Web pages. Hypertext authors construct a framework for an argument through the **homepage** (the site's introduction), the **navigation scheme** (the site's organizational structure), and the contents of individual pages, offering both internal and external links designed to guide readers through the various levels of argument and evidence. In effect, a *hypertext argument* is produced by the collaboration between the author's direction and the readers' participation; in this

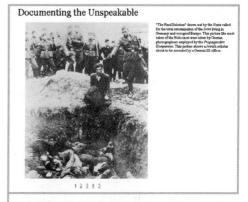

Documenting the Unspeakable

FIGURE 7.12. One of Ye Yuan's linked pages in his photo essay. Each link contains a single photograph with an explanatory caption.

AT A GLANCE

Designing a Photo Essay

1. Decide on the argument or thesis for your project.

2. Categorize your images, arranging them within the theme groups.

3. Organize them into different configurations: by chronology, theme, and subject.

4. Draft written text in the form of headings, captions, and paragraphs.

5. Determine your layout by experimenting with ways of formatting the words and images.

FIGURE 7.13. The Truth.com Crazyworld homepage demonstrates multiple strategies of effective Website composition.

way, the rhetorical situation of a Website as a visual argument becomes literally interactive, with readers playing an active role in the construction of meaning.

We see this dynamic determines the argumentative structure for a site such as the Truth. com's Crazyworld homepage, accessible through the Truth.com's archives of past pages (see Figure 7.13). The site's target audience might be young people inclined toward smoking. But by appearing on the Internet the site conveys its argument to the broader public, using the carnival motif to suggest what a "crazy world" we live in, where tobacco companies continue to sell—and consumers continue to buy and smoke—cigarettes that contain chemicals like arsenic, benzene, and cyanide. The site's primary *level of decorum* is plain style: through simple language, the carnival metaphor, and engaging visuals, the Website seeks to persuade viewers of the dangers of tobacco usage to both smokers and nonsmokers. This draws readers into the site, where they encounter the more explicitly argumentative indictments of Big Tobacco in the site's subsidiary content pages that reveal statistics, interviews, and indictments of cigarette companies.

The power of this visual argument lies in the flexibility of its design, which allows the audience to explore its many features. Although it resists relying on the sort of linear development typically found in paper texts, it still offers readers a variety of structured and clearly delineated pathways into its central arguments against Big Tobacco. On the surface, the site presents striking graphics and a visual *menu bar,* consisting of links to different aspects of the site. However, its primary *navigation toolbar,* the list of links that provide direct access to the interior of the Website, is actually hidden beneath the clown image. The toolbar only appears when the viewer rolls the mouse over the word *Navigate,* placed beneath the curved arrow that points at the clown. This Website, then, has been composed as a highly interactive piece of digital writing. There is no "right way" to navigate this site, and the writers are able to reach a wide audience and convey a powerful argument about the dangers of smoking.

COLLABORATIVE CHALLENGE

Perform a rhetorical analysis of several Websites: first, using the link from the *Envision* Website, look at "Error 404," a parody Webpage created during the U.S. war with Iraq; then compare http://www. whitehouse.org, a parody site, with the official http://www. whitehouse.gov site. How does the parody site use rhetoric, organization, style, and decorum to produce an argument? Working collaboratively, draft a sample homepage that makes the same argument as the parody page but without using parody. What rhetorical choices did you make in designing your page?

www.ablongman.com/envision/228

The process of authoring your own Website may seem daunting at first. However, in many ways drafting text for the Web resembles drafting the complex argument of a long research paper: in both cases, you need to identify the necessary elements of your composition, and then you need to follow a process of careful planning and organization.

In designing your Website, you will need to account for three levels of information: a *homepage* at the **primary level** (which will serve as the introduction to your site); a *series of topic pages* at the **secondary level** (which will contain both content and, sometimes, links to further, more specialized sub topic pages); and the *subtopic pages* at the **deep level** (which will contain

AT A GLANCE

Essential Elements for Composing a Website

- Decide upon your target audience.
- Select your content and main argument.
- Determine your purpose (to teach, persuade, or move to action).
- Compose your level of decorum.
- Design your site organization, navigation, and layout.

content and perhaps even more links). Although most sites contain only one homepage, some use a **splash page**—often featuring a single provocative quote, a flash animation, or gripping image—that functions as a hook or **gateway** to a more substantive introductory homepage. There is no limit on the number of topic and content pages you can include; you should determine the scope of your project and number of pages based on your assessment of how to make your argument most effectively.

In terms of design, composing a Website resembles the process of outlining a research paper. Yet there are important differences between digital writing and writing for print readers. First, you'll need to *chunk* your information—or divide it into manageable parts. Second, you'll want consistency of theme, font, and/or color throughout your site; avoid visual clutter and ineffectual use of images; think about the relationship between the words and images. Third, to achieve an effective design, you might want to create a *template,* or visual precedent, that establishes the key elements for the rest of the site, much as an introduction in a written paper often sets the style and conventions for the rest of the argument to follow.

Let's look at Sarah Douglas's research-based Website on Internet usage and isolation in forms such as instant messaging, online dating, and Weblogs. Her design challenge was to encourage her readers to explore each form of electronic communication in depth without losing perspective on the overall argument. Her solution entailed using design to structure her pages effectively (see Figure 7.14).

Her layers of navigation are embedded at the top of her site. First, in black, the title bar recurs from page to page. Beneath that, a navigation bar, also constant throughout the site, lists the major paths of her argument, color-coding each path with vivid, complementary colors. The third horizontal bar is the variable; it represents a secondary navigation bar for navigating within each node. Significantly, the color reproduces that of the major path from which it is derived. Therefore, at a glance, readers are oriented. In addition, in the blue box in the left margin, Sarah embedded key quotes that comment on the issues contained in that particular page. By choosing a color not

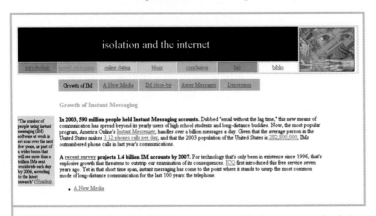

FIGURE 7.14. Sarah Douglas's Website on isolation and the Internet uses color design for effective navigation.

otherwise used by the site and also by setting the quotation box next to the main frame, Sarah creates an argument in the digital medium that captures the dynamic nature of her research project.

As you compose your own Website as a visual argument, be sure to consider **usability**—how user friendly your hypertext is and how accessible to users with disabilities. Even a site with professional design and a state-of-the-art graphic interface is ultimately ineffective if the audience cannot navigate it. You can test your Website for usability through the resources available on the *Envision* Website. Learning to write with attention to diverse readers will make you a more rhetorically savvy and effective communicator.

Making a Multimedia Montage

In this last section, we'll introduce you to writing projects such as visual collages, multimedia mixes using audio and video, hand-painted murals, self-produced films, startup magazines, and more. We'll call these texts **multimedia montages** because they involve the combination of numerous media (images, sound, writing, digital elements, and more) and because they often consist of nonlinear collections of evidence; the argument occurs in the project as a whole. Although the term *montage* is taken from film studies and refers to a sequence of still images, we'll extend it to refer to any combination of diverse media elements. The key to designing multimedia montages lies in understanding not only your audience, argument, medium, and form but also the purpose for the project.

Consider Yang Shi's decision to construct a visual collage based on his purpose. He began his project with the goal of creating a print photo essay on the subject of Mao Zedong's political impact on China, but he soon found that the photo essay's linear structure seemed to suggest a single definitive interpretation of Mao's influence. Since Yang was interested in exploring the complexity and contradictions inherent to the issue, he found the graphic possibilities of a visual collage preferable since this format allowed for a dialogue between simul-

AT A GLANCE

Designing a Website

- Draft a header; consider including an image in it.
- Map a logical organization for your site to help readers find information easily and understand your site's purpose and argument.
- Include a navigation tool, either at the top below the title or along the left margin.
- Develop clear content using words and images.
- Be consistent in using color, imagery, and font; avoid jarring color combinations or visual clutter.
- Resize images and locate them effectively on your pages.
- Create a series of links, either to subpages or to external sites.
- Provide a feedback link so users can email you comments.
- Include a "last updated" feature.
- Test your site for usability—both in terms of its general user friendliness and its accessibility to users with disabilities.

FIGURE 7.15. Yang Shi's photo collage about Mao Zedong and the Chinese Cultural Revolution.

taneous, competing images. By juxtaposing and intertwining numerous images from 1960s China, Yang Shi created a powerful, complex argument about the causalities of Mao's Cultural Revolution. Yang recognized that in a collage he could not only exploit the power of numerous images but also crop and arrange those images for rhetorical purpose. Accordingly, he created an overtly chaotic layout, one that he felt reflected the lack of focus of the Chinese Cultural Revolution (see Figure 7.15).

Despite the initial impression of randomness, however, there is an underlying order to Yang's collage: from the portrait of Mao heading the page, to the patriotic children surrounding him, to the statistics at the bottom, and finally to the outline of China as a faint red background at the poster's center in front of the protestors, all the visual elements structure the text's visual argument. In one sense, China encompasses all these representations—struggles and tragedies, ideals and victories. Yet the collage's inclusion of Mao's choice of political imagery—the propaganda drawings of happy workers—suggests that Mao undermined his own anti-West stance by "marketing" himself along the same lines as traditional

Student Writing

Read Yang Shi's reflection letter concerning his design decisions.

www.ablongman.com/envision/230

Western advertising. In this way, Yang's strategic use of the collage form produces a powerful statement through a careful arrangement of images and color.

Think carefully about your purpose, your argument, your audience's familiarity with the topic, and the organization of your materials as you design your own multimedia montage. You might decide to construct a dynamic text, using PowerPoint slide shows or film-editing software to produce a moving montage, slide show, or animation. KiYonna Carr, for example, in creating her visual argument on the enduring legacy of slavery on African-American women's self-image, paired a sequence of historical and contemporary photographs with her own voice-over commentary. Similarly, Derrick Jue chose a short-film format for his visual argument on protests over the war against Iraq. In what might be described as a photo essay set to music, Derrick developed his montage by carefully selecting images from the news that depicted scenes from the war, from protest demonstrations, and from footage of politicians speaking about the war, and then arranging them into a slide show set to the song "Wake Me Up," by Evanescence. Everything in the piece, from the order of images to their relationship to the accompanying sounds, serves a rhetorical purpose, working to convey Derrick's argument about the American public's sometimes angry, sometimes ambivalent reactions to the war against Iraq; the rapid succession of images paired with stirring music provokes an emotional reaction in its audience, without the need for written commentary.

Some of the most innovative multimedia montages convey their visual arguments not electronically but rather **tactilely,** using touch or physical form. Thus, when you think of *multimedia,* take it literally and don't rule out creating physical models, three-dimensional structures, and reproductions with material elements. You might follow Jessica Vun's example: she produced a hand-sewn manners book to give readers the "feel" for gender roles in the 1800s, the subject of her research paper. Or consider Allison Smith's project, in which she made drawings by hand and stained them with tea to suggest their age for a project on Margaret Sanger's political cartoons in her battle for legalized birth control. Perhaps Dexian Cai's work might inspire your invention strategies: for his visual argument against the globalization of McDonald's into Asian markets, Dex brought in traditional Chinese snacks as an alternative, food version of an op-ad. Finally, you might consider Lauren Dunagan's decision to transform her research argument about the visual rhetoric of graffiti into a 14-foot-long hand-painted mural that used graffiti itself to make an argument about the power of graffiti as a medium for social protest and self-expression. To paraphrase famous theorist Marshall McLuhan, in Lauren's project, the medium became the message.

In each of these cases, the student used the physical nature of the text itself (a model, a stained historical document, an edible artifact, and a mural) in a rhetorically purposeful manner. The range of possibilities for your visual argument suggests the ways writing has changed over time—and how it continues to evolve with the advent of new writing and composing technologies. From Weblogs to interactive multimedia exhibits and collaborative hypertext projects, the way we understand language, argument, and persuasion continues to evolve. With the ever-changing face of modern media, you have an increasing number of choices for designing arguments with purpose, power, and creativity.

Designing Your Own Arguments

In this chapter, you've learned how writing offers an opportunity to experiment with designing and producing your texts in ways that meet your purpose and match the expectations of your audience. Often this means knowing, understanding, and adhering to conventions set forth by a community of scholars, readers, or writers. This is the case for the document design of your research paper, cover page, abstract, and bio. At other times, this means exploring innovative approaches to design in multimedia contexts. It is also the case for the document design of hybrid compositions and visual arguments. All modes of design depend on your rhetorical expertise in choosing a level of decorum, in knowing what strategies best work for your situation, in deciding on your medium and your format, and then in having these choices support your purpose in designing your work. By examining academic essays, op-ads, photo essays, Websites, and multimedia montages, you have seen that the rhetorical principles of audience, argument, form, and purpose carry across diverse media. It's time now for you to make your contribution. Write out your brainstorming ideas, and begin to design your own argument.

PREWRITING CHECKLIST

Focus on Analyzing Design in Arguments

❏ **Argument:** What is the topic and the argument? What evidence is used to support the argument? What is the rhetorical stance and point of view on the topic? What role does verbal, visual, or multimedia play in persuasion in this text? Are words and images complementary or does the argument work primarily through one means?

❏ **Audience:** Whom is the argument intended to reach? What response seems to be anticipated from the audience? Sympathetic? Hostile? Concerned?

(continued)

- ❏ **Medium:** Is the medium used appropriate for the argument and its target audience? What type of interaction does the medium create with its audience?

- ❏ **Form:** What are the specific characteristics of the medium? Consider layout, images, style, font. How are these elements organized?

- ❏ **Purpose:** What is the purpose in presenting the argument to the audience in this design? To move them to action? inform them? teach them? What type of decorum or style (grand, middle, or plain) is used to realize this purpose?

WRITING PROJECTS

1. **Design elements to accompany your final revision:** Write an abstract and bio for your final research paper. Check that you have adhered to proper academic document design. Now compose a one-page op-ad featuring the argument from your research project. The op-ad should combine both images and written elements. Keep in mind those elements important to successful advertising, including consideration of audience and purpose; use of space, color, and image; strategies of development; and an appropriate hook. Indicate in a written note the intended audience (who would read it) and context (what magazine or newspaper they would read it in) for your ad. Post all your documents online as a showcase of your work as a writer and researcher.

2. **Visual Argument:** Create a photo essay based on the argument from your research paper or as part of an independent project. The images you use in your photo essay may be from your paper, or you can use a completely new set, particularly if you did not use images in your paper. Your argument may mirror that in your research paper, or you may focus on a smaller portion of your overall argument. The style, arrangement, medium, and rhetorical strategies of your photo essay should match your audience and your purpose. Include written text in your photo essay strategically. Once you have finished, write a one-page reflection on the strategies you used in this project.

3. **Multimedia Argument:** Transform your written essay into an electronic format that uses audio strategically as part of the text's persuasive power. You can match your images to a recorded argument. Alternatively, combine visual images with a soundtrack. Pick your music carefully, and time each image to match a particular mood or moment in the music or select music to match the sequence of your images. If you are transforming a paper essay into an electronic audio version, feel free to modify your organization, arrangement, text selection, and even treatment of images to accommodate this shift in medium. Once you have finished, write a one-page reflection on how the shift in medium affected your argument.

Visit www.ablongman.com/envision for expanded assignment guidelines and student projects.

CHAPTER 8

Delivering Presentations

Y ou've finished your written argument. You've submitted it to your instructor according to proper academic conventions as explained in Chapters 7 and 9, and maybe you have even translated it into a hybrid composition or visual argument. But sometimes you are asked to do more: to present your argument to an audience in the form of a "live" presentation. Both academic and public audiences call for oral or multimedia presentations on occasion, and you need to develop skills and strategies for designing and delivering presentations to take advantage of these opportunities. In this chapter, we'll learn from famous writers and speakers, such as Dr. Martin Luther King Jr., whose famous "I Have a Dream" speech offers one of the most powerful pieces of rhetoric in the English language. King's powerful presentation did not derive solely from the written script. As the image in Figure 8.1 captures, it was the convergence of well-crafted language, passionate delivery, and deliberate gesture that combined to produce that landmark articulation of the civil rights movement.

FIGURE 8.1. Martin Luther King Jr. presents to a crowd at the Lincoln Memorial during his "I Have a Dream" speech in Washington DC, August 28, 1963.

You might look to King and other orators as models for effective presentation strategies as you prepare to shape your writing for oral delivery. As you approach drafting your presentation, take time to explore the many possibilities available to you for this act of effective communication. You will need to base your decisions for picking certain presentation strategies on a solid rhetorical foundation, and to do so, you need to understand the *branches of oratory* as well as how to apply them to particular occasions. In this chapter, you'll learn effective strategies for selecting the appropriate branch of oratory for your rhetorical situation, for translating your written argument into a multimedia presentation, and for scripting and designing a memorable and effective delivery of your argument.

Chapter Preview Questions

- How can I transform a written argument into a visual or oral presentation?
- When should I use a speech, a poster session, a PowerPoint show, or a live performance? What rhetorical choices shape my decision?
- What are the branches of oratory, and how do they shape my presentation options?
- How can the canons of memory and delivery help my presentation?

Understanding the Branches of Oratory

As you prepare to draft, design, and deliver a compelling presentation, it is helpful to turn to classical rhetoric for ways of understanding the needs of your specific writing situation—your own purpose, audience, and persona. For even though today we turn to rhetoric to shape any visual or verbal communication, originally rhetoric evolved as a technique in classical Greece for teaching people how to speak both eloquently and persuasively in public. Classical rhetoricians such as Aristotle divided oratory into three "branches" or causes based on time, purpose, and content. Let's explore the way the principles behind these **branches of oratory** can be applied to your goal of writing a presentation.

The first branch, **judicial** or **forensic discourse,** involves defending or accusing, and it usually deals with the past. Think of this as oratory about *right or wrong.* The second branch, **deliberative** or **legislative discourse,** concerns politics or policy and focuses most often on the future. You might think of this as oratory about what is beneficial or harmful. The purpose of such oratory is to argue for or against specific actions that might take place in the future. Finally, **epideictic** rhetoric deals with the present time. Also called *ceremonial* or *demonstrative* oratory, this discourse is all about praising or blaming, and the purpose is to revel in the moment.

Since the rhetorical branches may not be familiar concepts, let's look at some contexts for them that you might encounter in your own writing and speaking situations:

- For *judicial* or *forensic discourse,* you might present a position on a past action in debate team, moot court, or law school, using verbal arguments as well as charts, graphs, photos, and other visual evidence arranged and designed to persuade your audience.

BRANCHES OF ORATORY: CONTEMPORARY EXAMPLES

Judicial or forensic discourse—involves accusing or defending	Deliberative or legislative discourse—designed to argue for or against specific actions	Epideictic discourse—involves praise or blame
Johnny Cochran's 1995 defense of O. J. Simpson represents a notable instance of forensic discourse when Cochran used powerful visual and verbal rhetoric to clear O. J. Simpson of murder charges.	In his documentary film *An Inconvenient Truth* (2006), Al Gore employs deliberative discourse to advise the audience of the necessary steps for reducing the future impact of global warming.	Eulogies, such as the speech Maya Angelou gave at Coretta Scott King's funeral in February 2006, are a typical form of epideictic discourse in that they center on praising and celebrating people's lives.

Notice the way Cochran makes his point visually by slipping on gloves that had been used in the crime to underscore his point "If it doesn't fit, you must acquit."	*An Inconvenient Truth* features Gore giving a series of lectures, many of which are rendered more powerful by carefully chosen background images and striking photographs.	Although Maya Angelou's tone in speaking of Coretta Scott King was celebratory, her demeanor was somber and respectful.

- For *deliberative* or *legislative discourse,* you might exhort or dissuade an audience if you speak at a conference to promote the launching of your own business, the development of new software, or a plan for a cross-country fundraising trip; you would write a memo, a financial plan, and the specifications concerning the worthiness of the enterprise; you might also use PowerPoint slides, charts, images, prototypes, models, and animation to persuade your audience.

- For *epideictic* or *ceremonial discourse,* you might engage in a rhetoric of display in a senior thesis, company report, advertising campaign, or even a political party statement designed to praise (or blame) a candidate.

As you can tell, although the branches of oratory may be unfamiliar in theory, we see them in practice all the time, from the professor's PowerPoint lecture defending the inclusion of "intelligent design" in high school science courses (forensic) to a Kappa Alpha Theta member's speech to her sorority sisters about the success of their community outreach program that year (epideictic). When you draft your presentations, you'll need to assess which branch of oratory best addresses the demands of your particular rhetorical situation.

Audience, Purpose, and Persona

The branches of oratory are only one of the resources from classical rhetoric that writers draw on in crafting successful presentations. Concepts such as attention to *audience, purpose,* and *persona,* which we've discussed in relation to written texts, are key elements for oral rhetoric as well. For instance, consider how attention to purpose, audience, and persona determines the presentations shown in Figures 8.2 and 8.3. What kind of audience might each of the speakers be facing? How does each one need to design a presentation, select words and visual material, and practice a form of delivery that is specific to the rhetorical situation? In each case, the speaker carefully constructed his or her presentation to be a powerful visual and verbal argument.

Consider the many kinds of presentations you encounter as part of your academic experience. Do you attend lectures on specific topics, with a single speaker standing at a podium and delivering a verbal argument? Have you been an audience member for a formal academic panel, where multiple speakers take turns presenting arguments, sometimes providing handouts to the audience or using a projection screen to convey their ideas? Or is your most frequent presentation experience the PowerPoint lecture, in

FIGURE 8.2. The Guerrilla Girls present at a symposium on the feminist role in contemporary performance art.

FIGURE 8.3. Steve Jobs discusses Intel technology at the 2006 Mac World convention.

which the speaker provides a point-by-point map of the material, includes images related to the subject matter, and sometimes posts a copy of the slides on a Website for future reading? Although these presentations might differ in format, they are similar in that all are designed to meet the needs of their particular audience and rhetorical situation.

CREATIVE PRACTICE

Keep a log of all the kinds of presentations you encounter in one week at your university. If possible, take a camera with you and document your observations of each kind of presentation. What are the differences between them? Write down as many details as you can and reflect on which type of presentation you would like to try. Write up your reflections in the form of a short narrative.

In your own work, you may find yourself presenting to your class, to a larger academic audience as part of a conference panel, to college administrators or a university forum, or even to a public audience. In each case, you'll have many choices to make. You can start determining the possibilities for your own presentation by using focusing questions such as those found in the "At a Glance" box, designed to help you identify your audience, purpose, and persona.

AT A GLANCE

Identifying Your Audience, Purpose, and Persona

1. What format will my presentation take (purely oral speech, multimedia slide show, interactive drama, etc.)?

2. Who is my audience? What do they know or not know about this topic already? How receptive will they be to my material?

3. What is my purpose? What do I hope to accomplish? What is my ultimate goal with this presentation?

4. What branch of oratory does my presentation represent? Is it designed to defend or accuse? To argue a position or policy? To celebrate or condemn?

5. What persona do I want to convey to my audience (knowledgeable, friendly, impassioned, concerned, expert, peer, etc.)? How do I visualize myself as a presenter?

6. What kind of tone do I want to use in my presentation (fun, serious, informative, sarcastic, concerned, alarmed, practical, etc.)?

7. What kinds of supporting materials do I plan to use in my presentation (quotes from research, photographs in a PowerPoint slide or on a handout, film or commercial clips, graphs, charts, posters, etc.)?

As the final point in the "At a Glance" box suggests, most presentations to-day include strategically chosen visual texts—what we used to call "visual aids"—that in fact perform a crucial rhetorical function: they collaborate with words to convey the speaker's argument. A photo of extensive crop damage can provide *evidence* in an environmental science lecture, and a chart can communicate economic trends to an audience quickly and effectively. Sometimes, moreover, visuals provide a stronger message than or even contradict the verbal component of the speech. A presenter might use a visual text ironically—for instance, showing a slide listing statistics that refute an opponent's argument or providing an emotional appeal while conveying information in a flat tone of voice. In these ways, visual texts communicate powerful arguments that you can use as part of your overall presentation.

Transforming Research into a Presentation

The process of transforming your research-based argument into a presentation can be quite challenging, for you need to take into account scope, content, and style. If you have 15 written pages of argument, this would probably take 40 minutes or more to read out loud. But of course, you would certainly not choose to simply read your written paper, for writing is often different when meant to be read silently versus when meant to be read out loud. Only in certain academic circles is there a preference for complex, written prose as a formal presentation style. In most cases, audiences desire clear, conversational speech that is easy to follow. To achieve this goal, you need to think about transforming your research argument from one kind of writing to another—from writing for readers to writing for listeners. You'll also need to cut down the sheer amount of material you can convey and think about ways to present it in an interesting, memorable way. You can accomplish all these goals through a process of *selection, organization,* and *translation.*

AT A GLANCE

Key Steps for Transforming Your Research Argument into a Presentation

- **Scope:** How do you convert 10, 15, or even 20 pages of argument into a 5-, 10-, or 15-minute oral presentation?

  Answer: Selection

- **Content:** How do you reframe the content so that it makes sense to your audience?

  Answer: Organization

- **Style:** How do you change the written word to a spoken, visual, and digital medium?

  Answer: Translation

Selection

Keep in mind that as you consider what materials to select, you should always plan for a shorter presentation time than what you actually have allotted. Most of us speak for longer than we realize; so if you are planning material for a 10-minute presentation, aim for 8; a 15-minute presentation, aim for 12; a 5-minute presentation, aim for 3. One way to keep your time frame manageable is to select a subset of material to present. That is, if your written argument comprises three main areas, plan to cover only one in your presentation. Also, if you plan on speaking extemporaneously (or improvising), be sure that you build this into your schedule for your presentation. Finally, remember to be as selective with your visual evidence as you are with your overall information; if your research relies heavily on images, charts, or graphs, be sure to carefully consider which to include in your presentation. You might opt to use only the most powerful images, or you might decide to center your presentation on a single case study or example and therefore feature only those materials relevant to that narrower focus.

You should find the focusing questions in the "At a Glance" box helpful for moving through the process of selection for your project. Question 1 will help you identify the crux of your presentation. This may be your thesis, but it may also *not* be your thesis. That is, in the course of writing your paper, you may have found that what really matters most is the need to raise awareness about an issue, the need to publicize potential solutions to a problem, or the need to advocate for a particular research agenda. Question 2 will help you narrow your project to a few points designed to convey your project's significance to the audience. Question 3 will help you confirm your purpose and begin to translate your main point into a medium that will persuade your audience: do you want to raise awareness, rally support, propose a change, offer new insights, or suggest avenues of future research? You need to select your materials with these goals in mind.

AT A GLANCE

Questions for Focusing Your Argument

1. What matters most about this project?
2. What two or three points can I make to convey my answer to the above question?
3. What do I want my audience to walk away thinking about when I am done?

Organization

As you move through the process of transforming your research into an oral presentation, you have an opportunity to **reorder** your written argument to meet the needs and expectations of a listening audience. You might, for instance, begin with your conclusion and then convey the narrative of your research. Or you might want to show your visual evidence first, ask questions, and then provide your thesis at the end. In other words, you don't need to create your presentation as a miniature version of your written talk. Be innovative in your choice of organization; think about what structure would be the most effective for your audience.

To help with this process, create a flowchart, outline, or block graphic of each element of your presentation. Don't forget your opening "hook" and closing message as you work on organizing your presentation. Try matching each component to a minute-by-minute schedule to make sure that you are within time limits. And finally, consider creating a **visual outline** by drawing or pasting in images next to your verbal cues to show how and when you will use visual rhetoric as a part of your presentation. Looking at a section of Tommy Tsai's presentation outline (see Figure 8.4) for his oral presentation on World War II propaganda, we can see that he carefully paired the words he intended to speak (on the right) with the slides he would show to his audience (on the left). In this way, he could clearly map the relationship between the visual and verbal elements of his presentation, creating a strong underlying organization for his argument. The key here is to see the presentation as its own genre of writing and draft a text that meets the needs of both your audience and your purpose.

AT A GLANCE

Key Questions to Shape Your Organization

- How do I want to "hook" my audience? What would be an effective way to open my presentation? Should I appeal to emotion? to reason? Should I establish my authority as a researcher? What parts of my researcher would help me do so?

- What strategies do I want to use to organize my presentation? Narration? Example? Cause and effect? Problem-solution? Process? Definition? Which strategies would be most useful for conveying my argument clearly and effectively to my audience?

- What main points do I want to use as the centerpiece of my presentation? Do I want

to focus on a single case study or on multiple examples?

- At what point do I want to present my thesis? Do I want to start with a question or line of inquiry and then end with my argument in my conclusion? Or do I want to start strong with my thesis within the first moments of my talk and then prove it with evidence?

- How do I want to close my presentation? Do I want to conclude by summing up my points or by pointing to the future or further implications? Do I want to end with a call to action or with a provocative question? What strategy would create the greatest impact on my audience?

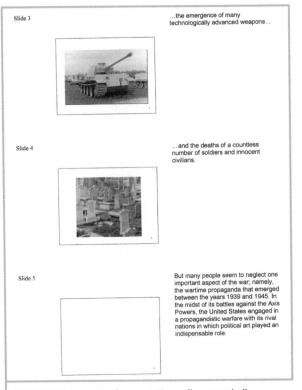

Slide 3 ...the emergence of many technologically advanced weapons...

Slide 4 ...and the deaths of a countless number of soldiers and innocent civilians.

Slide 5 But many people seem to neglect one important aspect of the war; namely, the wartime propaganda that emerged between the years 1939 and 1945. In the midst of its battles against the Axis Powers, the United States engaged in a propagandistic warfare with its rival nations in which political art played an indispensable role.

FIGURE 8.4. Tommy Tsai's presentation outline strategically juxtaposed the oral script with the visual evidence he would present in his slides. Note that he includes a blank slide.

Translation

The final step of the transformation is to translate your writing from text meant to be read to text meant to be heard. This is more important than it may first appear. Think about presentations you've attended where the speaker read from a complicated, verbose script, without looking up or changing the inflection of his or her voice. It's possible that if you sat down and read that same speech, you might have found it interesting; however, listening to the material presented in that way, you probably found yourself bored, confused, or both. The point here is that there are important differences between these types of writing, and you need to carefully *translate* your research into a form accessible to your listening audience.

The extent to which you modify your writing as you draft your script depends on your audience and purpose; for instance, if you were trying to persuade your college administrators to endorse a new recycling policy (an example of deliberative discourse), you would adopt a different style and mode of speaking than if you were accusing that same administration of inattention to the recycling issue at a student council meeting (an example of forensic discourse). However, in general, there are some steps you can take to facilitate the translation process. As you script your speech, examine the length of your sentences, the complexity of your prose, and the sophistication of your diction. Most listeners find shorter sentences, specific language, and clear transitions and prose structures important for understanding oral discourse. In addition, be sure to avoid jargon and to define any terms with which your audience might not be familiar. Consider adding to your script explicit

signposting—verbal "signs" that indicate the steps of an argument or the structure of your presentation. More often than not, listeners need more explicit signposting than do readers of papers.

Listeners also respond to humor, direct address, concrete examples, and even questions. These strategies are designed to directly engage your audience's attention. As you write your script, annotate your written copy with places where you pause, emphasize words, look up, or laugh. Also include reminders of when to point to visuals or advance your slides.

AT A GLANCE

Signposting

Help listeners by including these terms to structure your argument:

- First
- Second
- Third
- On one hand
- On the other hand
- For example
- Consider
- But
- Yet
- In conclusion

CREATIVE PRACTICE

Compare the very different styles of two speeches, both given by women, both concerning human rights, but presented to very different audiences and by very different personas: Eleanor Roosevelt's speech entitled "Adoption of the Declaration of Human Rights," delivered December 9, 1948, in Paris, France; and a speech by Cher (played by Alicia Silverstone) from the movie *Clueless* (1995) on "Whether all oppressed people should be allowed refuge in America." Look at the written versions of their speeches as you listen to them talk. What characteristics of the spoken word does each piece of writing share? How are they different?

www.ablongman.com/envision/231

Transformation in Action

Let's take a close look at how one student transformed her written research paper into a multimedia research presentation. As we saw in Chapter 4, Susan Zhang wrote a research proposal on the photo manipulation of media images. After finishing the written proposal, she was asked to present her proposal orally to her class. What follows is the written script for her presentation; as you read through it, you may want to reference her original proposal (see pages 124-129) in order to appreciate the way she transformed her written argument into an oral presentation.

Note how Susan has references to her slides.

Hi everyone, my name is Susan, and before I begin, a little bit about me.

[cue slide: "About Me"]

Last summer I vacationed with my family in Australia, and that was the beginning of my interest in photography, as you can see. **[cue animation: Mom & me]** And I had a really great time taking pictures of wildlife there, including this one of a duck. **[cue animation: duck]** Well actually that was all a lie. I've never been south of the equator, and that picture of my mom and me is grafted onto the background of Sidney harbor, and that duck is a digital rendering of the animal.

Her language is casual and low style. She even uses humor.

This prompts some unusual questions. If I can pass off a digitally altered photograph as real, why can't others, such as the news and the media for example? Can we trust the pictures that we see in the news?

[cue slide: title slide]

And that brings us to the topic of my proposal, which is titled "Little Photoshop of Horrors? Digital Manipulation of Media Images."

Let's start by looking at some examples.

Her explicit signposting helps the audience follow her argument.

[cue slide: OJ] This photo is from 1994 when O. J. Simpson was arrested. *Newsweek* kept his mugshot unaltered, while *Time* darkened the color of his skin. Minority groups protested that this made him look darker and more menacing and therefore presumed his guilt. The photographer claimed that he was only going for a more artful, more compelling image.

[cue slide: Martha Stewart] This is the *Newsweek* cover released last year when Martha Stewart was released from prison.

The caption is "Martha's Last Laugh: After Prison, She's Thinner, Wealthier and Ready for Primetime." This may be true, but the slim body pictured is not in fact hers.

[cue slide: Walinski]

This photo was taken in 1994, which is when a British soldier was photographed pointing a gun at an Iraqi citizen. It is actually a composite **[cue animation: original photos]** of these two photos. The photographer later apologized and was fired.

[cue slide: "Introduction"]

What happened? Before digital imaging, people trusted photography to be an honest medium. A photographer and his camera were deemed the unbiased purveyor of reality. How has the capacity for photo manipulation affected the credibility of photos in media? Some hypotheses I have are: **[cue animation: point one]** has it led to a loss of credibility due to more powerful image-editing techniques, or **[cue animation: point two]** has it led to increased credibility due to the evolution of stricter standards?

[cue slide: "Perspectives"]

Some perspectives I plan to take are number one historical. **[cue animation: historical]** I intend to look at photo manipulation before digital imaging to look at whether people doctored photos then and whether the guidelines are stricter then versus now. **[cue animation: public]** Also, I plan to look at the public response to digital manipulation. For example, where is the line drawn? Sometimes when the doctoring is obvious, it could be interpreted as social satire or commentary; however, if it's subtle,

She uses rhetorical questions and cuts down the length and complexity of her prose in order to convey her argument effectively to her audience.

people could perceive this as perception. Also, how easily can people recognize altered images? **[cue animation: photographer]** And for the photographer's point of view, what are some of the reasons for our digitally manipulated photographs. Could it be out of respect for the privacy of the subject, or for the sensibilities of the audience? Also, what are the guidelines and the various contexts in which they may apply?

[cue slide: "Methods"]

Some methods that I'll use for my research include books. **[cue animation: books]** I'll start with a kind of general approach to ethical photojournalism. Some books I have include *The Burden of Visual Truth: The Role of Photojournalism in Mediating Reality* and also some books on digital image ethics. I also plan at looking at **[cue animation: databases]** online databases to find some examples of digital image ethics and photo manipulation, some articles on recent controversies over altered photos, authoritative opinions by photojournalists and photographers, and some examples of how their public responded to the incidents.

[cue animation: Websites] And also I'll look at some other Websites such as news and media sites online and some smaller photojournalism sites to see how they address image authenticity and to see if they label their images as illustrations or as genuine photographs. And finally I'll look at online guidelines. The National Press Photography Association has a Website for a digital code of ethics, for example.

[cue slide: "Summary"]

In summary, we find digital imaging has made photo manipulation easier and perhaps more prevalent. For example, you could use aesthetic touch-ups, graft parts of pictures onto others, and even construct a picture entirely from scratch. As a result, there's a lot of public skepticism over the reliability of the images. So my proposal is to explore to what extent this skepticism is really justified.

Her strong and compelling conclusion provides an effective ending to her script.

Reading through Susan's proposal, we can see the effective ways in which she transformed her proposal for oral delivery.

Selection: Although she focused on a single pair of images in her original proposal, Susan used a series of current, recognizable examples of photo manipulation to persuade her audience in her presentation, including some photographs she "altered" herself. She also condensed her sources section and eliminated her timeline altogether, taking into account what information would most interest her listeners.

Organization: Susan's organization in the latter half of her presentation resembles that found in her proposal in moving through methods, to sources, to conclusion. However, her introduction is completely reworked, designed to better capture the attention of a listening—and viewing—audience.

Translation: Throughout, Susan simplified her language and moved to a more colloquial tone that matched the very colloquial introduction she used to hook her audience. Compare, for instance, the final line of her oral presentation with this one, which served as the final sentence for her proposal: "A closer look at the occurrences of digital manipulation today, as regulated by the evolving guidelines of photojournalism, could reveal to what extent such skepticism is warranted." In her presentation, the language is much more direct, clear, and succinct. It is tailored to a listening audience.

CREATIVE PRACTICE

Visit the *Envision* Website to compare the writing in Martin Luther King Jr.'s "Letter from Birmingham Jail" with the transcript of his famous speech, "I've Been to the Mountaintop." How does each one indicate either a reader or a listener as the primary audience? Now work on writing for different audiences: translate the letter into a speech and the speech into a written argument. What did you change? What rhetorical techniques work best for each form of writing? What can you apply from this exercise to your own process of translation?

www.ablongman.com/envision/232

Considering Strategies of Design

As you can tell from Susan Zhang's presentation, careful translation can be the key to communicating your argument powerfully and persuasively. Her combination of personal example, a series of persuasive case studies, a strong voice, clear structure, and solid delivery all combined to create a compelling presentation. Let's discuss some other examples to get your ideas flowing about the possibilities available to you for your presentation. These designs include *oral delivery, media components,* and even *embodied rhetoric*—that is, the use of the body to communicate visual information.

- Jessica Luo, presenting on the media coverage of the Tiananmen Square incident in 1989, decided to center her talk on a significant number of photographs from both the Chinese and European presses. She organized them into pairs to demonstrate the different persuasive arguments made through the photos by each media organization. She wanted to move a mainly American student audience into caring about an incident that happened in China more than 15 years ago. Thus, she decided to transform her "objective" writer's voice into a personal narrative and used rhythmic, repetitive terms that explained the rhetorical significance of each image.
- For a project on land mines, Stewart Dorsey decided to show two PowerPoint presentations side by side on two large projection screens. He placed himself in the middle of the two screens to suggest that his argument offered a feasible compromise between polarized camps.

- Max Echtemendy used a hands-on approach to design his research presentation on fantasy violence. First, he set up a table showing horror novels, DVD boxes, articles in magazines, music videos, and many other examples of "fantasy violence all around us." Then he asked students to complete a brief questionnaire, and he worked with their answers as he discussed the key elements of his argument. He ended by showing a clip from *The Lord of the Rings* and asking for audience response.

- Tom Hurlbutt, exploring the implications of Internet surveillance, created a dynamic PowerPoint presentation that linked to Websites, asked students to log on to Amazon, and revealed code that showed their search history from previous class sessions. In this way, he integrated graphic effects in a rhetorically purposeful way.

- Eric Jung, for a presentation on art and technology, transformed the classroom into a twenty-second-century museum, complete with "exhibits" of technologically produced art. He assumed the role of museum guide and gave the class a "tour" of the exhibit, concluding with a "retrospective" lecture about the early twenty-first-century debate over how digital media changed popular conceptions of art.

As you can tell from these innovative projects, there are many effective ways to use strategies of selection, organization, and translation to design the most intriguing, powerful, and appropriate presentation for your purposes.

COLLABORATIVE CHALLENGE

Take 10 minutes to brainstorm the design possibilities for your presentation. Complete the following questions:

1. What format will your presentation take?
2. What materials do you plan to use in your presentation?
3. What might be a potential outline for your presentation?

Now peer review your responses with a partner. Have each person suggest changes, new ideas, and alternative ways of designing the presentation. You might also use this time to begin practicing the presentation. Finally, to get a sense of how your presentation will change according to your audience, consider how your answers would change depending on whether you presented to a class audience or a group of friends in the dorm, a review panel at a company, or a potential employer. Experiment to find the most effective ways to design your presentation.

Using Visuals Rhetorically

Presentations can vary greatly in their design and delivery. At times, you may be asked to deliver an exclusively *oral presentation,* in which you make your argument without the use of any visuals. This form of public speaking is the one most of us are quite familiar with: great civil rights leaders, peace activists, and political leaders rarely cue up a PowerPoint slide to make their points. Yet, more frequently, even the shortest talks are augmented by strategically chosen visual texts that enhance the persuasiveness of an argument. For your own assignments, it is likely that you will be given the option of using visuals in your presentations, so it is important that you develop strategies for doing so effectively—that is, with rhetorical purpose.

Writing for Poster Sessions

One mode of presentation that communicates an argument both verbally and visually is the **poster.** This presentation style is used most frequently in the sciences, where information is presented through the format of the poster session. At science conferences, visitors walk through giant halls showcasing hundreds of posters, reading the ones of interest and often requesting a copy of the paper on which the poster is based. If you plan on pursuing a science major, you might want to use this presentation format to practice writing in that medium.

To write for a poster session, researchers take materials from their larger projects, select salient points, organize the material into shorter written summaries with complementary charts and illustrations, and attach the materials to a poster board. The goal of a poster session is that every contributor produces a visual-verbal display that conveys the research accurately, concisely, and in an engaging way. In Figure 8.5 and

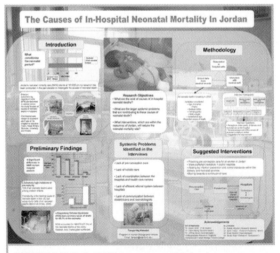

FIGURE 8.5. Tanja Haj-Hassan won awards for these posters, displayed at the 2005 Stanford Symposium for Undergraduate Research in Progress.

Figure 8.6, we can see examples of award-winning student posters produced for Stanford University's 2005 Symposium of Undergraduate Research in Progress.

Clearly, the authors of these posters designed them differently; however, we can see similarities in the strategies they used to create their visual arguments. In the words of the award committee, both demonstrate "visually exciting design" that conveys "intellectually compelling content" in a way that facilitates "overall excellent communication with a general audience." They accomplish these goals by signposting their posters with bold headers; structuring their information into a clear vertical hierarchy; pairing their concise, written content with powerful photographs and information graphics; and by presenting their visual-verbal argument in a way that effectively engages the interest and understanding of their audience.

When you turn to create your own poster, keep in mind the fundamental elements for writing this kind of presentation described in the "At a Glance" box. By following these guidelines, you can create effective visual-verbal texts that are consistent in format and easily understood by audience members.

Writing for PowerPoint or Slide-Based Presentations

In addition to poster sessions, PowerPoint presentations have become very popular in both academic and professional contexts. The software itself is just a tool, but it's an incredibly

FIGURE 8.6. Co-researchers Carlos Ortiz and Jonathan Hwang transformed their research into this award-winning poster for the 2005 Stanford Symposium for Undergraduate Research in Progress.

AT A GLANCE

Guidelines for Creating Posters for a Poster Session

- Make sure your poster is readable from a distance; size your fonts accordingly.

- Put the poster's title, authors, and academic affiliation at the top.

- Avoid visual clutter; consider using white space to offset various elements, including tables, figures, and written texts.

- Arrange materials in columns not rows.

- Avoid long passages of texts; rely primarily on visual persuasion.

- Always check with the conference organizers for their specific guidelines.

For more detailed advice, go to the *Envision* Website.

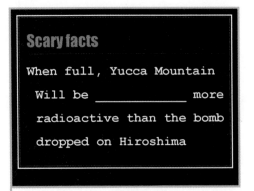

FIGURE 8.7. Natalie Farrell's presentation titled "Yucca Mountain and Nuclear Waste: Gambling with the Future of the Human Race, December 2002," slide 5.

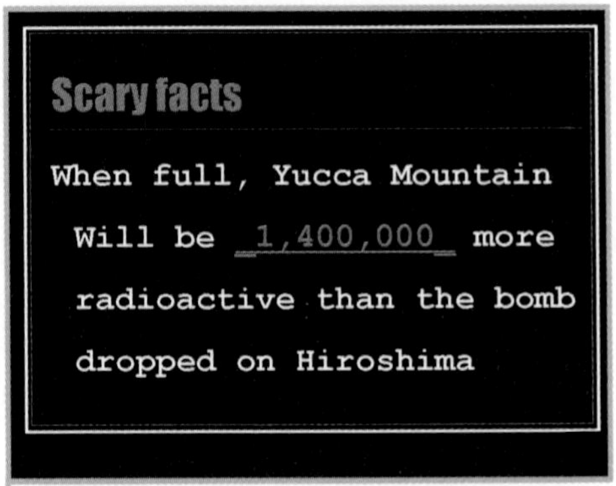

FIGURE 8.8. Natalie Farrell's presentation, slide 6, in which she dramatically fills in the blank

helpful and timesaving one that can organize and display your key points of argument and your visual materials into a series of slides. The more you become familiar with PowerPoint as a tool, the more you can use it effectively to offer a timed slide show of images, to emphasize points through visual design (highlighting text, blowing up images, sliding across a picture, engaging the audience by filling in blanks as you speak, and much more).

Alex Bleyleben, for instance, used PowerPoint to project slides of endangered rhinos for a paper on global activism. In one dramatic move, he included a black slide to shift the audience's attention from the gruesome images back to his own presence at the podium as he delivered the key points of his argument. He then concluded with an impressive image. Another student, Natalie Farrell, taught herself PowerPoint in one evening for her presentation on Yucca Mountain. She included slides with deliberate blanks left in the list of statistics to engage the class and ask them to calculate the projected environmental risk of a nuclear disaster (see Figures 8.7 and 8.8).

As Natalie clicked forward in her presentation, she elicited the class to guess at the power of radiation in Yucca Mountain before shocking the audience with the actual numbers. She succeeded in what cultural critic Stephen Shugart deems is the necessity of "transforming the concept of PowerPoint from 'presenting at' into 'a way of promoting discussion' or to use it in unconventional ways to create more effective learning situations." One way to think about writing with PowerPoint as a rhetorical tool is to return to our model of research as a conversation or dialogue. How can you engage your audience, as Natalie did, rather than throw data at them or run through a list of ideas?

When writing for PowerPoint, keep in mind the way you want your audience to respond. Remember that before this software was developed, a speaker needed to use slides to share visual material. If you think of using PowerPoint the way you would use slides in a presentation, you might be less likely to fill each slide with bulleted lists of information or large amounts of writing. Consider exactly how you plan to use each slide and then craft your presentation around your answers:

AT A GLANCE

Writing an Effective Power-Point Presentation

- Use purposeful visuals not clip art.
- Plan to spend time discussing the images on each slide.
- Don't put too much text on each slide or rely too heavily on bullet lists.
- Keep fonts consistent in style, size, and color to avoid distracting the audience.
- Break complex ideas into multiple slides.
- Give a handout with full quotations as necessary.
- Include sound effects and animation rhetorically rather than for flair or flash.

Find more detailed advice on the *Envision* Website.

- Do you want to show photographs, cartoons, or other visual images?
- Do you want to raise questions and then fill in answers?
- Do you want to show an interactive map or link to a Website?
- Do you want to embed a link to a movie clip or use animation?
- Do you want to include a blank slide for emphasis or use other creative methods of presentation?

These questions suggest many purposeful, rhetorical ways of writing for a PowerPoint presentation. Again, begin with your purpose and your audience, and then design your presentation to meet your needs. The guidelines presented here cover some of the more common techniques you should incorporate in your presentation. But realize that you can modify these "rules" to suit your own needs. Some students have told us they find it helpful to use PowerPoint rather than create a poster session or present a purely oral speech because the program provides a structure that they can use to pace their presentations or keep them on track. This seems to be particularly true for students presenting in a second language or those who experience a great deal of anxiety when speaking. PowerPoint's timed slide function and

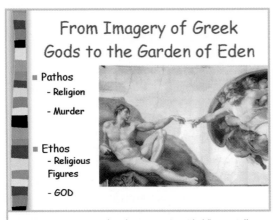

FIGURE 8.9. Tracy Hadnott's presentation titled "Stem Cell Research Through a Visual Lens," slide 2.

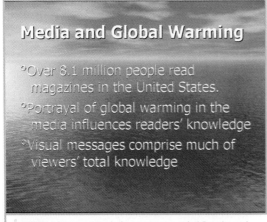

FIGURE 8.10. Sarah Trube's presentation titled "Media and Global Warming," slide 9.

ease for creating placeholders serve a *double rhetorical purpose* for such students: they actually find it helpful to read information off the slides, and in this way the presentation tool helps convey information and facilitate delivery. Consider your own needs as a speaker when you select your mode of presentation. Slide-based presentations in PowerPoint can be very compelling for an audience and very rewarding for you as a presenter.

Possibilities for PowerPoint

Using a conventional PowerPoint format, Tracy Hadnott created five slides to serve as placeholders for her research-based presentation on the morality of stem cell research. As shown in Figure 8.9, she used a simple design, preventing the paper from being too cluttered. In the colored line on the left side of the slide, the mosaic colors replicate strands of DNA. Thus the slide design conveyed the content of her argument visually while she presented it orally.

Similarly, Sarah Trube designed her slides with careful attention to the visual argument made by the slide background. For her presentation on global warming, humorously titled "Escaping the Frying Pan: The Media Fire and the Scrambled Egg of Global Climate Change," she used a background template that showed a watery image of the earth and sky to create the right mood (see Figure 8.10). She spent considerable time discussing each of the bullet points listed in her slide so that it served the rhetorical function of a brief outline.

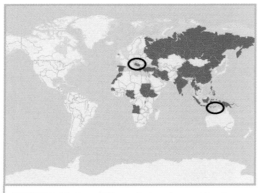

FIGURE 8.11. One of Morgan Springer's map slides from his PowerPoint presentation on self-determination in Kosovo and East Timor.

In an unusual application of PowerPoint, Morgan Springer created a dynamic, animated map that colored red those countries experiencing political wars and military dictatorships (see Figure 8.11). He ended by circling the two countries that were the focus of his research paper on self-determination in Kosovo and East Timor.

Student Writing
See Morgan Springer's map animation in action on his creative PowerPoint presentation.
www.ablongman.com/envision/233

Using a more humorous and interactive approach for his presentation on the visual strategies of political campaigns, Kavi Vyas got the audience thinking about his argument by pretending to hold an election for the new governor of California. He announced the election in the first slide and then gave everyone a handout of his second slide that showed himself ostensibly dressed up as different candidates. After taking a class "vote," he delved into his argument that often voters respond to effective visual appeals rather than the substantive platforms of the candidates. Figures 8.12 and 8.13 show two consecutive slides from his presentation. The obvious use of humor made his presentation both quite engaging and effective in communicating his critique of the two-party system.

FIGURE 8.12. Kavi Vyas's slide announcing the election.

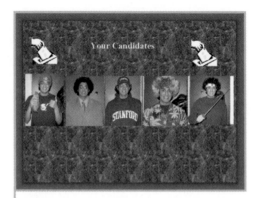

FIGURE 8.13. Kavi's slide showing the importance of embodied rhetoric for electorical candidates and public speakers.

CREATIVE PRACTICE

Experiment with designing slides for your presentation, using either PowerPoint or transparencies for overhead projection. First, create a title slide. Then try making slides that show only images, enlarged to fit the whole screen. Next, experiment with text slides. Should you use a bulleted list? a question followed by an answer? a blank to be filled in with the click of a mouse or an impromptu notation on a transparency? Finally, try some interactive or dynamic features, such as links to Webpages, animation to make images cascade and change, or even audio or video clips. Avoid using sounds or images as mere decoration; make every slide a rhetorical part of your persuasive presentation.

Choosing Methods of Delivery

As you can tell, the way you present your visual materials is just as crucial as drafting content for that presentation. In other words, after *selection, arrangement,* and *design* of materials, you need to think about ways of *delivering* the presentation. But why is delivery so important? Won't the content carry the persuasiveness of the presentation? If the writing is good, won't the delivery be good? Indeed, the writing must be skillful; the selection, organization, and translation of your argument into an appropriate, audience-centered design are crucial for your success. But you also need to attend to *how* you communicate your argument to your audience. In other words, you need to involve those last two canons of rhetoric, *memory* and *delivery.* In brief, **memory** entails both memorizing one's argument to communicate it to the audience and evoking memorable phrases, while **delivery** concerns strategies of presenting your argument to an audience.

We know that memory was crucial for rhetoricians before the invention of the printing press. Speakers would memorize phrases, stories, and histories to pass down from generation to generation. Significantly, this process occurred through a form of visual organization called an **architectural mnemonic technique,** a method in which you associate a phrase to a room or a part of a house so that as you look around during your presentation you receive visual clues to trigger your memory. Scholars William Covino and David Jolliffe explain that the rhetorician Cicero described this technique as "a set of visual images like the rooms of a house, which can be associated with the items in a long speech" (67). As you think about strategies of presentation, you might want to try memorizing key parts of your speech through this technique by creating a visual map of your script. Also, attend to the way your audience will remember your words, and choose your examples, your diction, and your pacing accordingly. In this way, memory leads naturally into delivery, the last canon of rhetoric.

When asked which three of the five canons of rhetoric he considered most significant, the Greek orator Demosthenes replied, "delivery, delivery, delivery." In other words, so crucial is this fifth canon that it can supersede the rest. One core aspect of the canon of delivery is the *sound* of the presentation: how speakers use tone of voice, pacing, strategic pauses, or changes in volume or inflection to make their arguments memorable and effective.

AT A GLANCE

Some Fundamental Elements of Delivery

- *Stance or posture:* also called embodied rhetoric
- *Gesture:* use of hands to communicate information
- *Voice:* pitch, tone, loudness, softness, and enunciation
- *Pacing:* of words, visuals, and argument
- *Rhetorical appeals:* use of logos, pathos, ethos
- *Visuals:* slides, posters, graphics, handouts
- *Embodied visuals:* not only stance but dress, appearance, mannerisms
- *Style:* elements such as repetition, allusion, metaphor, stories, personal narrative, jokes, and pauses

Delivery, as one of the five canons of rhetoric, deals primarily with the effectiveness of a speech's presentation. Oral communication, combined with variations in the presenter's voice and body movements, comprises the delivery of speech. The speaker's ability to manipulate auditory and visual techniques enables him/her to effectively convey his/her argument to the audience.

—Kelly Ingleman

If you think of some of the most prominent speakers of recent history— Illinois Senator Barack Obama, former president Ronald Reagon, former Congresswoman Barbara Jordan—you probably can hear in your head the rhetorically powerful ways they used the sound of language itself. You can likewise prepare yourself for effective oral delivery by annotating your script to indicate places where you will pause, emphasize a key word, or use the strength of your voice to underscore a point. Written cues like this can help you to deliver a memorable, moving, and convincing oral argument.

However, it is not just the *sound* of delivery that affects the persuasiveness of an oral presentation but the *look* of that presentation as well. How many times have you seen a talk in which the speaker dressed up to make a point or used the rhetoric of his or her body to persuade the audience? This form of presentation is a genre we call **embodied rhetoric,** a presentation in which the body becomes a visual means of communicating the message. Kavi Vyas, for instance, used embodied rhetoric prominently in his presentation, as seen in Figure 8.13. However, even in more traditional presentations, you employ the power of embodied rhetoric through the clothes you wear, how you stand, the voice you choose, and even how you hold the materials you use to convey your argument. When Liz Kreiner delivered her presentation on sexual assault on campus, for instance (see Figure 8.14), she made very strategic decisions about her embodied rhetoric: to emphasize the seriousness of her subject, she dressed conservatively and stood absolutely still at the podium as she recounted the disturbing stories of date rape that she had uncovered during her research. Her somber demeanor, reinforced by her serious tone of voice, produced an extremely powerful rhetorical moment.

However, in most cases, we see embodied rhetoric at work through gesture. Often, when we think about the term *gesture* in relation to public speaking, we think of very overt or intentional hand motions that public speakers make for emphasis, like

FIGURE 8.14. During her presentation on sexual assault on campus, Liz Kreiner opted against using multimedia, relying instead on her voice and embodied rhetoric to convey the seriousness of her subject.

FIGURE 8.15. In his presentation on recent developments in stem cell research, Jake Palinsky used gesture deliberately to help his audience understand a scientific diagram.

FIGURE 8.16. In a moment of explanation, Alina Lanesberg uses a subtle gesture to emphasize her point and draw her audience into her argument.

that made by Jake Palinsky in Figure 8.15, in which he directs the audience's attention by gesturing to the diagram he is describing. Our eyes follow his finger to focus on the part of the diagram he is explaining at that moment.

The gesture is a careful rhetorical move: it has purpose and works effectively as a strategy of communication. Sometimes gestures in public speaking seem less carefully composed, such as the one in Figure 8.16. Here we see the speaker in midsentence, her hands opened as if in an involuntary accompaniment to her words. But notice how the open palm, extended toward members of the audience, invites them to listen; it is tilted down to allow words to travel and open the space between the speaker and the audience. This subtle instance of embodied rhetoric invites the listeners into the argument and demonstrates a moment of explanation and connection.

Although we all use gestures without realizing that we do, it is in fact possible to train ourselves to use the rhetoric of the body more carefully, and even strategically, as an integral part of our overall presentation design. Your purpose in using gestures as part of a presentation should be to harness the power of the body effectively to communicate ideas. Therefore, as you draft and deliver your presentation, remember that your *entire* body—from body language to clothes, posture, expression, and gestures—participates in communicating your ideas and information.

CREATIVE PRACTICE

Analyze the gestures used by one of the most famous public speakers, Martin Luther King Jr. (see Figures 8.17 and Figures 8.18). Write a brief analysis of the suggested meaning and purpose of each gesture, describing each of the images as you make your argument. Then select the words you might match to the gesture. This exercise will help you explore strategies to use in your own presentations.

FIGURE 8.18. Martin Luther King Jr. emphasizes his point at a mass rally in Philadelphia, August 4, 1965.

FIGURE 8.17. Martin Luther King Jr. gesturing at a press conference.

COLLABORATIVE CHALLENGE

With a partner from class, conduct field research on the delivery strategies of three speakers. Write down your impressions using the fundamental elements of delivery listed in the "At a Glance" box. Then assess each speaker in terms of the effectiveness and appropriateness of delivery strategies based on the needs of the audience: Does a formal speaker put an entire lecture hall to sleep through monotone voice, lack of gestures, and a formal body language, or does the speaker use humor, vivid expressions, and clear pauses to keep the audience engaged? Does a teacher in a small seminar use direct eye contact and open body language to invite participation, or does the speaker stand towering over the group and silence others? Finally, identify key techniques that you can apply from each speaker in terms of excellent strategies of delivery and try to use them in your own presentation.

Practicing Your Presentation

Speakers like Martin Luther King Jr. dedicate much of their time to practicing their delivery. Similarly, two ideologically opposed political figures, Adolf Hitler and Winston Churchill, relied extensively on practice to develop their delivery. First-person testimonies about Hitler suggest that he incessantly recorded himself speaking and using hand gestures. Then, he would watch the films over and over again, selecting the motions that he felt were most powerful. Next, he would practice that form of delivery—the tone of voice, the pacing, the bodily stance, and the hand gestures—until he felt it was perfect. Finally, he would destroy the recordings so that no one would know how carefully he practiced. The practice made his delivery seem natural and his power seem real. At the opposite end of the spectrum, Winston Churchill used voice alone to persuade the British public to withstand the waves of Nazi attacks night after night in the bombing of Britain. Over the radio wires, his practiced and powerful words—delivered with the perfect amount of confidence and encouragement—helped the British persevere during those dark days. These examples reveal the power of practice in strengthening delivery and its capacity to persuade audiences.

Likewise, you should incorporate repeated practice into the process of drafting and revising your presentations. As with any assignment, your argument will benefit from peer review, so consider performing a "dress rehearsal" for a friend or roommate to get his or her feedback on the clarity of your ideas, your use of multimedia or visual aids, and the effectiveness of your delivery. Better yet, become your own peer reviewer by filming your "dress rehearsal" and then critiquing your performance. Sometimes, by becoming a member of the audience yourself, you can see how to revise your presentation into a truly powerful oral argument.

Winston Churchill could never have stirred the British public as he did were it not for the grave, serious, and controlled tone of voice that he employed in his radio speeches. His faith in the allied powers rang out in stentorian cadences that by their very vibrations instilled belief in the masses. His message was often cliché, but his delivery was never anything but spellbinding. Had he had a feeble voice, perhaps Germany would have fared better.

—Dr. Gideon Burton

COLLABORATIVE CHALLENGE

Have someone digitally record or film you while you practice your presentation to find out if you make any involuntary movements (such as rubbing your chin, clicking a pen, or twirling your hair) or verbal tics (such as repeating "umm" or "like"). Select two or three strong expressions, gestures, and verbal phrases that you can use with rhetorical purpose and effectiveness. Then practice these again on film until you feel completely confident. In addition to practicing your delivery, work on the canon of memory by trying to memorize some key points of your presentation to deliver them without having to look at your notes or script.

Anticipating Problems and the Question-and-Answer Session

As you practice your presentation, don't forget to consider problems that might arise, such as faulty technology, a bored or confused audience, or even hecklers. To troubleshoot technology, visit your room and test out your equipment in advance. Make sure you have backup for the technology: save your work on a CD or memory stick, or email it to yourself. But remember, even if your practice session goes smoothly, bring handouts in case your PowerPoint slides don't work, and be prepared to talk without technology if necessary. Also, be ready to cut down or extend the length of your talk by indicating on your speech places you might pause or points you might discuss in more detail. Realize that the more comfortable you are with your material, the more you can adapt on the spot to the needs of your audience.

Successful adaptation includes handling the question-and-answer session well; this part of a presentation, usually located at the end, serves as the final opportunity to clarify your argument and convince your audience. A successful presenter anticipates and, in some cases, even sets up the framework for the question-and-answer session. For instance, during his presentation on Marilyn Manson, Ben Rosenbrough realized he didn't have time to develop the link he saw between Elvis Presley and Manson in his formal presentation

Student Writing

Read Ben Rosenbrough's presentation script to see how he planned a "surprise slide" for the question-and-answer session.

www.ablongman.com/envision/234

and so he made only a passing reference to the connection, hoping that the audience would be intrigued and ask about it after his talk. When they did, he advanced his PowerPoint beyond his conclusion slide to one documenting these connections in a powerful way. His surprise preparation for the question-and-answer session made his presentation design exceptionally successful. Similarly, you can anticipate what questions your audience might have by delivering your presentation to a peer group member, seeing what questions your presentation generates and even practicing trial responses. Consider having some new evidence, a stunning visual, or even a handout prepared to answer a question that you hope might be asked after your presentation.

Documenting Your Presentation

Design. Delivery. Practice. What is left? After all your hard work on your presentation, you probably want to leave some kind of trace, a written artifact, or a form of textual memory of the presentation. **Documentation—** *some form of written or visual evidence of your presentation's argument*—is the answer. Documentation serves an important rhetorical function: to inform and persuade. This might take the form of a **handout** which provides additional information in the form of an annotated bibliography, a summary of your key points and thesis, visual rhetoric from your presentation, references for further reading, or a printout of your PowerPoint presentation. You should put your contact information on it so the audience can ask you further questions.

Documentation might also consist of a **text** or **script** for your presentation. This can either be the annotated printout of your PowerPoint presentation, a full speech, or a typed set of notes in outline form with placeholders for your slides or media aids such as shown in Tommy Tsai's visual outline (see Figure 8.4). More innovatively, you might document your presentation with a **creative take-away** that reflects a key aspect of your presentation. Consider Wendy Hagenmaier's handout for her project on media coverage of the bombing of Hiroshima and Nagasaki (see Figure 8.19). The cover of the *New York Times* from August 1945 is attached to a small candle; Wendy's caption reads, "Light this

Student Writing
See Courtney Smith's handout, designed to accompany her presentation on Palestinian female suicide bombers.
www.ablongman.com/envision/235

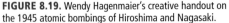

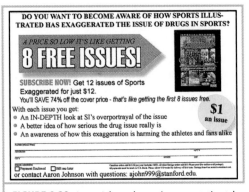

FIGURE 8.19. Wendy Hagenmaier's creative handout on the 1945 atomic bombings of Hiroshima and Nagasaki.

FIGURE 8.20. Aaron Johnson's creative presentation take-away for his research project on *Sports Illustrated*.

candle in remembrance of how the August 1945 atomic bombings of Hiroshima and Nagasaki have been remembered by Japanese and American photojournalists. The 'flashes' of its flame will serve to remind you that photojournalistic coverage is often an attempt to shape collective national memory and that remembrance is subjective." Another student, Falco Pichler, presenting his research finding on Nike marketing strategies, created a "backstage pass" to what he called the "Nike Show" and invited students to read his paper online. Aaron Johnson, presenting his research on media representation of athletes who take performance-enhancing drugs, made a mock subscription card with the distorted title "Sports Exaggerated" as creative documentation for his presentation (see Figure 8.20). Using Photoshop, he embedded a cover of *Sports Illustrated* into the subscription card and listed the main points of his argument as "advertising points" for his presentation. Notice his complete contact information at the bottom of the card.

These examples begin to show the range of creative documentation strategies you might pursue as the final part of your presentation. Taking the lead from Aaron, you might even craft an interactive visual take-away such as a graphic montage, a minibook, or other forms of visual argument. The importance of such texts—whether conventional prose handouts or compelling visual creations—lies in their power to make your presentation memorable, convincing, and engaging. So consider your strategies for documentation as carefully as you design your entire presentation.

Creating Your Own Presentation

In this chapter, you have explored possibilities for presentations; learned how to convert a written argument into a spoken, visual, multimedia presentation or performance; and worked through the different ways of writing for oral, poster, and PowerPoint presentations. Recall the strategies of design, arrangement, and delivery you have learned, and keep in mind the importance of both gesture and embodied rhetoric as ways of communicating your message and your purpose to your particular audience. Finally, as you begin to craft your own presentation, remember the old adage, "practice makes perfect." Peer review and revision are as important to your presentation as collaboration on drafts and revision are to your written work. They enable you to anticipate problems and harness your creativity as you shape your ideas into a memorable, moving, and persuasive form of rhetorical communication.

PREWRITING CHECKLIST

Focus on Analyzing Presentations

❏ What is the presenter's purpose? To inform? persuade? instruct? motivate? initiate discussion? Did the presentation successfully accomplish that purpose?

❏ What is the presenter's relationship to the topic he or she discussed? Is the presenter an expert? a novice? fairly well informed?

❏ Was the presentation appropriate for the audience? Consider language, organization, and explanation of technical or specialized concepts.

❏ Did the speaker present him- or herself as an authority instructing the audience? as a peer sharing information? Did the presenter make eye contact (indicating a direct relationship with the audience) or simply read from a prepared text (indicating a focus on the material rather than the audience)? How did this affect the structure and style of the presentation?

❏ How was the presentation structured? Was an outline or summary provided for the audience to follow? Was this done orally, on the board, in a handout, or on a slide? Was the development of the argument clear? Did it follow the designated structure?

❏ Did the presenter take into account the audience's reaction? For instance, did he or she notice some confusion in the audience and pause to explain a difficult point?

(continued)

❏ How did the presentation begin? Did the presenter use any effective oral or visual devices to "hook" the audience? Was there a clear conclusion?

❏ Were the main points clearly developed? How was the scope of the presentation? Was there too much information? too little?

❏ Did the presenter use word choices appropriate to the occasion, audience, and subject matter? Were the sentence structures too complex (as if to be read silently) or more colloquial (as if to be read aloud)? Did the presenter project his or her voice enough? Did he or she speak slowly and clearly or rush through the material?

❏ Did the presenter use any formal devices—figurative language, deliberate repetition, literary allusions?

❏ Consider the presenter's embodied rhetoric. Did he or she stand or sit? remain stationary, or move around? Did the presenter use gestures, facial expression, or even costume to add to the rhetorical effect of the argument?

❏ How did the presenter use visuals? Did he or she show slides, bring in posters, write on a blackboard, distribute handouts, engage in role-playing, pass around books, or bring in material evidence for the presentation? Were the visual components rhetorically purposeful or did they seem an afterthought?

❏ If the presenter used posters, Were they clear and accessible to the audience? Did they stand alone as arguments, or was their meaning only clear in conjunction with the oral presentation? Were the words large enough to read from a distance? Did the poster avoid visual clutter? Did it contain a clear title and use information graphics effectively?

❏ If the presenter used a slide program such as PowerPoint, Was the visual design of the slides effective? Did the slides have a unity of theme, color, and layout? Did the presenter avoid visual clutter on the slides? How much text was on each slide? Were placeholders used for emphasis or pacing? Were there innovations in the slideshow, such as using dual screens, animation, or embedded clips or Internet links? Were these effective or distracting? Did the presenter speak to the computer screen rather than the audience? Did the presenter's body block the screen, obscuring the slides?

❏ If the presenter used the blackboard or whiteboard, Did he or she write clearly and legibly? Were the notations on the board purposeful? Did the presenter block the board, making it difficult to read?

(continued)

❏ If the presenter used technology, Were there any technical difficulties? Did the presenter overcome them smoothly (for instance, having a backup plan), or have a difficult time recovering from the glitch, perhaps because of relying more heavily on technology than on the force of argument?

❏ Did the presenter finish within the allotted time? How did he or she handle the question-and-answer session?

WRITING PROJECTS

1. **Field Research:** As part of the necessary preparation for writing your own presentation, conduct field research in the form of observing three public speeches, presentations, or oral/ multimedia arguments, and type up a brief rhetorical analysis on the delivery, rhetorical strategies, and effectiveness of each one. These presentations can include lectures in any of your classes, speakers visiting campus or your dorms, or the practice presentation of a member of your class. Find three speakers or presentations to expand the possibilities available to you. Write a brief analysis of each one; try to be as specific as possible in your observations and make sure that you indicate what strategies you plan to use in your own presentation.

2. **Formal Presentation:** Create and deliver a timed presentation of your research argument for your class (ask your instructor for the precise time limit). You should include the appropriate media (visual rhetoric, PowerPoint slides, Websites, movie clips, performative or interactive aspects). In addition, the oral delivery of your presentation might include a handout that you distribute to the class to provide information—for example, an annotated bibliography, a summary of your key points and thesis, visual rhetoric from your presentation, references for further reading, or a printout of your PowerPoint presentation—formatted in the proper manner (or in a creative way if that works for your presentation) with your complete contact information on it. Make sure that you compose a script for your presentation. This can either be the annotated printout of your PowerPoint presentation, a full speech, or notes in outline form (with placeholders for your slides or multimedia). Include references in the text or script of your presentation to any materials you use (handouts and printouts of multimedia).

3. **Collaborative Presentation:** Work in groups of two to four to design and deliver a presentation to the class. You might want to divide the tasks of selecting material, brainstorming strategies of presentation, and designing your visual materials. Will you take turns speaking throughout the presentation, or will each person be responsible

for a distinct segment of the presentation? Will one person write the script, another person deliver it—perhaps from memory—while a third creates the slides? Choose the strategy that best suits your audience and your purpose. Don't forget to practice together, and when your group is presenting, look at the others who are speaking to keep the class' attention focused on your group presentation.

4. **Community Writing Presentation:** Either in groups or individually, design your presentation for a specific community audience. What happens if you present your research project on performance art to a group of politicians, to school administrators, to the theater department? Think about how your message can reach a broader audience in this way. What if your project is on the educational poster campaign to prevent the spread of AIDS? After you design one presentation for your writing class, rewrite it to meet the audience expectations of a not-for-profit organization, an international amnesty meeting, or an urban center continuing education class.

Visit www.ablongman.com/envision for expanded assignment guidelines and student projects.

CHAPTER 9

Documentation and Plagiarism

"Creativity always builds on the past." You probably learned this adage by basing your research paper on the many ideas you discovered through your extensive exploration of research sources or by composing a presentation of your research based on examples of effective delivery you noticed from your own classes. For many writers, the debt to those who have written before them is carefully acknowledged—whether through direct references, through parenthetical citations, or through a list of sources. Even visual artists and multimedia writers make their sources explicit to show that they belong to a larger community of writers and that they respect the work of others.

FIGURE 9.1. Justin Cone's film, *Building on the Past*, remixes visuals and sound to emphasize how all our ideas rely on the works of those before us.

But Justin Cone, a designer and animator based in Austin, Texas, makes this point more emphatically through the multimedia montage shown in Figure 9.1, a short film called *Building on the Past*, which won first place in a Creative Commons contest. *Building on the Past* recycles and modifies public-domain film footage from the Prelinger Archive to make an argument about the relationship between creativity and legislation. The visuals, only a fraction of which you see here, are accompanied by a musical score and a voice-over that repeats the same sentence intermittently throughout the film: "Creativity always builds on the past." In this particular scene, which occurs at the opening of the film, Cone reedited the public-domain footage to run in reverse, showing the children running backward uphill instead of forward downhill. In this way, even in the first few minutes of his piece he offers a powerful argument about how we rely on others for our own creativity; he expresses that idea visually, through his strategy of organization, word choice, and design.

Your research project, too, draws its strength from previous work on the subject. It is a merger of your argument and the already existing dialogue on the topic. So even as you "reedit it" to suit the purpose of your paper—by selecting passages to quote, paraphrase, summarize, or even argue against—it is crucial that you let your readers know *where* the ideas originated by providing what we call complete and ethical **source attribution,** or the acknowledgment and identification of your sources.

In this chapter, you'll learn how the rhetorical art of imitation—the process by which we all learn to write, compose, speak, and produce texts—differs from the theft of others' ideas, called plagiarism. We'll discuss intellectual property and why it is important to respect the work of others, and you'll acquire strategies for avoiding unintentional plagiarism. We'll provide a means of understanding the process of constructing in-text and end-of-paper citations, and we'll explain MLA, APA, CSE, and Chicago documentation styles.

Chapter Preview Questions

- What is the difference between rhetorical imitation and stealing intellectual property?
- How can I avoid unintentional plagiarism?
- Why is it important to learn the conventions of a documentation style?
- What are the proper methods for in-text citations and bibliographies?

Rhetorical Imitation and Intellectual Property

In ancient times, **rhetorical imitation,** or the practice of taking after others, was a celebrated form of instruction. Students would copy a speech out word by word, studying the word choice, organization, rhythm, and art of the work. Then they would write a rhetorical analysis (as you did in Chapter 1) of the speech to understand figures and tropes, strategies of argument, and organizational choices. Finally, they would use elements of the speeches they studied, including content (words) and form (arrangement), to draft their own speeches. Through this imitation, they learned to be great rhetors. Such imitative exercises helped students learn from models of excellence.

But, as Dr. Gideon Burton tells us, imitation signified only the beginning. It was "the bridge between one's reading and writing (or speaking). . . . Students moved from close imitations of their models to looser sorts, using these models increasingly as starting points for longer, more involved compositions of their own making." In other words, students started with imitation but soon moved on to create original texts.

This, too, is your task in the writing classroom. After analyzing articles and readings and emulating argumentative and organization strategies from samples of student writing, at some point you need to move on to create an original text. Yet, in the process, you may wish to refer back to those on whose work you are building. This is where **documentation** comes in—the responsible and correct acknowledgment of your sources and influences.

Today, it is common to talk about ideas, not just in terms of words and thoughts, but also in terms of **intellectual property,** that is, ideas that belong to someone as a form of property. People create patents and copyrights, go to court, and go to all sorts of extremes to protect their right to consider their ideas, inventions, and thoughts *as property.* In this increasingly litigious society, you need to understand when to stop imitation and when to start acknowledging your sources so that you preserve the rights of others and protect yourself as an emerging writer.

Understanding Plagiarism

Plagiarism means using another person's idea as your own. The etymological origin of *plagiarism,* according to scholars Peter Morgan and Glenn Reynolds, concerns stealing someone's work. In classical times, imitation was not a crime. But with the invention of printing technology, copyright law, and a cultural emphasis on intellectual property as profitable came a concern about taking someone else's ideas—and hence their earning potential—whether intentionally or unintentionally. The consequent demand for originality in writing, which continues in academic and professional circles today, is linked to profit margins and explains why plagiarism remains a punishable act.

In colleges and universities, plagiarism can often lead to suspension or even expulsion because the perpetrator is literally stealing the ideas and livelihood of someone else. Students and faculty members alike have been kicked out of universities on plagiarism charges pertaining to stolen words as well as stolen ideas, designs, and even computer code. In 2003, vice chancellor and physics professor B. S. Rajput of Kamaon University, along with his research assistant, was charged with replicating—word for word and equation for equation— significant sections of a published article by Professor Renata Kallosh of Stanford University's physics department. Both Rajput and his assistant were forced to leave their university, but, more importantly, the entire academic community felt that intellectual property had been stolen and a code of ethics broken.

As this example reveals, besides being aware of plagiarism for historical and economic reasons, there is another, even more compelling ethical reason for keeping the dialogue model of research in mind. As you work with sources, realize that the claims you are able to make are in fact based on the foundation provided by others. Identifying your sources thus becomes a writing strategy that you need to implement out of *respect* for those who have come before you. By acknowledging their names, ideas, and words, you contribute to a body of knowledge, graciously extending thanks to those who have paved the way. Therefore, while there are legal issues related to intellectual property, copyright law, and "fair use" that you need to know about, if you keep the *respect principle* in mind, it is unlikely that you'll fall into the trap of inadvertently "stealing" someone's work.

You can get started on including your sources by name in your research paper by listing them in your detailed outline at appropriate places. Include direct quotations whenever possible; don't forget to cite your sources for both paraphrase and quotations. Make sure you include the full names of your sources; cite them as people and put in page numbers to practice responsible and respectful writing strategies.

Avoiding Unintentional Plagiarism

To avoid accidentally taking someone else's ideas or words as your own, you might follow two practices. First, always keep in mind that you are contributing to a conversation with other writers interested in your topic. Think of each of your sources as an important participant in that conversation. When you are writing a research-based argument using a large number of texts, think of working with sources as responding to people whose works you **cite,** or quote, as a way of including them in the dialogue. Say to yourself, "I speak my part, I refer to another person's view, and I provide a citation of the statement." With research papers, you are having a conversation with an entire room of people, introducing each person in turn, and serving as the moderator.

Second, develop effective ways of note taking while reading through your sources. If you find an interesting quote, don't just underline or highlight it. Copy it into your research log with a notation about how you might use it. If you find an intriguing idea, write down the attribution in your research log.

Consider Michael Rothenberg's notations in his research log for a project on the design plans for the Twin Towers Memorial in New York City.

Safety: "there's no reason to believe the structures that replace the twin towers wouldn't also be targets." CNN? "they're a target forever"—Klemenic, president of an engineering firm Skilling Ward Magnusson Barkshire in Seattle.

Howard Decker, chief curator of the National Building Museum in Washington, DC said: the other target was the "squat pentagon." He said that shows terrorists choose targets because of their symbolism, not their height. "The desire to build tall buildings is an old one," he said. "The motivations for it are complicated. Commerce. Capitalism. Ego."

Michael lists his notes by category: safety. He then copies the source directly and writes down the full name and identifying information for the quote. He'll use this to build ethos in citing this authority within his paper.

Michael repeats this process for his second note. Here he puts the most interesting words in quotation marks and deliberately uses different words in composing his paraphrase of the source. (See Michael's complete paper on the *Envision* Website.)

This notion of considering your sources as people, as the cast of characters for your research paper, can help you avoid unintentional plagiarism, or the phenomenon that happens when we assimilate all the material we have read and then think that the ideas are our own. This can happen for many reasons: fatigue, oversaturation of information, poor memory, or sloppy note taking. Regardless, even the unintentional taking of others' ideas has very serious consequences, as we can learn from the plight of Doris Kearns Goodwin, a Pulitzer Prize–winning historian who was charged with stealing the words and ideas of others.

How I Caused That Story
A historian explains why someone else's writing wound up in her book
Doris Kearns Goodwin

I am a historian. With the exception of being a wife and mother, it is who I am. And there is nothing I take more seriously.

In recent days, questions have been raised about how historians go about crediting their sources, and I have been caught up in the swirl. Ironically, the more intensive and far-reaching a historian's research, the greater the difficulty of citation. As the mountain of material grows, so does the possibility of error.

Fourteen years ago, not long after the publication of my book *The Fitzgeralds and the Kennedys,* I received a communication from author Lynne McTaggart pointing out that material from her book on Kathleen Kennedy had not been properly attributed. I realized that she was right. Though my footnotes repeatedly cited Ms. McTaggart's work, I failed to provide quotation marks for phrases that I had taken verbatim, having assumed that these phrases, drawn from my notes, were my words, not hers. I made the corrections she requested, and the matter was completely laid to rest—until last week, when the *Weekly Standard* published an article reviving the issue. The larger question for those of us who write history is to understand how citation mistakes can happen.

The research and writing for this 900-page book, with its 3,500 footnotes, took place over 10 years. At that time, I wrote my books and took my notes in longhand, believing I could not think well on a keyboard. Most of my sources were drawn from a multitude of primary materials: manuscript collections, private letters, diaries, oral histories, newspapers, periodicals, personal interviews. After three years of research, I discovered more than 150 cartons of materials that had been previously stored in the attic of Joe Kennedy's Hyannis Port house. These materials were a treasure trove for a historian—old report cards, thousands of family letters, movie stubs and diaries, which allowed me to cross the boundaries of time and space. It took me two additional years to read, categorize and take notes on these documents.

During this same period, I took handwritten notes on perhaps 300 books. Passages I wanted to quote directly were noted along with general notes on the ideas and story lines of each book. Notes on all these sources were then arranged chronologically and kept in dozens of folders in 25 banker's boxes. Immersed in a flood of papers, I began to write the book. After each section and each chapter was completed, I returned the notes to the boxes along with notations for future footnoting. When the manuscript was finished, I went back to all these sources to check the accuracy of attributions. As a final protection, I revisited the 300 books themselves. Somehow in this process, a few of the books were not fully rechecked. I relied instead on my notes, which combined direct quotes and paraphrased sentences. If I had had the books in front of me, rather than my notes, I would have caught mistakes in the first place and placed any borrowed phrases in direct quotes.

What made this incident particularly hard for me was the fact that I take great pride in the depth of my research and the extensiveness of my citations. The writing of history is a rich process of building on the work of the past with the hope that others will build on what you have done. Through footnotes you point the way to future historians.

The only protection as a historian is to institute a process of research and writing that minimizes the possibility of error. And that I have tried to do, aided by modern technology, which enables me, having long since moved beyond longhand, to use a computer for both organizing and taking notes. I now rely on a scanner, which reproduces the passages I want to cite, and then I keep my own comments on those books in a separate file so that I will never confuse the two again. But the real miracle occurred when my college-age son taught me how to use the mysterious footnote key on the computer, which makes it possible to insert the citations directly into the text while the sources are still in front of me, instead of shuffling through hundreds of folders four or five years down the line, trying desperately to remember from where I derived a particular statistic or quote. Still, there is no guarantee against error. Should one occur, all I can do, as I did 14 years ago, is to correct it as soon as I possibly can, for my own sake and the sake of history. In the end, I am still the same fallible person I was before I made the transition to the computer, and the process of building a lengthy work of history remains a complicated but honorable task.

Goodwin explains how she unintentionally plagiarized one of her 300 sources; her new technological approach to note taking offers a concrete strategy for preventing this disaster. As you develop effective practices for avoiding unintentional plagiarism, consider how you can include your sources more immediately (as Goodwin learned to do), develop a dialogue with them in your research log (as Michael Rothenberg does), and be particularly vigilant about checking and cross-checking to ensure that you've made proper attribution.

Understanding Documentation Style

As a writer, you have a rhetorical choice to make between documentation styles. Different styles are preferred by different communities of writers, as shown in the following table. The format guidelines for each style actually have a rhetorical purpose corresponding to the way that knowledge is constructed for that community.

Documentation Style	Community of Writers	Defining Features	Purpose of Features	Example
MLA	Modern Language Association (language, literature, writing, philosophy, and humanities scholars and teachers)	Citation begins with author's name (last name first, full first name), then book title, then publication information, then date.	Knowledge advances based on individual author's contributions; thus, names are prioritized over dates; place of publication matters for building ethos	McCloud, Scott. Understanding Comics. New York: HarperPerennial, 1994.
APA	American Psychological Association (psychologists and social scientists)	Publication date immediately follows designation of author, multiple authors may be listed (last name and initials), titles are in sentence style (first word capitalized, rest lowercase)	Since knowledge advances based on dated contributions to the field, dates are prioritized; most writing is collaborative, so up to six authors are listed; titles, typically long and technical, are in lowercase.	Bruce, V., & Green, P. (1990). *Visual perception: Physiology, psychology, and ecology* (2nd ed.). London: Erlbaum.
CSE	Council of Science Editors (such as biology and physics)	References include last name and date; often superscript numbers are used	Like APA style, emphasis is on knowledge advancing through studies and scientific research; a heavily cited style of writing	[1]Goble, JL. Visual disorders in the handicapped child. New York: M. Dekker; 1984. p. 265.
Chicago	University of Chicago (business writers, professional writers, and those in fine arts)	Sources are listed as footnotes or endnotes and include page numbers	Knowledge is incremental, and readers like to check facts as they go along	[2]Scott McCloud, *Understanding Comics* (New York: HarperPerennial, 1994), 33.

For the purposes of this chapter, we focus on MLA style because the writing we've been discussing in this book belongs to disciplines in the humanities. The different styles, methods of organization, modes of argumentation, and conventions for writing in the social sciences, sciences, business, and fine arts communities are not covered in this book.

Documentation as Cross-Referencing

Documentation is not intended to be some surreptitious way to check up on you; rather, it is part of the research dialogue. The idea is that readers might be inspired enough by your research and your use of materials to want to read some of your sources themselves. In this way, documentation functions as a road map or signpost to your audience about how to locate the source—both in your bibliography and in the library or online. Accordingly, the central purpose of documentation is to point readers clearly and explicitly to the list of sources at the end of the paper.

Let's take a look at a citation in Michael Rothenberg's paper on the Twin Towers. We call this an **in-text citation** or **reference** because it occurs within the body of his paper. MLA style always places such references inside parentheses to set them off from the rest of the writing. Look at how the last name and page number of the citation in parentheses point the reader directly to the author's name in the "Works Cited" list.

. . . the Twin Towers were so enormous that together they encased a staggering 11 million square feet of commercial space (Czarnecki 31).

Works Cited

Bravman, John. Interview by Michael Rothenberg. 13 May 2003.

Bruno, Lisa D. "Studio Daniel Libeskind." 6 Nov. 2002. Sunspot. 1
June 2003 <http://www.sunspot.net/news/custom/
attack/ny-bzarch062993970nov06,0,2252478.
story?coll=bal%2Dattack%2Dstoryutil>.

Czarnecki, John E. "Architects at the Forefront as They Show Ground
Zero Aspirations." Architectural Record Nov. 2002: 31-50.

Notice that Michael has alphabetized the list by authors' last names, which corresponds to MLA style documentation placing author names as most important. Readers need only scan down the page to look for the last name of the source cited earlier. This makes it very easy, and once you understand that this **cross-referencing logic** governs all documentation rules, you can begin to understand how to document a wide range of sources—even new multimedia sources for which there are no set rules of citation.

For instance, Michael needed to document several quotes he obtained from a temporary PDF document posted on the Website of a city review board. By understanding documentation as *cross-referencing,* here's what Michael wrote:

> In particular, they required a memorial that would include both history and memory "such as the Libeskind's below-grade 'ground zero' space," as well as a proposal "that returns a much-lamented presence to the skyline" like Libeskind's tower, and finally, a plan that develops the site in the context of the community (Evaluation 3, 12).

> Evaluation of Innovative Design Proposals. Ed. Ernest Hutton. 13 Jan. 2003. New York: New Visions. 25 May 2003 <http://www.nynv.aiga.org/NYNV20030113.pdf>.

As you can see, the word within the parenthetical documentation sets up a *cross-reference* to the first word listed in the "Works Cited" list at the end of the paper. This makes it easy to compose a very concise reference within the paper and easy to find that reference at the end of the paper.

Using Notes for Documentation

Although MLA style relies primarily on in-text citations and a final bibliography—unlike Chicago style, which uses primarily footnotes or endnotes—sometimes you might occasionally need to include a note. What situations allow for the use of footnotes or endnotes in MLA style? You'll use notes in MLA style when you want to include extra explanatory information but don't want to break the flow of your argument.

Following are two notes from Michael's paper. In the first case, he wanted to define some of the key terms of his argument, but he felt it would be intrusive to pause and explain his terms within the paper itself.

> [1] Those in the public who influenced the design of the new World Trade Center include all of those concerned with the project and not just New York citizens. However, even though the majority of these motivated individuals live in New York, they represent every state and many nations. Hence, the collective group of citizens in the worldwide community who are interested in this project are referred to as "the public" throughout this document, but this phrase should be understood to include primarily New York citizens.

In the second case, he wanted to add more information from his research log, but again he felt it would break the flow of his argument. In this case, he was able to include direct quotations and statistics from his research; this built his ethos and allowed interested readers to learn more about the subject. Notice that he included the source for his research again through the cross-referencing system. A reader would only have to scan down to the *O* section of his bibliography to find the full source for this citation.

> [2] Five thousand people from the New York area participated in a two-week in-depth discussion starting on July 20, 2002. According to their Website, "This historic gathering—called 'Listening to the City'—gave participants an opportunity to help shape the redevelopment of Lower Manhattan and the creation of a permanent memorial to the victims of 9/11." At this gathering, the 5,000 committed individuals responded to many questions and polls. Of the respondents, 60% thought that new towers should be built at least as tall as the originals, 71% thought that adding a "major element or icon" to the skyline was "very important," and

> 87% thought it was "important" or "very important" to add
> something unique to the skyline (Online Dialogues).

In addition to providing explanatory information, notes can also point readers to a list of sources you would discuss or include if you had space to do so. In Michael's case, he wanted to discuss mammoth architectural designs more broadly but did not have the space in his paper to do so. His solution was a note pointing the reader to a source on this topic, which happened to be another paper he had written. This note would also be the place for a list of sources about this tangential topic.

> [6] See my paper, "The Two Towers," on the Petronas Towers as
> the world's tallest, February 2003.

Typically, such notes are formatted as **endnotes,** appearing at the end of your paper, before the bibliography. **Footnotes,** which appear at the bottom or foot of the page, would again break the flow of the argument. But ask your teacher for specific guidance about your own paper.

MLA-Style Works Cited Lists

You've seen how documentation works as a *cross-referencing system*, in which the in-text citation within parentheses points the reader directly to the source in the bibliography. In MLA style, the bibliography is called a **Works Cited** list because it refers explicitly to the works (or sources) you have cited (or quoted) in your paper. Sometimes a Works Cited list is accompanied by another section called a **Works Consulted** list, which names all the other sources you may have read and studied but did not actually quote from in your final revision.

Realize that a reference page is a moment of ethos building as well: by listing both works *cited* and works *consulted,* you demonstrate your research process and new knowledge. You also invite your readers to explore the topic in depth with you.

If your instructor agrees, you can organize or format your bibliographic materials in different ways. You can either list all your sources alphabetically, or you can divide your sources into various categories—if you want to showcase your primary research, for example.

Consider Sunthar Premakumar's reference page from his paper discussed in Chapter 6. Here, he loosely followed MLA form; he categorized his sources to show the range of his research and included some annotations, reminiscent of the annotated bibliography you learned about in Chapter 5.

Works Cited and Consulted

Books

- Devany, Arthur. <u>Hollywood Economics</u>. New York: Routledge, 2004.

- Ninian, Alex. <u>Bollywood</u>. Ipswich, MA: EBSCO, 2003.

- Ruckert, George E. <u>Music in North India</u>. New York: Oxford UP, 2004.

- Shankar, Ravi. <u>My Music, My Life</u>. New York: Simon, 1968.

- Waterman, David. <u>Hollywood's Road to Success</u>. Cambridge, MA: Harvard UP, 2005.

Journal Articles

- Henry, Edward O. "The Rationalization of Intensity in Indian Music." <u>Ethnomusicology: Journal of the Society for Ethnomusicology</u>. 46.1 (Winter 2002): 33-56. <u>Expanded Academic ASAP</u>.

- Mayrhofer, C. M. "Media and the Transformation of Religion in South Asia." <u>Indo-Iranian Journal</u>. 43.1 (Annual 2000): 80(2). <u>Expanded Academic ASAP</u>.

Films

- <u>Kabhi Kushi Kabhi Gham</u>—A movie by the famous Bollywood director Karan Johar. This movie explores the simple dynamics that prevails in Indian families and advocates the important

---

Sunthar decides to categorize his sources according to his iceberg of research.

He includes both works he quotes and works he has consulted for background knowledge.

Sunthar uses a bulleted list instead of the conventional hanging indent shown in the following sample.

The journal articles Sunthar lists include volume and issue numbers as well as page numbers. Since Sunthar found them through a library database, he includes the name of the database at the end of the citation.

Sunthar also includes the films he analyzed providing a brief annotation for each one.

message of understanding within families. This is confirmed by the tag line of the movie, "It's all about loving your parents."

- Kal Ho Na Ho—With a tag line of "A Story of a Lifetime . . . in a Heartbeat," this movie depicts a story of a person who is willing to help everyone he meets. The movie calls out to the public to be less selfish. Filled with many glorious songs, it was one of the biggest hits of its time.

- Lagaan—This is an inspirational movie produced by the famous Bollywood actor Amir Khan, who also plays the lead in the movie. This movie is about how a group of villagers come together to fight against the British army, which ruled India at that time. This movie promotes the idea of unity and transcending social and cultural differences to build a strong bond with fellow countrymen.

Interviews

Amritha Appaswami

He also lists the interviewees, providing information to build the ethos of each person.

—a second-year master's student majoring in biological sciences at Stanford University. Having trained in Carnatic classical music, Amritha is an avid listener of Indian film music.

A. R. Rahman

—hailed by *Time* magazine as the "Mozart of Madras," Rahman is one of the most successful artists of all time and, according to a BBC estimate, is said to have sold between 100 million and 150 million albums. In India, Rahman is recognized as the artist

who changed the face of music by successfully fusing traditional
Indian classical strains with the elements of modern technology
and evolving his own unique style.

Stuti Goswamy

—one of the biggest Bollywood fans on campus. I asked
her about the influence of Bollywood songs on her.
I also talked to her about the persuasiveness of these
movies.

Roopa Mahadevan

—one of the well-known Carnatic music singers on campus, Roopa
is a great admirer of Bollywood songs. She is a first-year master's
student in biological sciences.

In contrast, Dexian Cai, whose outline appeared in Chapter 6, more strictly followed conventional MLA style for his works cited, alphabetizing his list and using hanging indentation format.

Works Cited

Kincheloe, Joe L. <u>The Sign of the Burger: McDonald's and the
Culture of Power</u>. Philadelphia: Temple UP, 2002.

McSpotlight, 27 Oct. 2003 <http://www.mcspotlight.com>.

"The Merchants of Cool." <u>Frontline</u>. By Rachel Dretzin. Dir. Barak
Goodman. 2001. PBS. 27 Feb. 2001 <http://www.pbs.org/
wgbh/pages/frontline/shows/cool/>.

Dex alphabetizes the list by last name.

If there is no author, as for "Merchants of Cool," the title is listed first. Note that little words such as *the* are not considered for alphabetizing.

Ritzer, George. <u>McDonaldization the Reader</u>. Thousand Oaks, CA:

Pine Forge, 2002.

When an author's
name appears more
than once, three
hyphens (---) stand in
for the name.

---. <u>The McDonaldization of Society</u>. Rev. ed. Thousand Oaks,

CA: Pine Forge, 1996.

Smart, Barry, ed. <u>Resisting McDonaldization</u>. London: Sage, 1999.

Each entry is format-
ted with a hanging
indent so readers can
skim the names more
easily

Vidal, John. <u>Mclibel: Burger Culture on Trial</u>. New York: New Press,

1997.

Watson, James L. <u>Golden Arches East: McDonald's in East Asia</u>.

Palo Alto, CA: Stanford UP, 1997.

Documentation for Print and Online Sources

MLA style follows a particular logic in ordering information for a citation. Consult the "At a Glance" box and the table on page 305 to begin to understand this system. You might also study the list of examples provided in this chapter, but realize that sometimes for less conventional sources (i.e. Facebook wall posts) you may need to improvise the format based on your understanding of MLA style.

AT A GLANCE

MLA Documentation for Print and Online Sources

For the Works Cited list, follow the order below in listing details about your source

- Author or authors
- Title of book or article
- If an article, title of journal or book within which it is published
- Place of publication
- Publisher

- Date of publication
- If an online source, date you accessed it
- If a printed or PDF article, page span
- If online article from a database, the database or search engine
- If online source, the full URL

LOGIC OF MLA STYLE

Satrapi, Marjane.	Persepolis: The Story of a Childhood.	New York: Pantheon, 2004.
List the author's name first, by last name. If there are multiple authors, include them all, following the order listed on the publication.	The title comes next. For books and films, underline or italicize the title. For shorter pieces (such as articles, TV shows, songs, etc.), put the title in quotation marks with the larger publication (the collection of essays, TV series, or album) underlined or italicized.	Last comes publication information: place, publisher or company, and date. For shorter pieces, include the complete range of page numbers (for the article), and include URLs for online sources. Also include the date you accessed online sources.
If there is no author, use the publishing organization (if available) or jump next to the title.	If you need to refer to the title for in-text citations (and there is no author), use the first few keywords only.	

Single-Author Book

Satrapi, Marjane. Persepolis: The Story of a Childhood. New York:
    Pantheon, 2004.

Multiple-Author Book

Andrews, Maggie, and Mary M. Talbot, eds. All the World and Her
    Husband: Women in Twentieth-Century Consumer Culture.
    London: Cassell, 2000.

Introduction, Preface, Foreword, or Afterword in a Book

Gerbner, George. Foreword. Cultural Diversity and the U.S. Media.
    Eds. Yahya R. Kamalipour and Theresa Carillia. New York:
    State U of New York P, 1998. xv-xvi.

Article in an Anthology

Boichel, Bill. "Batman: Commodity as Myth." The Many Lives of
    the Batman. Eds. Roberta Pearson and William Uricchio.
    New York: BFI, 1991. 4-17.

Article from a Journal

Roberts, Garyn G. "Understanding the Sequential Art of Comic Strips and Comic Books and Their Descendants in the Early Years of the New Millenium." Journal of American Culture 27.2 (2004): 210-217.

Article from a Popular Magazine Published Monthly

Maney, Kevin. "The New Face of IBM." Wired July 2005: 142-152.

Sontag, Susan. "Looking at War." The New Yorker 3 Jan. 2003. 20 June 2006 <http://www.newyorker.com/printables/archive/050119fr_archive04>.

Article from a Newspaper

Cowell, Alan. "Book Buried in Irish Bog Is Called a Major Find." New York Times 27 July 2006. 31 July 2006 <http://www.nytimes.com/2006/07/27/books/27psal.html?_r=1&ref=arts&oref=slogin>.

Article from a Database

Chun, Alex. "Comic Strip's Plight Isn't Funny." Los Angeles Times 27 Apr. 2006, home ed.: E6. Lexis Nexis. Stanford University, Stanford, CA. 4 May 2006 <http://www.lexisnexis.com>.

Article from a Website

Yagoda, Ben. "You Need to Read This: How Need to Vanquished Have To, Must and Should." Slate.com. 17 July 2006. 20 July 2006 <http://www.slate.com/id/2145734>.

Anthology

Herndl, Carl G., and Stuart C. Brown, eds. Green Culture. Madison: U of Wisconsin P, 1996.

Anonymous Article

"Hillary's American Dream." The Economist 29 July 2006: 32.

Definition

"Diversity." <u>American Heritage Dictionary of the English Language</u>.
4th ed. Houghton, 2000.

"Greek Mythology." <u>Wikipedia.com</u>. 27 July 2006 <http://en.
wikipedia.org/wiki/Greek_mythology>.

Letter to the Editor

Tucker, Rich Thompson. "High Cost of Cheap Coal." Letter. <u>National
Geographic</u> July 2006: 6-7.

Letter or Memo

Greer, Michael. Letter to the authors. 30 July 2006.

Dissertation

Li, Zhan. "The Potential of America's Army: The Video Game as
Civilian-Military Public Sphere." Diss. Massachusetts Institute
of Technology, 2004.

Government Publication

United States. Census Bureau. Housing and Household Economic
Statistics Division. <u>Poverty Thresholds 2005</u>. 1 Feb. 2006. 20
May 2006 <http://www.census.gov/hhes/www/poverty/
threhld/thresh05.html>.

Cover

Adams, Neil. "Deadman." <u>Comics VF.com</u>. 1978. 23 Oct. 2005
<http://www.comicsvf.com/fs/17164.php>.

Interview

Tullman, Geoffrey. Personal interview. 21 May 2006.

Cho, Ana. Telephone interview. 4 June 2005.

Email

Tisbury, Martha. "Re: Information Overload." E-mail to Max
Anderson. 31 July 2006.

Online Posting

> Shelly, Ayla. "Visual Rhetoric, Girls, and Ads." Online posting. 5 Nov. 2005. GrrlChatSpot. 2 March 2006. <http://groups.google. com/group/grrlchtspt/ExchangeDetail.asp?i+2234981>.

Chat Room Discussion or Real-time Communication

> Zhang, Zhihao. "Revision Suggestions." 25 May 2006. Cross-Cultural Rhetoric Chat Room. 25 May 2006. <coursework-pilot.stanford.edu/ccrhet/chat>.

AT A GLANCE

MLA Documentation for Visual and Multimedia Sources

For the "Works Cited" list, follow the order below in listing details about your source

- Author or organization
- Title of the image, film, ad, TV series, or document
- If part of a collection, title of the collection
- Place of publication and publisher
- Date of publication
- If an online source, date you accessed it
- If online article from a database, the name of the database or search engine
- If online source, the full URL (not just Google or the search engine name)

Documentation for Visual, Audio, and Multimedia Sources

Because many of the materials you may work with fall into the category of innovative text produced by new technologies—such as Webmovies, Flash animation, Weblogs, three-dimensional images, storyboards, sound clips, and more—you need to learn how to construct a citation that provides as much detail as possible about the text. Even citing interviews and surveys can be tricky for some because the format does not match conventional books or articles. Just follow the logical steps for citing print and online sources, developing a rubric that works to offer as much information as possible. The key is consistency and adhering as closely as possible to the logic of MLA style.

Photograph or Visual Image

> "Golden Gate Bridge," San Francisco. Photograph by the author. 23 June 2004.
>
> Goldin, Nan. Jimmy Paulette & Misty in a Taxi, NYC. 1991. San Francisco Museum of Modern Art, San Francisco.

Sherman, Cindy. Untitled Film Still #13. 1978. The Complete
Untitled Film Stills of Cindy Sherman. Museum of Modern Art.
7 July 2006 <http://www.moma.org/exhibitions/1997/
sherman/index.html>.

Advertisement

Nike. "We Are All Witnesses." Advertisement. 3 Jan. 2006
<http://www.nikebasketball.com>.

Film or Film Clip

Beyond Killing Us Softly: The Impact of Media Images on Women
and Girls. Dir./Prod. Margaret Lazarus, Renner Wunderlich.
Cambridge Documentary Films, 2000.

"A Brief History of America." Bowling for Columbine. 2002.
Dir. Michael Moore. 13 June 2006. <http://www.
bowlingforcolumbine.com/media/clips/index.php>.

Comic Strip Online

Pastis, Stephen. "Pearls Before Swine." Comic strip. Comics.com
18 Apr. 2006. 16 May 2006 <http://www.comics.com/
comics/pearls/archive/pearls-20060418.html>.

Entire Internet Site

Cartoonists Index. MSNBC. 4 Nov. 2005 <http://cagle.msnbc.com>.

Individual Webpage from an Internet Site

Stevenson, Seth. "Head Case: The Mesmerizing Ad for Headache Gel."
Slate.com. 24 July 2006. 25 July 2006 <http://www.slate.com/
id/2146382>.

Personal Homepage

Corrigan, Edna. Homepage. 31 Jan. 2005. 24 Oct. 2005
<http://www.ednarules.com>.

Television Program

"The Diet Wars." Frontline. PBS. 2004. 16 Aug. 2006 <http://www.
pbs.org/wgbh/pages/frontline/shows/diet/view/>.

Computer Game

America's Army: Special Forces. CD-ROM. U.S. Army-Army Game
Project, 2002.

Full Spectrum Warrior. XBOX disc. THQ and Pandemic Studios,
2004.

Computer Game Online

Second Life. Your World. Your Imagination. Linden Labs. 7 May
2006 <http://secondlife.com>.

Screen Shot

Star Wars Galaxies. Screen shot. Sony Online Entertainment. 5 Feb.
2005 <swg.stratics.com/content/news/images/jawa.jpg>.

Radio Essay

"Book Marketing Goes to the Movies." Morning Edition. Narr. John
Ydstie. Natl. Public Radio. 18 July 2006. Transcript.

Sound Clip or Recording

Reagan, Ronald. "The Space Shuttle 'Challenger' Tragedy Address."
28 Jan. 1986. American Rhetoric. 5 Mar. 2006 <http://www.
americanrhetoric.com/speeches/rreaganchallenger.htm>.

Class Lecture

Connors, Fiona. "Visual Literacy in Perspective." English 210B.
Boston University. 24 Oct. 2004.

Speech

Rheingold, Howard. "Technologies of Cooperation." The Annenberg
Center for Communication. University of Southern California,
Los Angeles. 3 Apr. 2006.

Jobs, Steve. Commencement Address. Stanford University. 12 June

2005. 27 July 2006 <http://www.wiredatom.com/

jobs_stanford_speech/>.

Painting

Warhol, Andy. <u>Self Portrait</u>. 1986. <u>The Warhol: Collections</u>. 3 Aug.

2006 <http://www.warhol.org/collections/index.html>.

Map

Hong Kong Disneyland Guide. Map. Disney, 2006.

Performance

<u>Phedre</u>. By Racine. Dir. Ileana Drinovan. Pigott Theater, Memorial

Hall, Stanford, CA. May 10–13, 2006.

Copyright and Citing Sources

When you decide to integrate visuals or multimedia in your writing, it's not enough to just include the source and provide the citation for it. You need to spend a few moments thinking about issues of copyright and permissions. Whether you are dealing with images or print quotations, you are using materials produced or prepared by another person, and you must give that person credit for the work. In some cases—particularly if you plan to publish your work—you also need to obtain permission to use it. As you browse through catalogs of images, you need to record the source of each image you decide to use. If you have copied an image from the Web (by right clicking and choosing "Save Picture As"), you need to include as much of the full source information as you can find: the Website author, the title, the sponsoring organization, the date. If you have found a visual (photograph, chart, ad) from a print source and scanned it into a computer so you can insert it into your essay, you need to list the print source in full as well as information about the original image (the name of the photographer, the image title, and the date). Listing Google as your source is not sufficient; take pains to find the original source and list it in full. Keep careful track as you locate images, give appropriate credit when you use them in your essay, and ask for permission if necessary.

Student Paper in MLA Style

Tanner Gardner's research paper focused on the influx of international sports stars into professional leagues, like the National Basketball Association (NBA). He included a wide range of sources and worked hard to meet proper documentation style.

Tanner includes complete identifying information in the upper-left corner. The whole paper is double-spaced for MLA style.

Tanner centers his title. He also uses an epigram to kick off the paper; the reader will look for McCallum in the "Works Cited" list.

In a creative double opening, Tanner begins with a quote that builds off the epigram and introduces his theme of the economics of the NBA. The reader will look for Stern in the Works Cited list.

Tanner Gardner

Program in Writing and Rhetoric

Dr. Alyssa J. O'Brien

Final Research Paper

November 2, 2005

Show Me the Money! The Globalization of the NBA

"Tomorrow the world: NBA will be international by the end of

the Century"

—Jack McCallum, *Sports Illustrated* Columnist, 1988

"With the 11th pick in the draft, the Orlando Magic select

Fran Vazquez of Xantada, Spain." As David Stern, the NBA

commissioner, made this announcement, representatives of the

Orlando Magic couldn't help but smile. The team had just chosen a

6-foot-11 forward that would ideally return them to the glory days

of the early 1990s. Like the Orlando Magic, other NBA teams have

begun to increase their focus on players abroad and as a result, in

the past decade the league has seen the proliferation of foreign-

born players. Their impact has reached far beyond the court,

altering the culture of the NBA. These players have caused a

cultural overhaul in the league, creating a change of face in the

NBA. Extending even further are the economic implications, as the

Gardner 2

NBA and large companies have benefited in enormous ways. Thus, Jack McCallum's prediction of an international NBA almost 20 years ago has become reality today. In the past fifteen years, foreign-born athletes have been lured by the rhetoric of competition, money, and advertising rhetoric to migrate to America where bright lights and bucks hopefully await them. In the process, they have brought their culture to America while also bringing economic perks to the countries involved.

Yao Ming, Manu Ginobili, and Peja Stojakovic are all players who fit this description and bring to mind the new global face of the NBA. Theses players from China, Argentina, and Serbia have led to a new trend of globalization in sports. Economics are often the focal point of globalization as the World Bank defines it as "the integration of growing economies and societies around the world" (World Bank). It is also important to look at the cultural side of globalization though, as another organization identifies it as "a rapid increase in cross-border social, cultural and technological exchange" (ASED). An economic view on globalization ignores the cultural benefit, shedding a negative light on globalization and even causing America to be viewed as imperialists for their part in it. However, there are situations in which globalization has benefited both America and more importantly the foreign country involved. This is particularly relevant to the globalization of sports, specifically in the NBA. While whether the NBA is a positive model of globalization remains to be seen, the past 15 years in the league provide a good

Notice how Tanner links back to his epigram as he introduces his three-part thesis.

Tanner composes an effective transition by moving from the macro to the micro and naming specific players.

Tanner puts the name of the organization as the author in this parenthetical citation.

Here he uses ASED; look for it in the Works Cited list.

The transition in the last line sets up the scope and purpose of his argument.

Gardner 3

example of how economies and cultures can come together in a positive way.

When David Stern was named commissioner of the NBA on February 1, 1984, the league was in turmoil. Financially, many teams were experiencing difficulties and close to bankruptcy. Culturally, the league reputation was sub par at best and plagued by "thugs and drugs." Relationally, the league and the players' association were constantly at each other's throats. Perhaps most significant to Stern, television ratings were at an all-time low, as the 1980 NBA finals were not even shown live on TV. The NBA had lost it luster and turned into a one-man show rather than the team game it had been. There was no doubt it was time for an overhaul in the league. Stern needed to implement a change to save the failing league and needed to do it quick.

Stern, a brilliant marketer, quickly became allies with Boris Stankovic, head of FIBA, the worldwide governing body of basketball. Stern's relationship with Stankovic laid the groundwork for the NBA's interests in Europe, although the majority of the influx of foreign-born players would not take place until the middle to late 1990s. Although most NBA teams scouted in Europe by the late 1980s, the foreign players had not yet proven themselves in the competitive NBA. Nevertheless, Stern saw the economic potential in European markets for the NBA, specifically in television. At the time, a meager 20 foreign-born athletes were playing in the NBA, but this number would soon change.

There's no need for source attribution for "thugs and drugs" because it is a common expression.

Tanner's combination of narrative and research synthesis makes for quite an engaging style.

Gardner 4

If the numbers indicate anything, Stern's interest in Europe soon manifested itself. The 20 foreign-born athletes on NBA rosters in 1989 represented only 6% of the total players in the league. Fifteen years later, the 2004-2005 NBA season saw an unbelievable 81 international players, an increase of over 300% in only 15 years, as the graph below shows (see Figure 1). These international players now make up over 20% of the NBA.

While the actual increase in numbers is important, the underlying impact of these numbers is much more striking. In addition to signing as free agents, foreign-born players have dominated the NBA draft in recent years, as they have been taken as the top pick in four of the last nine drafts. In the most recent draft, international players represented almost a third of total

Tanner introduces his graphic effectively, setting up the numbers with prose first and then using the information graphic as evidence.

Generating this chart from the research he completed, Tanner inserts it here.

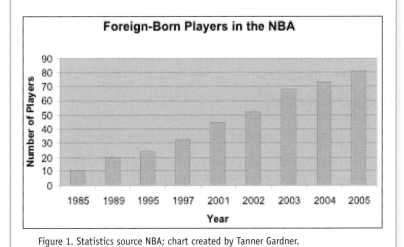

Figure 1. Statistics source NBA; chart created by Tanner Gardner.

Gardner 5

picks. Perhaps most important is the increase in diversity among players. In 1989, only 14 countries were represented in the NBA. 15 years later, 35 countries are now represented, integrating many new faces into the league. As Donn Nelson, president of basketball operations for the Dallas Mavericks comments, "You can't just label them foreign or international players any longer. They're just players who can do the same thing the other guys in the league can do" (qtd. in DuPree). Indeed these players are a norm in the NBA now. As the increase has occurred, NBA teams have reacted in an appropriate way, hiring new scouts focusing solely on players abroad.

A major factor that has contributed to the influx of foreign-born players in the NBA is foreign scouting. With the success of foreign players, developing contacts in the international markets is a must. The number of foreign-scouts employed by teams has increased drastically right along with the players. Today, most teams have numerous scouts focused on international talent. Europe tends to be the primary focus, but scouts in Asia and South America are also on the rise. Asia has been a recent target because of their abundance of big men, something the NBA has recently lacked. The point is clear though: foreign-scouting is essential. As Joe Ash, the Indiana Pacers' director of scouting notes, "Scouting foreign talent is a necessity, not an option. You have too" (Brunt). It is obvious the scouts have been pushing these foreign players to come over, but what exactly has been their prerogative for coming to America?

Citing a source within a source, Tanner uses "qtd. in" to show that Nelson is quoted in DuPree.

Notice how the repetition of highlighted words work to advance Tanner's argument and form an effective transition to focus on the next point: sports scouts in Asia and South America.

Placing the last name in the parentheses allows Tanner to refer to this source by title in the text.

Gardner 6

The main draw of foreign players to the NBA has been the intense and visible competition among the players. I call this phenomenon the rhetoric of competition. The 1992 Olympics was the turning point of this element. The USA fielded perhaps their strongest team ever at the Olympics in Barcelona, showing the world the competitiveness of US basketball. Rick Welts, president of NBA Properties Inc. at the time, called this event "the most important in the history of the sport" (qtd. in Desens). International athletes, many of whom strive to be the best, took note and longed for the competition of the NBA. Simply put: they want to test their skills against the best. Consequently, there has been a steady flow of athletes to the NBA lured by the rhetoric of competition since. The competition has also been a medium for them to improve their skills both directly by playing and indirectly by watching. As it turns out, these foreign players are just as competitive as Americans. In addition, playing in front of large crowds breeds a more competitive atmosphere, as more people create a more electrifying environment. The NBA is the place to find this, as in 2002 the average attendance in the NBA (16,683) was more than double that of the premier European league, the Basketball Clubs Association of Spain (5,700).[1] With more fans and more support in America, there is inevitably more money.

While competition has been a large factor, there is no way to ignore the economics of the situation. There are enormous

---

[1] Source: NBA and Eurobasket.com

On the previous page, Tanner ended the paragraph with a question to move the argument forward. Here he answers the question and creates a new term: "the rhetoric of competition." He then turns to the example of the USA Olympic team in Barcelona to support his point.

Tanner includes an explanatory note here because he has drawn this data from several sources. The notes can either appear as footnotes or be placed at the end of the document.

Gardner 7

economic benefits to playing in the NBA. Take, for example, 2002 salary statistics: The average salary in the NBA was $3.95 million while the minimum salary was $350,000 compared to the average salary in the Basketball Clubs Association of Spain, $242,000.[2] Thus, foreign-born players are guaranteed a minimum salary in the NBA that is greater than the average salary in the best league in Europe or Asia. The money does not come only from playing in the NBA though, as the side benefits of endorsements by major companies provide these athletes substantial sums of money and visibility, increasing the financial benefit for the players

Advertising rhetoric has been perhaps the most lucrative draw for athletes to come to America. These athletes have garnered multi-million dollar contracts from corporations, while simultaneously being the newest way for corporations to strike it rich abroad. There is no better example of this than Yao Ming. Ming has become the most prominent face of international advertising in sports. He has appeared in many commercials and advertisements for corporate giants like Apple Computers and Visa, projecting his face all over the world.

This advertisement shown on the right (see Figure 2) featuring Yao Ming and Verne Troyer, was released by Apple Computers in early 2003 as an international advertisement in the form of a commercial and a picture. In the picture, the face of Yao is cheerful and personable. By portraying him in this respect, it is

Tanner introduces visual evidence not just as decoration. He spends time offering a rhetorical analysis of the elements of this image.

---

[2] Source: NBA and Eurobasket.com

Gardner 8

obvious that Apple sees Yao as very marketable individual. Overall, the intent of Apple is clear: by using Ming in an international advertisement, they show that they feel international players can appeal to all audiences, regardless of race or ethnicity. This type of

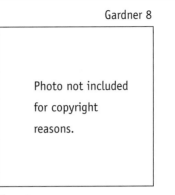

Photo not included for copyright reasons.

Figure 2.

rhetoric is not unique to Apple, as other companies like Visa and MasterCard have also used this tactic in their advertisements. While the target audience of the advertisements is not the athletes, there is no doubt international athletes are noticing them.

Seeing foreign athletes in advertisements is a direct economic appeal to other internationals looking to make it big in the US. The relationship is reciprocal: corporations like Apple and Nike tap into markets abroad by having these athletes wear there gear while the athletes themselves make a fortune simultaneously. Even in the midst of this, there are many other interests, namely the NBA, corporations, and the home countries of the foreign players, achieving substantial monetary returns.

While the financial benefit of international players coming to the NBA is no doubt substantial, the biggest financial winner in the scope of it all appears to be the NBA. Ironically, in 1989 Forbes' columnist Jeffrey Trachtenberg predicted in the future,

Tanner includes this image in his paper here instead of in an appendix as a strategic choice to serve as evidence for his claims about the persona of Yao Ming.

Make sure you get permission to reproduce the image if you seek to post your paper online.

Tanner provides supporting evidence through additional examples, but he does not need to spend time in the paper on these images since he is moving on to his next point: the economic benefit of ads to home countries.

Gardner 9

"David Stern and his conquistadors in short pants will be making a lot of people a lot of money" taking the game international (Trachtenberg). Trachtenberg's prediction was, appropriately, right on the money. Between 1985 and 1990, the broadcast of NBA games overseas doubled to 70 countries. These broadcasts generated $5 million for the NBA. Almost ten years later, the NBA's revenue abroad had increased, but the NBA still took a loss of $25 million, prompting <u>Business Week</u> to label their approach to globalization "too conservative" (The NBA). The NBA must have taken the comment to heart, as by 2003 the NBA broadcasted games in a staggering 212 countries, earning the NBA $35 million dollars. In addition, 20% of NBA merchandise was sold overseas for a profit of $430 million (Eisenberg). Stern has even predicted that in the next decade, foreign broadcasts will reach 50% of US television revenue. Along the way corporations will continue to benefit too.

Corporations tapping into foreign markets have been a direct result of the influx of international athletes. Historian Walter LaFeber once observed, "aside from the illegal narcotics trade, sports have become the world's most globalized and lucrative business" (qtd. in Larmer). LaFeber couldn't have been more correct as corporations have quickly recognized the migration of foreign-born players as an opportunity to make millions. Spalding's eagerness to acclimate to foreign markets has come as a great benefit, increasing their sales by an astounding 44% in 2002. Nike, who had a mere 33% of sale internationally in 1993,

This secondary source offers a key point of argument for Tanner. Notice, though, how he builds on it to advance his own argument his by returning to the key terms of his title with "right on the money." He is emphasizing his own voice as a writer and researcher.

As Tanner turns to logos in his argumentation, Eisenberg's name is placed in parentheses, using the cross-referencing logic of MLA style.

Now Tanner turns to the historical sources in his iceberg of research.

Gardner 10

increased this number by 53% in just 10 years.[3] The relationship
between Nike and basketball is actually reciprocal, as their
promotions actually promote basketball internationally by
providing publicity for the sport ("The Yao"). Reebok, a partner of
the NBA, derived 30% of its sales abroad in 2002, an increased of
10% in just two years (Eisenberg). 2002 also marked Rebooks
commitment to long-term growth in Asia, as they signed their
poster-boy, Yao Ming. Reebok is not the only one benefiting from
Ming, though.

China is a perfect example of a foreign-country benefiting
from globalization ("In the NBA"). The country has had a definite
interest in Ming migrating to the NBA. Ming, who carried China's
flag at the 2004 Olympics, is an economic benefit for China. China's
government has a policy where players who come to the NBA must
treat their salary as follows: 30% goes to the Chinese Basketball
Association, 10% to the player's home city, and finally 10% to the
State General Administration of Sports. This total represents 50% of
Yao's salary, which was almost $4.5 million in 2005. As many
consider Asia the world's fastest growing sports market, it seems
China will continue to benefit financially from their policy on
athletes playing internationally.

While money is a very important part in the equation of
foreign-born players playing in the NBA, the non-monetary

Here Tanner refers to a Website, using the key words of the title.

Despite the ample use of sources in his paper, Tanner keeps the spotlight on his argument. His voice as a writer emerges as the one synthesizing all this research to construct his own original argument.

---

[3] Locke, Richard M. "The Promise and Perils of Globalization: The Case of Nike."
MIT's Sloan School of Business Website. 8 Oct 2005. <http://mitsloan.mit.edu/
50th/nikepaper.pdf>.

Gardner 11

benefits to the league are more important. Foreign-born players in the NBA are a win-win situation for the league and the players. These players come from countries that stress the fundamentals of basketball and a team atmosphere. Rick Adelman, the coach of the Sacramento Kings, notes, "foreign players have added the skill factor back into the game" (qtd. in Eisenberg). Thus, the players not only improve their skills playing in the best league but also make the NBA more competitive. Along with this competitiveness comes a new exciting game.

The new and thrilling NBA has also been a result of a change in culture, which is perhaps the most significant effect of foreign-born players in the NBA. As stated earlier, "thugs and drugs" plagued the 1980's in the NBA. International players have helped change this image by bringing a more clean cut face to the NBA while at the same time bridging the cultural gap. These players don't talk trash: they simply play the game. Joe Davidson of the Sacramento Bee says it best: "They [foreign-born players] haven't been corrupted by ESPN highlights into thinking that dunking is the only way to succeed" (Davidson). The new culture and international element of the NBA has made it more fan friendly and accessible to all, providing an atmosphere in which almost any sports fan can be entertained regardless of ethnicity. Ultimately, the foreign-born players have brought fans back to the sport while simultaneously improving financial stability in the league. In this way, the change of face in the NBA has proven to be a success.

Gardner 12

The influx of foreign-born players in the NBA has clearly benefited professional basketball on numerous levels: financially for the players, the league, various corporations and foreign countries, and culturally for the NBA in general. However, it is important to note that not all international players are bolting for the NBA. Fran Vazquez provides the perfect example. Although he initially thought he was ready to come to the NBA, "the timing, as it turned out, was just not right for him. More than anything, I think it was a cultural thing," said Dave Twardzik, assistant General Manager of the Orlando Magic (Povtak). Vazquez is just a rare exception though, as most players are ready to make the transition. While the money is important to the players, it appears the chance to compete at the highest level, fame from advertising, and the freedoms and excitement of America are what ultimately draw them over.

Looking towards the future of the NBA, it does not appear like there is an end in sight to the trend. David Stern has even gone as far as to predict there will be a team in Europe in the next ten years. As international players continue to journey to America, the involved parties will continue to reap the benefits. Thus, the successful model of globalization in the NBA will continue. Overall, the trend towards globalization in the NBA is not unique: there is a search for global talent not only in other professional sports like the MLB and NHL, but also in all areas of society today. Yet, this has caused for some uneasiness. If other sectors of society use the NBA as a model for globalization, it may benefit all

Tanner pauses to consider the counter-argument and uses conditional language to assert his own thesis one more time.

One last citation gives Tanner's argument authority before he moves to his conclusion.

In his conclusion, Tanner looks to the future, thereby broadening out the scope and significance of his research-based argument.

Gardner 13

parties involved in a majority of situations and one day be viewed in a positive light.

Gardner 14

Works Cited

ASED. "Asia-Europe Dialogue on alternative political strategies." 2005. ASED. 25 Oct. 2005 <http://www.ased.org>.

Brunt, Cliff. "NBA Draft Gives Teams a Chance to Add International Flair." Associated Press 23 June 2005.

Davidson, Joe. E-mail interview. 15 Oct. 2005.

Desens, Carl. "The NBA's Fast Break Overseas." BusinessWeek 5 Dec. 1994. 10 Oct. 2005 <http://www.businessweek.com/archives/1994/b340279.arc.htm>.

DuPree, David. "Foreign-Borns Aren't Unique." USA Today 14 Oct. 2004: 2C.

Eisenberg, Daniel. "The NBA's Global Game Plan." Time 17 Mar. 2003: 59+.

Larmer, Brook. "The Center of the World." Foreign Policy 15 Sept. 2005. 66.

McCallum, Jack. "Tomorrow the World." Sports Illustrated 7 Nov. 1988: 58.

"The NBA Needs to Do Some Globetrotting." Business Week 19 July 1999: 19.

All sources are alphabetized.

He includes articles and interviews.

He lists full information for online sources, but he doesn't just use online materials; Tanner uses many print texts as well.

Povtak, Tim. "Spanish Forward Reiterates He's Not Coming to NBA

This Season." <u>Charlotte Observer</u> 3 Aug. 2005. 8 Oct. 2005

<http://www.charlotte.com/mld/charlotte/sports/

basketball/12297039.htm>.

Trachtenberg, Jeffrey A. "Playing the Global Game." <u>Forbes</u> 23 Jan.

1989: 90.

World Bank. "Globalization." 2001. 25 Oct. 2005 <http://www1.

worldbank.org/economicpolicy/globalization>.

"The Yao Crowd." <u>Economist</u> 9 Aug. 2003: 55.

Articles without authors are listed by title key words.

Works Consulted

Molina, Pablo Malo. "Spanish Basketball." <u>Eurobasket.com</u>.

Feb. 2002. 8 Oct. 2005 <www.eurobasket.com/

esp.intro.asp>.

"NBA Minimum Salary." <u>InsideHoops.com</u>. 10 Aug. 2005.

8 Oct. 2004 <http://www.insidehoops.com/

minimum-nba-salary.shtml>.

Tanner includes his works consulted to show more of his iceberg of research.

Documentation for Your Paper

Now that you've learned about the meaning of intellectual property, the dangers of plagiarism, the rhetorical purpose for documentation style, the cross-referencing logic of in-text citations, and the guidelines for MLA Works Cited and Consulted lists, it is time for you to review your own writing. Have you acknowledged all your sources in full? Did you include proper and concise parenthetical attributions in the paper? Does your bibliographic list provide an alphabetized reflection of your research? If so, then you have accomplished a great deal as a writer.

WRITING PROJECTS

1. **Documentation Log:** Develop your own system of note taking to avoid the kind of plagiarism trap that writer Doris Kearns Goodwin fell into.

2. **Peer Review of Citations:** Share your draft paper with a group of peers, and have them check to see which sources need citation. Does your paper contain knowledge you must have obtained from a source? If so, you need to acknowledge the source of that knowledge. Do certain passages seem to be common knowledge? If so, you don't need to cite them. What paragraphs could go into notes? What aspects of your paper need more explanation and could use a note?

3. **Draft Works Cited List:** As you compose your paper and formulate your "Works Cited" list, visit the online tools available through the *Envision* Website to help you generate your list, double-check your entries, convert MLA to APA, or learn more about documentation style.

4. **Writing with Technology:** You might find it helpful to turn to one of the scholarly tools for producing a Work Cited list. These include *Ref Works, End Note,* and *TermPerfect.* You can find links to these tools on the Envision website. Many researchers and scholars depend on these tools—such writers will keep notes right in the program, insert all identifying information for a source, and then select the documentation format needed for their papers. The technology then produces a list in the proper documentation style. You need to double check the list, of course, but it can save you lots of time.

 Visit www.ablongman.com/envision for expanded assignment guidelines and student projects.

Works Cited

CHAPTER 1

Aristotle. "Rhetoric." *The History and Theory of Rhetoric.* By James A. Herrick. Boston: Allyn & Bacon, 1998.

Blakesley, David, and Collin Brooke. "Introduction: Notes on Visual Rhetoric." *Enculturation* 3.2 (2001): Node 4. <http://enculturation.gmu.edu/3_2/introduction.html>.

Diamond, Matthew. "No Laughing Matter: Post-September 11 Political Cartoons in Arab/Muslim Newspapers." *Political Communication* 19 (2002): 251–72.

Gellis, Mark. "Six Ways of Thinking about Rhetoric." The Rhetoric Page at Kettering University. Par. 1. <http://www.gmi.edu/~mgellis/HANDT001.HTM>.

Holkins, Jerry. "The Hipness Threshold." Penny Arcade Blog. 12 Mar. 2004. 22 June 2006. <http://www.penny-arcade.com/comic/2004/03/12>.

Horn, Robert. *Visual Language: Global Communication for the 21st Century.* MacRovu Inc., 1999.

Huntington, Samuel P. "'Under God': Michael Newdow is right. Atheists *are* outsiders in America." *Wall Street Journal* 16 June 2004.

Lehrer, Jim. "Illustrated Men." *Online Focus.* Transcript. 31 Oct. 1996. <http://www.pbs.org/newshour/bb/election/october96/cartoonists_10-31.html>.

Marlette, Doug. "I Was a Tool of Satan." *Columbia Journalism Review* Nov./Dec. 2003: 52. < http://www.cjr.org/issues/2003/6/satan-marlette.asp>.

McCloud, Scott. *Understanding Comics.* New York: HarperPerennial, 1993.

Melandri, Lisa. "Drawing the Line." Philadelphia, PA. 18 Mar. 2003. <http://thegalleriesatmoore.org/publications/cartoons/politicalcartoons.shtml>.

Mitchell, J. T. "The Pictorial Turn." *Picture Theory.* Chicago: U of Chicago P, 1994.

Moore, Art. "'What Would Muhammad Drive?': Pulitzer-winner's cartoon terrorist spurs death threats from Muslims." WorldNetDaily.com. 28 Dec. 2002. 18 Mar. 2003 <http://www.worldnetdaily.com/news/article.asp?ARTICLE_ID530197>.

Plato. *Gorgias.* Trans. Robin Waterfield. New York: Oxford UP, 1994. 21.

Villanueva, Victor Jr. *Bootstraps: From an American Academic of Color.* Urbana, IL: National Council of Teachers of English, 1993.

Watterson, Bill. *Calvin and Hobbes Sunday Pages 1985–1995.* Kansas City, MO: Andrews McMeel Publishing, 2001.

CHAPTER 2

Bowen, Laurence, and Jill Schmid. "Minority Presence and Portrayal in Mainstream Magazine Advertising: An Update." *Journalism and Mass Communications Quarterly* 74.1 (2004): 134–46

Burgin, Victor. "Art, Common Sense, and Photography." *Visual Culture: The Reader.* Eds. Jessica Evans and Stuart Hall. London: Sage Publications, 1999. 41–50.

Caputi, Jane. "Seeing Elephants: The Myths of Phallotechnology." *Feminist Studies* 14.3 (1988).

Hacker, Andrea. *New York Times* 14 June 1984.

Kinneavy, James. "Kairos in Classical and Modern Rhetorical Theory." *Rhetoric and Kairos: Essays in History, Theory and Praxis.* Eds. Phillip Sipiora, James Baumlin, and Carolyn Miller. Albany: State U of New York P, 2002. 58–76.

"Merchants of Cool." *Frontline.* Dir. Barak Goodman. PBS. 27 Feb. 2001. <http://www.pbs.org/wgbh/pages/frontline/shows/cool/>.

Messaris, Paul. *Visual Persuasion: The Role of Images in Advertising.* Thousand Oaks, CA: Sage Publications, 1997.

Stevenson, Seth. "You and Your Shadow." Slate.com. 4 Mar. 2004. <http://www.slate.com/id/2096459/>.

Twitchell, James B. *Adcult USA.* New York: Columbia UP, 1996.

---. "Listerine: Gerard Lambert and Selling the Need." *Twenty Ads That Shook the World.* New York: Three Rivers Press, 2000. 60–69.

Williams, Roy H. "The Wizard of Advertising." *Secret Formulas of the Wizard of Ads.* Bard Press, 1999.

CHAPTER 3

Boese, Alex. *Museum of Hoaxes.* <http://museumofhoaxes.com>.

Cicero. *De Inventione.* Trans. H. M. Hubbell. Cambridge, MA: Loeb Classical Library, 1949.

Curtis, James. "Dorothea Lange, Migrant Mother, and the Culture of the Great Depression." *Winterthur Portfolio: A Journal of American Material Culture* 21 (Spring 1986) 1–20.

Dunn, Geoffrey. "Photographic License." *San Louis Obispo Times.* 17 Jan. 2002. <http://www.newtimes-slo.com/archives/cov_stories_2002/cov_01172002.html>.

Gottesman, Jane. *Game Face.* NewYork: Random House, 2001.

Harris, Christopher, and Paul Martin Lester. *Visual Journalism.* Boston: Allyn & Bacon, 2002.

Sontag, Susan. "Looking at War: Photography's View of Devastation and Death." *The New Yorker* 9 Dec. 2002: 82–98.

CHAPTER 4

Bizzell, Patricia, and Bruce Herzberg. "Research as a Social Act." *Background Readings for Instructors Using The Bedford Handbook.* 6th ed. Ed. Glenn Blalock. Boston: Bedford/St. Martin's, 2002. 321–26.

Booth, Wayne. *Craft of Research.* Chicago: U of Chicago P, 1995.

Drew, Elizabeth. *Poetry: A Modern Guide.* New York: Dell Publishing, 1959.

Gorgias. "Encomium of Helen." *The Older Sophists: A Complete Translation by Several Hands of the Fragments.* Ed. Rosamond Kent Sprague. Columbia: U of South Carolina P, 1972. 50–54. 7 Apr. 2003. <http://www.phil.vt.edu/mgifford/phil2115/Helen.htm>.

Hunt, Douglas. *The Riverside Guide to Writing.* Boston: Houghton Mifflin, 1991.

CHAPTER 5

Ballenger, Bruce. *The Curious Researcher.* 4th ed. NewYork: Longman, 2004.

Bowen, Catherine Drinker. *Adventures of a Biographer.* Boston: Little, Brown, 1959.

"Bush vs. Bush." *The Daily Show with Jon Stewart.* <http://www.comedycentral.com/tv_shows/ds/videos_corr.jhtml?startIndex513&p5stewart>.

Clark, Jocalyn. "Babes and Boob? Analysis of JAMA Cover Art." *British Medical Journal* (18 Dec. 1999): 1603.

Gonser, Sarah. "Revising the Cover Story." *Folio: The Magazine for Magazine Management* 1 Mar. 2003.

Huff, Darrell. *How to Lie with Statistics.* New York: Norton, 1993.

Rea, Alan, and Doug White. "The Changing Nature of Writing: Prose or Code in the Classroom." *Background Readings for Instructors Using The Bedford Handbook.* 6th ed. Ed. Glan Blalock. Boston: Bedford/St. Martin's, 2002. 217–30.

"Statistical Significance." Creative Research Systems, 2000. <http://www.surveysystem.com/signif.htm>.

"Stem Cells, Regenerative Medicine and Cancer." The Beckman Symposium. 14–15 Apr. 2003. <http://beckman.stanford.edu/events/symp_videos.html>.

Stewart, John. *America.* New York: Warner Books, 2004.

Vogel, Gretchen. "Can Old Cells Learn New Tricks?" *Science* 25 Feb. 2000: 1418–19.

Zimbardo, Philip G., Ann L. Weber, and Robert L. Johnson. *Psychology: Core Concepts.* 4th ed. Boston: Allyn & Bacon, 2003.

CHAPTER 6

Adamson, Eric. "Malleability, Misrepresentation, Manipulation: The Rhetoric of Images in Economic Forecasting." Boothe Prize Essay, Winter 2003. Program in Writing and Rhetoric, Stanford University. <http://pwr.stanford.edu/publications/>.

Antohin, Anatoly. "Storyboard." <http://afronord.tripod.com/film/storyboard.html.

Blast, Joseph. "Gorgeous Propaganda, Frightening Truth." *Heartland Perspectives.* June 2006. <http://www.heartland.org/Article.cfm?artId519239>.

Burke, Kenneth. "Rhetoric—Old and New." *New Rhetorics.* Ed. Martin Steinmann. New York: Scribner, 1967. 59–76.

Collier, John, Greg Daniels, and Paul Lieberstein. "Homer, Hank & the American Dream: Social & Political Satire on American Television." The Program in American Studies. Stanford University, Stanford, CA 7 Nov. 2003.

Gibaldi, Joseph. *MLA Handbook for the Writers of Research Papers.* 6th ed. New York: Modern Language Association, 2003.

Goodwin, Doris Kearns. "How I Caused That Story." 27 Jan. 2002. <http://www.time.com/time/nation/article/0,8599,197614,00.html>.

Hilligoss, Susan. *Visual Communication.* 2nd ed. New York: Longman, 2002.

Kaplan, Deborah. "Mass Marketing Jane Austen: Men, Women and Courtship in Two Film Adaptations." *Jane Austen in Hollywood.* Eds. Linda Troost and Sayre Greenfield: U of Kentucky P, 1998. 177–87.

Lamott, Anne. *Bird by Bird: Some Instructions on Writing and Life.* New York: Anchor, 1995.

"Merchants of Cool." *Frontline.* Dir. Barak Goodman. PBS. 27 Feb. 2001. <http:// www.pbs.org/wgbh/pages/frontline/shows/cool/>.

Moore, Michael. *Fahrenheit 9/11.* Sony Pictures, 2004.

Morgan, Peter W., and Glenn H. Reynolds. "A Plague of Originality." *The Idler.* <http://www.the-idler.com/IDLER-02/1-23.html>.

Paton, Alan. *National Observer* 8 Nov. 1965.

Phillips, William H. *Film: An Introduction.* 2nd ed. Boston: Bedford/St. Martins, 2002.

Rasch, David. "How I Write Interview." Stanford Writing Center. Stanford University. 17 Nov. 2003.

CHAPTER 7

Adbusters: Culturejammers. <http://www.adbusters.org>.

Agee, James. Foreword. *Let Us Now Praise Famous Men.* Boston: Houghton Mifflin, 1969.

Burton, Gideon. *Silva Rhetoricae: The Forest of Rhetoric.* <http://humanities.byu.edu/ rhetoric/silva.htm>.

Cody, Anthony. "Teaching Practices: Digital Photoessays." Apple Learning Exchange. <http://ali.apple.com/ali_sites/ali/neccexhibits/1000308/The_Lesson.html>.

Crowley, Sharon, and Debra Hawhee. *Ancient Rhetorics for Contemporary Students.* New York: Longman, 1999.

George, Diana. "From Analysis to Design: Visual Communication in the Teaching of Writing." *CCC* 54.1 (2002): 11–39.

Greenfield, Laura. *Girl Culture.* San Francisco, CA: Chronicle Books, 2002.

Levy, Matthew. "A Rescue Worker's Chronicle." <http://www.umbc.edu/window/levy.html>.

Lanham, Richard. *The Electronic Word: Democracy, Technology, and the Arts.* Chicago: U of Chicago P, 1993.

Landow, George. *Hypertext.* Baltimore: Johns Hopkins UP, 1992.

Nielsen, Jakob, and Marie Tahir. *Homepage Usability: 50 Websites Deconstructed.* Indianapolis: New Riders Publishing, 2002.

Sammons, Martha. *The Internet Writer's Handbook.* New York: Longman, 2004.

Stephenson, Sam, ed. *Dream Street: W. Eugene Smith's Pittsburgh Project.* New York: Norton, 2001.

CHAPTER 8

Burton, Gideon. *Silva Rhetoricae: The Forest of Rhetoric.* <http://humanities.byu.edu/rhetoric/silva.htm>.

Byrne, David. "Learning to Love PowerPoint." *Wired Magazine* Sept. 2003. <http://www.wired.com/wired/archive/11.09/ppt1.html>.

Covino, William, and David Jolliffe. *Rhetoric: Concepts, Definitions, Boundaries.* Boston: Allyn & Bacon, 1995.

Hocks, Mary. "Understanding Visual Rhetoric in Digital Writing Environments." *CCC* 54.4 (June 2003): 629–56.

Ingleman, Kelly. "Delivery." Rhetoric Resources at Tech. Georgia Institute of Technology. <http://www.lcc.gatech.edu/gallery/rhetoric/terms/delivery.html>.

Kilbourne, Jean. *Slim Hopes: Advertising and the Obsession with Thinness.* Dir. Sut Jhally. Northampton, MA: Media Education Foundation, 1995.

Parker, Ian. "Absolute PowerPoint." *The New Yorker* 28 May 2001: 76–87.

Shugart, Stephen. "Beyond PowerPoint." *Educator's Voice* 15 Aug. 2001. <http://www.title3.net/TechTips/misusingpp.html>.

Tufte, Edward. "PowerPoint Is Evil: Power Corrupts. PowerPoint Corrupts Absolutely." *Wired Magazine* Sept. 2003. <http://www.wired.com/wired/archive/11.09/ppt2.html>.

CHAPTER 9

Chicago Manual of Style. 15th ed. Chicago: U of Chicago P, 2003.

The Concise Rules of APA Style. APA, 2005.

Cone, Justin. "Building on the Past." <http://justincone.com/main.html>.

Gibaldi, Joseph. *MLA Handbook for the Writers of Research Papers.* 6th ed. New York: Modern Language Association, 2003.

Goodwin, Doris Kearns. "How I Caused That Story." *Time* 27 January 2002.

Publication Manual of the American Psychological Association. 5th ed. APA, 2001.

Scientific Style and Format. 6th ed. Cambridge: Cambridge UP. 1994.

Credits

Images

Page v: Copyright 2004 Nick Anderson. All rights reserved. Reprinted with permission of Nick Anderson in conjunction with Washington Post Writers Group and the Cartoonist Group.

Page 1: Abed Omar Qusini/Reuters.

Figure 2.2: Courtesy of RUSK PROFESSIONAL HAIRCARE.

Figure 2.4: © Chevron Corporation and used with permission.

Figure 2.5: © The Procter & Gamble Company. Used by permission.

Figure 2.6: Courtesy of Volkswagen of America, Inc.

Figure 2.7: Courtesy of Unilever/AXE.

Figure 2.8: Image courtesy of The Advertising Archives.

Figure 2.10: General Motors Corp. Used with permission. GM Media Archives.

Figure 2.11: Courtesy of Ford Motor Company.

Figure 2.12: © The American Legacy Foundation.

Figure 2.13: Image courtesy of The Advertising Archives.

Figure 3.1 and page vi: AP Images.

Figure 3.2: Margaret Bourke-White/Time & Life Pictures/Getty Images.

Figure 3.3: Todd Heisler/Polaris Images.

Figure 3.4: Library of Congress.

Figure 3.5: Library of Congress.

Figure 3.6: Bettmann/CORBIS.

Figure 3.7: "Triathlon Start" Harvey's Lake, Pa., 1994. Photograph by Mark Cohen.

Figure 3.8: "By a Nose" Philadelphia, Pa. © Norman Y. Lono, 1980

Figure 3.9: "Girl on a Swing" Pitt Street, NYC, 1938. Photograph by Walter Rosenblum.

Figure 3.10: Cordell Hauglie.

Figure 3.12: Courtesy of Deseret Morning News Archives.

Page 88: AP Images.

Figure 3.13: Abed Omar Qusini/Reuters.

Figure 3.14: Courtesy *Boston Herald*.

Page 105: Miramax/Photofest.

Figure 4.1 and page vii: Patrick Broderick/ModernHumorist.com.

Figure 4.2: Hoover Institution Archives Poster Collection.

Figure 4.4: Courtesy National Archives, 513533.

Figure 4.5: Courtesy National Archives, 516102.

Figure 4.6: Courtesy National Archives, 514597.

Figure 4.7: Library of Congress.

Figure 4.8: The Art Archive/Musée des 2 Guerres Mondiales Paris/Dagli Orti.

Figure 4.9: Library of Congress.

Figure 4.10: Image courtesy of The Advertising Archives.

Figure 4.14: Courtesy of Micah Ian Wright & AntiWarPosters.com.

Figure 4.15: © 2003-WHITEHOUSE.ORG.

Figure 4.16: Courtesy of Steve Horn.

Figure 4.17: Courtesy of Micah Ian Wright & AntiWarPosters.com.

Page 131: Courtesy National Archives, 513533.

Figure 5.1 and page vii: ArcticNet—NCE/Time & Life Pictures/Getty Images.

Figure 5.2: Cover text only from SCIENCE Vol. 311, No. 5768 (24 March 2006). Reprinted with permission from AAAS. Photo: Nevada Wier/CORBIS.

Figure 5.3: Time & Life Pictures/Getty Images.

Figure 5.4: Steve Bronstein/The Image Bank/Getty Images.

Figure 5.5: *Rocket Blitz* from the Moon by Chesley Bonestell. Bonestell Space Art.

Figure 5.6: Time & Life Pictures/Getty Images.

Figure 5.12: *Stem Cells*, March 2006 cover © AlphaMed Press.

Figure 5.13: Courtesy of the Yale Scientific Magazine.

Figure 5.18: Still courtesy of COMEDY CENTRAL.

Figure 6.1 and page viii: Courtesy of Universal Studios Licensing LLLP.

Figure 6.4: Miramax/Photofest.

Figure 6.5: Lions Gate/Photofest.

Page 225: Warner Bros./Photofest.

Figure 7.2 (left): Danjaq/Eon/UA/The Kobal Collection/Keith Hamshere.

Figure 7.2 (right): Paramount/Icon/The Kobal Collection/Andrew Cooper.

Figure 7.8: Reproduced with the kind permission of The Body Shop International, plc.

Figure 7.9: Courtesy www.adbusters.org.

Figure 8.1 and page x: AP Images.

Page 256 (left, right): AP Images.

Page 256 (center): Paramount Classics/Photofest.

Figure 8.2: © Die Höge, 1999. Photo by Monika Beyer.

Figure 8.3: AP Images.

Figure 8.17: Bettmann/CORBIS.
Figure 8.18: Topham/The Image Works.
Figure 9.1 and page xi: *Building on the Past* by
Justin Cone.

Text

American Association for the Advancement of
Science (AAAS). Screen shot of AAAS
Science & Policy web page, http://www.
aaas.org/spp/sfrl/projects/stem/index.
shtml. Reprinted with permission from
AAAS.

Bowen, Laurence and Jill Schmid. "Minority Pres-
ence and Portrayal in Mainstream Magazine
Advertising: An Update," *Journal and Mass
Communication Quarterly*, 74:1, 134-146.

CNN.com. Screen shot from "The Stem Cell
Debate," http://www.cnn.com/
SPECIALS/2001/stemcell/. © 2003 Cable
News Network LP, LLLP. All rights reserved.
Reprinted with permission.

Curtis, James. "Dorothea Lange, Migrant Mother,
and the Culture of the Great Depression,"
Winterthur Portfolio, 1986, 21. 1:2.

Do No Harm: The Coalition of Americans for
Research Ethics. Screen shot from http://
www.stemcellresearch.org/. Reprinted by permission from Do No Harm: The
Coalition of Americans for Research Ethics.

Dunn, Geoffrey. From "Documentary
Photography from the Outside In: Dorothea
Lange and Migrant Mother," *Deconstructing
Documentary: theory and Practice in Documen-
tary Film and Photography*, a dissertation
submitted in partial satisfaction of the require-
ments for the degree of *Doctor of Philosophy in
Sociology*, September 2004, pp. 106-11.
Reprinted by permission of the author.

Ephron, Nora. "The Boston Photographs," from
Scribble, Scribble: Notes on the Media.
Copyright © 1978 by Nora Ephron.
Reprinted by permission of International
Creative Management, Inc.

Goodwin, Doris Kearns. "How I Caused That
Story," *Time*, January 27, 2002. © 2002
Time, Inc. Reprinted by permission.

Gottesman, Jane. Screen shots from the online
version of *Game Face*, found at http://
washingtonpost.com/wp-srv.photo.
onassignment,gameFace/. Reprinted by
permission of Game Face Productions.

Holkins, Jerry. Blog entry for "The Hipness
Threshold," from *Penny Arcade*, March 12,
2004. Reprinted by permission.

Huntington, Samuel P. Excerpt from "Under
God." Reprinted from *The Wall Street
Journal*, June 16, 2004. © 2004
Dow Jones & Company. All rights
reserved. By permission of The Wall Street
Journal and the author.

Marlette, Doug. "I Was a Tool of Satan." Reprinted
from *Columbia Journalism Review*, November/
December 2003. © 2003 by Columbia
Journalism Review. Reprinted by permission
of the publisher and the author.

Marlette, Doug. "What Would Mohammed
Drive?" Cartoon courtesy of Doug Marlette.

McSpotlight/London Greenpeace. "What's Wrong
with the Body Shop?" Referenced version
from the "Beyond McDonald's" pages at
http://www.mcspotlight.org. Original
(unreferenced) version from London
Greenpeace leaflet.

Stem Cell Research Foundation. Screen shot from
http://www.stemcellresearch foundation.org.
Image appears courtesy of the Stem Cell
Research Foundation.

Stevenson, Seth. "You and Your Shadow,"
Slate.com, March 2, 2004. Slate.com and
Washingtonpost.Newsweek Interactive. All
rights reserved. Reprinted by permission of
United Media.

TheTruth.com. "Crazyworld," screen shot
from http://www.thetruth.com. Reprinted
by permission of the American Legacy
Foundation.

United States Army Office of Global
Communication. "Friendship," leaflet
air-dropped in Afghanistan, n.d.

Vogel, Gretchen. "Can Old Cells Learn
New Tricks?" Reprinted with permission from
Science 287: 1418-19, 25 February 2000.
Copyright 2000 AAAS.

Index

Abercrombie and Fitch advertisements, 50
Abstracts
 composing, 227–229
 summaries, 145
Academic writing, 223–227
 abstracts, composing, 227–229
 bios, shaping, 229–231
 design of, 225–227
 evaluating academic sources, 154–159
 key elements of, 223
 photo essays, producing, 242–245
 verbal and visual design, combining, 231–233
 visuals, incorporating, 224–225
Adams, Ansel, 73
Adbusters, 231–232, 241
Adcult USA, 38
Ad hominem fallacy, 58
Advance screenings, 196
Advertisements
 as arguments, 38–42
 celebrity endorsements, 55–56
 context and, 60–61
 documentation for, 309
 ethos in, 54–57
 false needs, creation of, 53
 Internet advertising, 140
 kairos in, 60–61
 local fallacies in, 47–53
 op-ads (opinion advertisements), 240–242
 parody and, 59
 pathos, use of, 48–51
 prewriting checklist for analyzing, 62–63
Agee, James, 243
Ali, Aisha, 90–92
Allard, William Albert, 243

Alternative Spring Break (ASB) program, 233–235
American Association for the Advancement of Science, 149–150
The Americans (Frank), 83–84
America (The Book) (Stewart), 162
Analogy
 in advertisements, 38, 42
 and persona, 79
Anderson, Nick, 25
Angelou, Maya, 256
An Inconvenient Truth, 191–193, 256
Annotated bibliographies, 167–169
 composing/constructing, 168
Anonymous article, documenting, 306
Anthologies
 article, documenting, 305
 entire anthology, documenting, 306
APA (American Psychological Association) documentation style, 296
Appendices, images placed in, 224–225
Apple "Switch" advertisements, 55–56
Architectural mnemonic technique, 277
Arguments, 2–3, 105–134.
 See also Drafts; Evidence; Presentations
 advertisements as, 38–42
 in annotated bibliographies, 168
 composing, 66–104
 constructing, 101–102
 designing, 220–252
 diversity in presenting, 189
 drafting, 194–200

freewriting, 120–122
 hypertext arguments, 245–246
 interpretation and, 19
 logos and, 44
 multiple sides, writing, 90–93
 in outlines, 188–190
 planning projects, 132–134
 prewriting checklists, 35, 133
 for public audiences, 233–235
 questions, asking, 107–110
 in thesis statement, 29
 visual arguments, 12–13, 239–240
 visualizing research, 138–139
Aristotle, 5, 54
Arrangement, 73–78
 defined, 67
 digital photography and, 77
 in Ephron, Nora's essay, 98–100
Art works, documenting, 311
Atheism, 16–17
"At the Time of the Louisville Flood" (Bourke-White), 68
Attribution of sources, 290
Audience, 8, 19–20
 of academic source, 154–156
 arguments, designing, 233–235
 delivery to, 257–258
 formatting for, 235–239
 hybrid composition, formatting for, 235–239
 for PowerPoint presentations, 273
 in prewriting checklist, 35
Audio
 delivery, sound of, 277–278
 documentation of sources, 308–311
 in photo essays, 243
Authority
 appeals to, 54–57
 over evidence, 58

Authors, 8
  academic sources, evaluation
    of, 155
Axe cologne advertisement, 51

Bachelet, Michelle, 220
Background for research
    proposal, 123
Bakker, Jim, 22
Bakker, Tammy, 22
Banner ads, 140
Basilio, Norma, 75, 76
Before-and-after strategy, 47
Begging the question fallacy, 47
Bibliographies. *See also*
    "Works Cited" lists
  annotated bibliographies,
    167–169
  citations in, 145
  for of integrated
    quotations, 193
Biographies
  in research proposal, 123
  shaping, 229–231
BIOsis, 153
Bird by Bird (Lamott), 195
BladeRunner—The Director's
    Cut, 196, 214
Blast, Joseph, 192–193
Bleyleben, Alex, 272
Block structure, 74
Body language, 280
Bollywood cinema, 196–200
Books
  documentation for, 305
  as primary sources, 141–142
Boondocks, 10–11
The Boondocks: Because I Know
    You Don't Read Newspapers
    (McGruder), 11
Booth, Douglas, 169
Bourke-White, Margaret, 68

Bowen, Catherine
    Drinker, 105, 158
Bowen, Laurence, 44
Brainstorming
  for arguments, 252
  graphic brainstorming, 115–117
  for presentations, 269
  for research log, 109
  titles, 82
Branches of oratory, 254, 255–256
Bubble webs, 173–175, 176
Budweiser advertisements, 57
Building on the Past, 289
Burton, Gideon, 281, 291
Bush, George W., 79, 164
  stem cell debate, 148–152

Cagle, Daryl, 14, 18, 28, 29
Calvin and Hobbes, 8–10, 26
Canons of rhetoric. *See also*
    Arrangement; invention;
    Style
  defined, 67
  position papers, crafting, 85–90
Captions
  for images, 225
  in photo essays, 243
Cartoons, 2
  analysis of, 8–13
  culture and, 19–20
  documentation for, 309
  editorial cartoons, 2, 13–15
  rhetorical analysis of, 7–13
Causality, fallacy of, 47
Cause and effect, 74
  in advertisements, 38, 40, 45
  outlines, 182
  and persona, 79
Celebrity endorsements, 55–56
Ceremonial oratory, 255–256
Chan, Jackie, 55
Character, appeals to, 54–57

Characters
  advertisement, analysis of, 62
  in prewriting checklist, 35
Chat room discussion,
    documenting, 308
Chicago documentation style, 296
Chronological outlines, 182, 183
Chronological structure, 74
Chunking Website information, 248
Churchill, Winston, 281
Cicero
  and architectural mnemonic
    technique, 277
  on decorum, 222
  on invention, 68
Citations. *See also* Documentation
  in-text citations, 297
  for quotations, 193
  of sources, 292–293
Clairol Nice 'n Easy advertisement,
    39–40
Clarkson, Kelly, 55
Classification and division
  in advertisements, 38
  and persona, 79
Class lecture, documenting, 310
Close, Glenn, 189
Clueless, 196, 263
Clustering, 115
CNN.com, 148–149, 243
Coca-Cola advertisement, 60–61
Cochran, Johnny, 256
Collaboration in peer review
    process, 195–200
Collier's magazine, 142–143
Columbia Journalism Review, 20
Comic strips. *See* Cartoons
Community service projects, 233
Comparison and contrast
  in advertisements, 38, 40,
    41–42, 46
  ethos, misuses of, 58

Composing arguments, 66–104
Composition in prewriting
    checklist, 35
Computers
  draft revisions on, 215
  games, documenting, 310
Concessions
  in drafts, 201
  multiple perspectives and, 100
Conclusions, 85
Cone, Justin, 289
Consistency of arguments, 201
Constructive feedback, 203
Contacts for interviews and
    surveys, 161
Content of advertisements, 62
Context, 2, 19–20
  and advertisements, 60–62
Conversation metaphor, 139
Cooper Mini advertisement, 50
Copyright issues, 311
Covers
  documenting, 307
  evaluation of, 154–155
Covino, William, 277
Crazyword homepage,
    Truth.com, 246
Creative take-aways, 283–284
Credibility, ethos and, 56–57
Crest Whitening Strip
    advertisement, 46–47
Cross-referencing documentation,
    297–298
CSE (Council of Science Editors)
    documentation style, 296
Culkin, Macaulay, 58
Culture
  advertisement, analysis of, 63
  cartoons and, 19
  in prewriting checklist, 35
Cum hoc fallacy, 47
Curtis, James, 71

The Daily Show, 164, 257
Databases
  documenting articles, 306
  evaluating, 152–156
  search terms from, 140
  usefulness of, 145
Date of publication,
    evaluating, 155
Decorum, 221–222
  of Websites, 246
Deep level of Website, 247
Deering, John, 17, 18
Deferred thesis, 74–75
Definition
  in advertisements, 38
  documenting, 307
  and persona, 79
Deliberative discourse, 255–256
Delivery. See also Presentations
  defined, 67
  fundamental elements of, 277
  gestures and, 278–280
  memory and, 277
  methods of, 276–281
  of PowerPoint presentations, 275
  sound of, 277–278
Demonstrative oratory, 255–256
Demosthenes, 277
Description in advertisements,
    38, 41
Design
  advertisement, analysis of, 63
  of arguments, 220–252
Development strategy, 63
Dialogue of sources, 164–167
Diamond, Matthew, 13
Difficulties in research proposal, 123
Direct quotations, 190–191
Disclaimers, 48
Discourse, 137
Dissertations, documenting, 307
Documentaries. See Movies

Documentation, 289–290, 291.
    See also MLA (Modern
    Language Association)
    documentation style
  for audio sources, 308–311
  copyright issues, 311
  as cross-referencing, 297–298
  of integrated quotations, 193
  of interviews and surveys, 161
  notes for, 298–300
  for online sources, 304–311
  of presentation, 283–284
  for print sources, 304–311
  student paper example, 312–325
  styles of, 296–300
  for visual sources, 308–311
Document design, 221–222
DoNoHarm Website, 152, 164
Doonesbury, 10
"Dorothea Lange, Migrant Mother,
    and the Culture of the Great
    Depression" (Curtis), 71
Double-spacing documents, 223
Drafts
  assessment of, 201
  collaboration in, 195–200
  for movie scripts, 172–173
  peer reviews, 195–200, 203
  research argument, 194–200
  revision of, 200–215
  summary of, 215
  visual form, organizing
    draft in, 173–176
Dress rehearsals, 281
Dunn, Geoffrey, 71–72

Editorial cartoons, 2, 13–15
Either-or-argument fallacy, 47
Email, documenting, 307
Embodied rhetoric, 278
  in presentations, 268
Emma, 196

Emotion, appeals to, 48–51
Encyclopedia of Bioethics, 153
End comments for quotations, 193
Endnotes, 298–300
Energy breaks, 195
Enlistment posters, 107–109,
        111–112
Ephron, Nora, 93–101
Epideictic rhetoric, 255–256
Epigraphs in introductions, 83
Ethics and plagiarism, 291–292
Ethos, 54–57
    bio establishing, 229
    defined, 43
    direct quotations and, 190
    grammatical mistakes and, 201
    misuses of, 58–59
    parody and, 59
    and persona, 79
Eulogies, 256
Evaluation
    of field research, 162–163
    of research sources, 148–163
Evans, Walker, 243
Evidence
    authority over, 58
    direct quotations as, 190
    images as, 225
    multiple perspectives and, 100
    in persuasive arguments, 34
Examples
    in advertisements, 38, 40, 41
    and persona, 79

Fahrenheit 9/11, 188–189
Fallacies, 47
    ad hominem fallacy, 58
    slippery slope fallacy, 52
False needs, use of, 52–53
Falwell, Jerry, 22
Fatal Attraction, 196
Feedback. *See also* Peer reviews

    constructive feedback, 203
    on presentations, 281
Field research, 158–160
    evaluating, 162–163
File sharing, 106
Film. *See* Movies
First drafts, 195
Fleshing out outlines, 194
Following up interviews and
        surveys, 161
Footnotes, 298–300
Ford Escape advertisement, 50
Forensic discourse, 255–256
Formal outlines, 178–183
Forman, Stanley, 94–98
Formatting
    for audiences, 235–239
    outlines, 188
Foundational information, 144
Frank, Robert, 83–84
Freewriting, 194
    research topics, 120–122

Game Face (Gottesman), 75–77
Gateway to Website, 247
Gestures and delivery, 278–280
Gibson, Mel, 189
Girl Culture (Greenfield), 243
Global warming, 135–137
Goals for research proposal, 123
Goodwin, Doris Kearns, 293–296
Google, 148
Google, documenting, 311
Gore, Al, 191–193, 256
"Got Milk?" advertisements, 55
Gottesman, Jane, 75–77, 82
Government publications, 144
    documenting, 307
Grammar, revising drafts for,
        201–202
Grand style, 222
    abstracts in, 228

    characteristics of, 223
Graphic brainstorming, 115–117
Graphic flowcharts, 173–174,
        175–176
Graphic montages with
        presentations, 284
Greenfield, Lauren, 243

Halitosis, 52
Hamlet (Zeffirelli), 189
Handouts for presentation, 283
Hasty generalization fallacy, 47
Header on Websites, 150
Headlines, 232
High, Hugh, 165–167
The Hipness Threshold, 12
"The Historical and the Icon"
        (Levine), 71–72
Historical context, 62
Hitler, Adolf, 281
Hoax Photo Gallery, 77
Hogarth, William, 13
Holkins, Jerry, 12
Homepages, 245–246, 247
    Crazyword homepage,
        Truth.com, 246
    documenting personal
        homepage, 309
Hook line in outline, 179
Humor
    in advertisements, 51
    appeals to, 43
    in bio, 230
    in PowerPoint presentations, 275
Huntington, Samuel P., 16–17
Hussein, Saddam, 85–90
Hybrid compositions, 231–233
    for online reading audience,
        235–239
Hybrid text, 7
Hypertext, 245–246
Hypothesis, drafting, 128–132

Iceberg of research, 138
  secondary sources in, 144
"I Have a Dream" (King), 254
Illustrations in advertisements,
  38, 40
Illustrative outlines, 182
Imagery in prewriting checklist, 35
Images. *See also* Photographs
  in academic writing, 224–225
  advertisement, analysis of, 63
  in bio, 230
  captions for, 225
  documentating visual sources,
    308–311
  in multimedia montages,
    249–252
  in photo essays, 244
  signposting, 225
  verbal and visual design,
    combining, 231–233
Implications of thesis statement, 29
Incorporated structure, 192
Indexes
  evaluating, 155
  usefulness of, 145
Indignation, appeals to, 50
Information in drafts, 201
Integrating sources, 190–191
  documentation requirements, 193
  final check for, 193
  images into academic writing,
    224–225
  quotations, 191–193
Intellectual property, 290–291
Intentions, hypothesis and, 130
Internet. *See also* Websites
  advertising, 140
  documentation for online
    sources, 304–311
  photo essays on, 243
  postings, documenting, 308
  reading audience, 235–239

site, documenting, 309
sources, documentation of,
  304–311
Interpretation and argument, 19
Interrupted structure, 192–193
Interviews
  conducting, 160–161
  documenting, 307
In-text citations, 297
Introductions
  hooks in, 82–85
  of quotations, 191–193
  style and, 82–85
Invasion (ABC), 60
Invention
  defined, 67–68
  in Ephron, Nora's essay, 98
  in texts, 72–73
IPod advertisement, 37,
  40–42, 54–55
"I Was a Tool of Satan"
  (Marlette), 20–26

James, LeBron, 55
JFK, 189
Jobs, Steve, 257
Jollife, David, 277
Jordan, Barbara, 278
Journals. *See* Magazines
  and journals
Judicial discourse, 255–256

Kairos, 60–61
Kallosh, Renata, 292
Kennedy, John F., 142
Kerouac, Jack, 83–84
Keywords for research, developing,
  139–141
Kill Bill: Volume 1, 176–178
King, Coretta Scott, 256
King, Martin Luther, Jr., 254, 268,
  279–280, 281

Lambert, Gerard, 52
Lamott, Anne, 195
Lange, Dorothea, 70–72
Language
  advertisement, analysis of, 63
  in bio, 229
  direct quotations and, 190
  multiple personas and, 91
  in prewriting checklist, 35
Lara Croft: Tomb Raider,
  174–175
Layout of advertisement, 63
LegalPeriodical, 153
Legislative discourse, 255–256
Letters, documenting, 307
Letter to editor, documenting, 307
Let Us Now Praise Famous Men
  (Evans & Agee), 243
Levels of style, 222
Levine, Lawrence, 71–72
LexisNexis, 140
Libraries
  evaluating sources, 153–156
  search terms, finding, 139–141
Library of Congress
  American Memory collection, 147
  search terms, 140–147
  Subject Headings (LCSHs),
    140–141
Life magazine, 243
Linear path for arguments, 194
Linking references to
  quotations, 193
Listerine advertisement, 51–53
Logical fallacies, 47
Logos
  defined, 43
  fallacies, logical, 47
  and persona, 79
  for public audience, 233–234
Logos for brands, 55
Luckovich, Michael, 13, 14–15

Macro to micro outlines, 182

Magazines and journals
documenting articles, 306
prewriting checklist for
evaluating, 170

Mao Zedong, 249–251

Mapping, 115

Maps, documenting, 311

Margins, 223

Markstein, Gary, 15–16

Marlette, Doug, 19, 20–26

Masters Settlement Act, 59

Materials
for research topics, 113
stacking and labeling, 174

McCloud, Scott, 7–8

McGruder, Aaron, 10–11

McLuhan, Marshall, 251

Media. *See also* Multimedia
advertisement, analysis of, 62
imagery, 125–128
in presentations, 268
radio essay, documenting, 310
television, documenting
programs, 310

MEDLINE, 153

Memory
defined, 67
and delivery, 277

Memos, documenting, 307

Menu bar for Website, 246

Merchants of Cool, 183

Merchants of Death
(White), 165

Message of advertisement, 62

Methods
delivery methods, 276–281
for research proposal, 123
reverse outline method, 194

Microrevisions, 202

Microsoft's "We See"
advertisements, 56–57

Micro to macro outlines, 182

Middle, writing from, 194

Middle style, 222
abstracts in, 228

Migrant Mother photographs
(Lange), 71

Minibooks with presentations, 284

MLA (Modern Language
Association) documentation
style, 296. *See also* "Works
Cited" lists
footnotes and endnotes in,
298–300
for in-text citations, 297
logic of, 305
online sources, documentation
of, 304–311
print sources, documentation
of, 304–311
student paper example, 312–325

Montages, 249–252

Moore, Michael, 188–189

Movies
collaboration in, 196
documentation for, 309
drafting stage for, 172–173
focus on analyzing, 216
outtakes, 201
trailers for, 176–178

MSNBC.com, 243

Multimedia
documentation for sources,
308–311
literacy, 8
montages, 249–252

Multiple-author book,
documenting, 305

Multiple sides of argument, 90–93

Narration
in advertisements, 38
and persona, 79

Narrative outlines, 182

Narrowing topics, 117–119

National Geographic, 243

Navigation scheme, 245–246

Navigation toolbar for Website,
246–247

Nelly, 55

Newdow, Michael, 16–17

Newspaper article,
documenting, 306

Note taking, 167–169
plagiarism, avoiding, 293
strategies for, 167

O, 196

Obama, Barack, 278

Observations for thesis statement, 29

Ocean's 12, 225

Op-ads (opinion advertisements),
240–242

Opposing arguments, 201

Oral delivery, 268

Oral presentations.
See Presentations

Oratory, branches of, 254,
255–256

Order for revising drafts, 215

Organization
of drafts, 201
example of, 267
of presentations, 260–261

Original documents, 143

Ortiz, Carlos, 271

Othello, 196

Outlines
arguments, spotlighting,
188–190
assessing, 188
fleshing out, 194
formal outlines, 178–183
reverse outline method, 194
sources, identification of, 188

strategies for, 176–183
with subheads, 184–188
with transitions, 184, 187
visual outlines, 261
Outtakes, 201
Overarching effect, 43
Over-sentimentalization, 52

Page numbers, 223
Paintings, documenting, 311
Paraphrasing sources, 190–191
Parody, 241
ethos and, 59
Passion in writing, 194–195
Pathos, 48–51
defined, 43
exaggerated uses of, 51–53
humor and, 43
and persona, 79
Patriotism, appeals to, 50
Payback, 226
PBS Frontline Website, 183
Peer reviews, 195–200
of drafts, 203
Peers as research source, 147
Performance, documenting, 311
Perfume advertisements, 50
Persona
constructing, 79–80
multiple sides of argument
and, 90–93
in position papers, 87–88
and presentation, 257–258
Personal narrative essays, 5
Perspectives
in Ephron, Nora's essay,
93–101
multiple personas and, 90–93
synthesizing of, 93–101
Persuasion in research proposal,
124
Phillip Morris advertisements, 57

Photographs
in bio, 230
documenting, 308
as invention, 67–69
perspectives in, 70–72
photo essays, producing,
242–245
in PowerPoint presentations, 273
prewriting checklist for analyzing,
101–102
as primary sources, 142–143
Pinochet, Augusto, 220
Place of publication, evaluating,
155
Plagiarism, 289–290, 291–296
defined, 291
note taking and, 293
unintentional plagiarism,
avoiding, 292–293
Plain style, 222
abstracts in, 228
for Website, 246
"Pledge of Allegiance" cartoon,
15–16
Pop-up advertisements, 140
Porsche advertisement, 50
Position papers, 85–90
Posters. *See also* Propaganda posters
in presentations, 270–271
Post hoc fallacy, 47
PowerPoint presentations
audience for, 273
placeholders, creating, 274
possibilities for, 274–276
for public audience, 234
troubleshooting problems, 282
writing for, 271–274
Practicing presentations, 281–283
Preliminary thesis statement, 29
Prelinger Archive, 289
Preparation for interviews and
surveys, 161

Presentations, 254–288. *See also*
Delivery; PowerPoint
presentations
audience for, 257–258
brainstorming for, 269
documentation for, 283–284
example of, 263–267
organization of, 260–261
persona and, 257–258
posters, use of, 270–271
practicing, 281–283
prewriting checklist for, 285–287
purpose of, 257–258
question-and-answer session,
282–283
reordering arguments for,
260–261
research, transforming, 259–268
selection of material for, 260
terms for signposting, 263
timing of, 260
translating writing to, 262–263
visual aids in, 259
visual outlines for, 261
Prewriting checklists
advertisements, analyzing, 62–63
for arguments, 35, 135
for comics and cartoons, 35
for design in arguments,
252–253
movies, analysis of, 216
photographs, analyzing,
101–102
for presentations, 285–287
propaganda posters, analyzing,
113
for research projects, 133
Primary level of Website, 247
Primary sources, 141–144
in annotated bibliographies,
168–169
finding, 142–144

Print sources, documentation of, 304–311
Problem-solution
outlines, 182
structure, 74
Process
in advertisements, 38
and persona, 79
Professional Cartoonist Index, 18
Progression of drafts, 201
Propaganda posters, 107–109
analyzing, 113
from World War II, 111
PTL Club, 22
Public audience, designing arguments for, 233–235
Public speaking. *See* Presentations
Publishers of academic source, 155
Punch, 13
Punctuation, revising drafts for, 201–202
Purpose
for academic-writing conventions, 223
for multimedia montage, 251
of oratory, 257–258

Qualification of multiple perspectives, 100
Question-and-answer sessions, 282–283
Questions
hypothesis, developing, 130
for interviews, 161
presentations, focusing, 260
research questions, asking, 107–110
for surveys, 161
Websites, evaluation of, 151–152
Quotations
direct quotations, 190–191
integrating, 191–193

in introductions, 83
in Website, 248

Radio essay, documenting, 310
Rajput, B. S., 292
Random samples, 162
Range of participants, 162
Rare books, 143
Reading and integrating sources, 192
Reagan, Ronald, 278
Real, writing for, 233
Real-time communication, documenting, 308
Reason. *See also* logos
appeals to, 44–47
Rebour, Laurent, 88
Rebuttal, 100
Recording and integrating sources, 192
Recording Industry Association of America (RIAA), 106
Red herring fallacy, 47
Relating and integrating sources, 192
Relevance of academic source, 155–156
Reordering arguments, 260–261
A Rescue Worker's Chronicle (Levy), 243
Research. *See also* Arguments
context, 137
field research, 158–160
hypothesis, drafting, 128–132
presentations, transforming to, 259–268
proposals, 123–132
recording searches, 146
Research logs, 109–110
dialogue of sources, 165–167
recording searches in, 146
for secondary sources, 144–145
using, 139

Research topics, 109, 137
focus for, 115–119
freewriting, 120–122
generating, 110–114
graphic brainstorming for, 115–117
narrowing, 117–119
in research proposal, 123
screening questions for, 114
suggestions for, 113
zooming in on, 117–119
Respect, plagiarism and, 292
Reverse outline method, 194
Revision
as continual process, 214–215
of drafts, 200–215
Rhetoric, defined, 5
Rhetorical analysis
practicing, 15–26
texts for, 34
writing, 27–34
Rhetorical appeals, 43–50
advertisement, analysis of, 63
Rhetorical function, 8–9
Rhetorical imitation, 290–291
Rhetorical moves, 26
Rhetorical situation, 2, 5, 60
Boondocks, analyzing, 11
Rhetorical stance, 80–81
of academic source, 155–156
multiple sides of argument and, 90–93
in position paper, 89
in research proposal, 123
Rhetorical strategies, 37
using, 61–62
Rhetorical texts, 3
understanding, 3–5
Rhetorical triangle, 17, 80–81
RJ Reynolds Tobacco Co., 165–167
Roethlisberger, Ben, 55

Roosevelt, Eleanor, 263
Ross, Carolyn, 233
Rydlewski, Norma, 72

"Safe Happens" advertisement, 49–50
Sanger, Margaret, 251
Scare tactics, 52
Schmid, Jill, 44
Science magazine, 135–137
SciSearch, 153
Scott, Ridley, 196, 214
Screen shots, documenting, 310
Scribble, Scribble: Notes on the Media (Ephron), 93–101
Scripting presentation, 262–263
Scripts for presentation, 283
Search terms, developing, 139–141
Secondary level of Website, 247
Secondary sources, 141–142, 144–147
   in annotated bibliographies, 168–169
   searching for, 144–147
Seib, Charles, 94–98
Selection
   example of, 267
   of presentation materials, 260
Sensationalist images, 93
Serenity, 172–173
Service-learning projects, 233
Settings
   advertisement, analysis of, 62
   in prewriting checklist, 35
Sexuality, appeals to, 50
Shakespeare, William, 189, 196
Signposting
   images, 225
   presentations, 262–263
Silverstone, Alicia, 263

Single-author book, documenting, 305
Slide-based presentations. *See* PowerPoint presentations
Slippery slope fallacy, 52
"Solace at Surprise Creek" (Allard), 243
Sounds. *See* Audio
Sources, 135–171. *See also* Documentation; Integrating sources; Primary sources; Secondary sources
   annotated bibliographies, 167–169
   attribution, 290
   citing, 292–293
   dialogue of sources, 164–167
   evaluation of, 147–163
   field research, 158–160
   iceberg of research, 138
   implementing skills, 170
   note taking, 167–169
   outlines identifying, 188
   peers as, 147
   perspectives on, 189
   process for finding, 141–147
   search terms, developing, 139–141
   working with, 190–194
Spears, Britney, 58
Speeches. *See also* Delivery; Presentations
   documenting, 310–311
Spelling, revising drafts for, 201–202
Splash page, 247
Springer, Morgan, 275
Stacking the evidence fallacy, 47
Stanford University's Symposium of Undergraduate Research in Progress, 271

Statistics
   evaluation of, 162–163
   significance, statistical, 162
Statue of Liberty cartoon, 14–16
Steichen, Edward, 71
Stem cell debate, 148–152
Stem Cell Research Foundation home page, 152
Stevenson, Seth, 40–42, 54
Stewart, Jon, 163, 257
Stone, Oliver, 189
Story
   advertisement, analysis of, 62
   in prewriting checklist, 35
Storyboards, 172
Strategies of invention, 68
Style, 78–85
   in bio, 229
   Cicero on, 222
   and conclusions, 85
   defined, 67
   in Ephron, Nora's essay, 93–101
   and introductions, 82–83
   persona, constructing, 79–80
   in position paper, 89
   rhetorical stance, 80–81
   synthesizing perspectives, 93–101
   titles and, 81–82
Summaries
   of sources, 190–191
   Website design, 249
Surveys, conducting, 161
Synthesizing perspectives, 93–101

Table of contents
   evaluating, 155
   in photo essays, 243
Tactile montages, 251
Tape recording interviews, 161
Television, documenting programs, 310
Templates for Website, 248

Texts, 8
images, references to, 225
invention in, 72–73
kairos and, 60–61
presentation, text of, 283
as primary sources, 144
for rhetorical analysis, 34
rhetorical analysis of, 7–13
strategies for analyzing, 13–27
Themes
advertisement, analysis of, 62
outlines, thematic, 182, 183
structure, thematic, 74
trailers showing, 178
Thesis
developing, 27–34
in outlines, 179, 188
in research proposal, 123
tentative thesis, 121–122
testing, 31
Thesis statement, 27–34, 74–75
Thompson, Mike, cartoon
by, 30–31
TheTruth.com advertisement, 59
"This Is Your Brain on Drugs"
advertisement, 39
Thompson, Florence Owens, 72
Thompson, Mike, 30–31
Three-paragraph model,
120–122
Time.com, 243
Timeline for research proposal, 123
Time magazine, 135–137, 143
Timing presentations, 260
Title bar for Website, 248
Titles, style and, 81–82
Tomorrow Never Dies, 226
Tone
in bio, 229
in prewriting checklist, 35
publication tone, evaluating,
155–156

Topics. *See also* Research topics
etymology of, 110
for photo essays, 245
in prewriting checklist, 35
Toyota "Global Earth Charter"
advertisements, 57
Trailers for films, 176–178
Transitions, outlines with, 184, 187
Translating
example of, 267
presentation, writing to, 262–263
Troubleshooting presentation
problems, 282–283
Trudeau, Gary, 10
Trust and ethos, 55
Truth.com, 246
Twitchell, James, 38, 52, 58

"Under God" (Huntington), 16–17
Understanding Comics
(McCloud), 7
University of Chicago
documentation style, 296
URLs (Uniform Resource
Locators), 152
U.S.A. Swimming, 169
Usability of Website, 249

Verbal and visual design,
combining, 231–233
Victoria's Secret advertisement, 50
Villanueva, Victor, Jr., 1, 2
Visual aids. *See also* PowerPoint
presentations
posters, use of, 270–271
in presentations, 259
rhetorical use of, 270–276
Visual annotated bibliographies,
168–169
Visual arguments, 12–13, 220,
239–240
in Websites, 246

Visual collages, 249
Visualizing research, 113, 138–139
Visual juxtaposition, 242
Visual literacy, 12–13
Visual outlines, 261
Visual persuasion, 6, 18
in advertisements, 46–47
Visual rhetoric, 6
of library sources, 154–155
in research proposal, 123, 124
Visuals. *See* Images
Vogel, Gretchen, 156–157, 164
Voice, 78
advertisement, analysis of, 63
in drafts, 201
publication voice, evaluating,
155–156
Volkswagen Jetta advertisement,
49–50

Walski, Brian, 77
Watterson, 10
Webbing, 115–117
Websites
article, documenting, 306
chunking information in, 248
composing, 245–249
documenting, 306, 309
elements for composing, 247
embedding quotes in, 248
evaluating, 148–152
formatting for online audiences,
235–239
list questions for evaluating, 152
photo essays on, 243
prewriting checklist for
evaluating, 170
search terms, finding, 140–141
summary of design, 249
visual arguments, designing,
239–240
Whedon, Joss, 172

White, Larry C., 165–167
Williams, Serena, 55
Wolcott, Marion Post, 72
Woods, Tiger, 58
Word choice, 84–85
Working thesis, 27, 29–30
"Works Cited" lists, 297, 298, 300–304
  order of entry in, 304
  student paper example, 324–325

"Works Consulted" list, 300
Writing. *See also* Academic writing
  for PowerPoint presentations, 271–274
  presentation, translating to, 262–263
  prewriting checklist, 35
  for real, 233
  rhetorical analysis, 27–34
  rhetorical attention to, 155–156

Yale Scientific, 154–155
Yancey, Kathleen, 219
Yuan, Ye, 175, 244–245

Zeffirelli, Franco, 189
Zimbardo, Philip, 162–163